Family, Kinship and State in Contemporary Europe

Family, Kinship and State in Contemporary Europe

Overall Editor: Patrick Heady

Vol. 1 The Century of Welfare: Eight Countries

Vol. 2 The View from Below: Nineteen Localities

Vol. 3 Perspectives on Theory and Policy

Hannes Grandits is professor of Southeast European History at Humboldt University, Berlin.

Patrick Heady is a research associate at the Max Planck Institute for Social Anthropology and an honorary research fellow of University College London.

Hannes Grandits (ed.)

Family, Kinship and State in Contemporary Europe

Vol. 1
The Century of Welfare: Eight Countries

Campus Verlag
Frankfurt/New York

This publication has been produced with the financial assistance of the European Community and the Max Planck Society. The views expressed herein are purely those of the authors and may not in any circumstances be regarded as stating an official position of the European Commission or of the Society.

Bibliographic Information published by the Deutsche Nationalbibliothek.
The Deutsche Nationalbibliothek lists this publication in the Deutsche Nationalbibliografie.
Detailed bibliographic data are available in the Internet at http://dnb.d-nb.de.
ISBN 978-3-593-38961-5

Cover illustration: Needy family accommodated in the hotel of the count of La Rochefoucauld, Paris 1912 © Ullsteinbild
Cover design: Campus Verlag, Frankfurt am Main

Printed on acid free paper.
Printed in Germany

For further information:
www.campus.de
www.press.uchicago.edu

Contents

Acknowledgements

These three books have emerged from a joint research project, and so our debts of gratitude are unusually far-reaching – both to our fellow authors in these volumes and to many others.

To start with, we must thank the European Union for funding our research into Kinship and Social Security as part of its Sixth Framework research program. We are also grateful to the Max Planck Society for additional contributions to research and publication costs – and to the other institutions within the KASS consortium who funded parts of their work from their own budgets.

We would also like to thank our EU desk officers, Vittoria Vittorino and Marc Goffart, for their patience and support, and Hanna Hacker, the academic assessor appointed by the EU, for her fair-minded and fundamentally supportive comments, which were very helpful even when we disagreed. And of course the project would never have happened without the intellectual support and practical commitment of our senior colleagues, Günther Schlee, Chris Hann, Keebet and Franz von Benda-Beckmann at the Max Planck Institute for Social Anthropology at Halle, and Karl Kaser at the History Institute of Karl-Franzens-University Graz.

Many people at MPI Halle contributed to the success of this project in organisational or technical ways, and our thanks go to:

- Heiko Kastner, who coordinated all aspects of the project administration with unflappable calm for four eventful years, and went on to see the books through to publication
- Silke Riemann for the dynamism and creativity with which she coordinated the application for EU funding; Karoline Haufe, Judith Orland and Frances Pine for helping her so effectively; and Bettina Mann who put the application team together and has continued to watch over the project's best interests

- Gordon Milligan and Christian Kieser for writing the program for the Kinship Network Questionnaire, and designing its visual layout
- Tuba Bircan, Siegfried Gruber, Zhonghui Ou, Michael Schnegg and Robert White who wrote the data-conversion and analysis programs
- Armin Pippel, Harald Nagler and Oliver Weihmann for background support with computing matters
- Julia Baumhauer, Sebastian Fritz, Carola Michaelis and Lorenza Wand for their assistance in developing the KNQ
- Tuba Bircan, Franziska Böde, Melanie Funk, Yvonne Hörnicke, Annett Mehlhorn and Rabah Melodie El-Hajj Moussa for helping to administer the field work and quality-checking the KNQ data
- Dorothee Braun for her work on the concluding conference and the publication process
- Kristin Magnucki, Jutta Turner and Oliver Weihmann for design work
- Kathrin Niehuus, Burgunde Seidel, Anke Schneider, Matthias Friedrich and Nadine Wagenbrett for managing the contractual and financial side of things.

Outside MPI Halle we would like to thank

- Zoran Cica for his contribution to the historical research in Croatia, and Jasna Capo Zmegac for her institutional support
- Philippe Chaudat for his contribution to historical research in France
- Ida Ohlsson for her contribution to historical research, and Susanna Larson and Yvla Preutz for their fieldwork in Sweden
- Simona Sambati for her contribution to fieldwork in Italy, and Gian Paolo Gri for institutional support
- Dimitry Rogozin for his contribution to fieldwork in Russia
- Ludmila Wisniewska for her contribution to fieldwork, and Stefan Kowal and Ziemowit Malag for their contribution to historical research in Poland
- Tilo Grätz for his contribution to fieldwork in Germany, and
- Sunniva Greve for the language editing of all three volumes.

Finally, and most of all, we should like to thank the many members of the public who helped our field researchers, including those who took part in the interesting, but also very lengthy, interviews with the Kinship Network Questionnaire.

Hannes Grandits and Patrick Heady

Family, kinship and state in contemporary Europe: introduction to the three-volume series

Patrick Heady

Background and research agenda

This volume is the first of a series of three dedicated to the theme of "family, kinship and state in contemporary Europe". The history of these volumes goes back to early spring 2003, and to an application for research funding under the social security sub-heading of the European Union's Sixth Framework programme. It was a time at which policies on "the family" were subject to conflicting political pressures. Given what were felt to be high and possibly rising tax levels, there was pressure for the state to save money by handing back some of its social security responsibilities to ordinary families and networks of relatives. But there were also pressures to increase state help to some families. Concern for gender equality, and the desire to draw more fully on the economic contribution of women, prompted interest in forms of public assistance that would make it easier for women to combine motherhood with paid work. Growing public awareness of the low birth rates in nearly all Europe, and exceptionally low birth rates in many countries, prompted arguments that increasing official help to young families now would encourage fertility and so eventually provide more working age adults who could, in thirty years time, help to bear the burden of taxes and informal care necessary to ensure a decent life to current generations of adults when they eventually reached old age.

Implicitly, at least, all these debates raise the questions of who is most aware of people's current and future needs and who is best able and most strongly motivated to provide for them. Theoretical discussion of these issues gradually accumulated during the second half of the twentieth century. Economists produced rational choice models which included family members in the set of people whose welfare a rational individual might wish to maximise (Becker 1981), while evolutionary theorists provided an account of how commitment to the welfare of close relatives might have arisen and of the circumstances in which an individual might prefer the welfare of a relative to her own (Hamilton 1964). Evolutionary theorists and economists went on to develop theoretical and experimental analyses of situations in which reciprocal help would be viable (Axelrod 1984; Henrich and Henrich 2007; Hammerstein 2003). These analyses of reciprocity are relevant to cooperation between kin, though they are not specific to it.

Towards the end of the twentieth century moves began to be made to document actual patterns of interaction and mutual assistance between relatives. The International Social Survey Programme (ISSP) included comparative questions on the closeness of residence of specified relatives, and on the importance of relatives amongst the set of people to whom one might turn for help in various specified circumstances (Höllinger and Haller 1990; Gruber and Heady, this volume). In 2002 the European Statistical Office produced a volume on the "life of women and men", reworking statistics collected in the course of EU-sponsored enquiries to provide a comparative picture of gender roles in different EU countries – and also of residence patterns and various other indicators of the strength of ties to relatives and non-relatives (Eurostat 2002). By the early twenty first century, there were moves to replace this initial, rather impressionistic data on mutual assistance between relatives with much more thorough survey documentation of specific relationships. In some countries sociologists had already conducted detailed studies of contacts and transfers between adult family generations – showing that these were much more intensive than commonly assumed (Attias-Donfut 1995; Kohli 1999). These pioneering studies led on to the Survey of Health, Aging and Retirement in Europe (SHARE), whose first wave took place in 2004, providing detailed comparable information about exchanges between generations of grandparents, parents and children in 10 European countries (Kohli et al. 2010). Some of the quantitative studies of intergenerational relationships have been linked to ethnographic studies (Attias-Donfut and Segalen 1998) in order to provide insight into the quality of the relationships concerned, their interaction dynamics, and the values on which they rest.

Kinship and Social Security (KASS), the project whose findings are presented in these three volumes, arose in part from this ferment of ideas – and shares several methodological features, and even researchers, with projects mentioned in the previous paragraph. However, the angle of vision is rather different – and this is reflected in the academic disciplines we draw on. While much of the work referred to above comes under the headings of sociology and economics, most contributors to these three volumes see themselves as anthropologists or historians. We do not wish to reject economic and sociological ideas, but we feel that anthropologists and historians have some important things to add to recent discussions of family relationships and policy which might otherwise be missed. It may be helpful to say something about how this idea first dawned on us, before going on to outline its implications for the work presented in these volumes.

At the start of 2003 Hannes Grandits and I were completing the editorial work on a volume about the history and anthropology of European inheritance systems and their implications for family life and social organisation (Grandits and Heady 2003). Looking at the Eurostat publication just mentioned (Eurostat 2002) we were struck, like others before us (Reher 1998; Viazzo 2010) by the close correspondence between contemporary residential statistics for different parts of Europe and the macro-regional patterns sketched by Laslett (1983) and Hajnal (1982) on the basis of case studies from previous centuries – and also by the inverse relationship between close family ties and statistics on involvement in formal associations. We concluded that there were "[...] clear differences between the northern, central-western and Mediterranean countries – with the arrangements of the latter placing more emphasis on kinship ties and those of northern countries placing more emphasis on other forms of association" (Grandits and Heady 2003, 22–23). It looked as though anthropological insights into cultural differences and the role of kinship in community life, and historical analyses of the roots of different family forms, would be able to add something to our explanations of contemporary family life which went beyond rational choice models and purely biological understandings of kinship altruism.

We thought that a research programme that combined these perspectives would enable us to test them comparatively, and perhaps also work towards a comprehensive approach to kin relationships that combined a universalistic understanding of the cognitive and emotional dispositions involved (such as, but not limited to, those highlighted by current economic and evolutionary theories) with a historical and anthropological understanding of the factors which shape the variable macro and micro-contexts within which these dispositions operate. This was the essence of the KASS research proposal which we and our colleagues successfully submitted to the European Union.

Relation to other explanatory approaches

This combination of the universal with the very particular was not the only possible explanatory strategy, and in working out its implications we have had to grapple with some well-established middle-range research traditions. Two in particular – modernisation theory (Inglehart and Welzel 2005; Lesthaeghe 1983) and the theory of different macro-regional welfare regimes (Esping-Andersen 1990; Albertini et al. 2007) – offer explanations of the distribution of "strong" and "weak" family systems in contemporary Europe. It is reasonable to ask why we think these approaches need improvement.

This question might be difficult to answer if there was just one established explanation. But the fact that there are two of them, offering quite distinct accounts, suggests that neither can really be the last word. Taken at its simplest, modernisation theory states that new forms of economic life (industry and commerce as compared to agriculture, and the knowledge-based economy as compared with earlier forms of industry and commerce) generate new and more individualistic values; these values in turn make earlier, more authoritarian forms of family life unacceptable, leading to "weak" family systems. A simple version of welfare regime theory, on the other hand, says that different systems of official benefits and taxes provide different incentives to individuals and families, to which they respond with something like economic rationality. Thus, according to this argument, southern European benefit systems, which are relatively parsimonious by European Union standards, primarily benefit elderly people – strengthening their bargaining position within the family and requiring younger adults to turn to them for support. Similarly, the more generous systems of northern Europe, and the help they extend to young as well as old, free kin relationships from the constraints of economic need – allowing a more distant, but perhaps emotionally warmer, relationship to emerge between adult relatives.

Of course, stated so baldly, both theses require considerable qualification, which they receive later in these volumes. However, even in these forms it is clear that they raise as many questions as they answer. Why are some public welfare systems more generous than others? And why are the welfare systems that encourage weak families found in precisely those countries where individualistic values are most developed – and where modernisation theory would lead one to expect weak families even without state encouragement? Might it be the case that the kind of family system depends on the economic system, and that politicians merely provide the benefits that are most helpful to the kinds of families that actually exist? Do benefits perhaps have a genuinely incentive character which, operating through the kinds of family they support, promotes or obstructs the development of a truly "modern" economy? Or do quite different factors, now or in the past, also exert constraints on the kinds of state welfare policy and family system that can develop in any particular society?

It would be possible to extend this list of questions, but hopefully the key point has been made. When we look critically at the middle-range models, even if the correlations between types of "economy", "family" and "welfare state" remain more or less in place[1], these correlations are not enough in themselves to establish the directions of causation. Instead we are confronted with a dynamic system in which the characteristics of these macro-entities are connected to each other through the activities of the people whose lives they help to shape. In this system, the causal forces are the perceptions, thoughts and motives of the people who live within it, influenced as they are by the economic, family and welfare state institutions themselves.

Fortunately such a system, though it may seem discouragingly complex, offers many more ways of identifying causal connections than simply looking at national-level correlations. Sociologists have insisted on the importance of the micro-macro link, and it is here that the value of historical and anthropological approaches also begins to tell. In dynamic systems time-ordering matters – both at the macro-level and at the level of interpersonal interactions – so both historical and ethnographic narratives can throw real light on the causal processes at work. Starting points matter too: as we have seen, historical accounts of family systems and provisions for public welfare before the onset of industrialisation and the modern welfare state may help us to identify the initial conditions for the different national trajectories of family and welfare state development over time.

Secondly – and this is a very important point – both history and anthropology can tell us a great deal about what happens at the conceptual boundaries of the system. Although it is convenient in many contexts to treat the connections between the economy, public welfare and family life as if they formed a closed system, this is essentially an analytic fiction. Each

1 The extent to which this is so is discussed at various points in these volumes.

of the main institutions in the system is linked to other aspects of social or political life. This means that decisions about measures to promote family welfare – whether taken by the state or by families themselves – are never *just* about family welfare. An example was given in the first paragraph of this introduction, which noted the current search for family policies that can promote gender equality and female labour-force participation. The political priorities change but, as Hannes Grandits and the team of authors show in Volume I, the mutual entanglement of welfare policy and other political objectives appears to be a constant.

Similarly the decisions which individuals and families make about mutual assistance and welfare have implications which link those involved into wider systems of "kinship". Anthropologists have typically seen kinship as standing at the intersection between public and private life. The rules that govern marriage, residence and inheritance can be viewed simultaneously either as arrangements for the business of everyday living (what Goody [1976] describes as the domestic domain of production and reproduction), or as arrangements which ensure the perpetuation of certain kinds of community and political structure – such as exogamous lineages, endogamous castes, closed corporate villages, social classes and so on. Kinship ties are often treated, implicitly or explicitly, as constituent parts of local systems that are at once domestic, economic and political.

If this is so, the demands of the local kinship system may well place another set of constraints on family behaviour, over and above those emanating from state and economic structures. However, there are differences of opinion even among anthropologists about the importance of kinship (as distinct from the immediate family) in European societies. Goody (1983) presents the history of the European family as a 2,000-year process in which, in response to economic change and under pressure from church and state, lineage structures and kindreds have given way to a common European system based on the conjugal family. Goody's thesis – which has parallels with modernisation theory, though it projects the initial decline of kinship much further back in time – is supported with some differences of emphasis by Mitterauer (2003), but has been challenged by Sabean and others (Sabean et al. 2007) who point to ways in which the development of state and market institutions actually strengthened kin ties, at least among elite families. There are also ethnographic indications that Goody may have overstated the mutual independence of modern European families. These include the studies of kinship networks in post-war Britain (Bott 1957;

Firth et al. 1968; Young and Wilmott 1957), and a considerable number of ethnographic studies, mostly in rural areas of southern and eastern Europe. The ethnographies and associated historical studies have highlighted such classical anthropological themes as descent – conceptualised both in terms of lineal and cognatic ties, as well as in terms of the continuity of "houses" – and the use of marriage, spiritual kinship and structured exchange relationships to bind together solidary communities (Augustins 1989; Cole and Wolf 1974; Delille 1985; du Boulay 1984; Halpern 1967; Hammel 1968; Heady 1999; Jolas et al. 1990; Just 2000; Kligman 1988; Loizos 1975, 1981; Ott 1993; Pine 1996; Rogers 1991; Segalen 1991). Unfortunately the ethnographic literature and the survey-based literature on family values and intergenerational ties have developed in almost total isolation from each other.[2] Given the potential influence of kinship on family behaviour, and *vice versa*, it seems high time to explore the empirical connections between the two.

Our research project, and how its findings are presented in these volumes

These fundamental ideas – the need to explore changing family patterns from multiple perspectives, and the importance of placing them in the wider contexts of historical processes and kinship ties – were the starting point of the programme of research whose findings are presented in these books.

We decided to focus the research on eight countries: France, (East) Germany, Sweden, Austria, Italy, Croatia, Poland and Russia. They represent a cross-section in terms of recent historical experience (four "western", three "post-socialist", and one formerly divided country), and in terms of longer historical and cultural trends (reflected in religious traditions, kinship terminologies, and historical patterns of household composition).

2 Segalen (1986) is a notable exception to this.

Volume I – The Century of Welfare: Eight Countries

Volume I is dedicated to an analysis of the long term developments that have led up to the situation at present – focusing particularly on the interaction between kinship and the state during the twentieth century. The introductory chapter describes the double movement that characterised the last hundred years. At the start of the twentieth century there was a wide divergence between the countries in our sample – whether seen in terms of demographic variables or state welfare policies. By mid-century, the countries had become much more similar in both respects, in what can be seen in retrospect as a "golden age" of marriage and child-bearing and of state welfare. Following this period, which lasted till about 1970, the trends began to diverge again in ways that partly reflected and partly contrasted with the pattern of divergences a hundred years before.

There then follow eight chapters on the evolution of state policy towards the family in each of the countries in our study, including what is known about the response of families themselves to these developments. All chapters cover certain common themes – relating to economic change, the institutional development of welfare provision, the political and intellectual background to these developments, and the gradual growth of quantitative knowledge about family circumstances and behaviour. At the same time the authors have been encouraged to develop themes that are specific to the country in question.

The final chapter of Volume I uses historical statistics to provide a comparative view of changing family patterns and the impact of economic and educational change. The chapter links these historical trends to contemporary survey data on family values in the eight countries, and on the extent of contact between close kin. Both kinds of data connect the specificities of national history to sociological debates about the impact of modernisation and different forms of social capital – setting the scene for the studies reported in the next two volumes.

Volume II – The View from Below: Nineteen Localities

The first volume is oriented predominantly towards national-level information, about political processes, and places a good deal of emphasis on aggregated statistical information about families. Widening the perspective to include other aspects of kinship required a parallel shift in the units of data-collection and analysis. It was no longer enough to present aggregate information about individuals and families: they must be shown in relation to each other in kinship networks and local communities. Furthermore, we needed solid information about the extent of help and interaction throughout the kinship networks, and not just between close relatives. Finally, we needed to place the data about mundane interactions in the context of values, ideas and emotions.

This led us to adopt an original research strategy – based on field research at 19 localities (one rural and one urban in each of the eight countries, a third intermediate site in France and Italy, and a second rural locality in Poland). We did not assume that kinship networks and local communities coincided (in the urban areas they certainly did not) but collected data independently on each aspect by participant observation and qualitative interviews in the nineteen areas, and by extended, computer-recorded, interviews with representative samples of informants which demonstrated the extent, and geographic range of their kinship networks – and the patterns of interaction and assistance within each network.

The results of this research at each field site are presented in the second volume. The first chapter introduces the themes of kinship and community. It discusses different anthropological approaches to the study of kinship, and goes on to outline the methodology of the KASS field studies. This is followed by a chapter that is designed to "place" the characteristics of the field locations in relation to national patterns, and to give an initial overview of some similarities and contrasts between the field sites themselves. It is based on local statistics and on certain key quantitative results from the kinship network questionnaires, and covers demographic, residential and economic patterns, the average size of kinship networks, along with summary measures of mutual assistance and kin-based interaction.

There follow eight composite chapters prepared by the national field teams, primarily on the basis of the qualitative aspects of the field research. The aim in each case was to present and illustrate an "ethnographic model" of kinship and mutual assistance in each of the field sites. The field teams were asked to cover certain common themes – including ideas about altruism, reciprocity and self-interest, kinship and social capital, cognition, symbolism and ritual, and the impact of economic and administrative circumstances – and to relate these to the provision of aid, to gender and life-cycle roles, and to fertility. As in the case of the historical teams, they were also encouraged to develop their own theoretical approaches and to explore themes of particular local interest.

The final chapter reviews the ethnographic chapters, bringing out commonalities and contrasts both in the situations described, and the models that have been proposed.

Volume III – Perspectives on Theory and Policy

The third volume presents the main findings of the quantitative network analysis, followed by a series of essays which review the findings of the project as a whole from different disciplinary and theoretical perspectives. The quantitative analyses cover: a comparison of local systems of family, kindred and marriage; memory of kinship connections; practical domestic assistance; structural help – setting up and financing the home; reciprocity and altruism in practical assistance; and birth rates in the context of network relationships, values and social patterns. One chapter presents comparative survey data from SHARE and discusses its implications. The viewpoints presented in the essays include an overview of the modern reality of European kinship; an analysis of macro-regional differences in kinship culture; a comparison between urban and rural family systems; the interaction between kinship, neighbourhood and community loyalties; gender, kinship and the market for social care; the connections between kinship vocabularies and family systems; and an analysis of KASS findings from the viewpoint of evolutionary theories of human behaviour. The opening and closing chapters attempt a synthetic view of the research findings, linking them to policy debates about the relative importance of the "crowding in" and "crowding out" effects of public welfare provision, and to the concept of different welfare regimes. The discussion concludes with some recommendations for policy.

Bibliography

Albertini, M., M. Kohli and C. Vogel (2007), "Intergenerational transfers of time and money in European families: common patterns, different regimes?", *Journal of European social policy* , 17, pp. 319–334.

Attias-Donfut, C (ed.) (1995), *Les solidarités entre générations. Vieillesse, familles, État*, Paris: Nathan.

Attias-Donfut, C and M. Segalen (1998), *Grands-parents: la famille à travers les générations*, Paris: Éditions Odile Jacob.

Augustins, G. (1989), *Comment se perpétuer? Devenir des lignées et destins des patrimoines dans les paysanneries européennes*, Nanterre: Société d'ethnologie.

Axelrod, R. (1984), *The evolution of cooperation*, New York: Basic Books.

Becker, G. (1981), *A treatise on the family*, Cambridge Mass.: Harvard University Press.

Bott, E. (1957), *Family and social network: roles, norms and external relationships in ordinary urban families*, London: Tavistock Publications.

Cole, J. and E. Wolf (1974), *The hidden frontier: ecology and ethnicity in an alpine valley*, New York: Academic Press.

Delille, G. (1985), *Famille et propriété dans le royaume de Naples (XVe–XIXe siècle)*, Rome: École Française de Rome.

du Boulay, J. (1984), "The blood: symbolic relationships between descent, marriage, incest prohibitions and spiritual kinship in Greece", *Man*, 19, pp. 533–556.

Esping-Andersen, G. (1990), *The three worlds of welfare capitalism*, Princeton NJ: Princeton University Press.

Eurostat (2002), *The life of women and men in Europe: a statistical portrait*, Luxembourg: Office for Official Publications of the European Communities.

Firth, R., J. Hubert and A. Forge (1968), *Families and their relatives: kinship in a middle-class sector of London*, London: Routledge & Kegan Paul.

Goody, J. (1976), *Production and reproduction: a comparative study of the domestic domain.* Cambridge: Cambridge University Press.

— (1983), *The development of the family and marriage in Europe*, Cambridge: Cambridge University Press.

Grandits, H. and P. Heady (eds.) (2003), *Distinct inheritances: property, family and community in a changing Europe*, Münster: LIT.

Hajnal, J. (1982), "Two kinds of pre-industrial household formation system", *Population and Development Review*, 8, pp. 449–494.

Halpern, J. (1967), *A Serbian village*, New York: Columbia University Press.

Hamilton, W. (1964), "The genetical evolution of social behaviour", *Journal of Theoretical Biology*, 7, pp. 1–52.

Hammel, E. (1968), *Alternative social structures and ritual relations in the Balkans*, Englewood Cliffs: Prentice Hall.

Hammerstein, P. (ed.) (2003), *Genetic and cultural evolution of cooperation*, Cambridge Mass.: MIT Press.

Heady, P. (1999), *The hard people: rivalry, sympathy and social structure in an alpine valley*, Amsterdam: Harwood Academic.

Henrich, N. and J. Henrich (2007), *Why humans cooperate: a cultural and evolutionary explanation*, Oxford: Oxford University Press.

Höllinger, F. and M. Haller (1990), "Kinship and social networks in modern societies: a cross-cultural comparison among seven nations", *European Sociological Review*, 6, pp. 103–124.

Inglehart, R. and C. Welzel (2005), *Modernisation, cultural change and democracy: the human development sequence*, Cambridge: Cambridge University Press.

Jolas, T., M.-C. Pinguad, Y. Verdier and F. Zonabend (1990), *Une campagne voisine*, Paris: Éditions de la maison des sciences de l'homme.

Just, R. (2000), *A Greek island cosmos: kinship and community on Meganisi*, Oxford: James Currey.

Kligman, G. (1988), *The wedding of the dead*, London: University of California Press.

Kohli, M. (1999), "Private and public transfers between generations: linking the family and the state", *European Societies*, 1, pp. 81–104.

Kohli, M., M. Albertini and H. Künemund (2010), "Linkages among adult family generations: evidence from comparative survey research", in P. Heady and M. Kohli (eds.), *Family, kinship and state in contemporary Europe, Vol. 3: Perspectives on theory and policy*, Frankfurt and New York: Campus, pp. 233–258.

Laslett, P. (1983), "Family and household as work group and kin group: areas of traditional Europe compared", in R. Wall, J. Robin and P. Laslett (eds.), *Family forms in historic Europe*, Cambridge: Cambridge University Press, pp. 513–564.

Lesthaeghe, R. (1983), "A century of demographic and cultural change in western Europe: an exploration of underlying dimensions", *Population and Development Review*, 9(3), pp. 411–435.

Loizos, P. (1975), *The Greek gift: politics in a Cypriot village*, Oxford: Blackwell.

— (1981), *The heart grown bitter: a chronicle of Cypriot war refugees*, Cambridge: Cambridge University Press.

Mitterauer, M. (2003), "European kinship systems and household structures: medieval origins", in H. Grandits and P. Heady (eds.), *Distinct inheritances: property, family and community in a changing Europe*, Münster: LIT, pp. 35–52.

Ott, S. (1993), *The circle of mountains: a Basque shepherding community*, London: University of Nevada Press.

Pine, F. (1996), "Naming the house and naming the land: kinship and social groups in the Polish highlands", *Journal of the Royal Anthropological Institute*, 2, pp. 443–459.

Reher, D. (1998), "Family ties in western Europe: persistent contrasts", *Population and Development Review*, 24 (2), pp. 203–234.

Rogers, S. (1991), *Shaping modern times in rural France: the transformation and reproduction of an Aveyronnais community*, Princeton NJ: Princeton University Press.

Sabean, D., S. Teuschler and J. Mathieu (2007), *Kinship in Europe: approaches to long-term development (1300–1900)*, Oxford: Berghahn.

Segalen, M. (1986), *Historical anthropology of the family*, Cambridge: Cambridge University Press.

— (1991), *Fifteen generations of Bretons: kinship and society in lower Brittany 1720–1980*, Cambridge: Cambridge University Press.

Viazzo, P. P. (2010), "Macro-regional differences in European kinship culture", in P. Heady and M. Kohli (eds.), *Family, kinship and state in contemporary Europe, Vol. 3: Perspectives on theory and policy*, Frankfurt and New York: Campus, pp. 281–304.

Young, M. and P. Wilmott (1957), *Family and kinship in east London*, London: Routledge and Kegan Paul.

Introduction: the reshaping of family and kin relations in European welfare systems

Hannes Grandits

At the beginning of the twenty-first century, Europeans are clearly living in the era *after* the expansion of the welfare state – not to mention its virtual collapse in parts of Eastern Europe following 1989. Furthermore, during the European process of unification, ideas on adjusting the welfare regimes in the European Union were seriously investigated. These examinations made it patently clear to policy-makers that the interaction between welfare state policy and family/kin in Europe had developed in often quite diverse traditions. And although it would not be wrong from a global perspective to speak of a shared "European history" in terms of the welfare state (Kaelble 2004), the beliefs as to how it should function and the nature of its obligations still vary even today. Despite these differences, almost all European national policy discourses in recent decades have progressively come to the conclusion that the welfare state is overburdened. Demands that individual citizens and their family/kin take more responsibility for their social security have become louder.

The context outlined here constitutes the starting point for the research involved in this book, which analyses and compares European family and kinship over the last century, focusing on their role in the provision of social security. The aim is to reflect on the embodiment of family and kin in the historical development and functioning of the welfare state: what was and is the role of kinship and family in providing social security in European welfare state societies? How has the welfare state influenced family and kin relations?

These are the key questions raised in this volume, as they are crucial to the KASS research as a whole. The ethnographies, quantitative findings and theoretical contributions in Volumes II and III will tackle these common themes from complementary points of view. Here they are approached historically. In a critical evaluation of the historically varying relations of European welfare states to family and kin, the chapters of this volume provide a detailed analysis of the twentieth-century development of kinship and social security in eight European countries. These eight countries represent individual welfare state ideologies in Europe and to some degree individual historical "cultures" of kinship in public and private life (or may at least hypothetically be regarded as such at the outset). Contrasts between the eight national examples can be outlined as follows:

- The contrast, for instance, between supposedly familistic *Italy* (studied by Viazzo and Zanotelli in chapter 2), which serves here as an example of a Mediterranean society, and the allegedly individualistic north European *Sweden* (analysed by Gaunt in chapter 3), a Scandinavian welfare state model.
- The contrast between *Germany* and *France*, which – not least as a result of the Second World War and the Nazi experience – pursued different ideologies in terms of how the state should be allowed to influence family life. While Germany (analysed by Rosenbaum and Timm in chapter 4) declared the family a private realm to be protected from state intervention, France (reconsidered by Augustins and Segalen in chapter 5) developed a distinctly interventionist "pro-family" welfare policy.
- *Austria* (investigated by Pflegerl and Geserick in chapter 6) can be seen as an example of a small European country that remained politically "neutral" during the Cold War decades, when the welfare state went through considerable expansion throughout Europe, and later joined the EU integration process.
- Three chapters on *Croatia* (by Grandits in chapter 7), *Poland* (by Dyczewski in chapter 8) and *Russia* (by Trotsuk and Nikulin in chapter 9) – deal with family and kinship within the variants of socialist and post-socialist welfare state developments. These three chapters (three and a half if the chapter on Germany is included, where developments in the GDR are analysed comparatively) will give a better understanding of processes in Eastern Europe and enable us to make more fruitful comparisons between Western and Eastern Europe.

In the eight country chapters, i.e., on Sweden, Italy, France, Germany, Austria, Croatia, Poland and Russia, we will unearth in detail the characteristics of the interrelation between welfare state developments and family/kin. Despite the many peculiarities involved, there are general trends common to all eight countries. In this introductory chapter an attempt will be made to address some of them comparatively.

We begin with reflections on the "golden age" of marriage and its interrelation with the "golden age" of the welfare state in Europe of the 1950s and 1960s. We will then briefly refer to the emergence in recent decades of a new demographic situation throughout Europe. In the remaining sections of the chapter, European welfare state expansions and contractions will be discussed in relation to their consequences for family and kin relations.

The golden age of marriage and the welfare state

Over the last thirty years social and family history has fundamentally altered our understanding of family life in Europe in the past. Projections about invariable or harmonious historical family relations have been deconstructed. A panorama has evolved of family models that differed according to region, class or the rural-urban divide, often to a pronounced extent. Discussions were launched, for instance, on the consequences of distinctive marriage or inheritance regimes, or with the aim of defining macro-regional specifics (see, for example, Laslett and Wall 1972; Mitterauer and Sieder 1988; Viazzo 1989; Segalen 1990; Gullestad and Segalen 1997; Rosenbaum 1998; Viazzo 2003; Plakans and Wetherell 2003; Kertzer and Barbagli 2003).

Ideas about specific macro-regional family patterns have been the subject of an ongoing scientific debate. Family history and historical demography gradually developed the knowledge that historically quite different household formation characteristics prevailed in the different macro-regions of Europe. A household formation system in northwest Europe with a high predominance of simple households was contrasted with systems in the Mediterranean or in Eastern Europe, where larger family households were historically more common. Late marriage with high proportions of people who had never married was found to be widespread in the northwest or west of Europe (or in the Alpine regions of Central Europe), quite the reverse of Eastern Europe and many parts of the Mediterranean. In addition, the last two macro-regions differed fundamentally with regard to inheritance practices: male-centred forms of inheritance were dominant in vast areas of Eastern Europe, while in southern Europe conjugal-centred forms of inheritance predominated.

However, by the 1990s, this image of historically contrasting macro-regional forms of European family life was being questioned by a growing number of historical, anthropological and historical-anthropological micro-studies. A picture evolved of much more variability within the supposedly homogeneous macro-regions, and was explained as the result of a complex interplay of economic, ecological, demographic or cultural factors.

Nevertheless, a renewed validation of macro-regional differences came with closer scrutiny of the amount, mode and quality of interfamilial or kinship helping relations. This new "turn" in discussing models of European family life was also influenced by a recent series of European comparative quantitative studies (e.g., SHARE, ISSP or the European Value Surveys (EVS)) that also dealt with the importance of family and informal relations in social security arrangements in contemporary Europe (for a far more detailed discussion of these subsequent trends in historical family research Viazzo 2010; see also various papers in Grandits and Heady 2003; see also Gruber and Heady in this volume).

In the light of this condensed portrayal of diversity in family life in the Europe of the past and from the perspective of family history, it is surprising that the 1950s and 1960s can be viewed in retrospect as a period of unprecedented homogeneity throughout much of Europe. Marriage behaviour and consequently several household formation characteristics grew distinctly similar throughout most of Europe during these decades. This applied in particular to variables such as the marriage rate, marriage age or rate of children born "out of wedlock".

In the initial decades after the Second World War, almost all societies in Europe experienced a marriage boom. Getting married became an almost universal part of the life-course. This was true for close to the entire generation of young men and women, even in countries where socio-economic constraints or cultural rules had precluded a substantial percentage of the population from marriage in earlier periods (the Princeton European Fertility Project provided us with highly detailed and comparative knowledge of the divergent proportions of the married and unmarried throughout large parts of Europe since the nineteenth century, as well as of transformation trends in the twentieth century (early second half); see, for instance, Coale and Treadway 1986). In addition, the marriage age for men and women, historically divergent throughout much of Europe, began to converge to a hitherto unknown degree (Watkins 1986).

In the 1950s and 1960s, the percentage of children born out of wedlock declined all over Europe. As a rule only ten per cent of children, or even less, were born to non-married couples and single mothers. In other words approximately 90 per cent, in some countries almost 95 per cent, of children were born in wedlock. For some countries this represented a radical departure from the past (see figure 1.1), most notably Austria, for example, where up until the 1950s the number of children born out of wedlock had as a rule constituted approximately 25 per cent (historically even more) of all new-born children. In Sweden, too, the number of so-called "illegitimate" children showed a marked decrease in the 1950s compared with the previous fifty or twenty years (Pflegerl and Geserick; Gaunt in this volume).

Figure 1.1: Percentage of births outside marriage between 1900 and 2007

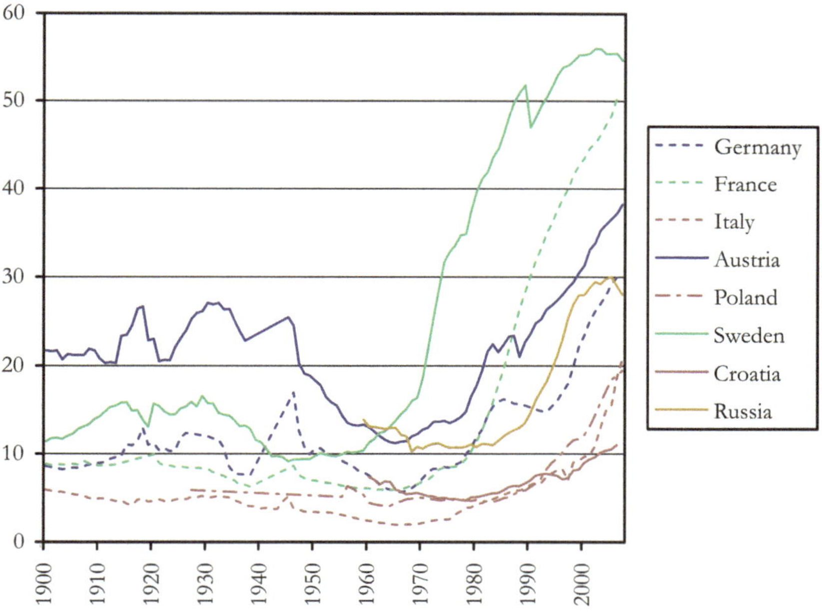

For sources see appendix

It is no coincidence that the marriage boom across Europe paralleled the period of post-war expansion of the welfare state and its "golden age" in Europe. The various types of welfare states that developed from the end of the 1940s up to the 1970s were essentially based on two major principles: full male employment and the stability of marriage (Raphael 2006, 62–66; Saraceno 2003, 256). Achieved, on the one hand, by stable economic growth in the early post-war decades, which brought prosperity to growing sections of Europe's populations, these principles were underpinned, on the other hand, by a new welfare state philosophy that successively developed existing "social rights" into a coherent whole and was primarily oriented almost everywhere in Western Europe towards the married-male-breadwinner family model. And despite ideological disparities, the daily practicalities of welfare state expansion in socialist Eastern Europe produced a similar outcome.

The expansion of the European welfare states has been discussed elsewhere (Alber 1982; Schmidt 1988; Esping-Andersen 1990; Bahle 1995; Tálos 1998; Kuhnle 2000; Kaufmann 2002; Schmid 2002; Esping-Andersen 2002; Kaelble and Schmid 2004; Tomka 2004). Its varying relation to family and kin is critically re-examined in the chapters of this volume. It is sufficient to conclude here that for a certain period of time the "new" welfare state of the post-WWII decades supported and even introduced an exceptional convergence of marriage and family structures throughout Europe.

Starting in the 1960s, socio-economic, cultural and eventually also legal changes began to alter this "uniform" pattern of marriage behaviour and family structures in Europe. Apart from common trends in transformation, however, this process did not take an identical course in the individual European countries. The percentage of people who married remained exceedingly high in southern European (see, for example, Italy) and in the socialist and post-socialist East, where rates of marriage in some countries exceeded 90 per cent. In northern and western Europe, on the other hand, marriage as a fixed element of the life course lost much of its earlier significance. Taking a closer look at the rates of children born "outside marriage", we see similar trends in geographical distribution. In Italy, Croatia or Poland, i.e., in southern and Eastern Europe, the percentage of children born out of wedlock remained extremely low (up to the beginning of the post-socialist transition, the pattern in Russia was also consistent with this development; see Trotsuk and Nikulin in this volume). Quite the opposite was the case, for instance, in Sweden. In the 1980s, more children were born here to non-married partners than to married couples (see figure 1.1). Also, in France and Austria marriage and having children were no longer as closely linked as they had been during the "golden age of the family". "Alternative forms" of family life had begun to spread and take root.

To some extent these newly emerging divergences in family formation characteristics once again resembled variations of the regional or "cultural" European marriage regimes of a more distant past. Meanwhile, however, the latter has frequently been forgotten by public memory, which was mostly due to the experience of the marriage boom in the early post-WWII decades, when "almost everyone" in Europe got married.

Falling birth rates and rising life expectancy

Numerous discussions about changes in family and kin relations have evolved in present-day Europe not least as a consequence of the ongoing so-called "second demographic transition" (Lesthaeghe 1983; Coale and Watkins 1986; Kaa 1987; Lesthaeghe and Willems 1999; Surkyn and Lesthaeghe 2004). Exceedingly low birth rates, a phenomenon that had emerged in the 1980s and persisted into the 1990s and 2000s, have become characteristic of Europe. Birth rates in almost all European countries have fallen below the replacement rate. The following figure on the "Total fertility rate between 1948 and 2003" clearly indicates general tendencies towards declining birth rates for all of the eight countries under review.

In some countries this process had already begun to accelerate in the (late) 1960s. Annual fertility rates dropped in many countries below the level of two births per woman, and by the 1980s had plunged in some countries below the 1.5 level. As the lines in the figure show, however, despite the general trend evident in all eight countries towards lower fertility rates, there were variations. In the case of Poland, Croatia and Russia, for instance, the beginning of the post-socialist transition produced an abrupt decline in the rate of fertility. The fertility rate in Sweden went through a period of ups and downs in the 1980s and 1990s but was still relatively high in a European comparison. In France fertility rates remained comparatively stable subsequent to the vast changes in the late 1960s and early 1970s. In fact France has shown a slight increase since the middle of the 1990s (to an average rate of almost two births per woman).

Figure 1.2: Total fertility rate between 1948 and 2005

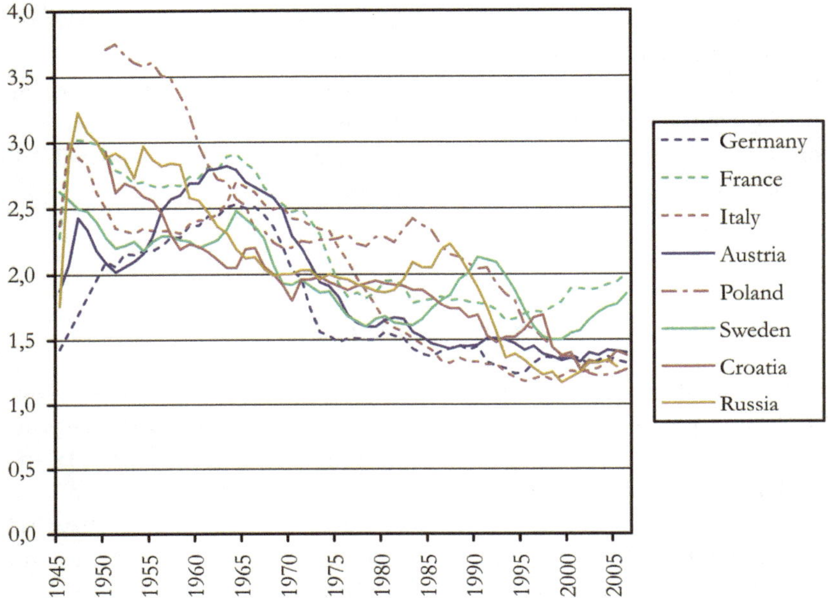

For sources see appendix

Of course these developments must be seen against the backdrop of a complex interplay of socio-economic and cultural settings, and the widely discussed value changes involved (see, for example, Surkyn and Lesthaege 2004; Billari and Kohler 2004; also Gruber and Heady in this volume). At least some of the variations evident in a European comparison are linked to attempts by the welfare state to "reconcile" parents' wage work and the family. Hence it would not be wrong to claim that the welfare state plays an important role in the development of European fertility rates (Saraceno 2006).

From a historical perspective this also applies to the second "dominant" demographic development in the twentieth century, i.e., the ageing of society. The following figure illustrates the steady growth in percentage of people over sixty years of age in the course of the last century.

Figure 1.3: Proportion of population aged 60+, 1901–2005

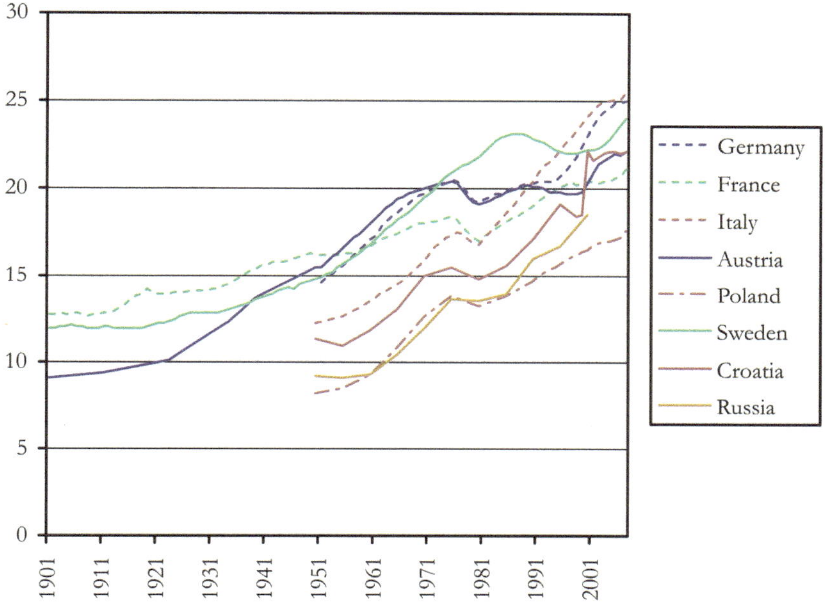

For sources see appendix

Life expectancy has greatly increased in all eight countries under study. The fact that in present-day Europe a substantial and continuously growing section of society belongs to "older stages" in the life-course – often described in the literature as "third age" (55–75 years) and "fourth age" (75 and over) – is a twentieth-century phenomenon (Kertzer and Laslett 1995; Kohli and Szydlik 2000) and would have been impossible without the health and care infrastructure that came with the expansion of the welfare state.

Welfare state reform

The demographic trends outlined here have undoubtedly influenced everyday family and kinship relations in recent decades. At the same time, however, family life – and thereafter the character of the European welfare states – was also affected by further socio-economic (and cultural) developments. Key among these was the massive (re-)entry of a growing percentage of (married) women (with children) into wage work outside the household, a development that had gained in importance in the "capitalist" West with increasing effect since the 1960s and begun even earlier in most of the socialist countries. Despite variations between East and West and from country to country in Europe, the growing participation almost everywhere of women in the labour market began to parallel full male employment (Pfau-Effinger 2000).

In the mid-1970s, however, the European welfare states were challenged by yet another "new" development: unemployment. Full male employment, a cornerstone of the welfare state in its "golden age", had begun to totter. In most European countries the post-war employment boom now appeared to be a thing of the past (for country details, see the statistics of the International Labour Organisation (ILO), e.g., at www.ilo.org). With the beginning of diversity in terms of marriage, which – as addressed above – also emerged in the late 1960s and early 1970s, the second all-important cornerstone, i.e., marriage, also lost its solidity, at least in some European countries.

State policies began to adapt the welfare state of the 1950s and 1960s to this spectrum of change in society with reforms. Towards the end of the century the above-mentioned ageing of the population and the decrease in birth rates in the long run turned out to be increasingly difficult challenges to deal with measures of welfare state reform. With the collapse of socialism in Eastern Europe, a much more fundamental reform of existing (welfare) state systems found its way to the top of the political agenda.

In retrospect, the national variation in policies aimed at adapting the European welfare state to all the changes above was also closely linked to concepts of family and kinship. In the course of welfare state expansion, family and kin were relieved of several social security responsibilities, which for large sections of society had been hard to shoulder in the past, if not impossible. Nevertheless, the welfare state did not fully replace family and kin obligations. It became apparent that the welfare state was being "incorporated" into kinship and family relations, leading to a "symbiosis" of family and state with regard to social security arrangements – one that impacted on kin relations and patterns of mutual aid throughout Europe (we will discuss the issue more thoroughly in the second half of this chapter).

In the initial dismantling of the welfare state throughout most of Europe, the individual countries did not necessarily share a similar understanding of the position of kinship and family in their respective societies (or welfare state systems), and the role they should play in the welfare state of the future. Adherents of the so-called "crowding-out" hypothesis claimed that a welfare state that was "too strong" would render private and interfamilial aid relations superfluous and thus further social isolation. Others tended to emphasize the "crowding-in" function of the welfare state, declaring that only a fully functional welfare system would enable relations of a voluntary or intense nature according to people's needs and desires. Indeed, several studies indicated that support from the welfare state or the community could further social integration substantially by preventing relations from becoming overtaxed with care and maintenance responsibilities. Accordingly relations would have the potential to become socially more "emotional" (for the different theories, see, for example, Lüdicke and Diewald 2007, 269; see also Wellman 1979; the introductory chapter by Heady and Schweitzer 2010).

This introductory chapter will now take a look at the significance of the normative setting and its development for the interrelation between the (welfare) state and family/kinship. Seen in the light of the country research chapters, all of which include in their analysis the basic trends of how family and kinship were legally defined and redefined in the respective countries during the nineteenth and twentieth centuries, the 1960s seems to have been a period that introduced a fundamentally new orientation.

Changing assumptions underlying family law

Despite the long process of secularization and reform of family law that began in the nineteenth century, a more fundamental redefinition of family was not to manifest itself in the legislation policy of most countries in Western Europe until the 1960s and 1970s. In the socialist countries in the eastern half of Europe, this legal redefinition had for the most part taken place one or two decades earlier (in the Soviet Union "experimental" and far-reaching family legislation reforms had even begun after the revolution of 1917; see Trotsuk and Nikulin in this volume).

Hence the comprehensive reorientation of how family was to be perceived in European legislation had finally moved forward in the 1960s or shortly afterwards. The assumption in the immediate post-war decades that women, once married, would withdraw into housewifery was to be increasingly shattered by changing values with regard to the place of women in society and mounting female employment. As the chapter authored by Augustins and Segalen in this volume describes in detail, what could be termed the "overthrow of patriarchy" began to unfold. The patriarchal construction of the family (i.e., the "legitimate family" concept, the husband as "household head", polarized gender identities etc.) was gradually dismantled, at least where family legislation was concerned. The aim of state legislative policy at the end of the 1960s was to follow cultural change (Ronfani 2003, 136; see also Rosenbaum and Timm; Pflegerl and Geserick in this volume).

This was to take place in Europe, however, at different times. The "reformed" family laws introduced by some countries, as distinct from others, made existing differences between individual countries more explicit for a certain period of time. While Sweden, for example, had implemented quite liberal divorce legislation long before the Second World War (see Gaunt in this volume), as late as the 1970s, countries like Italy only allowed divorce in narrowly defined circumstances. Despite the different courses these "legal adaptations" took, family laws in the last two decades have become more and more similar throughout Europe. In the 1980s, for instance, all European legislature accepted divorce by mutual consent. The final step in this process of legal convergence with regard to family came with the collapse of the socialist regimes and the integration of many former socialist countries in Central and Eastern Europe into the EU.

The reform of family legislation in the post-1960s decades was based above all on ideas of gender "equality". From a legal perspective the husband was no longer considered "head of the household". Spouses were legally defined as partners with reciprocal rights and duties. Furthermore, the "interests of the child" took increasing priority over "parental authority". Liberalization of the divorce laws reflected a transformed attitude towards marriage. Individual free choice began to supplant the earlier supremacy and sanctity of marriage as an institution. Gradually other forms of partnership were recognized by the state, whereby unmarried cohabiting couples were granted more rights, for example, in Sweden or France than in most other European countries (although this process is ongoing in many countries).

The convergence of family law in the countries of Western Europe and subsequently of Western and Eastern Europe did not result in a uniformity of family law (Rubellin-Devichi 1997, 61–75). National particularities remained relevant and some reforms gave rise to new divergence. Poland's post-socialist legal reforms, for instance, introduced a number of "Catholic" elements into family law, which no longer exist in the legislation of most other European countries (Dyczewski in this volume). In general, however, the marked trend towards homogeneity in European family law is unmistakeable. International conventions and the EU-wide need to conform legislation to the standards of the European Court furthers this process.

The majority of these legal changes were principally aimed at adapting family legislation to changing life-course patterns across Europe. Their impact, for instance, on gender equality was far-reaching and allowed for a more "flexible" attitude towards marriage in most European countries (albeit at different times). And although we can now see a "legal side" to family life in Europe in the direction of homogeneity (and an accelerated process towards greater convergence in the belief that a welfare state "à l'Europe" could be of significance to European societies; Kaelble and Schmid 2006), the understanding of what kinship and family would or should be in society did not necessarily follow in the wake of this process. Each European country has its own specific socio-economic development and legacy of welfare policy. Kinship and family relations are an integral part of this legacy, since the ideology and history of the welfare state strongly influenced the way in which family and kin relations have been embedded in society and the economy for the last fifty years.

Changes in relationships within the family and among kin

It used to be assumed that the process of "modernization" must lead to the "dissolution of family and kin networks". The chapters in this book strongly reject this argument and emphasise the continuing vitality of kinship ties in contemporary Europe. Indeed, despite the pluralization of family constellations and the rapidly growing incidence of marriage breakdown, there are some contexts in which the practical importance of kinship, and in particular of intergenerational ties, may even have increased during the second half of the twentieth century. It should, of course, be stressed in advance that further research is vital to confirm these trends. In particular, quantitative data on mutual assistance had rarely been collected before the 1990s – and so, as V. Bengtson (2001) recently emphasized, we still have insufficient "before" data from larger surveys to provide comprehensive quantitative "before and after" comparisons. Nevertheless, the chapter authors' careful evaluation of the existing scientific literature does allow us to reflect on commonalities and differences in the changes that occurred in different parts of Europe. So let us now turn to the trends which they have identified in family and kin relations in Europe's post-1945 history.

One sweeping change that impacted on kin relations was the social position assumed by the elderly as a result of expanding pension systems. Retirees acquired a relatively high standard of living. The older generation across all social classes lived longer and thus remained part of everyday relations for a much longer period than in the past, when grandchildren frequently experienced their grandparents for only a short time in their lives. Due to the establishment of viable pension systems, the elderly now disposed of comfortable incomes and were able to support both their children and grandchildren. Unlike in the past, the elderly in all classes were in a position to become "givers" in old age. Pensions began to revolve substantially between the generations and were invested in a circle of reciprocity. In the long run, this promoted solidarity between the generations (Kohli 1999; Ehmer 2000; Kohli and Szydlik 2000; Attias-Donfut 2001; Segalen 2003; see also Gaunt, for example, in this volume).

"New" forms of need for support from the older generation or from kin also began to emerge. Growing female employment rendered families more dependent on child-care support. The number of child-care institutions available for small children was insufficient for quite some time, a circumstance that still characterizes the situation in many countries today. Both grandparents and kin were and still are frequently an important element of child-care arrangements for "modern" two-breadwinner families (Segalen 2003; Rosenbaum and Timm in this volume).

In addition, the younger generation in many European countries has found it increasingly difficult in recent decades to achieve permanency on the labour market. Job protection policies made employment more secure for "privileged insiders", but the end of full employment all over Europe brought increasing uncertainty to young "outsiders" (Esping-Andersen 2002; Viazzo and Zanotelli in this volume). As a consequence numerous young people remain dependent on the parental generation for support. Moreover, education now constitutes a longer period in the life-course of the young and also has implications for family and kin relations. Today, investment in the education of (grown-up) children is a key aspect of intergenerational support (but also the flow of resources). The age at which young people marry and/or have their first child has increased, leading to an extension of youth, during which many remain – at least symbolically – "members" of their childhood families. The excessive cost of housing has led in many countries (particularly those with a predominant tradition of buying flats or houses) to a situation where accommodation for young people can only be obtained with support from the older generation – which is expected and given in an established culture of intergenerational support (Kohli 1999).

The greater instability of marriage has led kin to become a vital source of support in situations of family crisis. Unlike the "golden age" of family, when both stable and standardized family relations prevailed, this is no longer the case in many parts of Europe. When marriages collapse, grandparents and other kin provide emotional support or become key actors in child-care arrangements. Paradoxically, reduced family stability has not rarely led to an increase in kinship ties and their importance (see Gaunt in this volume).

One significant factor that has facilitated these developments and become a precondition for kin relations is the unparalleled expansion of all types of communication. Modern means of transport and communication promote keeping in touch with kin, even with those a great distance away. While in the past contact with kin was strictly limited once migration had occurred, regular contact can now be upheld across hundreds of kilometres. People have become more mobile in their daily lives and live family relations over large distances that would have been unthinkable in the past.

Our KASS research on family and kinship relations in present-day Europe, and indeed other recent research on this topic, has produced yet another finding, which has become evident to varying degrees throughout Europe, i.e., the comparatively high measure of proximity of kin in terms of residence structures. At the beginning of the twenty-first century, married couples almost everywhere in Europe express a strong desire to live independently. Co-residence of parents and married children has become less and less frequent, even in regions where it was once an important aspect of family life (see Viazzo and Zanotelli in this volume). Living in nuclear family or even one-person households is undoubtedly more predominant today than in the past. However, living independently is more often than not combined with living close to kin. Strategies to maintain the geographic proximity of generations seems to be a characteristic feature of European families. This is certainly the case in comparison with the situation in North America (Segalen 2003, 357; Varenne 2005, 59–90).

Nevertheless, the degree of residence proximity to kin varies from one country to another. It is more pronounced, for example, in southern than in northern Europe, where, in addition, closeness is often "evaluated" subjectively and hence differently (the KNQ results in Volume III and the accompanying discussion make this very clear). On the whole variations in the "style" and dimensions of kinship support appear to be widespread. We will now take a look at some of these trends in European family and kinship relations.

Distinctions in European kinship relations

European societies vary in terms of frequency of contact between kin. Different cultural patterns of sociability do exist, there is evidence of "more" sociability in southern and eastern Europe than in the north. In southern Europe, for instance in Italy, very frequent contact appears to be the social norm, while much further north, as in Sweden, the model of less frequent but often quite "intensive" family gatherings on special occasions (e.g., birthdays, joint holidays) is more common. European societies also differ as far as the age at leaving the parental home is concerned and the significance of the aforementioned proximity of residence structures (Höllinger and Haller 1990; Gaunt 1997; Reher 1998; Viazzo and Zanotelli in this volume).

A further distinction refers to the models of frequency and amount of financial transfers between generations and kin that prevail throughout Europe. The above-mentioned variances in sociability are not necessarily consistent with material transfer patterns. The chapters in this book as well as other research (Augustins 1989; Kaser 2000; Mitterauer 2003; Viazzo

2003; Grandits and Heady 2003) stress the fact that long-standing inheritance patterns from the past continue to influence current material transfer and support patterns between the generations and among kin. The inheritance norms of the past, however, were usually specific to the region and as a rule do not match current national frameworks. In Austria, for example, impartible inheritance ideologies have been foremost in structuring the rural social landscape of many Alpine regions up until now (see Pflegerl and Geserick in this volume). On the other hand, partibility has always been the convention in several other regions of Austria. The significance of historical inheritance regimes is discussed in this book, since it helps to explain current social security behaviour among kin, as in the chapters on France or Italy. It should be noted, however, that inheritance traditions seem to be of greater relevance in the rural spheres than they are in everyday urban life.

In general it seems that deep-rooted historical patterns of kinship ideology are undergoing a process of change. Historically, for instance, patrilineal ideas in Croatia or Poland had a particular relevance for the position of families in the wider kinship network. Although much of this ideology survived socialist modernization policies in public life, it is by no means the sole reality of kin behaviour today (see Grandits and Dyczewski in this volume). The organization of mutual assistance, particularly in the urban setting, is now primarily in female hands, a trend that has gained currency in most European societies in the course of transformation to the post-industrial era, notwithstanding the prevalence of patriarchal norms throughout Europe in the past (Segalen 2003, 372).

The aspects briefly touched upon in the above paragraphs serve to remind us that kinship ties do not necessarily function according to a European standardized world of values. Varying systems of intergenerational reciprocity or patterns of kinship solidarity can be encountered. And although kinship and family are undoubtedly important identity markers for the individual in all areas of the continent, they need to be understood within a particular historical tradition of cultural meaning. There is a certain "learned importance" with regard to intergenerational support and how it should function ideally. This "cultural" logic of kinship ties is analysed and addressed repeatedly in the chapters of this book and – adopting different perspectives – will be analysed further in Volume II and III of the KASS book series.

Conclusion: kinship and the challenges for welfare states

The variants of cultural "rationalities" are key to the understanding of how family and kinship now function in different parts of Europe. Reflecting on their "historische Gewordenheit" (historical making) is an integral part of this process. In this sense it is important to bear in mind long-term historical processes and decisive developments in earlier periods of the past, far beyond the twentieth century, or its second half, the focus of this chapter (see, for instance, Kaser 2000; Mitterauer 2003; Engelen and Wolf 2005; Sabean et al. 2007). This, however, is only one side of the coin. Diversity in today's family and kinship styles is also a result of the extent to which the welfare state intervenes in family life, of how policies have enabled families to reconcile employment with family, or of the type of care infrastructure made available by the state.

Today most European welfare states pursue policies that resemble each other in their recognition of the need for support in old age (although this does not apply to many of the post-socialist countries, where dramatic pension system cutbacks were implemented in the course of post-1989 reforms) but not in their policies on children and child care (Saraceno 2003, 2006). The challenge of reconciling employment and the family is huge throughout much of Europe and generally hits women hard, who – up to the golden age of the welfare state (and indeed thereafter) – have been the "chief carers" when it comes to family and kin. The extents of these trials, however, vary, as does the female employment rate (Pfau-Effinger 2000; Muszýnska 2004). Welfare institutions and arrangements across Europe have a tendency to be either helpful or obstructive in this struggle – with a variety of outcomes.

As outlined above, despite several common trends in Europe, there are considerable demographic variations. With regard to life expectancy they are perhaps less pronounced, although a certain divide between Western and post-socialist Eastern Europe is palpable, not least as a result of the socially difficult decade of "transition" in the latter. In terms of birth rates, on the other hand, they are quite conspicuous. Countries like France and Sweden currently have a higher birth rate than any of the other six countries dealt with in this volume. It is no coincidence that France and Sweden are the two countries in Europe that have developed a particularly capacious infrastructure of public child care, and among those with the highest percentage of women and mothers employed on the labour market.

In Italy as well as in Germany and Austria birth rates are exceedingly low. This goes hand in hand with a comparatively low percentage of working women, particularly those with small children. In contrast, the three former socialist countries analysed show a higher percentage of working women but almost certainly a more conspicuous climate of economic "insecurity" (e.g., widespread youth unemployment, limited housing market). In the countries with extremely low birth rates, it appears to be difficult for women to combine family with employment and career. Here too there is evidence that the public child-care sector has not adequately paralleled social change in recent decades or – similar to several post-socialist settings – even fell victim to welfare state reforms.

However, demographic indicators of social behaviour, similar to low birth rates, should be seen against the backdrop of the bigger picture of socio-economic change and welfare state development in Europe. Increasingly global economies as well as technological innovations have played a major role in changing the European economic order, which is currently in the process of becoming less and less similar to that of the "golden age" of the welfare state. European nations have been transformed from industrial to post-industrial societies with all that this entails, in particular for employment security (Esping-Anderson 2002, 2). This was and still is the reference point for numerous policy reform initiatives in the field of economics, a process that typically also has repercussions for the welfare state. Many politicians contend that employment must become more effective, more flexible and generally less charged with "superfluous welfare costs" if the respective nation's economy is to survive on world markets. The growing struggle to finance existing welfare state obligations, which are also relevant to the demographic situation, repeatedly serves as a pretext for the scaling down of welfare payments. In the current state of economic turmoil, political demands have been growing for more "responsibility" to be taken by the family or kin to ensure the social security of the individual citizen.

Can family and kinship fulfil these expectations and how realistic are they? On the one hand, they have already assumed key functions in the sphere of social integration. For the most part this manifests itself dramatically in the negative sense, i.e., in the absence of viable kinship ties in situations of crisis, social exclusion or old age. The chapters in this book illustrate how important family and kin are in the transfer of economic, social and cultural resources to the young, thereby enabling integration of the young and the old.

On the other hand, it should be stressed that recent kinship ties must be seen as part of a long process of welfare state development. Much of the potential of today's kin-based social security structures is closely linked to welfare payments, i.e., the public aspect of social security. The examples of post-socialist countries in this book show that drastic welfare state cutbacks can only be, if at all, partially "cushioned" by assistance from either family or kin (in addition also Hann 2002; Haukanes and Pine 2005). Today, growing poverty in certain sectors of society (e.g., among the elderly or single mothers) and continuous social stratification seem to be accessories in the struggle to survive in a less than "supportive" welfare state environment.

Given the severity of the developments and problems at stake, we may need to reconsider our approach towards family, gender, generational and employment policies. First of all, however, we need a greater appreciation of why we live in welfare states such as we have, and of the role that family and kin have assumed in the various European welfare regimes. By closely examining historical developments, the chapters of this volume make precisely this effort.

Bibliography

Alber, J. (1982), *Vom Armenhaus zum Wohlfahrtsstaat. Analysen zur Entwicklung der Sozialversicherung in Westeuropa*, Frankfurt/M. and New York: Campus Verlag.

Attias-Donfut, C. (2001), "The dynamics of elderly support: the transmission of solidarity patterns between generations", *Zeitschrift für Gerontologie und Geriatrie*, Bd. 34, Heft 1, pp. 9–15.

Augustins, G. (1989), *Comment se perpétuer? Devenir des lignées et destins des patrimoines dans les paysanneries européennes*, Nanterre: Société d'ethnologie.

Bahle, T. (1995), *Familienpolitik in Westeuropa. Ursprünge und Wandel im internationalen Vergleich*, Frankfurt/M. and New York: Campus.

Bengtson, V. (2001), "The Burgess Award lecture: beyond the nuclear family: the increasing importance of multigenerational bonds", *Journal of Marriage and the Family*, 63 (1), pp. 1–16.

Billari, F. and H. P. Kohler (2004), "Patterns of low and lowest-low fertility in Europe", *Population Studies*, 58 (2), pp. 161–176.

Börsch-Supan et al. (eds.) (2006), *Health, ageing and retirement in Europe – First results from SHARE*, Mannheim: Mannheim Research Institute for the Economics of Aging.

Coale, A. J. and R. Treadway (1986), "A summary of the changing distribution of overall fertility, marital fertility, and the proportion married in the provinces of Europe", in A. J. Coale and S. Cotts Watkins (eds.), *The decline of fertility in Europe: the revised proceedings of a conference on the Princeton European fertility project*, Princeton: Princeton University Press, pp. 31–79.

Coale A. J. and S. Cotts Watkins (eds.) (1986), *The decline of fertility in Europe: the revised proceedings of a conference on the Princeton European fertility project*, Princeton: Princeton University Press.

Ehmer, J. (2000), *Das Alter im Spiel der Generationen. Historische und sozialwissenschaftliche Beiträge*, Wien, Köln and Weimar: Böhlau.

Engelen, T. and A. Wolf (eds.) (2005), *Marriage and family in Eurasia: perspectives on the Hajnal hypothesis*, Amsterdam: Aksant.

Esping-Andersen, G. (1990), *The three worlds of welfare capitalism*, Cambridge: Polity Press.

— (2002), "Towards the good society, once again?", in G. Esping-Andersen, D. Gallie, A. Hemerijck and J. Myles (eds.), *Why we need a new welfare state*, Oxford, New York: Oxford University Press, pp. 1–25.

Gaunt, D. (1997), "Urban clannishness and the nuclear kin: trends in Swedish family life", in M. Gullestad and M. Segalen (eds.), *Family and kinship in Europe*, London: Pinter, pp. 103–128.

Grandits, H. and P. Heady (eds.) (2003), *Distinct inheritances: property, family and community in a changing Europe*, Münster: LIT.

Gullestad, M. and M. Segalen (eds.) (1997), *Family and kinship in Europe*, London: Pinter.

Hann, C. (ed.) (2002), *Postsocialism: ideals, ideologies and practices in Eurasia*, London and New York: Routledge.

Haukanes, H. and F. Pine (eds.) (2005), *Generations, kinship and care: gendered provisions of social security in central eastern Europe*, Bergen: Univ. of Bergen.

Heady, P. and P. Schweitzer (eds.) (2010), *Family, kinship and state in contemporary Europe, Vol. 2: The view from below: nineteen localities*, Frankfurt and New York: Campus.

Höllinger, F. and M. Haller (1990), "Kinship and social networks in modern societies: a cross-cultural comparison among seven nations", *European Sociological Review*, Vol. 6., No. 2., pp. 103–124.

Kaa, D. van der (1987), "Europe's second demographic transition", *Population Bulletin*, 42 (1), pp. 1–57.

Kaelble, H. (2004), "Das europäische Sozialmodell – eine historische Perspektive", in H. Kaelble and G. Schmid (eds.), *Das europäische Sozialmodell. Auf dem Weg zum transnationalen Sozialstaat*, 2. unv. Aufl., Berlin: Edition Sigma, pp. 31–50.

Kaelble, H. and G. Schmid (eds.) (2004), *Das europäische Sozialmodell. Auf dem Weg zum transnationalen Sozialstaat*, 2. unv. Aufl., Berlin: Edition Sigma.
Kaser, K. (2000), *Männerherrschaft, Besitz und Familie im östlichen Europa*, Wien, Köln and Weimar: Böhlau.
Kaufmann, F.-X. (2002), "Politics and policies towards the family in Europe", in F.X. Kaufmann, A. Kuijsten et al. (eds.), *Family life and family policies in Europe, Vol. 2: Problems and issues in comparative perspective*, Oxford: Oxford Univ. Press, pp. 419–490.
Kertzer, D. I. and M. Barbagli (eds.) (2003), *The history of the European family: Volume 3: Family life in the twentieth century*, New Haven and London: Yale Univ. Press.
Kertzer, D. I. and P. Laslett (eds.) (1995), *Aging in the past: demography, society, and old age. Berkeley*, Los Angeles and London: Univ. of California Press.
Kohli, M. (1999), "Private and public transfers between generations: linking the family and the state", *European Societies*, 1 (1), pp. 81–104.
Kohli, M. and M. Szydlik (eds.) (2000), *Generationen in Familie und Gesellschaft. Lebenslauf – Alter – Generation. Vol. III*, Opladen: Leske&Budrich.
Kuhnle, S. (ed.) (2000), *Survival of the European welfare state*, London and New York: Routledge.
Laslett, P. and R. Wall (eds.) (1972), *Household and family in past time*, Cambridge: Cambridge University Press.
Lesthaeghe, R. (1983), "A century of demographic and cultural change in western Europe: an exploration of underlying dimensions", *Population and Development Review*, 9 (3), pp. 441–435.
Lesthaeghe, R. and P. Willems (1999), "Is low fertility a temporary phenomenon in the European Union?", *Population and Development Review*, 25 (2), pp. 211–228.
Lüdicke, J. and M. Diewald (2007), "Modernisierung, Wohlfahrtsstaat und Ungleichheit als gesellschaftliche Bedingungen sozialer Integration. Eine Analyse von 25 Ländern", in J. Lüdicke and M. Diewald (eds.), *Soziale Netzwerke und soziale Ungleichheit. Zur Rolle von Sozialkapital in modernen Gesellschaften*, Wiesbaden: VS Verlag für Sozialwissenschaften.
Mitterauer, M. (2003), "European kinship systems and household structures: medieval origins", in H. Grandits and P. Heady (eds.), *Distinct inheritances: property, family and community in a changing Europe*, Münster: LIT, pp. 35–51.
Mitterauer, M. and R. Sieder (1988), *The European family: patriarchy to partnership from the middle ages to the present*, Chicago: The University of Chicago Press.
Muszyńska, M. (2004), *Family models in Europe in the context of women's status. Working Papers on Population, Family and Welfare No. 6*, Budapest: Hungarian Central Statistical Office.
Pfau-Effinger, B. (2000), *Kultur und Frauenerwerbstätigkeit in Europa Theorie und Empirie des internationalen Vergleichs*, Opladen: Leske&Budrich.
Plakans, A. and C. Wetherell (2003), "Households and kinship networks: the costs and benefits of contextualisation", *Continuity and Change*, 18 (1), pp. 49–76.

Raphael, L. (2006), "Europäische Sozialstaaten in der Boomphase (1948–1973)", in H. Kaelble and G. Schmid (eds.), *Das europäische Sozialmodell. Auf dem Weg zum transnationalen Sozialstaat*, 2. unv. Aufl., Berlin: Edition Sigma, pp. 51–73.

Reher, D. S. (1998), "Family ties in western Europe: persistent contrasts", *Population and Development Review*, Vol. 24, No. 2, pp. 203–234.

Ronfani, P. (2003), "Family law in Europe", in D. Kertzer and M. Barbagli (eds.), *The history of the European family. Vol. III. Family life in the twentieth century*, New Haven and London: Yale Univ. Press, pp. 113–151.

Rosenbaum, H. (1998), "Verwandtschaft in historischer Perspektive", in M. Wagner and Y. Schütze (eds.), *Verwandtschaft. Sozialwissenschaftliche Beiträge zu einem vernachlässigten Thema*, Stuttgart: Enke, pp. 17–33.

Rubellin-Devichi, J. (1997), "La permanence des spécificités nationales en droit de la famille", in J. Commaille and F. de Singly (eds.), *La question familiale en Europe*, Paris: L' Harmattan, pp. 61–75.

Sabean, D. W., S. Teuscher and J. Mathieu (2007), *Kinship in Europe: approaches to long-term developments (1300–1900)*, New York: Berghahn.

Saraceno, C. (2003), "Social and family policy", in D. Kertzer and M. Barbagli (eds.), *The history of the European family. Vol. III. Family life in the twentieth century*, New Haven and London: Yale Univ. Press, pp. 238–269.

— (2006), "The reproductive paradox of 'weak' and 'strong' families in contemporary Europe", in H. Kaelble and G. Schmid (eds.), *Das Europäische Sozialmodell, Auf dem Weg zum transnationalen Sozialstaat*, 2. unv. Aufl., Berlin: Edition Sigma, pp. 347–373.

Schmid, J. (2002), *Wohlfahrtsstaaten im Vergleich. Soziale Sicherung in Europa: Organisation, Finanzierung, Leistungen und Probleme*, Opladen: Leske+Budrich.

Schmidt, M. G. (1988), *Sozialpolitik. Historische Entwicklung und internationaler Vergleich*, Opladen: Leske+Budrich.

Segalen, M. (1990), *Die Familie: Geschichte, Soziologie, Anthropologie*, Frankfurt/M. and New York: Campus Verlag.

— (2003), "Kinship ties in European families", in D. Kertzer and M. Barbagli (eds.), *The history of the European family. Vol. III. Family life in the twentieth century*, New Haven and London: Yale Univ. Press, pp. 350–376.

Surkyn J. and R. Lesthaeghe (2004), "Value orientations and the Second Demographic Transition (SDT) in northern, western and southern Europe: an update", *Demographic Research: Special Collection 3*, Article 3, www.demographic-research.org.

Tálos, E. (ed.) (1998), *Soziale Sicherung im Wandel. Österreich und seine Nachbarstaaten. Ein Vergleich*, Wien, Köln and Weimar: Böhlau.

Tomka, B. (2004), *Welfare in east and west: Hungarian social security in international comparison, 1918–1990*, Berlin: Akademie Verlag.

Varenne, H. (2005), "Love and liberty: die moderne amerikanische Familie", in A. Burguière, C. Klapisch-Zuber, M. Segalen and F. Zonabend (eds.), *Geschichte der Familie. 20. Jahrhundert*, Essen: Magnus Verlag, pp. 59–90.

Viazzo, P. P. (1989), *Upland communities: environment, population and social structure in the Alps since the sixteenth century*, Cambridge: Cambridge University Press.
— (2003), "What's so special about the Mediterranean? Thirty years of research on household and family in Italy", *Continuity and Change*, 18, pp. 111–137.
— (2010), "Macro-regional differences in European kinship culture", in P. Heady and M. Kohli (eds.), *Family, kinship and state in contemporary Europe, Vol. 3: Perspectives on theory and policy*, Frankfurt and New York: Campus, pp. 281–304.
Watkins, S. C. (1986), "Regional patterns of nuptiality in western Europe, 1870–1960", in A. J. Coale and S. Cotts Watkins (eds.), *The decline of fertility in Europe: the revised proceedings of a conference on the Princeton European fertility project*, Princeton: Princeton University Press, pp. 314–336.
Wellman, B. (1979), "The community question: the intimate networks of East Yorkers", *American Journal of Sociology*, 84, pp. 1201–1231.

Welfare as a moral obligation: changing patterns of family support in Italy and the Mediterranean

Pier Paolo Viazzo and Francesco Zanotelli[1]

Italy and the debates on Mediterranean family and welfare patterns

David Kertzer once wrote that modern Italy had become "[...] a burial ground for many of the most ambitious, and well-known, theories of household and marriage systems proposed by historians, sociologists, and demographers" (1991, 247). The theories undermined by the Italian historical evidence were, of course, those put forward in the early 1980s by such scholars as Richard Smith (1981), John Hajnal (1982, 1983) and Peter Laslett (1983), and in particular their contention that southern or "Mediterranean" Europe had been characterized by a pattern of long standing, whose distinctive features included the near absence of neolocality, the prevalence of complex households, and the early marriage of women accompanied by late marriage for men.

Testing the "Mediterranean model" soon became one of the prime goals of research for historical demographers and family historians working on southern Europe, and by 1990 it was evident that the findings of a decade of unremitting investigation were contradicting many, or most, of the generalizations and predictions advanced by Smith, Hajnal and Laslett. The critics of the "Mediterranean model" were able to demonstrate, in particular, that in pre-industrial times southern Europe had exhibited an unexpected degree of regional and sub-regional variability. It was undeniable that in many areas women (and, often, men as well) had married

1 This chapter is based on common research, with Pier Paolo Viazzo responsible for the collection and analysis of historical-demographic material, and Francesco Zanotelli for research on legal history, policies, welfare, and intergenerational exchange. The division is reflected in the final text. Although jointly elaborated, the first, fourth and fifth sections have been authored by Viazzo, while the remaining four sections were written by Zanotelli.

young, but in others marriage had been as late as in north-western Europe. The geography of family forms had been equally chequered: while complex family households had apparently predominated in the northern regions of both Italy and Iberia, nuclear family households had prevailed in the south. As shown by a spate of studies published in the 1980s and early 1990s (Barbagli 1984, 1990, 1991; Barbagli and Kertzer 1992; Benigno 1989; Da Molin 1990a, 1990b; Kertzer 1984, 1989; Kertzer and Barbagli 1990; Kertzer and Brettell 1987; Kertzer and Hogan 1989, 1991; Viazzo 1989; Viazzo and Albera 1990), it was especially Italy that displayed a stunning variety of family forms and marriage patterns: a survey of the literature conducted by Marzio Barbagli (1991) revealed that no less than three quite different household formation systems were detectable in the eighteenth and nineteenth centuries, and local variants and hybrid forms abounded. This unsuspected heterogeneity appeared to bedevil any attempt to extend generalizations to the whole of Mediterranean or Western Europe.

This fairly well-known story has been chronicled elsewhere (Viazzo 2003, 2005). There is, however, a side to this story that has been neglected far too often, namely, that one of the less evident, albeit central, aims of the comparative study attempted by Laslett and his Cambridge colleagues was to shed light on how families or domestic groups had taken care of orphans, the sick and disabled, the elderly, and others in need. It was largely Laslett's passionate interest in the increasingly topical issue of elderly care that led him in the late 1970s to publish a seminal article (Laslett 1979). In his view, the discovery that in pre-industrial times neolocal simple-family households had prevailed in England, and more generally in north-western Europe, implied that many people were inevitably destined to be left without familial support, in conditions of actual or potential hardship. Far from being self-sufficient (as some scholars had maintained), the small and structurally simple households of England and north-western Europe were therefore vitally dependent on external support. But where did this support come from? Laslett's answer was that the existence in England of a deep-rooted and highly developed state system of poor relief suggested external support had come essentially from what he liked to call "the collectivity". The clearest formulation of this claim was provided by Laslett himself some ten years later in the form of his "nuclear-hardship hypothesis", which asserts that in England and north-western Europe, where nuclear families were dominant, transfers from the collectivity were of the highest importance, whereas transfers from the kin tended to be of little significance (Laslett 1988). Interestingly, the grounds on which these and other similar claims rested were partly demographic and partly cultural (Viazzo and Zanotelli 2006). Indeed, the nuclear-hardship hypothesis entailed a set of opposite predictions for southern Europe (and possibly Eastern Europe), where complex households were believed to have been dominant and the role of family and kinship was assumed to have been of much greater salience for primarily cultural reasons.

This hypothesis, too, was subjected to critical scrutiny and actually pronounced dead in the late 1990s by historians such as Peregrine Horden (1998) and Sandra Cavallo (1998), who argued that the supposed contrast between the relief systems of northern and southern Europe was either a figment of the imagination of historians unduly influenced by preconceptions shaped by the modern literature on the welfare state, or had at least been seriously exaggerated. Surprisingly, however, it has been resurrected in recent years by a number of scholars who retorted that broad and enduring differences in the strength of family and kinship ties did exist between northern and southern Europe, and that these differences crucially affected the ways in which welfare was provided (Reher 1998; Lynch 2003, 8–14; Micheli 2006).

David Reher's arguments have proved especially influential. One point worth noticing is that Reher, unlike Laslett, does not contend that neolocality and "simple" structure were distinguishing features of north-western European household formation systems vis-à-vis southern Europe, for he believes that extended or joint households were not as frequent in the south as postulated by some of his colleagues. Yet, he argues that a great divide did and *does* exist, since "family ties" in the past were unquestionably stronger in southern than in northern Europe, and still are today. Care of the elderly provides a critical test. Reher has no doubt that in Mediterranean Europe the family was far more essential for the well-being of its more vulnerable members than in northern latitudes, and that elderly care in particular fell almost exclusively on the family – as is evident today by the much higher proportion of old people living in institutions in northern Europe than in Italy, Spain or Portugal. There is, however, a significant specification: Reher (1998, 209) stresses that co-residence was not the only means of taking care of the elderly, and refers to "[...] the circulation of the elderly among the households of their offspring, or the spatial proximity between the homes of the elderly and those of their children' as comparable alternatives". In view of Reher's own proclivity to maintain that historically in southern Europe nuclear arrangements were also much more frequent than complex households, it is plain that he regards these two latter ways of providing welfare to have been much more important than co-residence.

But is southern Europe really as uniform as Reher seems to imply? This is a delicate question for our endeavour and for the KASS project as a whole, since Italy is the only "Mediterranean" country included in the study. Indeed, it is a question that readers should bear in mind constantly when reading this chapter. Nevertheless, by vigorously reasserting that long-standing contrasts between "cultural regions" do exist in Europe, Reher gives new life to those historical and sociological theories that, like Laslett's nuclear-hardship hypothesis, expect the role of family and kinship as providers of social security to have been and still be consistently greater in southern Europe than in its north-western countries. This is especially intriguing in view of other striking similarities that are apparently emerging among southern European countries as to the relative weight of the family and the collectivity as providers of welfare. For instance, mounting evidence pointing to the existence of a specific "Mediterranean pattern of immigration" – displayed by Portugal, Spain, Italy and Greece and related to the comparatively minor importance of collective bodies as providers of welfare (Pugliese 2002, 94–103; Boffo 2003; Sciortino 2004) – would appear to corroborate the impression that at least in certain significant aspects there are commonalities unifying virtually the whole of southern Europe. Even more significantly, in the past ten years or so a new strand of studies in the literature on the welfare state has suggested that the cluster of countries on the European shore of the Mediterranean is characterized by a specific model of the welfare state, whose distinguishing feature is a higher level of kinship solidarity within and beyond the household than in the other broad regions of Europe (Ferrera 1996; Jurado and Naldini 1997; Martin 1997; Naldini 2003).

Even if we provisionally accept that similarities do exist across Mediterranean Europe, it still remains to be established whether they are to be attributed to structural or cultural forces – an obviously intricate question, but one that can hardly be avoided. There are, however, other factors to be taken into account. Indeed, one stated purpose of the KASS project is to pay due attention to a dimension whose importance tends to be either overrated or almost ignored when talking of family and social security, namely, the legal dimension. Moreover, it is widely recognized that laws are not the only means of normative intervention by the state. Social policies may prove equally or even more effective in institutionalizing roles and regulating behaviour within the realm of kinship and the family. Before tackling the structural and cultural dimensions, in the next two sections we will therefore trace the historical development of both family law and family policies in nineteenth- and twentieth-century Italy.

The legal unification of Italy: continuities and changes

The work of legal historians suggests that Italian family law, as we know it today, is best seen as the result of a long-term process of continuous alternation between innovations and restorations ultimately revolving around two crucial issues: the exertion of parental authority over the offspring and the exertion of male power over women. Basically, the aim of legislation regulating rights and duties within the family and the formation of new households was to define and prescribe the type and duration of hierarchical relations between generations and genders. This was achieved through the regulation of a variety of institutions: marriage, dowry, succession, parental authority, residence, the patrimonial regime within the family, and the right to practice commercial activities. The outcome of the historical evolution of Italian family law is a relatively recent reform, passed in 1975, which was intended by its proponents to be a decisive effort to complete in a "modern" way a long-standing process towards the mitigation of such hierarchical relationships. The formal equality of men and women within marriage was sanctioned, and the legal status of legitimate and illegitimate children made almost equivalent. More generally, the individual was granted legal primacy vis-à-vis collective bodies, albeit still within the boundaries of a supra-individual unit such as the family. Today's transformations show that the story has not yet been fully written, as witnessed by current claims in favour of legal recognition of families without marriage as well as of unions between individuals of the same gender, or by the emergence and increased frequency of "blended" families.

In Italy, however, family law is marked not only by its changes over time, but also by a history of geographical diversity. Before the introduction of the *Code Napoléon* in 1804, the Italian territory was characterized – as legal historians are quick to point out – by the coexistence and historical stratification of legal systems of quite separate and distinct origins: Roman common law, German law, canon law, and royal constitutions, not to mention regional and local statutes. This legal diversity was partly reflected, and enhanced, by political fragmentation: while southern Italy had been virtually unified since the Middle Ages into the Kingdom of Naples (which included Sicily), around 1850 both central and especially northern Italy were still subdivided into a multitude of small independent states.

Although the historical, political and geographical origins and developments of legal formulations concerning the family were very different, it is nevertheless possible, following the lead of some scholars (Ungari 1969, 1970, 2002; Branca 1978; Vincenzi Amato 1988; Saraceno 1990, 1992), to pinpoint the fundamental principles underlying such formulations and identify the social actors who interacted in the arena of legislative production, either to protect or to modify these principles. Very sketchily, it seems justified to say that in pre-unitary Italy two different sets of interests favoured, respectively, convergence and divergence among the various sectors of the society. On one hand, what we might term a "supra-nuclear family" seems to have represented an ideal embraced by all social strata and occupational groups, from the peasant extended families that acted as work groups to the noble "lineages" headed by men whose position was secured by rigid rules of feudal succession. On the other hand, the rules governing the intergenerational transmission of family property tended to be a bone of contention between the nobility and the bourgeoisie, the latter being bitterly opposed to those legal institutions that restricted inheritance to a specified category of heirs (e.g., rights of primogeniture) and settled property in such a way that sale was not permitted and the heir obliged to avoid partition.

To sum up, the body of laws concerning family matters that obtained in pre-unitary Italy can be conceived of as the outcome of complex negotiations between social actors bearing multiple and often conflicting interests: families who give daughters and families who take brides, noble lineages and the rising bourgeoisie. There was, however, a common feature shared by all of these social actors: an ideal and legal model of hierarchical family structure, in which a male head presided over the other male members as well as over the female members of the family. The various statutes reflect a basic legal orientation that tended to protect first and foremost the *pater familias*, thereby generating an imbalance in terms of rights and duties between family members belonging to the same horizontal axis but of opposite gender: brothers and sisters, husbands and wives.

Italy was politically unified in 1861. One of the first major efforts of the new kingdom was the promulgation of a unitary code, known as the Pisanelli Code (1865). This was the first step in a process of legal unification guided by the determination of the Italian rulers to pursue a single model of the family instead of adapting law to the socially and culturally complex and heterogeneous fabric of the Italian population. This is a point worth pondering as it helps bring out the contrast between the legislators' representations of the family and the multiplicity of concrete family forms that existed in Italy in the late nineteenth and early twentieth centuries, which were highly differentiated along geographical and social lines. Moreover, the historical formation process of this code (largely inspired by the French tradition) is a caution against easy generalizations about legal commonalities presumed to characterize a "Mediterranean family model", since the unified family law that emerged in Italy obviously cannot be traced back to an exclusively southern European legal tradition. A significant episode mentioned by Ungari (1969, 81) provides a further cautionary tale. When in 1918 the eminent jurist and former minister of Justice, Vittorio Scialoja, promoted a legislative alliance between the "Latin" nations, his proposal was rejected: interestingly enough, his opponents argued that it was precisely family law that would pose the greatest problems, as it expressed a "different national spirit". In the political climate of the early twentieth century, the Italian parliament felt it necessary to affirm the autonomy and identity of the nation, and the family was used to serve this purpose, as it would be again during the fascist period. As a result of this search for national unity, both the extent of internal differences and the existence of similarities with other European legislations were clearly played down.

With the advent of fascism, for the first time in modern Italian history the state deliberately chose to meddle in even the most intimate of family affairs. In fact, concerning legislation on family and social security it should be stressed that the fascist government, while granting the utmost importance to the family, paid comparatively little attention to the regulation of rights and duties within and between families, especially with regard to such institutions as dowry and inheritance, with their obviously vital implications for social security. During the twenty years of fascist dictatorship, the state did not purport to act as an arbitrator between two private interlocutors, but rather to become an actor – indeed, the protagonist – in the family domain in order to regulate matters of ultimately public relevance. This goal was achieved more easily by promoting social policies than by simply mediating between individuals through the civil code. It is no accident, therefore, that the first public institutions in Italy specifically aimed at providing welfare and social security were established in those decades.

After the demise of fascism, a major preoccupation of the Constituent Assembly, which in 1948 wrote the new republican constitution, was to strip the state of the intrusive powers it had acquired during the *Ventennio*. The resulting notion of the relationship between state and family rested on the assumption that the family is an institution in charge of the socialization of the individual and as such must be protected by the state itself. Due to this general attitude, as well as to the heterogeneity of the political groups (liberals, Catholics, socialists, communists) who wrote the text of the constitution, the members of the Assembly ended up by questioning the principles that had ruled family law even before the fascist interlude. This extensive work of revision led them to declare equality between husbands and wives, and between natural and legitimate children, to discourage the division of goods between spouses, and to recognize the fundamental role of the woman, both as a worker (by affirming the principle of equal wages for men and women) and as a mother (by pledging the state to protect motherhood and ensure the welfare of infants and children). The new constitution assigned to parents the task of sustaining and educating their children, but in addition established that the state had the duty to organize a system of social support to help families fulfil these functions. Unlike fascism, the republican state made a principle of not using the family to force itself on the individual. Quite the contrary, the new constitution asserted that the state must make direct interventions to support the weaker categories in the population (primarily needy children) only when it was clear that the family was unable to do so. For almost thirty years, however, these principles remained a dead letter. Only with the reform of 1975, preceded in 1970 by the law introducing divorce, did legislative change finally come about, the foundations for which had been laid by the republican constitution of 1948.

In the concluding paragraphs of her important historical survey of family law in Italy since the late eighteenth century, Diana Vincenzi Amato (1988, 694) defined the body of laws that had emerged from the reform of 1975 as both "young" and "open". As a matter of fact, Italy has been one of the last European countries to "modernize" family law and seek equality in the rules governing the relationship between husbands and wives, and between parents and children within the family. In addition, this reform neither began nor ended in 1975, but, as mentioned above, was preceded by the law introducing divorce in 1970 and eventually followed by other critical laws, such as those concerning abortion (1978) and adoption (1983), and by the revision of the concordat between the Italian state and the Catholic Church (1984). This is why Vincenzi Amato called it an open code. Over the last two decades Italian family law has continued to remain open to change and innovation: Italian legislators have already been forced to adapt at least parts of it to several patent social transformations and are now faced, as we have noticed, with the dual challenge of ensuring social equality through welfare provision and of coming to terms with new family forms and co-residential arrangements, and the individual statuses they produce.

Leaving these contemporary (or future) issues and scenarios aside, it is useful to focus on the innovations introduced by the 1975 reform on matters of dependency and hierarchy within the family. First of all, as part of an effort to grant equality of rights and duties to husbands and wives, the institution of the dowry was abolished and the community of goods acquired after marriage became compulsory. The aim of the law was to preserve the unity of the married couple, but it was now believed that this could be achieved more successfully with common planning and mutual consent than by imposing the authority of one spouse (the husband) on the other. The new code expects spouses to live together, to be faithful, and to assist each other.

It is useful to dwell on this last point. Although the duty to be of assistance to each other had already been stated by the Napoleonic and Pisanelli codes, it should be noted that up to 1975 responsibility for sustaining the family was assigned to the husband in his capacity as head of the household. According to the egalitarian principles that inspired the new family law, the disposition of both husband and wife to collaborate and assist each other is now an essential feature of marriage, creating a dependent link between two individuals without domination of one partner over the other. Thus, assistance becomes the yardstick of the relationship between spouses, implying that help must be mutual in the running of the family, both in the material and the social sense, especially with regard to the upbringing and education of the offspring. If we then consider the family as a "legal union" comprising both parents and children, it is worth stressing the point – one of considerable relevance to an understanding of how the law conceives intergenerational relationships – that in the new code the notion of reciprocal help between individuals is placed at the centre of the "family contract", despite the fact that this union is not voluntary but the product of filiation. This inevitably entails a greater amount of responsibilities and duties for parents, although children do not only enjoy rights. Indeed, Italian family law sees the coexistence of a "duty to support", which distinguishes parents from children and places them in hierarchically different positions, and a "duty to contribute", which separates them but does not grant hierarchical superiority to one or both of the parents vis-à-vis their children.

It is also important to note that the issuing of norms intended to improve conditions for disadvantaged children was paralleled by a weakening of those institutions – at first private and charitable, and subsequently, with fascism, increasingly run by the state – whose task had been for centuries to take care of illegitimate, orphaned and otherwise needy children. Although some jurists interpret the 1975 reform as an individualistic turn in family law (Fumagalli Carulli 1989, 310), these and other provisions seem rather to suggest that the "new family law" was (and is) based on a conception of the family as the social group on which the whole of society ultimately rests, particularly as far as the upbringing, education, and care and welfare of children are concerned.

Policies: family, welfare and the state

The previous section has shown that family law has always been a contested arena: each change of power has entailed a change in the norms concerning the family, or at least an attempt to do so. It has also shown that in Italy, as elsewhere in Europe, law-makers have interpreted the "family" as an increasingly shrinking social field. In the Italian case, however, sweeping generalizations about the "legal demise" of the family (especially in its broader sense of "kinship", the entire set or network of kin relations irrespective of co-residence) are to be treated with caution. We will see that while family law tends to strengthen the nuclear family and, to use a metaphor, evict "kinship" or the "extended family" by pushing them out the front door, social policies that the state has implemented, on the other hand, or failed to implement, tend to favour a return of the extended family through the back door. The same applies to relations between the individual and the state: family law, particularly in recent times, has paid more and more attention to the individual, giving them equal rights regardless of gender or generational position. Nevertheless, the social policies implemented by the Italian state throughout the twentieth century have tended to reinforce the dependence of women on men and children on parents. It would thus appear that the importance of the family as a provider of social security not only depends on legal regulations and everyday practice, but also on the attitude of the state towards the family. This is a crucial point, since it is from the norms of welfare provision to people in need of care and economic support, rather than from the legal codes that define parental authority or the rules of succession that the specificities of the so-called "Mediterranean welfare model" ultimately emerge.

This, of course, does not imply an almost exclusive focus on the role of the state, as the historical, sociological and economic literature on social policies has done for a long time. In fact, as Manuela Naldini (2003, 1) has rightly remarked, "[...] the growing awareness of the limits of the welfare state and stronger pro-market ideologies have led to a reappraisal of the role of the market, the family and of voluntary organizations as alternative mechanisms of resource allocation for the provision of social protection and welfare". As a consequence, the family has eventually been recognized as one of the variables that characterize the different welfare state models to be found in Western Europe.

Such belated recognition can largely be credited to the impact of the feminist literature and, in the 1990s, of another significant strand in the analysis of welfare systems, which draws both on feminist studies and previous typological exercises, and whose main thesis is that a specific type of welfare state can be detected in the cluster of countries on the European shores of the Mediterranean (Leibfried 1991; Ferrera 1996, 2005; Gonzalez et al. 2000; Jurado and Naldini 1997; Martin 1997; Naldini 2003; Rhodes 1997a, 1997b). Some authors (e.g., Leibfried 1991, van Kerbergen 1995) have emphasized the role played by the Catholic Church in stressing the principle of "susbidiarity", according to which priority should be given to smaller social groups (including the family and the local community), voluntary associations and the private sector over the state. Other students (e.g., Ferrera 1996) consider Mediterranean welfare – especially in its Italian version – as characterized, in political scientist jargon, by "particularistic-clientelistic" relationships as well as by a "dualistic" system, whereby stable and dependent jobs are protected and unstable autonomous jobs are not.

While not disputing the significance of these dimensions in defining a Mediterranean type, some scholars believe that the specificity of the Southern European model is most effectively revealed by combining a gender perspective, which would emphasize the interdependence of man, woman and the state, with an intergenerational perspective, which would help to bring out kinship links and solidarities, and their institutionalization through norms and regulations (or even through failure by the state to intervene in situations of hardship and distress, leaving the family or kinship network to take over). Naldini, in particular, has insisted on the need to bring the family and kinship fully into welfare state analysis, since it is crucial, in her view, "[...] to detect how public and private obligations and responsibilities were legally defined in legislation and social policy with regard to the needs of economically *dependent* individuals on the basis of age, generation, gender and degree of kinship" (2003, 28–29). Starting from these premises, she distinguishes three main family models broadly corresponding to three different types of welfare state in Europe: the "male-breadwinner model" to be found, for instance, in Great Britain, the "dual-earner" family model (France, Scandinavian countries), and a third model – the "family/kinship solidarity model" – which is best exemplified by the countries of southern Europe. Not unlike the "male-breadwinner model", this third model, too, prescribes breadwinning for men and homemaking for women, but not exclusively. Women are entitled to derived social rights, and intergenerational ties and kin solidarity are expected to be found within and between households. The family/kinship solidarity model is occasionally taken for granted and norms may be implicit; family dependencies, even among adults, are institutionally recognized and supported as valuable.

Although it would be a mistake to assume that in previous centuries there were no institutionalized forms of assistance or that those in existence did not interact with family behaviour, the relationship between social policies, family and kinship becomes explicit during the twentieth century. Following the four-stage periodization proposed by Naldini (2003), we will briefly summarize this recent chunk of history, starting from the initial take-off period, advancing from about the turn of the nineteenth century to the end of the First World War and the advent of fascism in 1922.

A first set of provisions specifically intended to provide social security to the weaker categories of the population was the legislation on the protection of women and children passed in 1902, which fixed minimum age limits and maximum working hours per day, and regulated female and child labour at night, in dangerous places and the degree of demanding activities. A few years later, with the institution of the National Fund on Maternity Leave in 1910, both married and unmarried women were entitled to an allowance that covered both childbirth and miscarriage. One point worth stressing is that these laws only applied to women working in factories, and that during this period the social policy of the Church, too, was directed to protecting women and children at the stage of life – pregnancy and childbirth – seen as most risky, whereas the trade unions and the socialist movement felt a duty to put forward the demands of working women as workers. Perhaps not surprisingly, the promulgation of these laws was paralleled by, and partly caused, a considerable decline in the number of women employed in industry, a trend that was to be reversed only during the First World War. It should also be remarked that in these decades Italy, in spite of being a "Mediterranean" country, was basically on a par with countries like Germany, Austria or Belgium, where similar regulations had been introduced only a few years before.

During the fascist *Ventennio*, family policies grew significantly and the regime was the promoter of an organic set of reforms meant to enhance a patriarchal model of the family submitted to the control of the state. Since the principal aims were to fight the decline of fertility and to support fathers and fatherhood, women's participation in the official labour market was thwarted. This ideology was reinforced by means of discriminatory laws hampering women's employment, but also through the establishment of institutions devoted to the assistance of pregnant mothers, newborn children and working mothers (Saraceno 1990, 436–438). The family benefits paid to the male breadwinner were initially directed only to industrial workers through the Fascist National Institute of Social Insurance, whose tasks included the administration of pensions, unemployment benefits, and tuberculosis, sickness and maternity insurance. These benefits soon became the most important means of spreading the regime's pronatalist ideology: in 1937, it was established that the amount of each allowance would depend on the number of children; in the same year, a "bachelor tax" was instituted and a fiscal scheme for large families with children approved. All in all, measures related to insurance and pensions were devised to fit in with a specific family model: the protected categories were industrial workers and their family members.

The transition from fascism to democracy was marked by patent discontinuity in terms of family policies. The prevailing attitude for at least two decades was to avoid or reduce to a minimum interference by the state in family matters: only in the late 1960s and through the 1970s would a tendency towards "decommodification" – to use Esping-Andersen's (1990) term – emerge. This attitude was favoured by the convergence of the ruling conservative party (the Christian Democratic Party) and the main opposition party (the Communist Party). The former was predictably sensitive to the calls of the Catholic Church, the main bearer of the ideology of "subsidiarity", also in view of the extensive involvement of ecclesiastical structures in the provision of services for the family. The latter, on the other hand, tended to exert pressure primarily to defend the rights of the dependent worker, thereby making a neat ideological choice in favour of the male-breadwinner model. However, these elements of discontinuity coexisted with attitudes and practices explicitly or implicitly working towards continuity with the past. Firstly, social policies tended to reproduce a system pivoted on the principle of protection for the workers – an "occupational" model, therefore, rather than one founded on the rights accruing to each individual as citizens. Secondly, at least until the 1970s, social policies appear to have indirectly favoured the reproduction of a gendered division of labour by attributing the role of mother and housewife to the woman, or, when she worked, that of an unstable and irregular worker. Thirdly, social policies in the initial decades after the war reaffirmed the close link between the breadwinner and his relatives, who were either expected to look after him or to be helped if they were assumed to be economically dependent on him – a close link regarded by Naldini (2003) to be a distinguishing feature of the Italian system or, indeed, of the Mediterranean model.

The two periods of welfare state enlargement (during the fascist *Ventennio*) and subsequent consolidation and institutionalization (from the end of the Second World War to the 1970s) were followed by a period of crisis that has lasted to the present day. Young adults, in particular, have been affected, not least because the Italian social security system is mainly of the "occupational" type, which means that there is no provision for a minimum wage to which everyone is entitled based on the principle of citizenship. Thus, young people are neither helped nor encouraged to become independent. If we look at housing policies, the situation is similar. This lies in the complete lack of facilities for young singles to buy a house in a context where renting has become extremely expensive. Besides discouraging attempts to live outside the family, the Italian fiscal system has also badly hit unions not formalized through marriage.

When it comes to pregnancy and the upbringing of young children, the picture looks somewhat rosier. Introduced during the fascist period and subsequently reformulated in 1951 and 1971, the law on maternity leave provides for five compulsory months of absence and entitles new mothers to extend paid leave (at reduced wages) for a further six months and unpaid leave until the children have reached the age of three, while at the same time retaining their jobs. The other vital instrument offered by the state was the institution, between 1968 and 1971, of a system of day care for children. However, whereas infant schools (catering for children aged three to five) were rapidly organized and spread throughout the national territory, nursery schools (for children up to three years) still show vast regional and municipal differences. In the mid-1990s almost 95 per cent of all children aged three to five were enrolled in infant schools, with relatively modest differences between the southern regions (just over 90 per cent) and the rest of the country. If we look at nursery schools, on the other hand, we find that in 1992, only six places were available for every hundred children under the age of three, ranging from ten places in the North to just two in the South (Naldini 2003, 158–159), the likely effect of the widespread notion, ambiguously held also by public institutions, that child care up to the age of three is mostly a private and family matter.

In Italy, the elderly are the sector of the population that has enjoyed the highest degree of social sheltering: in 1998, old-age cash benefits accounted for over 50 per cent of all public social expenditure, compared to less than 40 per cent in Germany and France, and less than 25 per cent in Sweden (Viazzo 1992, 19–24; Cioni 1999; Sciortino 2004, 113–114). It is worth noting that the minimum social pension guaranteed to the elderly is, apart from disability pensions (and, in another sphere, access to the National Health Service), the only benefit provided on the basis of citizenship. Moreover, in addition to pensions for retired workers, another 10 per cent of total public social expenditure – again, a much larger portion than in most European states – is channelled towards pensions for surviving relatives (irrespective of age) who had been partly or totally dependent on the wages of the deceased: spouses, orphans, parents (since 1952) and siblings (since 1965). This is a significant recognition by the state of the importance of kinship as a source of welfare. Less spectacularly, but perhaps no less revealing, kinship again comes to the fore when social services are asked to provide assistance to an elderly person in need. In order to evaluate whether forms of outdoor or indoor relief should be conceded, social services – besides checking the economic and health conditions of the person in question – are also expected to conduct a wide-ranging investigation to ascertain the economic and health conditions of his or her co-resident relatives as well as of other kin obliged by law to provide support. Those affected are relatives (spouses, legitimate and illegitimate children, parents, sons and daughters-in-law, parents-in-law, siblings and half-siblings) whose support rights and duties are specified by the Italian civil code, which states that in the case of need kin must provide each other with financial support in proportion to their income, rather than their degree of kinship.

This examination of the historical development of social policies in Italy, however cursory, has been useful to put the "Italian pattern" in perspective and avoid the trap of assuming that relationships between family and state have been almost exclusively marked by long-term continuities. We have seen that during the relatively short time span covered by the democratic period at least three distinct phases can be detected. The first, which lasted roughly from 1948 to 1968, saw the withdrawal of the state from family matters and an emphasis on the principle of subsidiarity, ultimately augmenting the significance of family and kinship as welfare agencies (although the role of other agencies, first and foremost the Catholic Church, cannot be overlooked). From the late 1960s to the early 1990s, a move towards decommodification, peaking in the 1970s, became manifest. This phase of increasing commitment on the part of the state was eventually followed by the current crisis period. Once again, we are witnessing a retreat of the state, this time apparently dictated by economic rather than political circumstances, combined with a renewed emphasis on the principle of subsidiarity.

Two points should be underlined. Firstly, it would be wrong to infer that throughout modern Italian history there has been a stark contraposition between the state and the family. We would rather suggest that, according to varying circumstances, different relationship patterns and different attitudes of the state towards the family have obtained. When surveying Italian history, the impression gained is that the family dimension is present at all times, in other words, that state welfare, if provided at all, goes to the family or through the family to individuals. However, in periods of abundant public welfare, the family is the beneficiary; in leaner times, the family becomes a provider of welfare, making up for the lack of state assistance.

The second point to note is that families are currently being asked to take over an increasingly heavy burden of support duties from the state. This sequence of retreats and involvements by the state may well have cyclical features: but the family, which is now being charged with these duties, is not what it was in the initial decades after the war. It has meanwhile experienced the end of the economic boom, deep structural transformations in the labour market and massive demographic changes that have led to a shrinking of kinship networks. Exploring the structural factors affecting the size and composition of both co-resident domestic units and kinship networks is the task of the next section.

Demographic change and the "nuclearization" of the Italian family

Of all the changes that have taken place in European society during the last century, few have been as significant as the steep decline in both death and birth rates, usually referred to as the "demographic transition". This transition was particularly marked in a southern European country like Italy, where mortality and fertility had previously been higher than in the northwestern countries. Around 1900, life expectancy at birth in Italy (e_0 = 42.8) was much lower than in countries like France (47.4), Germany (49.0) and especially Sweden (57.9). By 1960 the gap had been greatly reduced, mostly because of the drop in infant and child mortality: Italian men and women could be expected to survive to 66.5 and 71.4 years of age respectively, compared to 67.0 and 73.5 in France, 66.9 and 72.2 in Germany, and 71.4 and 75.2 in Sweden (Pozzi 2000, 15). The same is true of fertility: in 1901, the estimated total fertility rate was considerably higher in Italy (4.6 children per woman) than in France (2.8) or Sweden (3.7); sixty years later it had dropped to 2.4, and while still slightly higher than in Sweden (2.2), it was lower than in France (2.7), the great forerunner of fertility control (Coale and Treadway 1986, 80–152; Council of Europe 2005, 76). Between 1892–1901 and 1952–1961, in Italy crude birth rates declined from 33.5 per cent to 18.1 per cent, and crude death rates from 23.1 per cent to 9.6 per cent (Del Panta 1996, 137).

But even more dramatic changes were still to come. Starting from approximately 1970, Italian fertility began to fall well below both the European average and the replacement level, while life expectancy continued to rise so rapidly that at the beginning of the twenty-first century, the chances of survival were greater in Italy than in most other European countries. While partly explained by the further decline of infant mortality, which has dropped from 40 per cent in the 1960s to less than 5 per cent today, these gains in life expectancy are mainly to be credited to improved survival rates at later ages: in 1980, the life expectancy of Italian men and women who had reached the age of forty-five was 25.4 and 32.4 years respectively, in 2002, e_{45} increased to 34.0 and 39.1 years; in 1980, e_{65} was 13.4 for men and 16.8 for women, it has now grown to 16.9 and 20.8 (Council of Europe 2005, 102–105). Thus, Italy has come to display an accentuated version of the so-called "second demographic transition" (Micheli 1995). Suddenly and unexpectedly, Europe's "demographic ranking" has been turned upside down and Italy has moved to the uppermost echelons.

Prolonged life, coupled with the "crisis of births" (Krause 2005), has resulted in major changes in the age structure of the Italian population. From a total population of 57,888,200 on 1 January 2004, Italy had 11,122,200 inhabitants aged 65 or over (19.2 per cent), compared with 8,216,700 boys and girls aged 0–14 (14.2 per cent) and 38,549,300 adults aged 15–64 (66.6 per cent). When turned into dependency ratios (table 2.1), these figures indicate that social security issues related to old age are critical in present-day Italy, and likely to become even more so in the future.

According to the theorists of the second demographic transition (van de Kaa 1987), these strictly demographic changes should be expected to be part of a "package" comprising massive transformations in a wide range of other social phenomena: big changes in both the mean age at marriage and the proportion married, and even more revolutionary shifts in patterns of household formation and composition. However, changes have not proceeded simultaneously in all places or at the same speed. Italy, in particular, is in the vanguard as regards fertility and mortality decline but clearly in the rearguard when it comes to nuptiality and residential patterns. Indeed, some scholars have suggested that there might be an "Italian path" – possibly shared with other Mediterranean countries – to the second demographic transition (Dalla Zuanna and Castiglioni 1995; Rosina and Fraboni 2004).

Table 2.1: Dependency ratios in the eight KASS countries on 1 January 2004

	65+/15–64		0–14 and 65+/15–64		65+/0–14	
Country	%	Rank	%	Rank	%	Rank
Austria	22.8	6	46.8	6	95.2	5
Croatia[a]	24.2	5	48.9	4	98.2	3
France	25.5	4	53.7	2	88.1	6
Germany	26.8	2	48.7	5	122.2	2
Italy	28.9	1	50.2	3	135.4	1
Poland	18.6	8	43.3	7	75.2	8
Russia	18.9	7	41.0	8	85.3	7
Sweden	26.4	3	53.8	1	96.4	4

[a] 1.1.2003.

Source: Council of Europe 2005, 52

Italian national statistics indicate that in the two decades from 1981 to 2001, the mean age at marriage has risen from twenty-seven to over thirty years of age for men and from twenty-three to twenty-seven years of age for women, and, even more remarkably, that the crude marriage rate has been in continuous decline from 7.7 per cent in 1960 to just 4.5 per cent today. Other statistical evidence explains, however, why the Italian case is puzzling demographers and sociologists. As we have seen, divorce was introduced in 1970, but over three decades later divorce rates remain low, as do other forms of union dissolution; cohabitation rates are also comparatively low, and the decline of marriage has by no means been matched by a rise in the percentage of births out of wedlock similar to that recorded in other west European countries (Del Panta 1996, 186; Crisci and Guarneri 2001, 4; Council of Europe 2005, 55, 72).

This is symptomatic of differences that seem to go deeper than simple statistics might suggest. It hints, first of all, at different attitudes to reproduction in different parts of Europe (Dalla Zuanna 2001, 136–138). Moreover, there are reasons to surmise that cohabitation may possess specific features in Italy due to the timing of its inception in the individual life course. In particular, there is solid evidence that the low cohabitation rates recorded in Italy are closely related to the "abnormally" late departure of both men and women from their parental homes (Barbagli et al. 2003, 17–28). Comparative data for the mid-1990s collected by Maria Iacovou (2001, 14) reveals that in Italy the median age at leaving home was 29.7 years for men and 27.1 for women. While these figures are only slightly higher than those estimated for Spain and Portugal (and Greek men), they are decidedly higher than those for the rest of western Europe: in Austria the median ages for males and females were 27.2 and 23.4 respectively, in Germany 24.8 and 21.6, in France 24.1 and 22.2, and in Denmark 21.4 and 20.3.

The relationships between age at leaving home and age at first marriage (or, nowadays, at first union) are effectively demonstrated for men in figure 2.1, where other classic markers of the transition to adulthood are also plotted. All in all, the two lines tend to almost overlap throughout the century, and the same could be shown to be true for women. Needless to say, corresponding graphs constructed for a north-western country such as England or Denmark, past or present, would look strikingly different. Such overlapping would seem to corroborate Reher's claims about the persistent contrast between north-western and southern European countries and the partly similar theses of those Italian scholars who believe that there is a basic continuity in the behaviour of north-western youngsters, who once left home early to work as servants and are now doing so to live on their own, with friends or with partners, as opposed to the long-term pattern displayed by their southern European counterparts, who had already shown a tendency in the past to leave home late to get married – or not to leave home at all, since they began and spent most of their married life in the parental households (Dalla Zuanna 2001, 138; Barbagli et al. 2003, 28–73).

Figure 2.1: Median age at which Italian men ended studies, started work, left home and got married (birth cohorts)

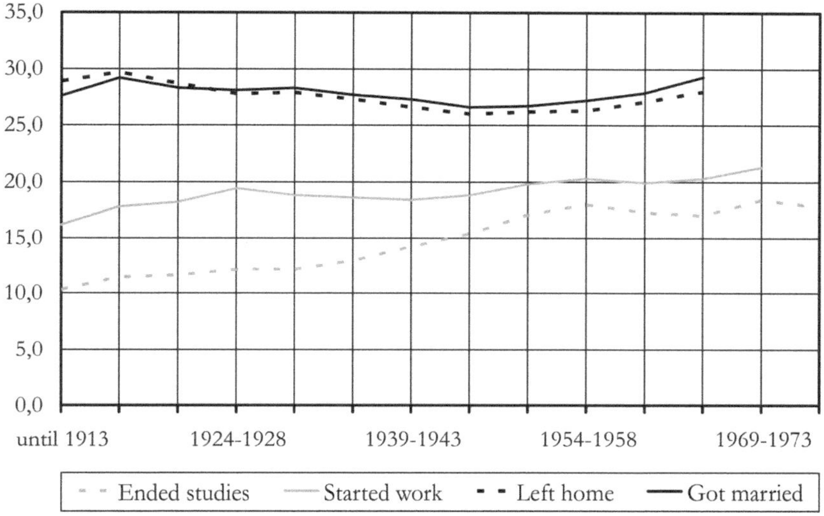

Source: Barbagli, Castiglioni and Dalla Zuanna 2003, 34

A key point to be noticed is, however, that the "national lines" in figure 2.1 actually tend to average out the different and, at times opposite, regional patterns. Table 2.2 shows that differences in the age at marriage between those born in the north-western regions and those born in the rest of Italy were significant. Perhaps even more interestingly, the figures in table 2.2 indicate that in the north-eastern and central regions men belonging to the oldest birth cohort tended to get married more than three and a half years before leaving home. This finding is especially intriguing: since it refers to men born before the First World War, it suggests that the geography of Italian family formation patterns in the past was varied and differed greatly from the one that progressively emerged in the course of the twentieth century, thereby cautioning against the lure of an oversimplified "continuist" argument. The issue of continuity and change in residential arrangements and family formation models is one of primary relevance to a study on the role of kinship and family as providers of social security. It is therefore necessary to subject it to closer inspection.

Table 2.2: Median male age at leaving home and at marriage in Italy by birth cohort and cluster of regions

	North-western regions			North-eastern and central regions			Southern regions, Sicily and Sardinia		
Birth cohort	Age at leaving home	Age at marriage	Difference	Age at leaving home	Age at marriage	Difference	Age at leaving home	Age at marriage	Difference
–1913	29.3	29.0	0.3	30.8	27.2	3.6	26.3	27.6	- 1.3
1929–33	27.6	28.3	- 0.7	28.7	28.7	0.0	27.0	27.8	- 0.8
1944–48	25.3	26.0	- 0.7	26.6	26.7	- 0.1	26.1	27.0	- 0.9
1964–68	27.8	29.7	- 2.0	28.6	29.8	- 1.2	27.6	28.8	- 1.2

Source: Barbagli et al. 2003, 36

Indeed, a survey of thirty years of historical research on household and family in Italy (Viazzo 2003) brings to light at least two relevant points. The first is that marked geographical differences did actually exist in the past. Back in the fifteenth and sixteenth centuries, both northern and central Italy displayed high proportions of "complex" households clearly related to the prevalence of sharecropping or similar forms of agricultural organization. Subsequently, in north-western Italy the decline in sharecropping and the shift to capitalist agriculture entailed a precocious process of "simplification" of family structures, whereas in north-eastern and especially central Italy the incidence of joint or otherwise "complex" households remained high, quite often exceeding the threshold of 50 per cent. By contrast, in southern Italy and Sicily neolocality and simple-family households prevailed throughout the modern age. As a second point, Italian historical evidence shows that in areas characterized by joint family systems, the great majority of elderly people lived in complex households; instances of elderly men or women living alone were extremely rare, corroborating Laslett's thesis that such systems provided most elderly or needy people with a reliable insurance policy against the risk of "nuclear hardship". But what about southern Italy, where neolocality was apparently the dominant residential pattern at marriage?

Before tackling this question, it should be emphasized that in southern Italy structurally complex households were not as uniformly infrequent as rapid generalizations would have us believe. Studies of a large number of towns and villages in early modern South Italy and Sicily (Benigno 1989; Da Molin 1990a, 57–67, 1990b, 505–509; Delille 1985, 170–197; Douglass 1980, 1991) have brought differences to light both within and between communities, and a strong association between joint family formation systems and the small-plot, mixed-agricultural regime of the hilly and mountainous parts of some southern Italian regions, whose distinctive ecological features and demographic patterns contrasted with those of the predominantly monocultural, large-estate, grain-growing agricultural communities of the plains. No less relevant for us, these studies have also revealed that even in places where neolocality was the rule, a sizeable proportion of elderly people lived in complex households with their married children or other relatives – arguably the effect of a cultural norm of solidarity imposing that the needy and the vulnerable should not be abandoned by their kin, and in particular that married children should take in their frail or widowed parents (Da Molin 1990a, 98–103; Benigno 1992, 196–202).

This is a useful reminder that the dominant concern with household formation rules fostered by Hajnal's essays has made family historians blind to the fact that even where simple-household formation systems prevailed, many people could nevertheless spend significant portions of their lives in complex households thanks to what Kertzer (1995, 376–377) has named "reincorporation rules". It should be noticed, however, that whether the focus is on family formation at marriage or on later extensions of the household to cater for old or needy relatives, the underlying assumption tends to be that social security was best provided by means of co-residence. Yet, as Franco Benigno (1989, 185) has aptly remarked, the evidence from southern Italy is also a warning that the domestic group did not isolate family members from other kin or from neighbours.

According to Benigno, "[...] the clearest example of the need to consider all kin ties in an assessment of the role of the co-residential group [...]" is offered by Gérard Delille's influential book on *Famille et propriété dans le Royaume de Naples* (1985), which has demonstrated that throughout the modern age, family life in the Italian South was moulded by a surprising variety of inheritance and residence patterns. Although neolocality and nuclear households were dominant in both regions, the contrast between Apulia and some parts of Campania was particularly striking. In Apulia, a land of extensive cultivation and massive in-migration of male workers, marriage was often uxorilocal, property was frequently transmitted in the female line, surnames were multiplied, and the continuity of descent lines became socially irrelevant. This pattern is reminiscent of what John Davis (1973, 1976) described in his classic studies of Pisticci, a town in the adjacent region of Lucania, where female inheritance of houses and the related rule of uxorilocality led to the formation of matrifocal neighbourhoods. In Campania, on the other hand, and particularly in those areas where shrub cultivation and small landownership prevailed, virilocal residence and the transmission of property through males combined to produce a distinctive settlement pattern consisting of hamlets inhabited by people bearing the same family name. Delille (1985, 90–132) identified these groupings of patrilineally connected kinsfolk as "lineages" and called the settlements they lived in *quartiers lignagers*.

Following in Delille's footsteps, more recent studies have now documented other cases of "lineage quarters" in Campania (Palumbo 1992, 1997, 221–271) as well as other neighbourhoods containing significant clusters of maternal kin in Apulia (Colclough 1994, 1998, 2003). Altogether, these and other works (e.g., Fazio 2004, 264–269) have shown that, although much of social life was characterised by the residential and economic independence of the nuclear family, in domains such as mutual aid, and the care and upbringing of children the nuclear family proved to be less independent. These findings have been widely used to denounce as fallacious the widespread tendency both in family history and in the history of charity and welfare to treat households as completely separate and isolated social and economic units (Levi 1990, 570–571). Moreover, by drawing attention to forms of constant practical support, such as childminding and the mutual exchange of goods, services and minor favours, they help to broaden the very notion of social security and rescue the historical-demographic study of the Italian family as a welfare institution from its near-obsession with elderly care and the more or less tacit assumption that support can only be provided through their absorption into the household. Indeed, a very relevant feature of the patterns unearthed by these studies is that in southern Italy both uxorilocal and virilocal rules generated a pattern of "spatial proximity", where neighbours were mostly relatives: this is a point to keep in mind when examining and interpreting the broad process of declining incidences of complex households, which sociologists like to term the nuclearization of the Italian family.

Only a tiny fraction of these historical studies were available when Marzio Barbagli, one of Italy's leading family sociologists, published his pioneering book *Sotto lo stesso tetto* (1984). At that time, the long-term historical developments of the Italian family could only be deduced on the basis of comparatively recent sources such as national population censuses, which pointed unambiguously to a process of increasing "nuclearization" of domestic groups: between 1951 and 1981 the average household size had declined from nearly four to just three members, and the proportion of people living in nuclear families has steadily grown from 67 per cent to almost 80 per cent. The story seemed simple enough: spurred by the combined effects of the parallel processes of industrialization and urbanization that Italian society was undergoing at an accelerated pace, the individualistic and modern nuclear family was eventually ousting the traditional, patriarchal family of old. However, Barbagli's analysis of the 1951 census revealed that the aggregate figures for the whole of Italy concealed marked geographical differences: as shown in table 2.3, the weight of complex households was greatest in the cluster of central regions where sharecropping had been most widespread and most resilient (Emilia-Romagna, Tuscany, Marche, and Umbria), and not so different in the north-eastern regions, where the organization of agricultural work approached that of sharecropping.

Table 2.3: Distribution of the population by household type and cluster of regions in Italy, 1951 and 1981

Household type	1951				1981			
	North-West	North-East	Centre	South	North-West	North-East	Centre	South
Solitary	4.1	2.2	2.1	2.3	8.0	5.9	6.2	5.0
Nuclear	68.0	56.6	53.7	75.0	79.4	75.5	70.6	82.9
Extended, multiple and without structure	27.9	41.2	44.2	22.7	12.5	18.6	23.2	12.1
Total	100.0	100.0	100.0	100.0	99.9	100.0	100.0	100.0

Sources: Barbagli 1984, 125 (1951); Barbagli 1997a, 118 (1981)

A contrasting picture was offered by the southern regions, where the proportion of people living in nuclear families was highest, whereas the North-west displayed intermediate levels. For sociologists and demographers these findings acted as a cautionary tale against any easy generalization concerning the whole of Italy and led them to speak of "three Italies" (Barbagli 1984, 113–121; Golini 1988, 343–346); in the course of the 1980s the first wave of historical studies proved that these geographical differences were of long standing.

Interestingly, the evidence provided by subsequent censuses indicated that in the decades marked by the massive industrialization of the Italian economy unmistakable signs of continuity with the past were still visible: in 1981, nearly a quarter of the inhabitants of central Italy lived in complex households. Since then, typological comparisons over time have been made increasingly difficult, or meaningless, by the inception of the "second demographic revolution", which has entailed unprecedented change in both marriage and residential patterns. Nevertheless, it is no accident that even today – to judge from the results of the 2001 census – the proportions of both "extended" and "multiple" households are significantly higher in central Italy (approximately six per cent and two per cent respectively) than in the rest of the country. Intriguing as these figures are, it is undeniable that between 1951 and 1981, the nuclear family was gaining ground everywhere in Italy and the number of complex households had fallen dramatically. Table 2.4 shows that this decline continued thereafter.

Table 2.4: Mean household size (MHS) and distribution of households by type in Italy, 1951–2001

Household type	1951	1961	1971	1981	1991	2001
Solitary	10.6	11.5	13.5	18.3	21.1	24.9
Nuclear	67.0	69.1	69.6	70.4	67.2	66.6
Extended, multiple and without structure	22.4	19.4	16.9	11.3	11.7	8.5
Total	100.0	100.0	100.0	100.0	100.0	100.0
MHS	3.9	3.6	3.4	3.0	2.8	2.6

Sources: Barbagli 1984, 124 (distribution of households, 1951–1971); Barbagli 1997a, 117 (distribution of households, 1981); ISTAT 2002. Prospetto 11 (mean household size). ISTAT 2005a (distribution of households, 2001)

It is also true that the proportion of nuclear families has slightly declined, but this has been more than counterbalanced by the steady growth of households consisting of solitaries, the proportion of which increased from 10.6 per cent in 1951 to just under 25 per cent in 2001.

It would seem that this convergence towards an overwhelming prevalence of either the conventional nuclear family or its permutations associated with the second demographic transition ultimately amounts to a final break with the past. However, other indications concerning residential patterns question this by suggesting the existence of an underlying cultural continuity – this time, however, no longer signalled by a strong tendency for relatives to co-reside in complex households but instead, for close relatives to live in spatially close proximity.

Kinship as welfare: from co-residence to spatial proximity

The process of "nuclearization" experienced by Italian domestic groups in the second half of the twentieth century was initially interpreted by sociologists and historians as part of a wider transition from a traditional to a modern social order entailing, among other things, Italy's belated convergence with northern European styles of family life. In his renowned book published in the mid-1970s, Edward Shorter (1977 [1975], 16) singled out the "[...] shearing away of the traditional couple's ties with the community, kin and lineage [...]" as essential to the making of the modern family. Like most of his colleagues, Shorter maintained that two major components in the reshaping of the family, which had been under way for some time in northern Europe, were the growing emphasis on the autonomy of the nuclear family and the severing, or at least loosening, of links between newly married couples and their relatives. Of course, by weakening the links with parents and kin, the modern couple was also, to a large extent, relinquishing their help. In northern Europe this had been made possible at a comparatively early stage by the benefits married couples were entitled to receive from the state; it seemed legitimate to surmise that in Italy, too, this move had been favoured by the policies promoted by the state especially in the 1970s, when a number of measures specifically intended to support the family had been enacted.

More recently, however, an alternative interpretation has been put forward by several Italian sociologists and demographers, who have contended that the "break" with parents and kin is far less dramatic than suggested by the declining proportion of complex families, since the old patterns of *co-residence* have actually been replaced by new patterns of *proximity* between parents and children and, more generally, between relatives (Barbagli 1997b; Barbagli et al. 2003). Indeed, such a shift from co-residence to spatial proximity is demonstrated to great effect by the retrospective evidence on the residential behaviour of Italian marriage cohorts collected by the Italian Institute of Statistics in 1998 for a large sample of 20,153 families. This evidence (ISTAT 1998) shows that the massive decline in the number of couples who began their married life living together with at least one parent (from 44 per cent around 1950 to just over ten per cent in the 1990s) is balanced by a substantial increase – from eight per cent to 22 per cent – in the proportion of those who set up new households at marriage but selected, or were forced, to reside in a flat in the same building in which at least one of the parents lived. And even most of those who moved to a different building actually settled at a distance of less than one kilometre from the spatially closest parent.

These figures tally with the results of other national and international surveys – first and foremost those of the famous 1986 International Social Survey Program (ISSP) on "Social relations and social support", which have been discussed, among others, by Finch (1989), Höllinger and Haller (1990) and, with special reference to the Italian case, by Ginsborg (1994, 82) – which have been signalling for the last twenty years that very high levels of spatial proximity are a distinctive feature of contemporary Italian society and would seem to confirm that the predicted convergence of Italy with northern Europe is still to come. Yet, it would be unwarranted to state that the convergence thesis is refuted altogether by the Italian evidence. In fact, if we shift our analysis from the comparative international scene to the national setting and focus on the regional level, the question of continuity and convergence, and the whole issue of the relations between co-residence and proximity take on quite a different appearance. Properly reworked, the data collected by the ISTAT investigation on the residential behaviour of Italian couples married between 1948 and 1997 reveals a twofold process of convergence of the "three Italies" towards increasingly low levels of co-residence (especially dramatic in the central and north-eastern regions) mirrored by a simultaneous and contrary convergence towards the high levels of proximity that are a distinctive feature of Italy in the wider European context (figure 2.2).

Figure 2.2: From co-residence to close proximity[2]: residence at marriage in Italy with respect to at least one parent of either spouse by marriage cohort and cluster of regions, 1948–1997

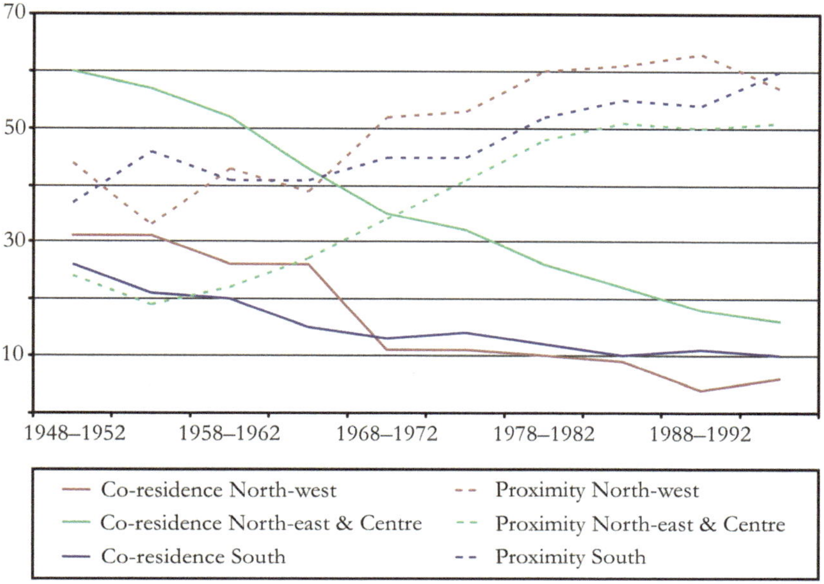

Sources: ISTAT 1998; Barbagli et al. 2003, 181

Although the indisputable primacy of the nuclear family is certainly indicative of a change in the values that had buttressed the complex family, the seeming metamorphosis of co-residence into proximity appears symptomatic of significant continuity in terms of the role and importance of close kin as sources of social security. On the one hand, it points to a growing desire on the part of the younger generations to seek privacy and greater autonomy through the creation of separate households at marriage, but suggests, on the other hand, that both the new couples and their parents continue to seek residential proximity. The immediate motivation behind this search for proximity is mainly the parents' wish to "help downwards", for example by buying or even building their children a house located not

2 "Close proximity" has been obtained by adding the couples who started their married lives living in the same building as at least one parent of either spouse, but residing in a separate flat, to those who settled at a distance of less than one kilometre.

far from their own. In the longer term, however, this residential choice comes to comply with a widespread moral value that asks adult children to "help upwards" by taking care of their elderly parents.

This remark about care of the elderly prompts a further consideration. We have noticed that the prevailing concern with household formation rules led historians to concentrate on residence at marriage and not pay sufficient attention to the possible existence of the "reincorporation rules" that provided for the absorption of elderly or otherwise vulnerable people into different households. Yet, in the southern Italian regions characterized by neolocality, such mechanisms did exist and allowed nuclear households to be expanded in order to accommodate old or needy relatives. Recent or contemporary evidence on social proximity is also heavily focused on marriage. In order to reach a more balanced view on the role of the family as a welfare institution it is therefore necessary to see whether, how and to what extent comparable mechanisms are at work today. Ownership of the houses where the elderly live seems to be a sufficiently reliable indicator to quantify a phenomenon that is of special import in the Italian social and demographic context, where the second demographic transition has brought about a massive ageing of the population. Evidence supplied by Elisabetta Cioni (1999, 129) indicates that in the mid-1990s approximately 40 per cent of the elderly who lived with their married children resided in houses owned either by their children or their children's spouses. If this figure is disaggregated by gender, we find that the arrangement was far more frequent for elderly mothers (45.8 per cent) than for fathers (28.8 per cent). If they resided with their unmarried children, on the other hand, the majority of both men (73.8 per cent) and women (57.8 per cent) lived in their own houses. These figures point to large processes of absorption of elderly parents into their children's households after periods – possibly lasting several decades – during which the nuclear families of both the parents and the children lived separate lives. They also suggest that the process of nuclearization of Italian households does not entail a severing of the links between generations. In times of need, these links may be reinforced to such an extent as to lead to renewed co-residence.

Cioni (1999, 51) observes that "[...] the coresidence of spouseless elderly people with their kin is exceedingly more frequent in Italy than in many other European countries [...]", and regards this to be the counterpart of the much lower proportion of aged men and women who live in homes for the elderly – another distinctive feature of Italy and other southern European countries (Reher 1998, 224), and one of the main symptoms, according to many analysts, of the state's inability or unwillingness to channel a substantial portion of public expenditure towards the establishment of nursing homes for the elderly despite a rising demand for this type of institution. Once again, however, overall national figures – quite apart from broad similarities between Mediterranean countries – conceal significant regional differences within Italy itself. Some data provided by Barbagli (1997b, 38) suggests that in central Italy, where living together in joint households was a deep-rooted custom, the mechanisms and values conducive to the reincorporation of elderly people are still stronger than in the north-western regions or, even more so, than in the southern regions where neolocality and nuclear families had been the norm for centuries. This would seem to impose the conclusion that especially in those regions where the process of nuclearization has gone farthest – either because of historical continuity with the past or massive transformations associated with industrialization, urbanization and internal migration – a large portion of the elderly population is abandoned both by the family and by the state.

Such a conclusion must, however, be resisted, as it would be predicated on the lurking assumption that co-residence is the only possible way of providing family support, and the institutional services offered by homes for the elderly its sole alternative. The possibility that the elderly may be "absorbed" not through co-residence but rather, so to speak, through spatial proximity must clearly be considered. As a matter of fact, very recent data collected by the Italian Institute of Statistics indicates that over 80 per cent of the Italian elderly who are either widowed or belong to couples in "empty nests" reside in the same municipality as at least one of their children (see table 2.5). Perhaps even more telling, nearly 60 per cent of the widows and widowers, and older couples with no co-resident child live at a minimum distance from their children: either in the same building or within one kilometre. The fact that the percentage is lower for the younger couples "in empty nests" suggests that it is when parents reach approximately seventy-five years of age that the pressure on descending generations grows to the point of leading, if not to "full absorption" into the children's households, at least to moves favouring greater spatial proximity. The only category that departs from this pattern consists of elderly parents who are separated or divorced. Significantly, they tend to reside in the same municipalities as their children, but at greater distances, almost to signify a break with a relational model where physical proximity is blended with affective closeness and social approval.

Table 2.5: Residential distance of elderly people from children, Italy 2003

Residential distance from only child or from the child living closest	Couples with women aged 65–74 in "empty nest"	Cum. %	Couples with women aged 75+ in "empty nest"	Cum. %	Elderly living alone (widowed)	Cum. %	Elderly living alone (separated or divorced)	Cum. %
Same building	18.3	18.3	25.5	25.5	27.4	27.4	14.7	14.7
< 1 Km	34.9	53.2	32.3	57.8	31.4	58.8	19.4	34.1
Same municipality	27.5	80.7	22.8	80.6	25.1	83.9	32.4	66.5
More distant	19.3	100.0	19.4	100.0	16.1	100.0	33.5	100.0
Total	100.0		100.0		100.0		100.0	

Source: ISTAT 2005b, 276

All in all, this evidence concurs to portray an image of the Italian family in which both the generations of the children and those of the parents appear to be involved in complex dynamics of help and exchange. However, categories such as co-residence and spatial proximity do nothing to reveal the subjects or the nature of their involvement, nor do they say enough about the networks to which they belong and the specific issues they have to confront. It is therefore necessary to turn to other exchanges and other data sources, in particular to investigations that have dealt with the topic of help and solidarity within the family and the kinship network.

Help in practice: intergenerational exchanges of time and goods

In his widely quoted overview of family and kinship in late twentieth-century Italy, Barbagli (1997b) singled out the extensive exchange of goods and services between relatives belonging to different generations as one of the most unambiguous indicators of the strong ties that link parents and grown-up children in Italy. Largely relying on a pioneer survey conducted by the Italian Institute of Statistics in 1983 (ISTAT 1985), he underlined the significance of both the exchanges that are made up of continuous flows (e.g., aid for child care) and those that occur only in crucial moments, such as a marriage or death in the family. In the mid-1990s, however, Barbagli was struggling with a dearth of empirical information. Things have changed considerably in the past ten years. A survey specifically devoted to kinship and solidarity networks was carried out in 1998, again by the National Institute of Statistics (ISTAT 2001), and another in 2003 (ISTAT 2005b). In addition, valuable information has come from several other studies, most notably from a recent survey concentrating on a number of aspects of the transition to adulthood of direct relevance to the theme of kinship and social security.

Perhaps the greatest merit of the 1998 survey is that it makes it possible for the first time to identify the socio-demographic contours of the main categories of "caregivers" and "care receivers". In her analysis of the evidence emerging from this survey, Linda Laura Sabbadini (2002, 329–330) demonstrates first of all that it is women as caregivers who devote the greatest number of hours to support non-co-resident relatives (on average twelve hours per month, compared to eight hours for men), and secondly that in 1998 the highest frequency of caregivers was to be found in the 55–64 age bracket. By ingeniously cross-tabulating the data on the socio-demographic features of the caregivers, and the amount and kind of help they provide, with the characteristics of the care receivers, Sabbadini (2002, 339) is able to draw a makeshift chart of the relations of free, non-institutional help in Italy. Two specific relations stand out due to the amount of time offered and the high degree of involvement entailed. The first connects a category we might call "daughters and daughters-in-law" as caregivers and a reciprocal category of "elderly mothers and mothers-in-law" as care receivers, whereas the second connects "grandmothers" as caregivers and "grandchildren" as care receivers (the former are indeed mainly mothers or mothers-in-law of working mothers, and childminding takes up an average of ten or more hours of their time every week). These findings are confirmed by the 2003 survey indicating that in the last two decades the mean age of caregivers has risen from 43.2 years in 1983 to 48.4 in 2003, and that the age groups 55–64 and 45–54 are now those with the highest proportions of women and men providing free help: child-minding turns out to be the most important form of help and mainly the task of women, who also play a more significant role in providing assistance to the elderly and helping with housework, whereas men give assistance in filling out administrative forms and performing non-domestic jobs (ISTAT 2005c, 281–285). The 1998 and 2003 surveys also indicate the type of households that benefit most from assistance channelled through the kinship network. Households that have a working mother and at least one child aged fourteen years or under come first in this ranking, followed by those that contain at least one man or woman aged eighty or over (ISTAT 2005c, 287).

By showing that flows extend both upwards and downwards and that it is especially women between the ages of forty-five and sixty-four who act as givers, these surveys demonstrate that in Italy, too, a crucial role is played by those cohorts of middle-aged people who have been variously labelled the "sandwich generation" (Miller 1981; Zal 1992), "pivotal generation" (Attias-Donfut 2001; Segalen 2003) or, perhaps more appropriately, "women in the middle" (Brody 1981, 1990). The results of these surveys also suggest that the Italian system of intergenerational exchange should in fact be seen as involving four generations rather than three, as originally implied by the model of the sandwich generation caught between growing children and ageing parents. Indeed, the pivotal generation G_0 (which tends more and more to include people aged over sixty-five) is increasingly engaged in transferring money and property to the generation of their children (G_{-1}) and providing care to the generation of their grandchildren (G_{-2}), as well as to the generation of their often no longer self-sufficient elderly parents (G_{+1}). It should be noticed that G_0 is the only generation to benefit from steady jobs and a sheltering welfare state. It is also the generation that is currently reproducing, through these help practices, the specific "culture of family care" taken to be typical of Italy and other Mediterranean countries.

Summarizing a view shared by many authors, Rosina and Fraboni (2004, 154) recently stated that the "strong relationship" at the core of this Mediterranean nexus of values and practices expresses itself, among other things, in the support of the young adult by the parental family until he/she has gained satisfactory employment, substantial help when he/she gets married (in particular purchase of a house), and continual help even after the children are married. It is worth stressing that this distinctive pattern of intergenerational behaviour is closely linked to a no less distinctive mix of three main sources that make up the individual incomes of young Italians, namely, the market (i.e., salaries or wages from regular or casual jobs), state benefits and financial support from their families.

Table 2.6 shows that, as far as employment is concerned, young Italians (and especially young Italian women) aged fifteen to thirty-four are at a serious disadvantage compared with the older generations. Moreover, not only are women in Italy allowed less space than men in the labour market, their position is also affected by lower salaries, partly because of the "segregative" effect of the kind of jobs reserved for or precluded to women, and partly – jobs being equal – because of lower remuneration. For our purposes, it is highly significant that such a dismal overall situation is judged by ISTAT (2005c, 217) to be "[…] probably due to the fact that women's working careers are more fragmented, owing to interruptions caused by maternity or to their duty to help their relatives'.

Table 2.6: Unemployment rate in Italy by gender, age and macro-region, 2004

	Males			Females			All		
	15–34	>35	Total	15–34	>35	Total	15–34	>35	Total
North-west	5.8	2.1	3.4	8.8	4.4	6.1	7.2	3.0	4.5
North-east	4.1	1.7	2.5	8.5	4.0	5.7	6.1	2.6	3.9
Centre	8.8	3.0	4.9	14.1	5.6	8.7	11.2	4.1	6.5
South	21.1	6.8	11.9	32.4	12.1	20.5	25.6	8.6	15.0
Italy	*11.3*	*3.7*	*6.4*	*16.7*	*6.6*	*10.5*	*13.6*	*4.8*	*8.0*

Source: ISTAT 2005c, 176

Comparative evidence that is even more striking is supplied by the results of a study conducted in the late 1990s by Milan's IARD Institute (IARD 2001). As shown in table 2.7, where data for six KASS countries is presented along with figures for Spain and the United Kingdom, the proportion of young people stating that a regular job was an important source of income is indeed far lower in Italy (just 26.1 per cent) than in all other countries. No less startling is the proportion of Italian youth who listed state benefits as a significant source of income: a mere 1.3 per cent mentioned training allowances and educational grants, and virtually no none (0.1 per cent) acknowledged unemployment subsidies and social security benefits as sources of income worth considering – an attitude and a condition matched only, at some distance, by young people in Poland and Spain, and a far cry from the answers provided in Sweden and especially in the United Kingdom. It comes as no surprise that over two-thirds of Italian youth regarded their parents or their family as a major source of financial support – a proportion again matched, revealingly, only by Spain and to a lesser degree by Poland and France, with the United Kingdom at the opposite end of the spectrum.

Table 2.7:
Sources of income for young people aged 15–24 in selected European countries, 1997

	Austria	France	Germany	Italy	Poland	Spain	Sweden	U.K.
Regular job	45.5	40.1	51.2	26.1	47.1	35.9	29.5	56.8
Casual work	8.2	14.6	15.8	15.5	5.1	10.9	18.6	6.2
Training allowance or educational grant	13.6	5.4	5.8	1.3	1.7	1.5	10.4	2.8
Unemployment/social security benefit	4.7	5.6	7.8	0.1	1.3	2.1	11.7	18.3
Parents/family	41.0	47.8	37.7	67.6	50.7	62.4	34.2	17.3

Source: IARD 2001, 42

It also comes as no surprise, for the authors of the IARD report (2001, 43), that young people in Italy and Spain (and other Mediterranean countries like Greece) run the highest risk of falling below the poverty line, "[...] the family of origin [being] an economically weaker institution than the state or the market'. Indeed, two Italian demographers (Mencarini and Tanturri 2006; see also Aassve et al. 2006) have recently argued that "[...] if Italian youth are not poorer than in the rest of Europe, this depends essentially on their living arrangements [...]", i.e., on their decision to continue living with their parents for a longer period than their counterparts in most European countries.

In view of these findings and the hypotheses they have prompted, it becomes all the more important to get a better understanding of the economic transfers to young people that take place within the realm of kinship. Unique opportunities to shed light on two central aspects of the exchanges between parents and children that occur before and after the children's departure from the parental home – flows of financial support and the ability to live in one's own house – is offered by a very recent investigation specifically devoted to the transition to adulthood. Carried out on a nationally representative sample of more than 3,000 young people, subdivided into two cohorts aged 23–27 and 33–37, the I.D.E.A. ("Inizio Dell'Età Adulta" – Beginning of Adulthood) survey has attempted to break new ground by introducing a "relational" perspective to capture the importance of certain key actors, such as parents, partners and siblings of interviewees and the members of their peer groups. Special attention has been given to the role of parents in affecting the behaviour of young adults, which explains why extensive efforts have been made to collect evidence on the material and immaterial support provided by parents throughout the life cycle (Mencarini et al. 2005; Mazzuco et al. 2006).

The analysis of the information on financial support yielded by this survey (Mencarini and Tanturri 2006, 225; Finocchiaro and De Domenico 2006, 313) reveals that in the six months before the interview, the sons belonging to the younger cohort who had already left home were those who received the largest share (40 per cent of them were given money by their parents, on average 300 euros or more per month), whereas the children belonging to the older cohort and already living on their own received least. If we consider this relation the other way around, it comes out that in both cohorts the proportion of children who help their parents is noticeably lower than the proportion of children who are helped. Whatever the size and regularity of the flows from parents to children, the latter can always count on parental help in case of need, whether they still live at home or have left home to study elsewhere or to get married.

In addition to providing regular or occasional financial support during the various phases of the transition to adulthood, the family of origin proves fundamental in subsidizing the purchase of a new house, backing a credit guarantee, or directly transferring property assets to children. From the early 1970s onwards, Italian society has witnessed a generalized "rush" to purchase houses, paralleled by a corresponding decline in the previously widespread habit of living in rented accommodation (the proportion of families in possession of their own houses has risen from approximately 50 per cent in 1971 to over 80 per cent today) and Barbagli et al. (2003, 193) have actually suggested that in Italy "[...] owning a house has almost become a prerequisite to get married". Again this is corroborated by the results of the I.D.E.A. survey, which indicate that over 65 per cent of young people were supported by their parents in buying a house and that this crucial form of help was mostly provided on the eve of the children's marriage. On the other hand, as pointed out by Mencarini and Tanturri (2006, 226), it appears that young people whose parents are separated or divorced are likely to receive little or no help at the moment of leaving home. This is in agreement with a set of hypotheses already advanced by Barbagli and his colleagues, who have also found that new couples tend to live close to the relatives who helped them to buy their house.

These findings confirm that in Italy relationships linking household arrangements, intergenerational transfers and the transition to adulthood make up a pattern that departs considerably from those observed in other parts of Europe. As has been noticed, "[...] in Nordic nations young men and women can live on their own because of the transfers from the state; in the United Kingdom because of the efficient performance of the labour market; and in some Western and Central European countries for the effective combinations of both market and state provisions' (IARD 2001, 44). Young men and women in Italy, on the other hand, are obliged to rely for the most part, sometimes exclusively, on their parents. Although no one would dispute this broad picture, there is, however, a certain amount of disagreement about the reasons for this state of affairs. Some authors (e.g., Mencarini and Tanturri 2006) believe that the tendency of Italian youth to stay at home for so long, and to depend on parents when it comes to buying the house that has now become a prerequisite for marriage and entry into adulthood is the result of structural constraints ranging from the difficulties young people have in finding a job to the weakness of the Italian welfare state. Other leading scholars are, on the other hand, inclined to grant "cultural" factors a decisive role. Interestingly, Barbagli and his colleagues, although not denying the importance of structural factors, seem to consider the aspiration, so marked in Italy today, to own a family home as a distinctive feature of a (Mediterranean) "familistic" culture. The increasingly strong interdependence of owning a house and getting married, the crucial support provided by parents and the married children's tendency to live close to the relatives who have made the purchase of their house and hence their marriage possible, are considered largely the effects of a traditional cultural pattern, and at the same time, instrumental in reproducing and perpetuating this pattern.

Conclusion: moral obligations, intergenerational dependencies and the role of culture

These partly divergent interpretations are currently generating lively, at times even heated, debates in Italy. However, simply pitting structuralist explanations focusing on present-day economic and political circumstances against explanations that stress long-term historical and/or cultural continuities may easily push these debates into an iron cage, as both types of explanation tend to deny the participation of social actors, or to relegate their role to a merely mechanistic function. If Sgritta is right in asserting that what distinguishes Italy and the other southern European countries is "[...] a strong emphasis on the responsibilities and obligations of the family [...]" (2003, 61), then it becomes essential to look at the meanings individuals attach to such obligations. To choose between a historical and a political-economic explanation is to see what are most likely two aspects of the same dynamics as contesting with one another. Individual behaviour can be more thoroughly grasped if seen as the outcome of decisions made by the actors who live in, and are constrained by, a specific economic and political context, and who are presented with a limited range of possibilities, some of which are drawn from the memory of what actors believe to be their past.

In this perspective, kinship is more than a web of social relations within which the subjects act alternately as providers or receivers of help and care. It is also a set of practices and discourses, a repository of moral obligations that individuals can tap, or with which they at least must come to terms when orienting their actions. Greater analytical attention should therefore be paid to the concrete manifestations of kinship and at the same time to the meanings kinship bears today for the actors in a given context. Instead of giving free rein to dichotomous oppositions – whether between structuralist and culturalist explanations or, within the culturalist camp, between countries displaying strong and weak kinship ties – it seems more fruitful to make a methodological point that helps to highlight features specific to the various national cases, and in particular to Italy and other countries belonging to what Jane Millar and Andrea Warman (1996) have called the "Mediterranean family of nations".

Martine Segalen (2003, 358) has suggested that in order to grasp kinship relations in twentieth-century Europe one must look at three basic dimensions: sociability, financial transfers and the transmission of family property. These dimensions clearly lend themselves to be used as criteria to measure the "strength" of kinship, and to pinpoint and quantify cross-national differences in the levels of interdependency between generations. Indeed, if we apply this grid to the Italian case we find that sociability between generations is reinforced by persisting high levels of residential proximity, that flows of financial support are continual and sizeable, and that the transfer of houses from the older to the younger generations (or the help parents provide in buying new houses) is a crucial factor affecting the transition to adulthood.

However, Segalen also suggests that modern kinship has a fourth dimension, i.e., "as a source of memory and identity". Taking this dimension into account compels us to scrutinize how kinship is perceived by the actors, how they pass moral judgements on their relatives' behaviour, and ultimately how feelings of family obligation have developed over time out of a complex skein of relationships involving notions of reciprocity, reputation and fairness (Millar and Warman 1996, 7). It is our feeling that in order to understand the nexus between kinship and social security in Europe, past and present, it is necessary to take these four dimensions together and to analyse their interaction. It would be undoubtedly wrong to see culture as a "factor" separated from the legal, political, economic and demographic domains, and equally misleading merely to regard it as a cover, a sort of fetish that conceals mechanisms of exploitation of women by men, or of families by the state. It is probably at this juncture that anthropology can most profitably take over from history, sociology, demography and economics. As a discipline for which the study of cultural processes has been central right from its beginnings, anthropology looks well-equipped to bring out how and where the practice and ethics of assistance meet and clash, and to explore the moral tensions that urge grandparents to look after their grandchildren, parents to help their children, and the young to take care of the elderly.

Bibliography

Aassve, A., M. Iacovou and L. Mencarini (2006), "Youth poverty and transition to adulthood in Europe", *Demographic Research,* 15, pp. 21–50.

Attias-Donfut, C. (2001), "The dynamics of elderly support: the transmission of solidarity patterns between generations", *Zeitschrift für Gerontologie und Geriatrie 34*, pp. 9–15.

Barbagli, M. (1984), *Sotto lo stesso tetto. Mutamenti della famiglia in Italia dal XV al XX secolo*, Bologna: Il Mulino.

— (1990), "Sistemi di formazione della famiglia in Italia", in Eugenio Sonnino (ed.), *Popolazione, società e ambiente. Temi di demografia storica italiana (secc. XVII-XIX)*, Bologna: Clueb.

— (1991), "Three household formation systems in eighteenth- and nineteenth-century Italy", in D. I. Kertzer and R. P. Saller (eds.), *The family in Italy from antiquity to the present*, New Haven and London: Yale University Press.

— (1997a), *Sotto lo stesso tetto. Mutamenti della famiglia in Italia dal XV al XX secolo, 3rd ed.*, Bologna: Il Mulino.

— (1997b), "Family and kinship in Italy", in M. Gullestad and M. Segalen (eds.), *Family and kinship in Europe*, London & Washington: Pinter.

Barbagli, M., M. Castiglioni and G. Dalla Zuanna (2003), *Fare famiglia in Italia. Un secolo di cambiamenti*. Bologna: Il Mulino.

Barbagli, M. and D. I. Kertzer (eds.) (1992), *Storia della famiglia italiana, 1750–1950*, Bologna: Il Mulino.

Benigno, F. (1989), "The southern Italian family in the early modern period", *Continuity and Change*, 4, pp. 165–194.

— (1992), "Per un'analisi del gruppo coresidente nella Sicilia moderna: il caso di Noto nel 1647", in G. Da Molin (ed.), *La famiglia ieri e oggi. Trasformazioni demografiche e sociali dal XV al XX secolo, vol. I*, Bari: Cacucci.

Boffo, S. (2003), "Il modello mediterraneo nel quadro delle nuove migrazioni internazionali", *La Critica Sociologica 143/144*, pp. 88–104.

Branca, G. (1978), "Relazione storica introduttiva", in Giuseppe Branca et al., *La riforma del diritto di famiglia*, Rome: Accademia Nazionale del Lincei.

Brody, E. M. (1981), "'Women in the middle' and family help to older people", *The Gerontologist 21*, pp. 471–480.

— (1990), *Women in the middle: their parent care years*, New York: Springer.

Cavallo, S. (1998), "Family obligations and inequalities in access to care in northern Italy, sixteenth and seventeenth centuries", in P. Horden and R. Smith (eds.), *The locus of care: families, communities, institutions, and the provision of welfare since antiquity*, London: Routledge.

Cioni, E. (1999), *Solidarietà tra generazioni. Anziani e famiglie in Italia*, Milan: Franco Angeli.

Coale, A. J. and R. Treadway (1986), "A summary of the changing distribution of overall fertility, marital fertility, and the proportion married in the provinces of Europe", in A. J. Coale and S. C. Watkins (eds.), *The decline of fertility in Europe*, Princeton: Princeton University Press.

Colclough, N. (1994), "Continuity and change in marriage patterns and group formation in a South Italian town", *L'Uomo, n.s., 7*, pp. 17–38.

— (1998), "Famiglia e parentela nell'Ascoli del Settecento", *Atti del 16° Convegno sulla preistoria, protostoria e storia della Daunia*, San Severo.
— (2003), "Capitoli matrimoniali in ancien régime Ascoli", in H. Grandits and P. Heady (eds.), *Distinct inheritances. Property, family and community in a changing Europe*, Münster: Lit.
Council of Europe (2005), *Recent demographic developments in Europe, 2004*, Strasbourg: Council of Europe Publishing.
Crisci, M. and A. Guarneri (2001), "Demotrends in Italy", *Demotrends 4 (2)*, pp. 4–5.
Dalla Zuanna, G. (2001), "The banquet of Aeolus: a familistic interpretation of Italy's lowest low fertility", *Demographic Research 4*, pp. 133–161.
Dalla Zuanna, G. and M. Castiglioni (1995), "Una 'via italiana' alla transizione?", in G. A. Micheli (ed.), *La società del figlio assente. Voci a confronto sulla seconda transizione demografica in Italia*, Milan: Franco Angeli.
Da Molin, G. (1990a), *La famiglia nel passato. Strutture familiari nel Regno di Napoli in età moderna*, Bari: Cacucci.
— (1990b), "Family forms and domestic service in southern Italy from the seventeenth to the nineteenth centuries", *Journal of Family History 15*, pp. 503–527.
Davis, J. (1973), *Land and family in Pisticci*, London: Athlone Press.
— (1976), "An account of changes in rules for the transmission of property in Pisticci, 1814–1961", in J. G. Peristiany (ed.), *Mediterranean family structures*, Cambridge: Cambridge University Press.
Delille, G. (1985), *Famille et propriété dans le Royaume de Naples (XVe-XIXe siècle)*, Rome & Paris: École Française de Rome & École des Hautes Études en Sciences Sociales.
Del Panta, L. (1996), "Dalla metà del Settecento ai giorni nostri", in L. Del Panta *et al.*, *La popolazione italiana dal medioevo a oggi*, Rome & Bari: Laterza.
Douglass, W. A. (1980), "The south Italian family: a critique", *Journal of Family History 5*, pp. 338–359.
— (1991), "The joint-family household in eighteenth-century southern Italian society", in D. I. Kertzer and R P. Saller (eds.), *The family in Italy from antiquity to the present*, New Haven & London, Yale University Press.
Esping-Andersen, G. (1990), *The three worlds of welfare capitalism*, Princeton, N.J., Princeton University Press.
Fazio, I. (2004), "The family, honour and gender in Sicily: models and new research", *Modern Italy 9*, pp. 263–280.
Ferrera, M. (1996), "The southern model of welfare in social Europe", *Journal of European Social Policy 6 (1)*, pp. 17–37.
— (ed.) (2005), *Welfare state reform in southern Europe: fighting poverty and social exclusion in Italy, Spain, Portugal, and Greece*, London: Routledge.
Finch, J. (1989), "Kinship and friendship", in R. Jowell, S. Witherspoon and L. Brook (eds.), *British social attitudes: special international report*, Aldershot: Gower.

Finocchiaro, G. and D. De Domenico (2006), "Prossimità abitativa e aiuti della famiglia d'origine", in M. Livi Bacci *et al.*, *Famiglie, nascite e politiche sociali*, Rome: Accademia Nazionale dei Lincei & Bardi Editore.

Fumagalli Carulli, O. (1989), "Innovazioni legislative e giurisprudenziali sulla famiglia", in P. Donati (ed.), *Primo rapporto sulla famiglia in Italia*, Cinisello Balsamo: Edizioni Paoline.

Ginsborg, P. (1994), "Familismo", in P. Ginsborg (ed.), *Stato dell'Italia*, Milan: Il Saggiatore.

Golini, A. (1988), "Profilo demografico della famiglia italiana", in P. Melograni (ed.), *La famiglia italiana dall'Ottocento a oggi*, Rome & Bari: Laterza.

Gonzalez, M. J., T. Jurado and M. Naldini (eds.) (2000), *Gender inequalities in southern Europe: women, work and welfare in the 1990s*, London: Frank Cass.

Hajnal, J. (1982), "Two kinds of preindustrial household formation system", *Population and Development Review 8*, pp. 449–494.

— (1983). "Two kinds of pre-industrial household formation system", in R. Wall, J. Robin and P. Laslett (eds.), *Family forms in historic Europe*, Cambridge: Cambridge University Press.

Höllinger, F. and M. Haller (1990), "Kinship and social networks in modern societies: a cross-cultural comparison among seven nations", *European Sociological Review 6*, pp. 103–124.

Horden, P. (1998), "Household care and informal networks: comparisons and continuities from antiquity to the present", in P. Horden and R. Smith (eds.), *The locus of care: families, communities, institutions, and the provision of welfare since antiquity*, London: Routledge.

Iacovou, M. (2001), *Leaving home in the European Union*, ISER Working Paper n. 2001/18, Colchester, Institute for Social and Economic Research, University of Essex.

IARD (2001), *Study on the state of young people and youth policy in Europe*, Milan: Istituto IARD Franco Brambilla.

ISTAT (1985), *Indagine sulle strutture e sui comportamenti familiari*, Rome: Istituto Nazionale di Statistica.

— (1998), *Indagine"Famiglia, soggetti sociali e condizione dell'infanzia"*, Rome: Istituto Nazionale di Statistica.

— (2001), *Parentela e reti di solidarietà: indagine multiscopo sulle famiglie*, Rome: Istituto Nazionale di Statistica.

— (2002), *14° Censimento generale della popolazione. Primi risultati*, Rome: Istituto Nazionale di Statistica.

— 2005a), *14° Censimento generale della popolazione*, http://dawinci.istat.it.

— (2005b), *Indagine multiscopo sulle famiglie: Famiglie e soggetti sociali*, Rome: Istituto Nazionale di Statistica.

— (2005c), *Rapporto annuale. La situazione del paese nel 2004*, Rome: Istituto Nazionale di Statistica.

Jurado Guerrero, T. and M. Naldini (1997), "Is the South so different? Italian and Spanish families in comparative perspective", in M. Rhodes (ed.), *Southern European welfare states: between crisis and reform*, London: Frank Cass.

Kertzer, D. I. (1984), *Family life in central Italy, 1880–1910*, New Brunswick, N.J.: Rutgers University Press.

— (1989), "The joint family household revisited: demographic constraints and household complexity in the European past", *Journal of Family History 14*, pp. 1–15.

— (1991), "Introduction to part three", in D. I. Kertzer and R. P. Saller (eds.), *The family in Italy from antiquity to the present*, New Haven & London: Yale University Press.

— (1995), "Toward a historical demography of aging", in D. I. Kertzer and P. Laslett (eds.), *Aging in the past*, Berkeley: University of California Press.

Kertzer, D. I. and M. Barbagli (eds.) (1990), "Italian family history, 1750–1950", *special issue of the Journal of Family History 15 (4).*

Kertzer, D. I. and C. Brettell (1987), "Advances in Italian and Iberian family history", *Journal of Family History 12*, pp. 87–120.

Kertzer, D. I. and D. P. Hogan (1989), *Family, political economy, and demographic change: the transformations of life in Casalecchio, Italy, 1861–1921*, Madison, Wis.: University of Wisconsin Press.

— (1991), "Reflections on the European marriage pattern: sharecropping and proletarianization in Casalecchio, Italy, 1861–1921", *Journal of Family History 16*, pp. 31–45.

Krause, E. L. (2005), *A crisis of births: population politics and family-making in Italy*, Belmont, Ca.: Wadsworth/Thomson.

Laslett, P. (1979), "Family and collectivity", *Sociology and Social Research 63*, pp. 432–442.

— (1983), "Family and household as work group and kin group: areas of traditional Europe compared", in R. Wall, J. Robin and P. Laslett (eds.), *Family forms in historic Europe*, Cambridge: Cambridge University Press.

— (1988), "Family, kinship and collectivity as systems of support in pre-industrial Europe: a consideration of the nuclear-hardship hypothesis", *Continuity and Change 3,* pp. 153–175.

Leibfried, S. (1991), *Towards a European welfare state? On integrating poverty regimes into the European Community*, Bremen: Zentrum für Sozialpolitik.

Levi, G. (1990), "Family and kin – a few thoughts", *Journal of Family History 15*, pp. 567–578.

Lynch, K. A. (2003), *Individuals, families, and communities in Europe, 1200–1800*, Cambridge: Cambridge University Press.

Martin, C. (1997), "Social welfare and the family in southern Europe", in M. Rhodes (ed.), *Southern European welfare states: between crisis and reform*, London: Frank Cass.

Mazzuco, S., L. Mencarini and R. Rettaroli (2006), "Similarities and differences between two cohorts of young adults in Italy: results of a CATI survey on transition to adulthood", *Demographic Research 15*, pp. 105–146.

Mencarini, L., R. Rettaroli and A. Rosina (2005), "Alcuni primi risultati dell'indagine I.D.E.A. ('Inizio Dell'Età Adulta')", http://www3.unicatt.it/pls/unicatt/consultazione.

Mencarini, L. and M. L. Tanturri (2006), "Vincoli economici per la transizione allo stato adulto", in M. Livi Bacci *et al.*, *Famiglie, nascite e politiche sociali*, Rome: Accademia Nazionale dei Lincei & Bardi Editore.

Micheli, G. A. (ed.) (1995), *La società del figlio assente. Voci a confronto sulla seconda transizione demografica in Italia*, Milano: Franco Angeli.

— (ed.) (2006), *Strategie di family formation. Cosa sta cambiando nella famiglia forte mediterranea*, Milan: Franco Angeli.

Millar, J. and A. Warman (1996), *Family obligations in Europe*, London: Family Policy Studies Centre.

Miller, D. (1981), *The 'sandwich' generation: adult children of the aging, Social Work 26*, pp. 419–423.

Naldini, M. (2003), *The family in the Mediterranean welfare states*, London: Frank Cass.

Palumbo, B. (1992), "Casa di mugliera, casa di galera'. Identità, residenza e parentela in un paese del Sannio", *La Ricerca Folklorica 25*, pp. 7–24.

— (1997), *Identità nel tempo. Saggi di antropologia della parentela*, Lecce: Argo

Pozzi, L. (2000), *La lotta per la vita. Evoluzione e geografia della sopravvivenza in Italia tra '800 e '900*, Udine: Forum.

Pugliese, E. (2002), *L'Italia tra migrazioni internazionali e migrazioni interne*, Bologna: Il Mulino.

Reher, D. S. (1998), "Family ties in western Europe: persistent contrasts", *Population and Development Review 24*, pp. 203–234.

Rhodes, M. (ed.) (1997a), *Southern European welfare states: between crisis and reform*, London: Frank Cass.

— (1997b), "Southern European welfare states: identity, problems and prospects for reform", in Martin Rhodes (ed.), *Southern European welfare states: between crisis and reform*, London: Frank Cass.

Rosina, A. and R. Fraboni (2004), "Is marriage losing its centrality in Italy?", *Demographic Research 11*, pp. 149–172.

Sabbadini, L. L. (2002), "Le reti di aiuto informali", in Osservatorio Nazionale sulla Famiglia, *Famiglie: mutamenti e politiche sociali*, Bologna: Il Mulino.

Saraceno, C. (1990), "Women, family, and the law, 1750–1942", *Journal of Family History 15*, pp. 427–442.

— (1992), "Le donne nella famiglia: una complessa costruzione giuridica, 1750–1942", in M. Barbagli and D. I. Kertzer (eds.), *Storia della famiglia italiana, 1750–1950*, Bologna: Il Mulino.

Sciortino, G. (2004), "Immigration in a Mediterranean welfare state: the Italian experience in comparative perspective", *Journal of Comparative Policy Analysis 6*, pp. 111–129.

Segalen, M. (2003), "Kinship ties in European families", in D. I. Kertzer and M. Barbagli (eds.), *Family life in the twentieth century: the history of the European family, Vol. 3*, New Haven & London: Yale University Press.

Sgritta, G. B. (2003), "Family and welfare systems in the transition to adulthood: an emblematic case-study", *Österreichisches Institut für Familienforschung – Materialensammlung Heft 16*, pp. 59–86.

Shorter, E. (1977), "The making of the modern family", London: Fontana Collins 1st ed., New York: Basic Books, 1975.

Smith, R. M. (1981), "The people of Tuscany and their families in the fifteenth century: medieval or Mediterranean?", *Journal of Family History 6*, pp. 107–128.

Ungari, P. (1969), *Ricerca sul diritto di famiglia (Parte prima: Il diritto di famiglia in Italia)*, Roma, Camera dei Deputati, Servizio Studi Legislazione e Inchieste Parlamentari, 2 vols.

— (1970), *Il diritto di famiglia in Italia. Dalle costituzioni giacobine al Codice Civile del 1942*, Bologna: Il Mulino.

— (2002), *Storia del diritto di famiglia in Italia*, Bologna: Il Mulino.

van de Kaa, D. J. (1987), "Europe's second demographic transition", *Population Bulletin 42*, pp. 1–57.

van Kerbergen, K. (1995), *Social capitalism: a study of Christian democracy and the welfare state*, London: Routledge.

Viazzo, P. P. (1989), *Upland communities: environment, population and social structure in the Alps since the sixteenth century*, Cambridge: Cambridge University Press.

— (1992), "Introduzione all'edizione italiana", in Peter. Laslett, *Una nuova mappa della vita. L'emergere della terza età*, Bologna: Il Mulino.

— (2003), "What's so special about the Mediterranean? Thirty years of research on household and family in Italy", *Continuity and Change 18*, pp. 111–137.

— (2005), "South of the Hajnal line: Italy and Southern Europe", in T. Engelen and A. P. Wolf (eds.), *Marriage and the family in Eurasia: perspectives on the Hajnal hypothesis*, Amsterdam: Aksant Academic Publishers.

Viazzo, P. P. and D. Albera (1990), "The peasant family in northern Italy, 1750–1930: a reassessment", *Journal of Family History 15*, pp. 461–482.

Viazzo, P. P. and F. Zanotelli (2006), "Parentela e assistenza: quali contributi dall'antropologia?", in I. Fazio and D. Lombardi (eds.), *Generazioni. Legami di parentela tra passato e presente*, Rome: Viella.

Vincenzi Amato, D. (1988), "La famiglia e il diritto", in P. Melograni (ed.), *La famiglia italiana dall'Ottocento a oggi*, Rome & Bari: Laterza.

Zal, H. M. (1992), *The sandwich generation: caught between growing children and aging parents*, New York: Insight Books.

Strengthening weak ties: Swedish welfare and kinship

David Gaunt

This article deals with several seeming paradoxes in the relationship between Swedish kinship and social services. The first of these is the paradox of kinship awareness. Swedes live in small households, the average size of which is one of the lowest in Europe. Extended households are rare. However, Swedes possess considerable kinship awareness and socialize a great deal with a selected group of relatives. The second paradox is that Swedish social and welfare services are well established and provide broad coverage. Swedish families rely on public services for child and elderly care. Pensions, illness insurance, unemployment insurance and student loans are designed to relieve families of the considerable burden of economic support. Nevertheless, Swedish families look after elderly and disabled kin to a considerable extent; particularly noteworthy is the amount of care given to kinsmen living in separate households. Twenty-three per cent of Swedes between sixteen and eighty-nine years of age give some sort of care to a relative, with 5 per cent given to a relative living in the same household and 18 per cent to kin in separate households. Since these figures represent an average, the percentage of those who give substantial care at a certain moment in their life cycle is much greater. A third paradox concerns the strong female representation on the Swedish labour market and the comparative rarity of career "housewives". Almost 80 per cent of adult women are employed. This notwithstanding, most care, including what is termed "heavy" care, is carried out by working women, who take measures to adjust their working lives to their caring functions (Socialstyrelsen 2006).

It is not unlikely that the contemporary Swedish welfare state has attained a symbiosis with basic kinship structures. Kinship is now part of social policy thinking and social services build on a continuum of care, where kin play a decisive role. Care of the oldest age group and the infirm is currently the most prominent interface between kinship and social policy. Since the early 1990s, care of the elderly by the next-of-kin has become the subject of much government interest and consequently been flooded with expert advice, academic research, social work projects and legislative support. The Foucauldian climate of "governmentality" that pressures families into mobilizing their resources to take care of elderly and disabled kin coincides with legitimating cuts in public services. In this light, the public sector, legislators, administrators and experts are attempting to reinvigorate and strengthen the latent kinship ties that had been largely ignored in the course of modernization.

Kinship – the cultural roots of rediscovery

By 2005, the Swedish population had exceeded 9,000,000 inhabitants. Recent decades have seen a steady increase in the average life expectancy. In 2003 it had reached eighty-two years for women and seventy-eight for men, an increase of approximately twenty-five years since the early 1900s. This means that more people than ever before have reached a grandparent or great-grandparent age, thereby increasing the living generational depth of kin groups, which in turn could account for the growing importance of genealogy in society and the media. During the autumn of 2005, for example, Swedish Radio broadcast "Släktband" (ties to relatives), while Swedish Television showed a programme on "Din släktsaga" (saga of your relatives). Affiliated to the national archives, a special state agency with its own premises and staff caters to the needs of amateur genealogists.

The ideal form of agrarian family life in Sweden was a variant of what the French sociologist Le Play termed the "stem family", where three generations lived together, i.e., grandparents, parents and children. The stem family was a relatively narrow group compared with the "extended family", since unlike the latter, it did not normally include a large number of married siblings and their children. As a rule, by the nineteenth century Swedish farmers would either have owned the land outright or been in permanent possession of it, thus making landed property the most valuable element of inheritance.

With few remarkable exceptions, villages in the central and northern provinces of Sweden generally contained only a few farms, which were situated in range of each other but rarely adjacent. Single farms were in the majority. Compact villages with farmhouses close together did occur, but were an ethnographic curiosity and are now on the tourist circuit. The Swedish variant of the stem family was a kin group of three or more generations living in the same farmyard, but with a separate cottage for the elderly. Thus households were physically separated, while propinquity gave them a common economic base. This allowed for a common group to share work tasks and a primary group for socialization, child care, and care in illness and old age. The generations were separated with regard to private behaviour in everyday life, such as cleaning, cooking or sleeping. The material grounds for separate dwellings in one farmyard was the easy availability of timber for construction, which explains why Swedish farms habitually had numerous buildings for storage, haybarns, toolsheds, and occasionally separate quarters for servants. In some regions farms even had alternate dwellings for summer and winter. It was common for teenage children to sleep in barns or storage houses, at least during the warmer seasons. Household size, defined as the number of people sleeping behind the same door and under the same roof, varied with the seasons.

There were some exceptions to the ideal described above. Comparatively less wood was available in southern Sweden, and farm buildings were traditionally made of clay with a timber frame. Historically, villages here were large and owned by a feudal lord, so that families had only a limited possibility to expand. The basic shape of the farm was a square farmyard surrounded on all sides by a narrow one-story rectangular building divided into separate rooms. In the poorer households, at least in winter, both families and their animals shared the same room. On larger farms, however, two families shared the farm and the farmyard but lived in separate rooms. Researchers in this area discovered frérèche households comprised of two brothers, each with his wife and children, who shared agricultural tasks (Hanssen 1976).

It was customary for young people to work as servants in the households of other farmers. It is not known to what degree these households belonged to their kin or to strangers. It was possibly a combination of the two. Children from poor families began their servant period early in life to ease poverty in their families of origin. For the most part, however, service began after confirmation and first Holy Communion. The period of service ended in the case of marriage, when the newlyweds took over a farm. Married servants were found in only a few regions with large estates of feudal origin; their families were referred to as *statare* and constituted one of the lowest social and economic groups in society.

Since the Middle Ages Swedish inheritance laws have been of the basic Germanic type. Heirs are divided into different priority groups. The first category of heirs (*bröstarvingar*, breast heirs) are the descendents, i.e., children and grandchildren regardless of whether they are male or female. In the absence of children, the second category (*bakarvingar*, back heirs) consists of the ascendents, i.e., the parents and siblings and their respective children, as well as the surviving wife or husband of the deceased. If there are no surviving descendents or ascendents, the third priority category can inherit. This is comprised of all other relatives in order of closeness in their blood relationship. However, even in medieval times the inheritance rights of distant kin was limited by the principle of *danaarv*, whereby the property of those who died leaving no blood relatives beyond cousins and were hence considered to be without heirs was taken over by the crown. As of the twentieth century and unless there was a will, even cousins were excluded from inheritance rights, and since 1928 such estates have flowed into a state fund known as the *Allmänna arvsfonden* (the general inheritance fund), used by the government as subsidies for activities involving children. Legislation in modern times gives full inheritance rights to children born outside marriage and to adopted children, both of whom are placed in the first priority category.

Women gave birth to a great many children. Many of them died before adulthood, however, leaving relatively few heirs. Since early modern times the inheritance laws have treated children equally and thus gravitated towards the division of property. Nevertheless, inheritance customs varied regionally. In some areas, such as the province of Dalarna, land division created a complex mosaic of smallholdings, and thus a need for extra income. It became tradition to leave the home village for seasonal work in Stockholm and return in the winter. Other areas with smallholdings developed a tradition of peddling wares throughout the countryside.

Families in many areas did not wait until shortly before death to divide up their property, but took to doing so upon the marriage of the child designated to assume control, while the older generation moved into a separate building. This phenomenon was called *sytning* (dialect for care) or *undantag* (exception, or something taken away) and a common term for the separate cottage is *undantagsstuga* (exception cottage). In the late seventeenth century, a legal contract was drawn up for the sale or transfer of the farm from the owner to a son or son-in-law. The contract specified the details of the price (if any) and other conditions such as the promise to supply the older generation with a cottage, firewood, food, clothes, pocket-money, depending on their personal desires. Contracts also stipulated that the younger generation bind itself to taking care of the elderly in sickness and infirmity, and to providing a decent burial when the time came (Gaunt 1982, 1988). In principle it was possible to close this contract with non-kin; as a rule, however, it was drawn up between different generations of the kin group. This practice continued up to World War II. Hence the farm remained intact and was not affected by division on the death of the previous elderly owners. Siblings who did not take over the farm had to be compensated, since they were disadvantaged and had lost their inheritance. Contracts frequently stipulated that the younger generation help siblings to set up farms elsewhere, or that siblings receive an immediate cash payment, several farm animals, and the promise of a contribution to a future wedding.

Conditions for people unable to marry in an agrarian society were precarious. This applied to the very poor, the non-inheriting children of large families, the chronically ill and the disabled. Many parishes, and some feudal estates and industrial enterprises erected "poor houses" or hospitals for those regarded as the deserving poor, in other words those who could not be blamed for their destitution. Up until modern times these institutions were small and cramped and most of the inmates were widows and widowers without kin. The number of poor people constantly exceeded the number of places available in the poorhouse. The solution was to allow the adult poor to rotate throughout the parish, staying a set number of days with food and rest in each household. Orphaned children of the poor were auctioned out to the household that agreed to take them in for the lowest annual payment from the parish poor relief fund. This procedure, which led to an almost slave-like situation for the children auctioned off to foster homes, persisted in several rural parishes up to the end of the nineteenth century.

Historically, class divisions in the agrarian community influenced the opportunities of those who lived in a family setting and were integrated in a kinship network (reserved for farmers in the possession of land), and those who lived as servants in the households of strangers, as foster children or inmates of poor-law institutions (a growing section of the population).

Kinship structure

Uniquely, Sweden has retained terms for kinship that in many other European languages had already disappeared in the Middle Ages. Swedish kinship terminology builds on a common Germanic type, with specific names for various relations. Thus there are four designations for grandparents: *mormor* (mother's mother), *farmor* (father's mother), *morfar* (mother's father) and *farfar* (father's father). There are two designations for aunt: *moster* (mother's sister) and *faster* (father's sister). Similarly, uncles are distinguished as *farbror* (father's brother) and *morbror* (mother's brother). Grandchildren are divided into *dotterdotter* (daughter's daughter), *sondotter* (son's daughter), *dotterson* (daughter's son) and *sonson* (son's son). Extensions to further generations, such as *mormorsmor* or *farmorsfar*, are still possible, similar to *sonsonsson*, for example. Cousins are divided into *sysslingar* (originally sister's children) and *bryllingar* (originally brother's children); designations also exist for cousins up to a certain degree of distance, such as *tremänningar* (third men) for second cousin, *fyrmänningar* (fourth men) for third cousin. In-laws were designated *svärfar* (father-in-law), *svärmor* (mother-in-law), *måg* (son-in-law), *svärdotter* (daughter-in-law), *svåger* (brother-in-law), and *svägerska* (sister-in-law). The survival of the specific terminology perhaps indicates that kinship awareness was a latent tie, weak but having the potential to be mobilized at the appropriate moment. This type of designation may have been necessary in a culture where surnames were almost unknown up to the nineteenth century. Children used patronymics such as Anders Persson or Anna Persdotter, i.e., Anders, son of Per or Anna, daughter of Per. In some families this type of naming is still tradition, with many bearing the surname Andersson, Hansson, Karlsson, Larsson, Nilsson or Svensson (Gaunt 2001).

The international word *familj* (family) entered the Swedish language in the late seventeenth or early eighteenth century as a borrowing from French. It was accompanied by other French terms for relationships, such as *kusin* (cousin), *tant* (aunt), *onkel* (uncle). These did not replace previous terms, but became synonyms used in polite conversation. The oldest Swedish term for kin group is *ätt*, which has a clan connotation oriented to a particular farm. The term is rarely used today, except to denote a group with an unusually long genealogical line. A medieval term for kin is *släkt* (adopted from the German *Geschlecht*), which is still common today. Its habitual meaning is one of the acknowledged group of blood relatives living outside the household. Some Swedes distinguish between close *släkt*, i.e., siblings, elderly parents and parents-in-law and grandparents, and distant *släkt*, i.e., all other blood relatives and in-laws (Gaunt 1997). Modern research indicates that Swedes are aware of their kin, but prefer to recognize only a certain number. In this sense, personally acknowledged kinship overlaps with friendship, and large numbers of blood relatives or in-laws who are known, are not acknowledged (Ekman 2003). This observation was also made in the ethnographic studies carried out in Sweden by Hans Marks during the KASS project.

The historic lack of surnames in Sweden made it difficult to keep track of kin. However, places with little geographic mobility and a tight network of kin and neighbours kept kin knowledge alive. In all likelihood, it would have been difficult for those who moved away from their home villages to pass on kin awareness to coming generations, where at the most they might have known the name of their place of origin and perhaps the first names of their ancestors.

Kin responsibility

In the medieval law codices, kinsmen were held responsible for the actions of one of their number. Thus if a murderer could not be caught, his relatives were forced to pay the fine to the injured family. Failure to do so meant possible entrapment in a blood feud between kin. The degree of responsibility for paying a fine varied with the degree to which the person was related to the perpetrator. Although the laws on kin responsibility were clear, there is little solid evidence that distant kin actually paid fines or were caught up in blood feuds. A complex detail was the fact that kinship could be traced through both mother and father, making it possible for a cousin to belong to the kin group of both the victim and the perpetrator. Evidence from the sagas indicates that close relatives settled vengeance: sons, brothers, and fathers but rarely cousins. Blood feuds and kin responsibility disappeared from legal practice with the establishment of a centralized court and jury system in early modern times.

Until 1956, the various poor law regulations contained statutes that obliged kin to take care of impoverished parents. Swedish civil law contained a similar statute up to 1979. However, these laws fell into disuse long before they were removed from the law books. As kin networks functioned differently depending on class and region, modern national legislation was ambivalent towards the involvement of kin. At times, legislators were aware of the potential of kinship networks. One instance is the current Social Services Law specifying that social services are to provide welfare benefits or social care only "when other alternatives" have been exhausted. Hence the availability of close kin becomes the explanation of why public care cannot be granted to an elderly or handicapped person. In the case of the Social Service Law, kin are termed *anhöriga* (next-of-kin, from the German word *Angehörige*), a word that has been common usage only in the last twenty years. The term *anhörig* entered everyday speech from administrative and legalistic language and designates the next-of-kin to a person who is no longer independent, such as the terminally ill, the seriously disabled, or the recently deceased. It thus defines the next-of-kin as those recognized as socially and culturally responsible for a dependant, or who would be in a position to assume this role. Although the word in itself is rather old, it was rarely used up to the 1980s, when hospitals and social services needed a generic term for next-of-kin. The presence of an *anhörig* in the same household or neighbourhood can result in delayed assistance from the municipality or county council (Bergh 1997). The parents of severely handicapped or chronically ill children and youth suffer in particular from this practice.

Historically, Swedish social laws were always designed with the notion of a stereotyped "needy" individual, unable to survive without outside support. The latter is perceived not merely as poor, ill, lonely and desperate, but also as socially isolated in terms of being estranged from family and friends, or as a member of a dysfunctional family. The latter was seen as positioned in the lower ranks of the working class. Traditionally, upper and middle-class families were treated as if their ties both within the immediate family and with relatives were strong. During the early twentieth century, the figure of the dominant aged grandmother or female head of kin, the "terror-aunt" (*skräcktanten*), was a common literary stereotype. In novels and plays her function was to hinder romantic young lovers from marrying by establishing a series of conventional social barriers, which the young lovers were forced to overcome. When working-class families showed signs of cohesion, however, it was usually interpreted within a discourse of potential social risk and reaction against modern society. Thus many Swedish social service innovations, foremost public child care, were readily incorporated into middle-class family lifestyles, while adoption by the working classes was shown to be slow and less enthusiastic. With the expansion of day care in the early stages of the 1970s, it was observed that working-class families were underrepresented. They preferred child care provided by relatives and neighbours in their homes. Working mothers occasionally arranged their jobs, i.e., worked part-time or night shifts, so as to be at home for most of the day. To some propagators of the benefits of day care, the preference for care within the family and social network was seen as disadvantageous to the child, who would be better served in a day-care unit with professionally trained personnel. The working-class preference for care within the immediate social network persisted through to the 1990s (Rosenberg 1991).

First steps towards a welfare state

On the whole, Swedes have a sceptical attitude towards institutionalization. This may be a legacy of the ill-reputed institutions run by the Poor Law administration, which were known for their harshness. Institutional solutions are commonly deemed acceptable in the initial phase of recognizing a new social problem, but are cast aside once the problem has become standard. In the wake of the nineteenth-century trauma of emigration, an era of liberal reforms brought a massive upswing to ideas on the usefulness of social work in ameliorating the plight of the poorest sections of society. Part of this movement had roots that went back to the 1890s, when a number of philanthropists had given advance warning of what they called the "worker question", i.e., how to improve the living conditions of the urban poor and detract them from revolutionary politics. This was basically a matter of constructing better housing, increasing wages, and propagandizing for sobriety and personal improvement. The new element that emerged in the twentieth century was the intellectualization, professionalization and institutionalization of philanthropy combined in the influential organization Central Association for Social Work (*Centralförbundet för socialt arbete*), founded in 1903. Another important voice was Ellen Key, a radical thinker who published the international bestseller *Barnets århundrade* (The century of the child) in 1900. This initiated a discourse on improving parenting, pedagogy and institutional settings (Key 1900).

The Central Association for Social Work quickly became a renowned liberal champion of social reform. In 1909, it began to train among others the directors of homes for the elderly, and inspectors of workplaces and child care. It pressured parliament to enact laws that would put the government via new central agencies in control of the thousands of municipalities, with their diverse routines and practices. In a sense, it was pressing for the state, which they termed "Society", to take over poor law relief from the municipalities. The state was also to regulate how the various social care institutions were run and ensure that they were managed by professionally trained personnel. It pioneered setting the agenda of social problems in Sweden and how they could be statistically presented. In 1920 it established the Social Political Institute in Stockholm, which later became the Stockholm School of Social Work.

The progressive social work movement propagated institutional care and saw many of its ideas bear fruit when in 1911 a liberal government was installed for the first time. As part of the pressure to reorganize social work under central government control, a special agency, *Socialstyrelsen* (literally the Social Board), was established in 1913. Part of its assignment was to control industrial working conditions, while other tasks were of a social nature, e.g., care of alcoholics, inspection of housing, statistics on the cost of living, and inspection of municipal child care and homes for the elderly.

The law of national pension insurance from 1913, the new poor relief act of 1918, and the emergence of the Swedish National Board of Health and Welfare in 1912 and the Ministry of Social Affairs in 1919 are all examples of concrete reforms backed by philanthropic organizations. Many of the leading representatives from the philanthropic associations became inspectors of the new government supervisory activities, which further underlined the close cooperation between voluntary social work and governmental social policy in the early decades of the twentieth century (SOU 1993, 82).

The social work movements declared that families and children needed protection and numerous steps were taken to implement their demands: in 1917, for example, new laws concerning children born out of wedlock were passed. Detailed regulations made the state responsible for the protection of illegitimate children and allowed intervention in the family home. Unwed mothers were assigned a personal child-welfare officer and negligent family breadwinners were forced to provide financial support for the upbringing of their children or face a jail sentence. Full adoption was introduced with these laws. The new child-welfare act passed in 1924 enjoined each municipality to set up a child-welfare board, which would assume responsibility for all issues concerning children and the improvement of their circumstances (Ohrlander 1992).

During this period the marriage laws that gave husbands legal power over their wives were altered. Gender equality, albeit not fully achieved at that time, was established as the goal of legislative reform. Henceforth both spouses were considered legally and financially independent, equal owners of their household property and jointly responsible for family maintenance. Divorce was liberalized and a no-fault principle introduced for both husbands and wives. In the case of divorce, family assets were to be divided into two equal parts. The children remained in the care of one parent, while the other was obliged to pay alimony to support the children (Melby et al. 2006).

The major acceptance of state intervention in social problems and family affairs resulted in the resolution of a number of long-standing political debates. First and foremost was the growing problem of poverty in old age. Debates on old-age insurance for workers began in 1884 and had been investigated in committees a number of times without reaching a final proposal. In this new climate of opinion it suddenly became possible in 1913 to pass a law on the *Folkpension* (literally the People's Pension) guaranteeing small cash payments to every citizen over the age of sixty-seven. Although pensions were negligible (even in the eyes of contemporaries) for elderly rural women it was often their first time ever to receive money. The People's Pension established several principles to be followed in the future, e.g., that social problems could be solved by establishing insurance funds to which individuals made regular payments. This became standard for unemployment, health and work accident insurance. Another principle defined that welfare legislation should be as universal as possible and cover all citizens, striving for class and gender equality. This was motivated by a feeling that programmes focused on the poorest strata of society would stigmatize the beneficiaries. Extra payments or services required for the deprived were achieved via additions to the legislation, which were regulated meticulously and administered by a heavy-handed bureaucracy accustomed to being ungenerous. This gave rise to a kaleidoscope of complex rules and a local administration that was difficult to supervise, with a puzzling division of the country into regions where citizens were entitled to various additional social benefits as a result of perceived higher or lower costs of living. A further complication in this context was the different pension sums drawn by men and women, with women throughout receiving the smaller amount, despite the principle of gender equality.

It is difficult to determine how the People's Pension changed relationships within the family and among kin. It can be argued that once the older generation enjoys an independent economy, the burden placed on the younger generations to give economic support will disappear. However, since the pension sum was extremely small from the start, it is highly unlikely that families experienced less economic responsibility, particularly if the elderly were penniless. In this case, the additional money from the People's Pension would have had no overall economic effect, since poor relief was adjusted downwards in proportion to the increase in the pension sum. Legislation on children also changed the status of children born outside wedlock. Up until 1917, these children were termed "illegitimate" (*oäkta*) and painfully stigmatized. The new law introduced the neutral term "children born outside marriage". Although the change in terms did not immediately reduce the stigma, these children now had a number of rights, including the right to inheritance and financial support from their fathers. This legislation was crucial not only as child protection but also because it ameliorated the plight of unmarried mothers, the cause of much public concern. The new laws also regulated the grounds for the forcible removement of children from their parents and placing them in social care. In 1922, about 108,000 children were in some form of social care, removed from their families and under the supervision of the poor law administration. Municipalities established child-care boards to inspect the home life of children at risk of becoming delinquent or who were born out of wedlock. Each child born out of wedlock was assigned to a professional child-care inspector (*barnavårdsman*), whose task was to give advice and support to the mother and "see to it that the rights of the child are properly upheld" (Nordlöf 1997, Bergman 1999).

Another concern of early twentieth-century Swedish social policy was the reform of *fattigvård* (poor care) relief institutions. Reform in 1918 marked a turning point in the greater responsibility of the municipalities for the support of paupers and those who were dependent. As mentioned above, this responsibility was previously divided. It now became obligatory for municipalities to establish homes for the elderlsy, while the previous pejorative term "poorhouse" was phased out. The law specified pleasant homelike facilities that were clean and tidy, which apparently proved easier to say than do, so that the negative stigma of institutional care remained in place. Other institutions, e.g., workhouses for homeless vagrants, were planned. The thrust of this legislation was to separate the elderly poor, who were considered blameless in their dependency, from the younger needy, who were treated in a punitive manner as if their plight had been self-inflicted. On the other hand, numerous municipalities simply altered the sign outside the poorhouses, renaming them homes for the elderly, but retained the same mixture of inmates and staff. By the mid 1940s, it was obvious that the clientele of these homes was still dominated by younger inmates because municipalities had nowhere else to put them. Even the newly built homes for the elderly were problematic for the inmates, since the latter were deprived of their voting rights and homes were often run with harsh discipline along the lines of paternalistic local rules of behaviour.

Several private philanthropic initiatives are also worth mentioning, since some of their activities were later integrated into public services. During World War I, Manfred Björkquist, a leading Lutheran theologian, began to train *hemsystrar* (home sisters) and *hemvårdarinnor* (female home caregivers) according to a model he had observed in Britain. They were to be of assistance to working-class families when a mother was ill or a child whose mother had to work. Björkquist had noted that working-class families frequently lived at some distance from their relatives and needed outside help. The presence of a home sister ensured that children did not have to be sent away from home when their mother was ill or had just died. A school for home sisters was established in Uppsala in 1920 and students were trained in household tasks, child care and nursing. Graduates were employed by the Red Cross and the Lutheran Church organizations (Gaunt 1996). Stockholm introduced its social *hemhjälp* (social home-help) in 1924 and by the 1960s employed 250 people who helped families with children in their homes. Home helpers were able to tend both sick mothers and the sick children of working mothers. In 1963, 11,000 families were provided with home help, by which time the service was no longer free. Families paid a small sum unless they passed a means test and were given a reduced rate.

In essence, the reform era established a political consensus that the state must intervene to create acceptable social conditions, since the population might otherwise emigrate or rebel. Social reforms were to be universal and apply to both industrial and agrarian families, and attempt to be gender equal. The philanthropic input resulted in a profusion of institutional care scattered throughout the country and a number of large institutional buildings optimistically staffed with experts and trained professionals. As a rule this meant that in a first step, the social services removed the person with problems from his or her family and home, and placed them under long-term observation.

The "family-friendly" welfare state after World War II

A major breakthrough for family policy occurred in the 1960s when the Social Democratic party recognized that the problems of families with children were more of a social than an economic nature. The party shifted the direction of its programme to a more child-friendly stance, which meant a more "women-friendly" perspective, instead of the male-breadwinner focus. The new programme included the following points:

"Active family policy. A more child friendly society. Support to families with children. Support to parents in their child fostering tasks. Family counseling and sexual education. Necessary reduction of homemakers' work burden through rationalization of work in the home."

A noteworthy omission, however, was a discussion on the need for formal child care. Inga Thorsson, a leading Social Democrat, Stockholm's mayor for social affairs and later a government minister, commented on the new pro-active focus on the family.

"The family plays a large, perhaps the decisive, role in the formation of improper development. And family influence is of major importance, more than the influence of gangs, the street or peers. In most cases it isn't the gangs that influence children, but rather the unsatisfactory home setting expressed by means of these gangs [...] Changes in social structures affect children primarily through the family. It has often been pointed out how the changes in social structures following industrialization altered the functions of modern families and how this has affected our social norms [...] The family has shrunk. There are fewer children per family. Grandparents no longer belong to the close family circle. Ties to kin, neighbours and the home town have diminished or disappeared. Added to fathers working outside the home is now the numerous cases of mothers in paid employment. Many of the smaller children spend the day in institutional care, while school children have to fend for themselves."

The above line of reasoning led Thorsson to propose even greater state intervention and support for families in general (Thorsson 1960).

This pointed to a new focus on working together with mothers and parents rather than on child protection. But it also signalled the impact of social work expertise in formulating the policies of the 1960s and early 1970s. Further parliamentary interest aimed at improving the situation of single mothers, who were identified as a major risk group. Many forms of state tax transfers were greatly increased and expanded to the relevant groups. The means-tested assistance to recent mothers, for instance, was replaced in 1963 by a one-off motherhood payment (*moderskapspenning*) to all families. A parliamentary investigation of *familjestöd* (Support to Families) recommended substituting motherhood insurance with parental insurance, which could be allocated to either the mother or the father. This symbolized a higher awareness of the parental role and the responsibility of the father. This issue was linked to the increasing debate on the heavy burdens placed on working mothers as a result of fathers' refusal to participate in household tasks, and found expression in the new gender policy terms *jämlikhet* (equality) and its successor *jämställdhet* (equal status).

In 1964, financial support for families with children comprised benefits such as the monthly child allowance, which increased with each additional child born into the family. Mothers received a maternity allowance and had the right to supplementary sickness benefits for 180 days if they suspended their employment. The family could also apply for housing allowances, and school meals were free of charge. Single parents were also catered for in the expanded family policy and were recipients of extra support measures.

The 1960 census was the first to register all gainfully employed women with children under the age of sixteen. Twenty per cent of all women with children worked outside the home. Most of them were between thirty-four and forty-four years of age and had one child. Of the women under the age of thirty-four without children at home, approximately 70 per cent were gainfully employed. Children obviously impinged on women's ability to work outside the home – less than 10 per cent of the women with four or more children were wage-earning. Even the birth of the first child reduced the proportion of working women under the age of twenty-four from 70.5 per cent to 21 per cent.

Social Democratic family policy slowly began to envision a two-breadwinner family model, where child care was to be tax-financed and distributed, and inspected by public agencies. However, the expansion of municipal child care was a response to the huge demand – which took politicians and administrators somewhat by surprise – when mothers began working to an unexpected degree. Public child care was plainly not a universal solution; non-socialist parties considered the provision of private child care an interesting option (Hinnfors 1992). Nevertheless, Swedish child care extended according to Social Democratic guidelines, and state subventions to private child care had to wait until 1991. In 1972, 12 per cent of children between one and six years of age availed of municipal day care. By 1980, this share had increased to 36 per cent and by 2003, 83 per cent of this group attended public day-care facilities (Skolverket 2003).

After years of preparation, the Child Care Committee released its final report in 1972. This document detailed the future expansion of public child care up to 1986, by which time the goal of full coverage was to be reached. Population growth disappeared from the social policy agenda, and prominence was now given to social aspects and employment. Industrial expansion in the 1950s and 1960s and the respective labour policies affected child-care policy as a result of the constant demand for workers. As female wage work was perceived as indispensable to Swedish industry, existing child-care policies proved to be no longer adequate. All-day nurseries, described in the 1950s as undesirable emergency solutions, were reinvigorated and advanced as the primary solution to the needs of children, women, families and the job market. The social motive and the pedagogic motive Social and educational motives merged to one child-care institution, a move that would have been inconceivable only a decade before. The Committee suggested a new name for child care to emphasize this fresh vision: instead of day nursery and playschool, child-care activities were to be bundled and forthwith referred to as pre-school, stressing the pedagogic rather than the childminding aspect, and pointing to the role of moulding children into future citizens (Statens offentliga utredningar 1972a, 26, 1972b, 20).

The 1970s saw a vast increase in the number of gainfully employed married women. A significant backdrop here was the separate taxation in 1971 of husbands and wives instead of the previous practice of taxing their combined incomes. In an instant, the tax reform had succeded in making the employment of wives and mothers outside the home more rewarding. Up until then, the wife's income had been combined with that of the husband, and progressive taxation took a proportionally larger bite out of this additional income (Blomquist 2001, 27). The growth of wage-earning mothers with children under the age of seven was uninterrupted, and increased from 60 to 84 per cent between 1975 and 1985. Child-care institutions had difficulty in expanding in proportion to the growing rate of female participation in paid labour (Blomquist 2001, 30f.). During the 1980s, new problems arose as mothers began to work full-time or longer hours. The majority of women in paid employment had previously chosen to work part-time. In each succeeding generation women worked longer hours than their mothers, and child-care soon became a prerequisite for female employment (Hinnfors 1992, 41f.).

The 1970s also saw a number of interventions aimed at supporting parents, while at the same time influencing their family lives. Step by step, new laws prolonged parental leave and increased financial compensation for lost income. The 1974 reform that introduced parental insurance was intended to bring more equality to parental roles, a key step in the gender equality goal. Another important aspect of the same reform was the right of either the mother or the father to stay at home for ten days per year with a sick child. The number of months in the parental insurance has since increased. At the beginning of the 1990s, parents could stay at home with a child for 360 days and receive 90 per cent of their income. In addition, parents gained the right to stay at home with a sick child for 120 days per year. The right of parents to shorter working hours was introduced in 1979, i.e., six instead of eight hours per day until the child reached the age of eight. Child-care allowance to stay-at-home mothers entered the political debate in the early 1960s but no consensus has been reached (Blomquist 2001, 28ff.). Thus pre-school expansion was integrated into labour market policy, with increased support for working parents in the form of time off to look after children at home.

Cohabitation instead of marriage

From the mid-1960s and throughout the 1970s, Sweden was noted for increased cohabitation among young people. At first cohabitation was perceived as a trial marriage, which after a short interval was expected to lead to a wedding. However, it gradually became apparent that many couples continued with cohabitation, to the extent that it finally found a permanent place in Swedish culture. Not only did couples live together without being married, they also had children and to all intents and purposes led ordinary family lives. In Swedish culture almost all those who married went through a period of cohabitation beforehand. Neither was it unknown in Sweden prior to this time. In the 1800s, cohabitation was known as "Stockholm marriage". However, its frequency among those born in 1936 rose from 30 per cent of all women under twenty-six years of age (1962) to almost 80 per cent of women born around 1960 (Qvist and Rennermalm 1985, 39). Cohabitation was popularly referred to as sambo, which for the abbreviation of sammanboende (literally, together living), and Swedes frequently speak of their sambo, for example, or their sambo's brother. In matters of taxation and inheritance the state treats married and cohabiting couples equally (Trost 1993).

Elderly Care

Although elderly care and child-care policies are considered separately, both impact on families, particularly on the ability of kin to combine care with working life. Because the proportion of elderly people in the population expanded greatly in the years after World War II, the problems concerned were treated at an early stage. To begin with, the role of the public sector as the supplier of care and services was unchallenged. However, the negative response to institutionalization also came early and a series of scandals involving homes for the elderly resulted in the universal rejection of these institutions at the start of the 1950s. The focus shifted instead to home care and other types of assistance that promoted independent living. Fulfilling the new goal of aging in place meant the creation of a support system for the next-of-kin, who bore the brunt of caring tasks.

A government commission recommended in 1963 that: "Everything must be done so that as many old people as possible can remain in established settings. In the effort to limit the need for institutional care one must take special steps to help the elderly in their homes, so called open elderly care." However, institutional care was still required and pensioners in homes for the elderly were to have their own rooms rather than share. It was anticipated that those who lived in homes would be made up of the frail and infirm to an increasing degree, thus turning them into nursing homes (Statens offentliga utredningar 1963, 47, 10–11).

In 1965, the state began to allocate subsidies to municipalities if they provided elderly care in private homes. The expansion of municipal home help culminated in 1975, when 328,000 elderly or disabled people were provided with this service. Between 1965 and 1975 services had increased to cover 23 per cent of the elderly population (over sixty-five years of age). Most of the help received by the elderly at home was minimal. However, despite the expansion of home help, the amount of institutional care in long-term hospitals and homes for the elderly remained stable. In 1965, more than 7 per cent of the elderly were in institutional settings, and this had increased to over 8 per cent by 1975 (Sundström and Berg 1988, 5). Researchers and politicians found this increase disturbing, since it was believed that the expansion of home care could reduce the need for care in institutions. Instead, it seems that home care merely delayed the institutionalization of the frail. Long-term care of chronic or terminal illness underwent rapid expansion. In the years after 1975, public services for the elderly declined. The sole exception to this category was housing for the elderly in the form of service houses, which were municipal housing projects for those able to live independently once they had moved to a modern apartment (Szebehely 1995, 30–31). As a rule, service houses were equipped with a staff of home helpers who provided a limited amount of assistance.

The general trend was one of increasing life expectancy coupled with improved general health of the elderly. In each survey carried out, fewer older people declared that they needed help. In 1954, the proportion of the elderly who claimed they needed help was 71 per cent; this declined to 60 per cent in 1975 (Sundström 1983, 20). The issue of loneliness and social isolation seemed to have become less pressing as contact with relatives increased. Fifty-nine per cent of the elderly reported they had contact with their children at least once a week, and by 1980 this had increased to 65 per cent. Whereas 4 per cent in 1954 stated that they rarely if ever had contact with their children, this fell to a mere 1 per cent in 1980.

In the early 1960s, about 4,000 elderly people were recipients of a home-care subsidy in the case of illness (*hemsjukvård*) from the county councils. Twenty per cent were looked after by a wife or husband, 21 per cent by a daughter living at home, while 31 per cent were cared for by a relative living outside the household, and 28 per cent by non-kin, typically a friend or neighbour (Statens offentliga utredningar 1963, 202).

The Discovery of Informal Care

In the 1970s, social workers and researchers became aware of the existence of what they called "informal care", i.e., unpaid care provided by kin within the family. It was anticipated that informal care would decline with the growing availability of "formal" care, but this did not happen. "There is little evidence of deteriorating informal relations. Rather it appears to be the case that the majority of the population has extensive social contacts even if knowledge of the contents or quality of these informal relations is very incomplete" (Sundström 1983, 24). One discovery was the existence of a group of women who had never married, but instead had remained in the homes of their parents in order to care for them in old age. They were known as *hemmadöttrar* (home daughters) and caused great concern because they had never held a job and therefore had no social insurance and only a tiny pension in their own old age, forcing them to turn to social services for welfare payments. The size of this group is not known, but inquiries have shown that municipalities throughout the country had contact with several thousand people in this category. An investigation in Stockholm in 1965 revealed that four per cent of the single women between the ages of fifty and sixty-six were permanent caregivers to old and frail parents, and a further nine per cent gave sporadic care to their parents (Inghe 1970, 188–189). It was acknowledged that these daughters had done great service in taking care of their parents.

The contemporary division of labour between public and kin

Throughout the 1980s the scope of publicly financed elderly care declined in the attempt to control rising costs. The number of people receiving home help diminished from 250,000 in 1980, representing almost 15 per cent of the elderly, to 200,000 in 1990, or 9 per cent. The percentage of those in nursing homes and homes for the elderly declined from 8 per cent in 1975 to approx. 5 per cent in 1990 (Szebehely 1995, 30–31). Closure of mental hospitals and the transfer of inmates to independent living was implemented in the mid-1990s. Behind these reductions was the awareness of run-away costs coupled with the growing difficulty to recruit suitable personnel. Although home help was supplied to less people, total costs mounted, since those who received home help were the most dependent, and many who would previously have been hospitalized were treated medically in their own homes. The number of people who received more than ten hours help a week increased from 10 per cent to approx. 25 per cent between 1986 and 1994 (ibid, 34).

A new appreciation of the care given by the next-of-kin emerged and the authorities began to provide them with support. A government committee estimated in 1987 that next-of-kin, neighbours and friends probably gave twice or three times as much care to the elderly as the municipalities (Statens offentliga utredningar 1987, 91; Johansson 1991). Research estimated the extent of caregiving in kinship networks. A comparative study of a rural and an urban region in 1981 and 1982 found that middle-aged women provided a considerable amount of care. A fifth had spent more than ten hours per week in looking after relatives living outside their own households (Gaunt 1988, 143).

Statisticians working with regular standard of living investigations include questions on social networks. Some of their findings show that Swedes felt more and more isolated in their residential neighbourhoods and have increasingly lower rates of social interaction with their neighbours. This is particularly the case with young adults aged between twenty-five and thirty-four and for recently retired elderly people aged between sixty-five and seventy-four years of age. In contrast, the Swedes report a high and growing frequency of contact with kin living outside the household. In any given week an average of 60 per cent of adult Swedes say they meet with a close relative who lives outside the household (Davidsson 1997, 287, 290).

During the past fifteen years the foundations of Swedish social welfare have changed radically. There has been a retreat from certain forms of care – particularly large-scale institutional settings – but also after-school activities for school children, for instance, and home care for the elderly. At the same time, the supply in other domains has been expanded, e.g., the variety of tailor-made care settings in elderly and child care, a development that is, to some extent, related to privatization in the social sector. On the other hand, it is also related to specific activities for the elderly with different illnesses or who speak different languages. Finally, it is related to the 1992 decision to give municipalities more independence from central government.

The privatization of care became a major political issue and a vast amount of care, hitherto a public monopoly, is now in the hands of private companies, parental or employee cooperatives, or voluntary associations. There is greater freedom of choice. In parent cooperative day-care, parents participate in caregiving on a regular basis. Some variants of elderly care focus on elderly immigrants and create services that are tailored to certain ethnic and religious groups most likely to have abstained from care up to that point.

Public and political debate has seen a dramatic upswing of interest in the nuclear family, parenting and kin relations. A key concern is the ability to combine parenthood with gainful employment outside the home. Advice books have proliferated (Björkman 2002; Dükler 2004; Zilg et al. 2005; Hougaard 2004; Carling and Cleve 2005). There is also a growing body of research and statistical investigation (Bygren et al. 2004; Tjänstemännens centralorganisation 2002; Lövkrona 1999; Magnusson 1998; Bernhardt 1992). With the expansion of higher education, attention has recently been paid to the economic situation of married university students with children (Morild 2002). The number of publications on being the next-of-kin to seriously ill relatives is vast. Much of these came about as a result of the political interest in creating municipal support for the next-of-kin, quietly mobilizing them for an overall caring strategy. (Fant 1988; Jeppsson-Grassman 2001; Janouch 2004). Because the next-of-kin are being used to fill care functions that had previously been carried by the social services, the enormous support given to caregiving next-of-kin resembles the self-discipline that Foucault has termed governmentality, according to which individuals are persuaded or persuade themselves to behave in accordance with the tasks that governments have designated.

Researchers have noted several changes in political attitudes toward the family and relatives. In the period from the mid-1950s to the late 1970s, the state and its agencies viewed parents with some degree of distrust. They organized family support from the standpoint that the family when left to itself would be dangerously isolated from society and that parents in general were in need of expert guidance. The idea of parental education flourished. In the 1980s and increasingly in the 1990s, however, parents were perceived as competent, and the state and its agencies tended to respect the authority of parents and their ability to utilize freedom of choice (Gleichmann 2004).

Social and family policies in the 1990s split from a semi-coherent whole into a number of individual spheres, each with its own dynamic and inner logic. This was partially caused by the emergence of "interest group" politics, which brought group-specific issues to a political agenda that had previously sought universal solutions. Each group demanded acknowledgement of its specific needs and the application of its "perspective". Child policy came into its own with its unmistakable "child perspective". Among other things this resulted in the establishment of an *ombudsman* office for children (Regeringskansliet 2001). A separate category dealing with the next-of-kin was added to the policy on age, and resulted in heavily funded governmental programmes (Socialstyrelsen 1999, 2002, 2003). Other perspectives with on-going influence over developments in family-related policy are: feminism and homosexual (including bisexual and transsexual), refugee and asylum issues. While the perspectives are different, they join in making policy more sensitive to the situation of the individual and the need to individualize approaches.

The modern Swedish fertility rate is closely related to the general economic situation, as the majority of all social insurances are based on individual income through gainful employment. The strong link between employment and childbearing makes Swedish population development highly susceptible to economic depression (Jonson and Dlab 2003). The first part of the 1990s was a period of deep economic decline, and although it was succeeded by a more favourable period, this did not result in increased employment. Further, entrance to the labour market was difficult and most young people worked in temporary jobs in the form of projects with little job security. This partly explains the high age of first-time mothers and the rapidly decreasing birth rates during the economic crisis in the 1990s. The number of births in Sweden during the 1980s was among the highest in Europe, with 124,000 births in 1990. However, this number declined dramatically during the 1990s to 88,000 in 1999, and although on the increase has not yet fully recovered.

Child perspective

In 1985, the *Riksdag* took the historic decision of introducing pre-school for all children aged one and over as of 1991. This implied that parents who either worked or studied would be able to place their children in some form of child care. Children who could not get a place in a day nursery would be placed in a part-time group or admitted to an open pre-school. The decision indicated a clear recognition of the educational value of pre-schools and the right of all children to enjoy these activities from an early age. Public child care expanded more rapidly in the 1980s than in previous decades, bringing a total increase of 129,000 new places. However, the 1985 vision of pre-schools for all children by 1991 could not be fulfilled. To the dismay of the politicians and local authorities, the growing demand still exceeded the supply (Johansson and Åstedt 1996, 35). A member of the *Riksdag* stated in a hearing in 1991 that several municipalities intended to raise the entrance age from twelve to eighteen months. Apologizing, the minister for social affairs admitted that both childbearing and women's partipation in paid employment had increased more than had been anticipated in 1985 (Schyman 1991).

The present Swedish mosaic is characterized by a strong attention to individuals and specific conditions rather than to a general family policy aimed at levelling the differences between families. Despite cutbacks, the state increased its engagement in family issues and reforms. During the 1990s and early 2000s, however, the pattern was one of policy-making for specific groups or family categories, such as one-parent or student families and close attention to detail. The expansion phase of Swedish welfare and family policy was initiated in the 1960s. Child-care institutions aimed at achieving full coverage by 1991. In the 1980s, however, the declining birth rates reversed abruptly and soared to become one of the highest in Europe. This was not the sole reason for the unfulfilled promise. Comprehensive reforms with standard solutions no longer appeared to be an adequate strategy, although for some time this remained the preferred policy. All children were to attend municipal day care, regardless of individual differences. This "medicine" was obviously not the universal cure for all families, and some fell through the safety net. Moreover, there was a growing demand for individualized solutions.

As the last decade of the twentieth century unfolded, Swedish welfare institutions were called more and more into question and underwent a phase of reorganization. The first years of the 1990s brought a more finely tuned child perspective, as laid down in the UN Convention of Childrens Rights that was adopted by the Swedish state in 1990. Issues primarily concerning the protection of children at risk, such as immigrant, adopted, abused and mentally handicapped children were discussed in the *Riksdag*. For a short period the government even included a minister for "child and family issues", a previously unheard of position. In 1993, the authority *Barnombudsmannen*, an ombudsman for children, was established and assigned the task of representing the interests and rights of children and youth from the perspective of the UN Convention.

The adoption of the children's rights perspective in the 1990s gave voice to one of the weakest elements in society. Asylum-seeking families with minor children were also given priority where possible. Legislation on the sexual abuse of children was tightened and sentences prolonged; media attention soared. After 1995 divorce courts were obliged to take children's will into consideration. The anthology *Barnets bästa* [The Child's Best] (Statens offentliga utredningar 1997, 116) was released in 1997. Socialstyrelsen triggered municipal social projects on the subject "The child in focus".

Ingrid Söderlind of the Swedish Institute for Futures Studies investigated the position of children in governmental committee reports from 1950 to 1999 (Söderlind 2005). The child perspective and children's right to take part in decisions that concern them were some of the issues initially discussed in the 1990s. Official investigations concerned children, empowerment and democracy, albeit major reductions were carried out at the same time. These issues were not related; the goal of increasing children's influence could not be realized since children and families with children became poorer. Official investigations conducted since the 1950s have dealt primarily with the type of support society should give to families with children and what efforts society expects of parents. In 1983, the investigation *Barn kostar* (children cost) established that the child allowance barely covered the costs for children. The Committee urged that the general child allowance be designed to cover all costs, but realized that achieving this goal meant considerable tax redistribution. The subsequent investigation of the economy of families with children was conducted in 2001, i.e., almost twenty years later (Statens offentliga utredningar 2001, 24). The economy of families with children had deteriorated considerably during the 1990s and the task of the Committee was to investigate the situation and propose solutions. The investigation was entitled *Ur fattigdomsfällan* (out of the poverty trap) and stated that a number of family benefits had been abolished or reduced during the 1990s. The value of parental insurance was only half of what it had been on introduction in 1974. It was essentially a matter of change in attitude: it was anticipated in 1983 that state benefits would cover the cost of children, by 2001, however, the economic responsibility for children was said to lie first and foremost with the parents (Flygt Högberg 2003).

In 1991, a coalition of non-socialist parties formed a government and announced a thorough "system change" with deregulation, privatization and freedom of choice. Family policy now became an expansive area of national politics. Child allowance was raised in 1993, and in 1994 the decision was taken to launch a child-care allowance. The socialist parties, on the other hand, advocated budget restraint in 1994. The Left Party suggested that child care should have its own crisis programme. In the same year, when the Social Democrats returned to government, the opposition continued to defend the family, but with increased economic depression the promised family policy reforms, such as extension of parent insurance and an increase in child benefits, were withdrawn. The entire social insurance system met with reductions in 1995, payments for maternity leave, parental leave etc. were to comprise 75 per cent instead of 80 per cent of the wage or salary income.

The baby boom that had begun in the 1980s came to a halt in the 1990s. Birth rates measured in the number of children per woman plummeted to the lowest level ever recorded. In 1999, fertility was 1.5 children per Swedish woman of fertile age. But, once again, the low number of births in 1999 reversed and began to increase: from 88,173 births in 1999 to 100,928 in 2004. Swedish birth levels now rank in the mid-range of European countries. Marriage rates have also gone up while divorce rates indicate a slight decline. In 1999, 35,628 couples married, and no less than 43,088 in 2004. The divorce rate decreased from 21,502 in the year 2000 to 20,106 in 2004 (Statistical Central Bureau 2004).

Cohabitation has increased greatly since the 1960s; approximately a third of all couples cohabit today. This is partly due to the significant number of old-age pensioners who now cohabit, whereas previously cohabitation was found predominantly in young adults. There is also an apparent rise in the number of people who regard themselves as couples, although they have separate residences. They are referred to as *särbo* (living together apart) or *delsbo* (part-time living together). Around 50 per cent of the children born in 1990 were born outside of marriage, but most of these births take place within a stable cohabitation relationship (Blomquist 2001, 15).

Wage-earning women was no longer a small category in the society of the 1990s and most labour markets were available to them. The share of women who were gainfully employed was 79 per cent in 2003. As the main objective of Swedish family policy since the 1970s has been to enable the combination of parenthood and gainful employment, family policy reforms were forced to meet the need for more diversity in employment and family forms.

In terms of child care, the 1990s was a turbulent decade for the municipal authorities. Fluctuating local birth rates made long-term planning difficult and the economic depression prevented major efforts. In 1991, the beginning of compulsory education was made flexible and six-year-olds were invited to start school when places were available (the previous school-beginner age was seven). The share of school beginners at the age of six, however, was small, i.e., 7.5 per cent in 1994/95. However, many municipalities moved the preparatory school year of six-year-olds from day nurseries to schools, thereby reducing the cost of pre-school activities and vacating places in child care for the younger "baby boom" children (Johansson and Åstedt 1996, 144). The number of children per employee/staff member increased during the 1990s and ignited yet another debate on the quality of pre-schools, where the actual existence of child care for the smallest children has been challenged (Kågeson 2005).

In the course of 2002, the number of children in child care soared from 315,000 to 333,600. The majority of "new" children were in fact already in child care, but had one parent on parental leave. The attendance of children of unemployed parents has also increased. The number of children in this category, however, remained stable due to sinking unemployment rates. After the reform, parents on sick leave were more likely to leave their children in public child care. 20,000 children, i.e., three times the number in 1999, have one parent who is on long-term sick leave or has an invalidity pension. Around 80 per cent of these children attend pre-school, compared to 60 per cent prior to the reform (www.skolverket.se 2005-09-22).

Mosaic of elderly care

In 1992, a long-discussed but major reform that transferred nursing homes and other forms of nursing for the elderly from the county councils to the municipalities came into effect. A key reason for the reform was the inability of county councils and municipalities to cooperate on the administrative level, which had produced numerous difficulties for senior citizens. Another reason for the reform, which led to a renaissance of institutional care, was recognition of the consequences of dementia, and especially Alzheimer's disease. The latter created the temporary panic necessary to legitimate institutional solutions. The breakthrough came with the portrayal of Alzheimer's disease as a deadly illness of epidemic proportions that was affecting an increasing number of those over eighty years of age. The personality disorders that accompanied the disease meant that many families were incapable of providing the necessary care without outside help and institutional resources (Gaunt et al. 1993). The new awareness of dementia created sufficient pressure to introduce a new, "homelike" form of institution, the *gruppboende* (group dwelling); the Social Board administered a special fund for municipalities that wished to construct them. Funds were granted when the group dwelling met specific demands, i.e., size, staffing and architecture. This step brought about a re-institutionalization of elderly care and the abandonment of traditional home help.

As early as the 1980s, small group dwellings had been proposed for the care of those suffering from Alzheimer's disease. Researchers and the responsible authorities were in conflict over how dementia care should be organized. The National Board of Health and Welfare saw the group dwelling as a comprehensive solution, whereas researchers considered them no more than a link in the chain of caregiving institutions. They insisted that there was also a need to expand nursing homes and terminal care for the victims of dementia (ibid, 73). From 1991, municipalities began to receive state subventions from the National Board of Health and Welfare to build group dwellings. The dwellings were planned to enable the demented patient to receive visits from kin. The rooms were considered the patients' "homes" and architectural regulations stipulated that each room was to have cooking facilities, whereby forgotten pots and pans on stoves id cause numerous fires. In 1987, sixty group dwellings existed in the whole of Sweden. The state planned an expansion to cover 25,000 places, which was to encompass about a fourth of those affected by dementia. The growth of formal care for the elderly aimed to ease the burden of the next-of-kin, since Alzheimer's caregivers were gradually being recognized as the "hidden victims". As recently as 2002, it was stated that next-of-kin supplied 75 per cent of all care, or three times the amount of care given by the municipal authorities. Subsequent research has come to similar high estimates of the level of kin care (Szebehely 2005). As already mentioned, a number of state-funded programmes involving municipal support for next-of-kin were initiated at the turn of the century.

Developments in elderly care are characterized by the stark demographic growth of the highest age groups, i.e., those most in need of care. Between 1980 and 1997, the number of people over eighty years of age increased from 263,000 to 427,000. Since those in the highest age categories are more frequently affected by diseases such as dementia, services are in the process of transforming their work from social to nursing care, and municipalities are obliged to employ staff with medical expertise. The new forms of institution, i.e., group dwellings, homes for the elderly and nursing homes, increased rapidly at first, while the former flagship of independent living, the *servicehus* (service houses), was often converted into institutional settings. A new generic term was created for institutional care: *särskilda boendeformer* (special forms of residence) and various types of state subsidies were promised to the municipalities. The first decade of the twenty-first century, however, has seen a reappearance of the anti-institutional principle and a decline in the number of places in special residence forms.

Throughout the 1990s, there was a growing awareness that elderly migrants were increasing in numbers and that standard municipal care had difficulty in taking care of them. There was also a suspicion that many of the elderly who needed care abstained as a result of language and cultural differences. In some cases young granddaughters stayed away from school to take care of a grandparent, increasing the difficulty of integrating into Swedish society (Ronström 1996; Heikkilä 1994; Karupää 1994; Hajighasemi 1994). The creation of ethnic-sensitive elderly care became a primary concern and resulted in the establishment of institutions or other forms of care, e.g., for elderly Finns, Spanish-speakers, Italians, Oriental Christians or Iranians. Demands for their own elderly care were raised by other ethnic groups, for instance by the Sami (Lapps). The background to many family conflicts was the inability of immigrant families to recreate the three-generational care environments they were familiar with from their homelands. Despite much good will, it proved no easy task to combine daily life in Sweden – particularly education and female employment – with ethnic customs. At times the only solution was to break up the three-generational household and have the elderly move into a service-house apartment.

Next-of-kin who take care of demented elderly people in their own homes have attracted considerable attention. Since the early 1990s, a several lobby organizations have supported the next-of-kin of dementia victims and a number of influential books have found a wide audience (Fant 1988). In 1987, the government introduced legislation to increase freedom of choice in terms of elderly care. New principles were forwarded: "Self-determination and integrity" gives the elderly the right to decide how they want to live their lives. Service and care must therefore be altered to the extent that individuals have greater freedom of choice to remain in their homes and familiar environment. "Security" emphasizes the need for the elderly to be close to relatives and neighbours. Elderly care should be characterized by continuity and, if necessary, staffed around the clock. "Freedom of choice" gives people the right to influence the content and form of public service and care. Municipalities should strive to create a broad spectrum on this front.

The 1997 revision of the Social Service Law takes into consideration the situation of relatives who take care of the frail elderly. It orders municipalities to give support and practical assistance to the next-of-kin who look after the long-term ill, the elderly and those with functional disabilities. This support can either be in the form of additional home help or temporarily placing the person concerned in an institution so that the care-giving relative can get rest and recreation. In 2000, the Social Board distributed money to the municipalities for projects designed to enhance conditions for the next-of-kin.

Conclusion

This survey of the relationship of kinship and social services in Sweden has concentrated on the development of child and elderly care since the 1900s. It found a number of principles and trends leading to a symbiosis of kinship structure and the way social services have been designed. The following are some of these trends and principles:

The principle of gender equality leads to the process of adjusting laws and regulations to equalize the manner in which legal and administrative systems treat women and men. This regulates the labour market, social services and basic societal values. Thus several adjustments to the social services were introduced to facilitate the combination of employment with cultural obligations to care for kin. Here there is a vast increase in state support for working parents, who are obliged for various reasons to engage in child care at home.

The principle of anti-institutionalization was strong in the second half of the twentieth century. It meant the rejection of institutional care as a long-term solution and the prioritizing of home care or care in "homelike" settings. New institutional forms are introduced temporarily and then only when a social or care problem first emerges. After a certain period of time, these innovations are terminated. The priority of the home setting invariably leads to a continuum of care shared by municipal caregivers and the next-of-kin. This has emerged as the clearest interface of interaction between kinship and the social services.

Traditional kinship thinking has been preserved in everyday Swedish language through the retention of kinship terms, which in numerous other languages have long since vanished. Thus kinship awareness was latent and has been mobilized in recent decades to fill the gap produced by the withdrawal of the welfare state from some of its commitments. Governments have rediscovered kinship as a resource to be counted on to step in when it comes to helping their next-of-kin.

Swedes claim they acknowledge only part of their kin network as morally important, in the sense of obligations and rights. Socialization and help is concentrated within this small group, thereby accounting for the reporting of smaller kinship groups than in many other European cultures. However, the size in this case can be an advantage, as it increases the ability to fulfil the moral obligation to help members of the kinship group and be gainfully employed at the same time.

Bibliography

Bergh, A. (1997), *Anhörigvård*, Lund: Studentlitteratur.

Bergman, H. (1999), "En familj som andra: barnavårdsmän och genuspolitik i den tidiga välfärdsstaten", in *Historisk tidskrift vol. 119*, pp. 227–252.

Bernhardt, E. M. (1992), *Working parents in Sweden: an example for Europe*, Stockholm: University Demography Unit.

Björkman, A. (ed.) (2002), *Uppdrag: Mamma, Berättelser från en ny generation mammor*, Stockholm: Bonniers.

Blomquist, B. (2001), Förskolebarnets relation till sin familj Förändrade förutsättningar och föreställningar 1950–1990, Göteborg: Göteborg Studies in Sociology 4.

Bygren, M., M. Gähler and M. Nermo (2004), *Familj och arbete: vardagsliv i förändring*, Stockholm: SNS.

Carling, M. and E. Cleve (2005), *Sopa lagom! Bättre balans i curlingfamiljen*, Stockholm: Wahlström & Widstrand.

Davidsson, G. (1997), *Sociala nätverk, Välfärd och ojämlikhet i 20–årsperspektiv 1975–1995*, Stockholm: Statistiska centralbyrån.

Dükler, H. (ed.) (2004), *Uppdrag: Pappa*, Stockholm: Bonniers.

Ekman, A.-K. (2003), "Too much kinship? Managing social relations in a small village in Sweden", *Etnofoor* 16:1, pp. 97–114.

Fant, M. (1988), *Att bli mamma till min mamma*, Stockholm: Natur och Kultur.

Flygt Högberg, C. (2003), *Barn osynliga i offentliga utredningar*, Från riksdag och departement 32.

Gaunt, D. (1982), "The property and kin relations of retired farmers in northern and central Europe", in R. Wall and P. Laslett (eds.), *Family forms in historic Europe*, Cambridge: Cambridge University Press, pp. 249–280.

— (1988), "Rural household organization and inheritance in northern Europe", in T. Hareven (ed.), *Family history at the crossroads*, Princeton: Princeton University Press, pp. 121–142.

— (1996), "Hemvård istället för vårdhem: den öppna vårdens uppkomst i Hemmet i vården, vården i hemmet", in D. Gaunt and G. Lantz (eds.), *Hemmet i vården – vården i Hemmet*, Stockholm: Liber, pp. 39–64.

— (1997), "Urban clannishness and the nuclear kin: trends in Swedish family life in family and kinship in Europe", in M. Gullestad and M. Segalen (eds.), *Family and kinship in Europe*, London: Pinter, pp. 103–128.

— (2001), "Kinship: the thin red line and the thick blue blood: extended kinship and households in history of the European family", in D. I. Kertzer and M. Barbagli (eds.), *Family life in early modern times 1500–1789*, New Haven: Yale University Press, pp. 257–287.

Gaunt, D., M. Öhlander and R. Schwarz (1993), *Demenser och demensvård, Medicinska, sociala och kulturella aspekter*, Stockholm: Liber.

Gaunt, L. (1988), *Familjekretsen: bosättning, umgänge och omsorg*, Gävle: Byggforskningsrådet.

Gleichmann, L. (2004), *Föräldraskap mellan styrning och samhällsomvandling: en studie av synen på föräldrar och relationer mellan familj och samhälle under perioden 1957–1997*, Stockholm: LHS.

Hajighasemi, F. (1994), *Invandring på gamla da'r – sextio äldre iranier berättar*, Stockholm: FoU byrån.

Hanssen, B. (1976), *Hushållens sammansättning i österlenska byar under 300 år*, Rig, pp. 33–60.

Heikkilä, K. (1994), *Mer än halva livet – en studie om äldre finländska invandrare i Stockholm*, Stockholm: FoU byrån.

Hinnfors, J. (1992), *Familjepolitik: Samhällsförändringar och partistrategier 1960–1990*, Stockholm: Almqvist & Wiksell.

Hougaard, B. (2004), *Curlingföräldrar och servicebarn – En handbok i barnuppfostran*, Stockholm: Prisma.

Inghe, G. (1970), *Den ofärdiga välfärden*, Stockholm: Tiden.

Janouch, K. (2004), *Anhörig*, Stockholm: Piratförlag.

Jeppsson-Grassman, E. (2001), *Medmänniska och anhörig: en studie av informella hjälpinsatser*, Stockholm: Sköndal institutet.

Johansson, G. and I. B. Åstedt (1996), *Förskolans utveckling – fakta och funderingar*, Stockholm: HLS.

Johansson, L. (1991), *Caring for the next of kin*, Uppsala University: Almqvist & Wiksell.

Jonson, A. and B. Dlab (2003), "Sysselsättning och fruktsamhet i Sverige och Finland", *Political economy*, Stockholm University.

Kågeson, P. (2005), *Tid för barn? En analys av samhällets omsorg om de minsta*, Stockholm: SNS.

Karupää, M.-A. (1994), *En koffert i Tallinn, Estniska pensionärer i Stockholm*, Stockholm: FoU byrån.

Key, E. (1900), *Barnets århundrade 2 vols*, Stockholm: Bonniers.

Lövkrona, I. (1999), "Kön, familj och arbeite", in B. Meurling, B. Lundgren and I. Lövkrona (eds.), *Familj och kön*, Lund: Studentlitteratur.

Magnusson, E. (1998), *Vardagens könsinnebörder under förhandling: om arbete, familj och produktion av kvinnlighet*, Umeå: Umeå universitet.

Melby, K., A. Pylkkänen, B. Rosenbeck and C. Carlsson Wetterberg (2006), *Inte ett ord om kärlek, Äktenskap och politik i Norden ca 1850–1930*, Lund: Makadam förlag.

Morild, K. (2002), *Styvmoderligt behandlade föräldrar: studenter med barn*, Stockholm: TCO.

Nordlöf, B. (1997), *Barnets rätt och bästa, En studie i barnavårdsmannaverksamheten i Stockholm*, Stockholm: Stockholmia förlag.

Ohrlander, K. (1992), *I barnens och nationens intresse: socialliberal reformpolitik 1903–1930*, Stockholm: Almqvist & Wiksell.

Qvist, J. and B. Rennermalm (1985), *Att bilda familj, Samboende, äktenskap och barnafödande bland kvinnor födda 1936–60*, Stockholm: Statistiska centralbyrån.

Regeringskansliet (2001), *Barnafödandet i fokus, Från befolkningspolitik till ett barnvänligt samhälle*, Stockholm: Regeringskansliet DS 2001: 57.

Ronström, O. (1996), *Vem ska ta hand om de gamla invandrarna?*, Stockholm: FoU byrån.

Rosenberg, A. (1991), *Två barn och ett eget hus*, Stockholm: Carlsson & Skaraborgs länsmuseum.

Schyman, G. (1991), "Tre månaders glapp mellan barnledigt och dagis", *Från Riksdag och Departement*, nr. 7.

Skolverket (2003), *Childcare, 1972–90*, Stockholm: SCB.

Socialstyrelsen (1999), *Anhörig 300: stimulansbidrag för utvärdering av anhörigstöd*, Stockholm: Socialstyrelsen.

— (2002), *Kommunernas stöd till anhörigvårdare: anhörigas erfarenheter och synpunkter*, Stockholm: Socialstyrelsen.

— (2003), *Ett år efter Anhörig 300: arbete med utveckling av anhörigstöd 2002*, Stockholm: Socialstyrelsen.

— (2006), *Omsorg människor emellan, En översikt av omsorgsgivande i den svenska befolkningen*, Stockholm: Socialstyrelsen.

Söderlind, I. (2005), *Var kommer barnen in?: Barn i politik, vetenskap och dagspress*, Stockholm: Institutet för framtidsstudier.

Statens offentliga utredningar (1963), *Åldringsvårdens läge, Undersökning utförd av socialpolitiska kommittén*, Stockholm: SOU.

— (1964), *Ökat stöd till barnfamiljer: promemoria angiven av Familjeberedningen*, Stockholm: SOU.

— (1972a), *Barnstugeutredningen*, Stockholm: SOU.

— (1972b), *Förskolan*, Stockholm: SOU.

— (1987), *Äldreomsorg i utveckling, Betänkande av äldreberedningen*, Stockholm: SOU.

— (1993), *Frivilligt socialt arbete: kartläggning och kunskapsöversikt*, Stockholm: SOU.

— (1997), *Barnets bästa*, Stockholm: SOU.

Statistical Central Bureau (2004), *Befolkningsstatistik 1749–2004*, Stockholm: SCB.

Sundström, G. (1983), *Caring for the aged in welfare society*, Stockholm: Studies in Social Work 1.

Sundström, G. and S. Berg (1988), *Vad har egentligen hänt inom äldreomsorgen? Har vård i hemmet ersatt institutionsvård? Erfarenheter 1965–1985*, Jönköping: Institutet för gerontologi.

Szebehely, M. (1995), *Vardagens organisering, Om vårdbiträden och gamla i hemtjänsten*, Lund: Arkiv.

— (2005), *Anhörigas betalda och obetalda äldreomsorgsinsatser*, Stockholm: SOU.

Thorsson, I. (1960), *Ett mänskligare samhälle*, Stockholm: Rabén & Sjögren.

Tjänstemännens centralorganisationen (2002), *Arbetstider och livspusslet/ jobb och familj*, Stockholm: TCO.

Trost, J. (1993), *Familjen i Sverige*, Stockholm: Liber.

Zilg, B., L. Sunna and K. Salmson (eds.) (2005), *Uppdrag: Familj, Berättelser från en ny generation familjer*, Stockholm: Bonniers.

The relationship between family, kin and social security in twentieth-century Germany

Heidi Rosenbaum and Elisabeth Timm[1]

Introduction[2]

In international comparative research on the relationship between family, kin[3] and social security[4], and on the relationship between family, kin and the modern welfare state[5], the Federal Republic of Germany is considered

---

1 Translation: John Bendix.

2 This chapter was completed in 2006 and updated in parts in 2007. It is a much shorter version of our report "Kinship and Social Security in Germany in the Twentieth Century" (Göttingen/Wien 2006), which was published in German in a completely revised, updated and enlarged version (Rosenbaum and Timm 2008).

3 "In the following, the term 'family' is used for the group that lives together in a household and consists of parents and children who are either minors or unmarried. Family thus means nuclear family. 'Kin' encompasses all other relations beyond this" (Rosenbaum 1998, 18). The use of the terms "family" and "kin", however, is ambiguous in the German-language research tradition. In research on the family into the 1980s, "family" typically meant nuclear family; those who examined networks tended instead to focus on "kin."

4 "Social security" is a topos both of ordinary usage and in analytical work on the post-World War Two era in Europe. When Alber (1982, 56) uses the term, he means the development of social insurance systems. This usage is also international; in Article 22 of the UN Declaration of Human Rights (1948) the "right to social security" is defined as a human right (Kaufmann 1973, 96).

5 Here the term "welfare state" is a "general term" (Motel-Klingebiel 2000, 16) and hence understood and used as an analytical term. It connotes "a modification of market forces through state support for the social security of the individual" (Bouvier 2002, 21). This definition is widely used in historical and sociological research, particularly in comparative analyses of European nation states (Esping-Andersen 1990; Schmid 2002). By contrast, the term Sozialstaat refers to a specifically German model of political and social policy (enshrined in the Basic Law), in which the political goal is "to supersede the opposition between traditional forms of state governance and the industrialized class-based society with social integration." In addition, the term "welfare" is to be avoided in order to distance the concept politically from older welfare state regulatory mechanisms that were seen as tied to poverty relief and thus carried connotations of lower social position

an example of a "conservative welfare regime" (Esping-Andersen 1990). Central to this type of regime is the role of the family and of kinship, while the market takes up only a marginal position. The state, or more precisely, the legislature, legalizes and regulates social security in a corporatist manner, following the principle of subsidiarity. Also typical is the institutionalization and regulation of quasi-public welfare associations (Bahle and Pfenning 2001).

Historical and sociological research on family and kin networks has shown that common practice in the provision of security is not exclusively a function of what is legally mandated by social, taxation or labour market policies. Instead, these practices should be seen as "[...] an interaction between cultural ideals, institutional conditions, social structure and social action, [...]" where constraints engendered by historically evolved "cultural contexts" also play their part (Pfau-Effinger 2000, 235, 22).

Chronology and dynamics of institutionalized social security in Germany

Long-range tendencies before and after the nineteenth century

In the context of family, kinship and social security relations in Germany up to the nineteenth century, four main tendencies can be identified: a) separate households, b) separate housing of generations, c) significance of kinship between households, d) collective retirement arrangements. These tendencies have governed developments since the nineteenth century and are still visible in the current situation as described below.

Living in separate households

As a result of the different social, economic and denominational factors involved, separate households have constituted a key form of living arrangement since the high Middle Ages (Ehmer 1990). Although commonly assumed, extended families and households containing more than two generations were not the dominant pattern (Mitterauer 1977). In Germany,

---

and dishonour unworthy of a democracy (Bouvier 2002, 21; similar definitions in Ritter 1998, 4f. and Kaufmann 2003).

as in other West and Central European countries, the importance of nuclear families and their lack of spatial integration in strong kinship networks is a traditional pattern rather than a consequence of industrialization and modernization (Rosenbaum 1998).

Separate housing of the generations

It was common for relatives to live in separate households. This was also true for parents and their adult married children, regardless of the varying regional inheritance patterns. Admittedly, households shared by parents and one married child were more prevalent in regions with impartible inheritance (Schlumbohm 1994; Rosenbaum 1996). Financial constraints were frequently the reason for young and old to share a household.

There is considerable evidence that joint housing of generations, where possible for demographic and economic reasons (Imhof 1981), was quite often avoided – most probably to forestall the conflicts inherent in such constellations. One example is the separate house for retired landholders (*Altenteiler*) on prosperous farms; another is the practice common in several German regions of paying off the oldest generation (*Geldausgedinge*); clauses detailed in agreements on handing over property (*Übergabeverträge*) can be seen as a third example (Gaunt 1982; Rosenbaum 1996). Multigenerational households first emerged with the economic and demographic developments of the nineteenth century, and then largely in the rural areas (Mitterauer 1977).

In the late nineteenth century members of the working classes shared their households with married children, albeit rarely, and if so, primarily as a living arrangement for the aged. The municipal authorities occasionally demanded that households be shared, as they represented the most economical solution (Reif 1982). Thus, even in the working-class milieu, multigenerational living arrangements, e.g., the older generation with married children, was a practice born of necessity rather than free choice.

Importance of kinship

Notwithstanding the preference for separate households and the relevance of collective retirement arrangements in Germany, kinship relations were neither unimportant nor irrelevant. On the contrary, they carried key functions in the economic and social realm, and were pertinent to the production and protection of political power (Bergeron 1981; Lipp 1982; 2006; summary in Rosenbaum 1998; Sabean 1998). Support provided by relatives and kinship networks was vital, particularly in an economic crisis. This remained true of working-class families up to the early twentieth century (Rosenbaum 1992) and became relevant once again in the years immediately after the First and Second World Wars. Under these difficult circumstances, relatives grew close, even spatially, accepting the conflicts that habitually accompany such living arrangements.

Collective arrangements for retirement

Separate households for the oldest generation were more common in urban centres than in the rural areas. Here monetary forms of retirement arrangements enabled older people to be more independent than was the case in the barter-oriented rural economy (Borscheid 1987; Ehmer 1990). In the pre-industrial era, the poor relief made available by the church and the state compensated for the absence of relatives or their inability to provide support.

Municipal organizations or city guilds also had traditions of collective retirement arrangements, with ordinances such as the 1570 *Polizeiverordnung*, which even demanded support for the local needy (Sachße and Tennstedt 1980, 107). Over and above, more prosperous groups could create security by making additional monetary provisions (such as savings, buying into the local hospital, or taking out a life annuity). Several professions organized widows' funds (*Witwenkassen*) in the seventeenth and eighteenth centuries (Borscheid 1987).

The eighteenth century marked a turning point, since the decline of the guilds also meant a decline in the forms of social security the guild system had provided. Pauperism emerged with the arrival of manufacturing, and the politics of social security now became the politics of disciplining the poor (*Armenzucht*) (Wendt 1995, 129). The primary purpose of the latter was to suppress begging, and was accompanied by institutionalization (jails, workhouses) as well as compulsory work for the poor.

Although some German states, most notably Prussia, with its *Allgemeine Landrecht* of 1794 (Hattenhauer 1994), provided public support in the case of need, these efforts remained inadequate, especially with regard to illness and old age, the two central factors in poverty at the time. Moreover, there was no legal basis for this support; it tended to take the form of publicly-funded rather than religiously-based alms. In short, old age was almost synonymous with poverty for the majority of the population in pre-industrial society, both for the urban and rural lower classes, as well as for peasants on small subsistence farms.

The growth of the industrial working class in the late nineteenth century and the concomitant development of the "social question" was to lead to the abandonment of the old policies for the poor and the introduction of a new social policy for the workers. Nevertheless, it would take another seventy years for the close connection between old age and poverty in Germany to be finally severed.

Developments up to 1945

The institutionalization of social security as a form of social insurance got under way in Germany in the course of the 1880s. Health and accident insurance, as well as disability and old age pensions, were introduced between 1883 and 1889 (Ritter 1998). Several features of these schemes have survived up to the present day, e.g., the principle of mandatory insurance, employment as the insurance basis, equal contributions by employer and employee, and graduated contributions based on income or risk. The older forms of poor relief were left unchanged, subject merely to minor legislative and administrative acts.

The support provided through social insurance and poor relief was meagre, however, particularly for the elderly. As in the past, they remained dependent on their relatives for support, whether in the form of general assistance or as specifically and legally defined transfer obligations with respect to livelihood[6]. These obligations were viable for the sole reason that married women and mothers in Germany rarely belonged to the wage labour force, a reality that endured well into the second half of the twentieth century (Willms 1980). However, it can be assumed that shouldering such obligations was not unproblematic, particularly during an economic crisis. When relatives were forced to support needy kin following massive recourse to the family by the state, severe internal conflict was frequently the result (Homburg 1985; Crew 1990).

---

6 The Civil Code (BGB Para. 1601) defines support obligations between lineal relatives in direct, ascending or descending line.

Social security was written into the 1919 Weimar Constitution (Arts. 119, 122, 142–65), and poor relief legally anchored, standardized, and differentiated by needy groups or the nature of the need (Ritter 1998; Frerich and Frey 1996, Vol. 1, 171–235). In addition, quasi-public welfare associations were given legal status and state support in 1922 and 1927, respectively. In the course of the Weimar Republic, industrial relations were officially reorganized, and supplemented with elements uniquely characteristic of social security in Germany. With the introduction of the new labour laws, the state created a balance between employer and employee interests, which was referred to as the Fordist[7] class compromise. Workers could share in societal wealth up to a point, but only at the cost of abandoning their efforts – long a political goal – of gaining access to the means of production. Unemployment insurance was added in 1927. For the first time in Germany, specific provisions for the unemployed were introduced; prior to this, they had been reliant on poor relief, or as it was called after 1918, poor relief for the unemployed (Frerich and Frey 1996, Vol. 1, 196, 199–203).

The Nazi regime largely perpetuated the existing social insurance system (ibid. 289–305), maintaining its dual character (Hammerschmidt 1999). In principle, however, all benefits were revocable, making it possible to characterize the Nazi state as a "good conduct state" (*Wohlverhaltensstaat*) rather than a "welfare state" (Wohlfahrtsstaat) (Teppe 1977, 196). The legal differentiation of needy groups, for example, with regard to those on war relief or on small pensions, had already begun during the Weimar Republic and led to diverse discrimination or privileging (including a veto on recourse to relatives). The Nazi state radicalized these distinctions further by introducing racial ideology into welfare laws and practices (Sachße and Tennstedt 1992). In terms of industrial relations, the regime brought the Fordist class compromise to an end or rather radicalized it by smashing the

7 The term "Fordism" derives from Antonio Gramsci, the regulation theory approach mainly from French social scientists and economists (Aglietta 1976, Boyer 1986, Lipietz 1985). It designates a particular relationship between mass production and mass consumption. See Lutz (1984) and Kind and Ronneberger (1996) for a discussion of the Fordist phase of the German Federal Republic. For the use of this approach in more recent sociological research on topics addressed in this paper, see, among others, Schmid (2002, 47), Kohli (2003, 528) or Lange 2003. Especially useful in this context is the combination of a feminist or gender perspective with the regulation theory, since this points to private networks and non-commodified reproductive work (e.g., care) as a precondition for capitalist economy (Chorus 2007).

unions and redefining work relations in terms of the "works community" (*Betriebsgemeinschaft*) rather than specific interests (Hachtmann 1998).

Developments from 1945 to 1989

East Germany (German Democratic Republic)

Understood in East Germany as the responsibility of the state, social security was anchored in the country's 1949 constitution. It was ensured through a uniform system of social insurance for all citizens (Frerich and Frey 1996, Vol. 2, 15–20; Bouvier 2002), and a broad spectrum of social benefits was made available by the state.

Child-care provisions were particularly relevant for the interrelationship of family, kin, and social security. East Germany established an extensive system of crèches, nurseries, kindergartens, and day-care centres for schoolchildren as part of the state-run school system (Erning et al. 1987, 93; Niebsch 1989, 88). A very high coverage rate (80–90 per cent, depending on type) of places was thereby achieved (Ochs 1993, 59). For both ideological and economic reasons, the goal was to mobilize as many women as possible for the labour force. Other opportunities available to women, including maternity leave, parental leave, reduced working hours, and child sick leave, were earmarked to enable their participation in paid employment (Kreyenfeld 2004, 7). East Germany also introduced pronatalist policies that led to specific payments to women, mothers or families, including birth grants and child benefits. Interest-free loans were granted on marriage, while the birth of a child either cancelled or reduced in part the amount to be paid back, if the marriage succeeded in producing a sufficient number of children. This was jokingly known as *abkindern* – paying off (*abzahlen*) a debt via childbirth.

Pensioners in East Germany, in contrast, had poor coverage (Frerich and Frey 1996, Vol. 2, 81–86; Boldorf 1998, 32; Schmidt 2001, 749f.; Bouvier 2002, 202, 221–228, 242f.). Consequently, it was typical for retirees to continue working and at the same time draw state pensions (Conrad 1998, 109; Bouvier 2002, 336f.). The labour shortage in East Germany reconciled the state to the fact that retirees continued to work (Matthesius and Waldschmidt 1989, 139).

Despite the comprehensive provision of social benefits by the state, poor relief was maintained in the GDR. It provided support, albeit at a low level, for those unable to work, and was used as a disciplinary instrument (Boldorf 1998; Rudloff 1998; Lindenberger 2005). In 1945/1946, the realm of quasi-public welfare was unified to become the *Volkssolidarität,* the "People's Solidarity", and placed on a new institutional footing. The religiously-based quasi-public welfare associations *Caritas* and *Diakonie* were also active, though to a limited degree (Frerich and Frey 1996, Vol. 2, 26; Angerhausen et al. 1998; Bouvier 2002, 234–43; Rudloff 1998, 225).

Unemployment insurance was continued, and primarily served as a steering mechanism with respect to labour, in the context of what de facto was a duty to work. After 1961, this became a *de jure* obligation (Frerich and Frey 1996, Vol. 2, 36f.; Boldorf 1998, 39). All in all strong efforts were made to free family and kin from having to make their own provisions, most successfully so in the area of child care. Less effective were state provisions for the elderly and the disabled, and plainly inadequate. As before, the onus to provide support for these groups was on family and relatives.

West Germany (Federal Republic of Germany/FRG)

West Germany reconfirmed the basic decisions of Bismarck's late nineteenth-century social policy. In doing so, it placed an unmistakable emphasis on the principle of subsidiarity, a notion derived from the Catholic social doctrine (Münch 1990, 207, 210; Becker 2000, 294; Niehuss 2001, 180) that had already formed part of the Weimar social policy and accentuated individual self-reliance and responsibility. Support in an emergency was first and foremost to come from relatives; societal or state aid would only be granted when family resources were in such short supply as to be unavailable to the person in need (Becker 2000, 186). Inherent in the principle of subsidiarity is the tendency to regard responsibility for financial or other security as resting with relatives, a propensity interrupted solely by the introduction of social insurance and its attendant legal requirements. The pension reform of 1957, in particular, created – for the first time in Germany – a system that guaranteed an adequate income in old age. Pension levels became wage index-related, thereby making retirees independent of support from their relatives to a large extent. The close link that existed between old age and poverty in substantial sections of the population in Germany was broken for the first time. The Federal Social Assistance Act (*Bundessozialhilfegesetz,* 1961–2004), which supplied the legal basis for disability claims, for example, provided basic assistance in a subsidiary manner following maintenance liabilities of relatives as defined in the German Civil Code.

With regard to family and child-care policies, the FRG was fighting on two fronts. On the one hand, there was a strong desire for distance from the deep incursions of the Nazi state into the private sphere of the family as well as into education. On the other hand, there was a need for detachment from the pro-natalist policies pursued in East Germany, including state insistence that mothers and women work (Moeller 1989, 162). Following the advice of social scientists (Schelsky 1967 [1953], 1967 [1954]), politicians underlined the freedom and sanctity of the family, indeed the necessity for the state not to interfere in any way, as the family was considered the "nucleus" of the state.

Correspondingly, the so-called "Family allowance" (*Familienlastenausgleich*) was not introduced until 1955, and then merely in the form of minimal child support for the third child born (Kuller 2004, 170, 186, 215f.; Schmidt 2000, 155f.; Kaufmann 2003, 289). In doing so, the state defined "family" as "the housewife and male-breadwinner marriage" (Pfau-Effinger 2000, 111). The consequence was an underdeveloped financial support system for children or families with children, particularly when compared with the expanding coverage available to pensioners.

In the context of work relations, West Germany revived the Fordist class compromise characteristic of the Weimar Republic. The employed in West Germany enjoyed extensive legal protection, both in terms of work and of benefits (Schmidt 2000, 155), guaranteed by an "elaborate labour law" (Kaufmann 2003, 279). In the wake of the "conservative transformation of the welfare state" (Borchert 1995), however, unemployment and other benefits were to suffer cutbacks beginning in the 1980s. Furthermore, in accordance with deregulation policies, employment underwent significant change, the main effects of which were flexibilization of and increase in the average number of working hours, and a rise in non-tariff employment (Eberlin et al. 2004; Hockerts 2007, 28; Kratzer and Sauer 2007, 241; Szydlik 2007). In addition, a growing low-wage sector was politically promoted and legally institutionalized; today, over 17 per cent of those in full-time employment are in this income bracket (Andreß and Seeck 2007, 466).

Key current structures and dynamics

When the two Germanies reunified in 1990, West German social and family policies, with their corresponding laws and structures, were implemented in East Germany (see below for consequences in everyday life). The most marked changes included the abolition of uniform insurance in the eastern German states, the integration of "People's Solidarity" into the existing West German system of associations, and a reduction in child-care places to almost half the previous capacity (Klein et al. 1996, 68). Although child-care provision in the eastern German states is still superior to what is available in the western states, especially for infants and toddlers (Engstler and Menning 2003, 120), it has nevertheless entailed a "reprivatization of the work of upbringing" (Schmidt and Schönberger 1999, 185–189, 196f.).

At very high cost to the German state, the eastern states were transformed, including the reorganization along free market principles of what had been state-sponsored social security (Frerich and Frey 1996, Vol. 3, 642f.). The result was a massive shift throughout unified Germany towards delegating responsibility to family and kin for aid and financial transfers with respect to ensuring social security. In addition, the legal basis for calling upon family members to provide support for needy kin has been broadened. This is particularly evident in the area of child care and care of the elderly; increasingly, it is also true for care of the disabled.

Broadening the legal definition of kin and strengthening the subsidiarity principle

Throughout the decades, West German social policy has responded to changes in private living arrangements. A formal aspect was the legal recognition of and guarantees provided to the new forms families and partnerships were taking, in line with developments in other western countries (Willekens 2003, 70). This has led to an ongoing extension of the concept of family relations, for example through the (almost) equal status accorded to children born in or out of wedlock (the most recent formulation appears in the *Kindschaftsrecht* of 1998)[8] and the recognition of (same sex, unmar-

8 The constitution of the GDR of 1949 had already rescinded the German Civil Code provisions on illegitimacy; with the changes in 1966 to family law, children born both in and out of wedlock were treated as equal with respect to support and inheritance rights.

ried) long-term relationships or partnerships (for example in the *Lebenspartnerschaftsgesetz* of 2001). The result is that a larger circle of individuals is now obliged to provide mutual support than was the case under the older definition of family and marriage in the German Civil Code. Current social policy in Germany, similar to that pursued elsewhere in Europe, is oriented towards "[...] fully utilizing the existing potential informal aid holds [...]" (Schmid 2002, 404), which again underscores the principle of subsidiarity.

With respect to the "normative orientation of social policy," the focus on "vertical income and wealth inequality" has shifted towards "[...] inequality between the generations, between childless and child-rich families, between children and adults, between women and men, and between foreigners and locals" (Leisering 2000, 74). This does not presuppose that the old question of social inequality – originally addressed by the labour relations reform – has disappeared. On the contrary. It is the middle classes that are now increasingly threatened by a decline in their social and economic status; they live in a state of "precarious prosperity" (Vester et al. 2001, 83f.).

This can be clearly seen in the four most recent (2003–2005) laws governing aspects of labour in the service sector. The fourth of these laws (2005) combines unemployment relief with public assistance, and in so doing has dealt a radical blow to the distinction drawn during the Weimar Republic between security provision for the unemployed and aid for the needy (later referred to as *Sozialhilfebedürftige*, i.e., those in need of public assistance). The earlier principle aimed at maintaining the social status of those affected (*Berufsschutz*). Conditions have now tightened. Coverage has been undermined by the demand for willingness to work in a different job despite possible wage cuts and for more reliance on personal savings or other financial resources. In effect, this law exacts more from family or kin, inasmuch as the maximum duration of unemployment benefit has been reduced from two years to one. The income or wealth of relatives legally obliged to provide support, or of those with whom the unemployed person lives (in a so-called "community of needs" or *Bedarfsgemeinschaft*), are now included in state calculations on the level of support to be granted after one year of unemployment benefit.

A reform of the laws concerning shared parental rights in the context of bringing up children born out of wedlock, which was to take place in former East Germany in October 1990 within the framework of a family law reform, could not be realized (Schumann 1998, 133f.).

Political promotion and legal support for the male-breadwinner model

Although new forms of cohabitation are taken into consideration in estimating support needs, numerous regulations still revert to the male-breadwinner model. This includes, in particular, the spousal income-splitting taxation system, the weak expansion of child care, half-day schools, parental leave, and the child-raising allowance.

Spousal income-splitting system: A key policy in the German national budget concerns the tax treatment of married couples (Conrad 1990, 311). Introduced in 1958, it was structured in such a way as to benefit families with both growing and adult children as well as married couples without children. (Kuller 2004, 14). This tax policy benefits male-breadwinner marriages, in other words marriages where one partner (usually the husband, fully employed) earns considerably more than the other (usually the wife, employed part-time or unemployed) (Dingeldey 2002; Gottfried and O'Reilly 2002, 48; Kuller 2004, 174f.; Vollmer 2004). This and other aspects of the German tax laws (Dingeldey 2002, 157) led to a situation of "[...] considerable redistribution of income towards marriages that follow the pattern of the 'male-breadwinner model'" (Pfau-Effinger 2000, 129f.).

Child care: After 1945, the ideal of child care provided by the mother had structure-generating consequences for child-care policies in Germany. By the mid-1960s, this picture had begun to change, as arguments in favour of the emancipation of children, particularly from the lower classes, and with regard to education policy, began to impact on the child-care discourse. In addition, the "Sputnik shock" or sense of being unable to keep up internationally, not least with the Russians, meant education policies were accorded greater status (Konrad 2004, 206, 209; Kuller 2004, 294, 339). However, the rejection of child-care provision outside the home remained the dominant policy until the late 1970s (Haines 2000, 53f.).

This approach changed fundamentally with the introduction of kindergarten places for three to six-year-olds, for which a legal title has existed since 1996. To an overwhelming degree, and typical of Germany, this has meant half-day kindergartens (Konrad 2004, 206f.). 1974 saw the launching of the "day-care mothers" (*Tagesmütter*) project, although unlike in neighbouring France, it was not institutionalized at state level (Becker 2000, 189, 198). In addition, private efforts were made to provide group care for toddlers or infants, primarily in the former West German states and particularly among the middle classes. The latter was less a question of working women's requirements than of the need for social contact between the mothers concerned (Hoecklin 1998; Wendt and Maucher 2000, 91; Hoecklin 2002). Even the most recent law in this area, intended to create more child-care places for pre-school children (*Tagesbetreuungsausbaugesetz* 2004), has brought little substantive change, as there is no legal claim to such places, and expansion is foreseen in the existing day care provided by "day-care mothers".

A further institutional feature of child care in Germany is the fact that public schooling does not exceed half days. Consequently, some form of private care must be provided for children over six years of age, since a public scheme for after-school care does not exist (Knijn et al. 2003, 185f.). To date, no fundamental decisions have been taken to extend public school attendance beyond half days. Several pilot projects or model endeavours (such as the "dependable elementary school") were launched, although the forms they take do not permit legal claims to be made for their provision or extension (Ludwig et al. 2002, 187f.; Kaufmann 2003, 304). In short, the upbringing and education of children has been and continues to be regarded first and foremost as "a private matter," and is treated accordingly in laws and regulations (Scheiwe 1994, 72).

Parental leave, child-raising allowance and parental allowance: In conjunction with the inadequate provision of child care, regulations releasing women from employment are also relevant. The parental leave introduced in 1986/88 (referred to as *Elternzeit* since 2001) and the federal child-raising allowance introduced in 1986 (known as *Erziehungsgeld, and as of 2007: Elterngeld/parental allowance*) are of particular importance here (Pfau-Effinger 2000, 130; Farahat et al. 2006). Both of these welfare state measures were created to ease pressure on the labour market (Schäfgen and Spellerberg 1998, 78; Gerhard et al. 2003, 20; Lewis 2003, 52; Morgan and Zippel 2003, 61f.). The regulations governing parental leave contain the right to be temporarily exempted from an employment relationship, but at the same time include protection against wrongful dismissal should parental leave be taken. Since 1992, it has been possible to extend parental leave up to three years. The relatively modest child-raising allowance can be drawn for twelve (in certain circumstances, twenty-four) months. Beyond a certain income level, parental leave is not available at all. It is almost exclusively taken by the mother (Vaskovics and Rost 1999; Engstler and Menning 2003, 118), and the low level of the child-raising allowance leads to dependence of the family on the (usually higher) income of the male partner.

Hence both forms support the male-breadwinner model and having the children looked after by the mother, who is either unemployed or, at best, works part-time. (Pfau-Effinger 2000, 131; also Morgan and Zippel 2003; Scheiwe 1994, 62).

In 2007, parental allowance (67 per cent of the average monthly net income available prior to birth, or a maximum of 1,800 euro) replaced the former child-raising allowance, and is awarded in the case of parental leave to either the mother or the father for a maximum of twelve months. A further two months are subsidized if the second parent takes parental leave for that amount of time. Apart from the intended improvements for couples with higher qualifications and incomes, first analyses here again find a continuation of the male-breadwinner model, resulting from the income differences between male and female employees, and a worsening of the financial situation for lower-income households (Farahat et al. 2006). Due to their fostering of stratification, the effects of the parental allowance settlement have been characterized as "selected emancipation" (*exklusive Emanzipation*) (ibid. 985).

Overall, therefore, German family policy measures (child allowance, maternal leave, parental leave, child-raising allowance, spousal income-splitting) reinforce the model of the male as the principal breadwinner of the family. Furthermore, these regulations and benefits create "a consecutive order" for women with respect to career and family (Schmid 2002, 271),[9] which is clearly reflected in the distinctive career paths taken, especially in western German states. It remains to be investigated how the recent shift in German family politics towards greater legal, financial and cultural support for mothers' employment (BMFSFJ 2006) will change these dynamics. They are clearly not the effect of enforced emancipation alone, but also a consequence of the neoliberal orientation that recommends ensuring the family income with the employment of not one but two parents in the face of precarious job market conditions (BMFSFJ 2006, 87).

9 Other than an increase in child sick leave, which was raised in 1992 from five (granted in the 1980s) to ten days for the first child and twenty days for the second (for single parents, twenty-five days for the first, fifty for the second) following East German practice, (Kreyenfeld 2004, 11), little has been done to make wage work and raising children compatible.

Policies on the elderly

The welfare coverage of elderly people in Germany is crucial to the relationship between family/kin and social security provision (see below). After reunification, West German pension regulations were extended to cover former East Germany, and led to a significant improvement in the lives of the elderly there. However, the costs incurred have worsened the budgetary plight of the pension system and made its financial recovery and stabilization almost impossible to achieve.[10]

A fundamentally new measure that focused on security provision for the elderly was the law on long-term care insurance (*Pflegeversicherungsgesetz*) passed in 1995, which provides benefits for the elderly in need of care previously covered by Public Assistance. The law targeted families and relatives who provide elderly care and guarantee support, a goal that has largely been achieved (Berger-Schmitt 2003, 9; Pabst and Rothgang 2000, 362; Eisen 2001, 90f.). There was also an increase in the availability of outpatient nursing services (Pabst and Rothgang 2000, 364).

A variety of options that would increase the financial security of the elderly is currently under discussion, including pension tax, pension cutbacks, higher retirement age, increased participation of women in the workforce, more immigration, stronger support for families with children (to increase the birth rate), and the supplementing or conversion of the given current disbursement system to a system of capital cover. Newer political initiatives have called for, or promoted, having older citizens do more unpaid work or take on honorary posts in Germany (BMFSFJ 2005a). These initiatives have "[...] a tendency, in the medium and long term, to shift the relationship between earned income and pension income to the detriment of retirees" (Motel-Klingebiel 2000, 287; similarly Schmid 2002, 117). One anticipated outcome is the "[...] negative consequences for private intergenerational relations, which could on the whole affect welfare state arrangements to a greater extent than is normally admitted" (Motel-Klingebiel 2000, 289).

10 Current discussions in political circles and in the media, and many of the more serious academic calculations with regard to the future financing of pensions and health insurance, pay relatively little attention to the vertical distribution of income and wealth. Instead, calculations deal almost exclusively with demographic change and advances in medical technology. Several researchers, however, have noted that "the consequences of German reunification for the pension system... serve to point to the fact that the problems of future financing are not only of a demographic nature" (Schmid 2002, 296).

Historical development and current state of family and kin

Demographic Trends

Population and birth rates

In 1914, Germany had the second-largest population in Europe after Russia (Ehmer 2004, 7). Yet the birth rate in the bourgeois middle classes had already begun to decline in the nineteenth century, a trend that had spread to more and more strata of the population by the interwar period. Prior to the Second World War, the two-child family had become the norm.

Despite the growth in population, the falling birth rate led to an intense discussion on quantitative and qualitative population policy, which had little or no practical consequences during the Weimar Republic (Usborne 1994). The pro-natalist policies adopted by the Nazi regime brought about a temporary increase in both marriage and birth rates (Marschalck 1984; Ehmer 2004). In 1946, at the end of the Second World War, only 63.4 million people lived in the territory that was to become East Germany and West Germany, a consequence of wartime population and territory losses, as well as of the racist criteria that determined qualitative population policy under the Nazi regime (Marschalck 1984, 147).

In the ensuing decades, the number of births increased, peaking at 17.7 live births per 1000 residents in West Germany in 1965, and 17.0 in East Germany in 1960 (Mittelbach 1994, 62f.). This was followed by yet another drop in the birth rates in both German states (Marschalck 1984, 98f.).

Today, more precisely as of 2003, the total fertility rate of 1.34 for Germany is one of the lowest in Europe, comparable to that of Italy (1.29) and Poland (1.24) (cf. Annex I., "Total fertility rate"), leaving Germany now below the demographic replacement rate. Falling birth rates have led to projections that the population of Germany will have dropped from the current 82 million to between 65–70 million by the year 2050 (Engstler and Menning 2003, 94).

One significant characteristic, long noted in West Germany, was the shift towards persistent childlessness – something virtually unheard of in East Germany. In 2003, approximately 23 per cent of women born in 1960 in West Germany, and 10 per cent of those born in East Germany, were childless.[11] In an international comparison, this represents a "high level of

11 www.bpb.de/wissen/B17WEQ.html (17 Aug. 2005).

persistent childlessness" and is one of the "striking characteristics" of the German way of life (Dornseiff and Sackmann 2003, 346).

Age and kin structure

The age structure of the German population in the nineteenth century remained stable, unlike that of the twentieth century, which was subject to fluctuation. Up to 1950, this was primarily due to a decline in birth rates, whereas thereafter, increased life expectancy was the main cause (Ehmer 2004). In 2001, 16.6 per cent of the German population was over sixty-five, the third highest percentage in Europe after Italy (18.2 per cent) and Sweden (19.2 per cent). As a result of the downward trend in the number of children per marriage evident since the early twentieth century, the number of lateral relatives has declined. Coupled with increased life expectancy, this makes it now more likely that three or more generations will share a certain life span. However, very few relatives exist in each of these generations. Consequently, we can speak of a "verticalization" of the kin structure (Bengtson and Schütze 1992, 503). This tendency is particularly marked in the former East German states, where 76 per cent of the middle generation (aged forty-four to fifty-five) have children and grandchildren compared to 52 per cent of this age group in the former West German states (Kohli et al. 1997, 167f.; Vaskovics et al. 1994, 144). In the context of the relationship between family, kin, and social security, this means "[…] that the structural opportunity to integrate older members into the family is fundamentally higher in the eastern German states' (Kohli et al. 1997, 167). Due to the increase in remarriage, or as a result of consecutive partners who bring children into the relationship, a "social broadening of relations" also comes about (Hettlage 1992, 196, cited in Vaskovics et al. 1994, 145).

Marriage and divorce

Marriage rates in both German states have continuously declined from their very high levels during the 1950s and 1960s. In the aftermath of re-unification, the marriage rate in eastern Germany sank precipitously, but is now showing signs of a gradual increase. Overall, however, marriage rates have reached a historic low, with only 5.1 (East 5.4; West 3.9) marriages per 1000 inhabitants as of 2000 (Statistisches Bundesamt 2004).

East/west parallels with respect to birth and marriage rates can also be found in the rising incidence of divorce. While levels in East Germany were higher than in West Germany, the trends began to converge after reunification. During the transformation process and by the mid-1990s, the divorce rate in the eastern German states had declined by about 10 per cent, whereas it continued to climb in the western states. The divorce rate in the eastern states has begun to rise again, and in 2003 showed 37.1 divorces for every 100 marriages; in the western states, the rate was 43.5.[12]

Differentiating ways of life

In both East and West Germany, "an increase in the heterogeneity in forms of partnership" had been taking place since the 1980s, in other words, a "pluralization" (Vaskovics et al. 1994, 89; Brüderl and Klein 2003, 213f.; Kohli 2003, 534). The absolute number of nuclear families has declined, while the variety of household arrangements that includes children (single parent, step-families, patchwork families) has increased, as have forms without children (unmarried couples, childless married couples, singles) (Vaskovics id.; Engstler and Menning 2003, 23). This growing differentiation is due in part to a greater distinction between marriage and family (Napp-Peters 1985; Meulders-Klein and Théry 1998; Alt 2003, 241; Marbach 2003, 183), and in part to the dissociation of marital partnership from cohabitation (Vaskovics et al. 1994, 151; Schneider and Ruckdeschel 2003), but also due to the – still comparatively rare – emergence of families composed of homosexual parents and children (Rauchfleisch 1997; Wegener 2005).

Overall, however, marriage remains the most common form of cohabitation in partnerships in Germany. The proportion of unmarried partnerships in the population is higher in the eastern than in the western German states (Engstler and Menning 2003, 45). Most children in Germany live with their married parents, although here, too, an east/west difference is apparent (Engstler and Menning 2003, 24): nearly half of the children in the eastern states grow up – at least for the first few years – in households with unmarried partners or single parents (Alt 2003, 242; Engstler and Menning 2003, 25f.). A substantial percentage marry at a later

12 www.bpb.de/wissen/NHXRDM.html (24 March 2006, Statistisches Bundesamt).

date. In other words, the link between starting a family and marriage is weaker in the east than in the west.

Single parents and their children constitute approximately 10 per cent of the German population,[13] the vast majority of whom are "mother-child families". Most single parents are divorced, whereby the percentage of unmarried single parents is higher in the east than in the west (Engstler and Menning 2003, 40–41).

Hence differentiating private "ways of life" is more a reflection of household and personal arrangements "prior to marriage [...] and after divorce" than it is a matter of replacing traditional family forms (Pfau-Effinger 2000, 142). The fact that young adults have tended to delay – if not dispense with – marriage and starting a family since the 1980s has led to a situation where no more than a third of all households are households with children (Engstler and Menning 2003, 34).

Institutionalizing the life course

As in other bourgeois societies, "institutionalization of the life course" developed in Germany in the twentieth century. That is, "[...] life course and age need to be regarded as an autonomous structural and structuring dimension of society" (Kohli 1985, 1). In the FRG, this meant a "'normal work biography' that included continuous, full employment" for men, while for women it meant no employment or a (repeatedly interrupted) career of mostly part-time employment (Kohli 2003, 529, 531f.), in a form that typically implied "[...] wage work until the birth of the first child; career interruption until the child reaches school age; re-entry into the labour force thereafter" (Schäfgen and Spellerberg 1998, 78). Part-time employment is characteristic of the re-entry of mothers into the work force after the family phase (von Oertzen 1999). One striking difference between the GDR and the Federal Republic was the similarity between male and female life courses in the former with respect to employment (Matthesius and Waldschmidt 1989; Conrad 1998, 109; Bouvier 2002, 236f.). While this has lessened somewhat, the east/west difference in female life courses is still plainly visible when economically active women and mothers in Germany are compared.

13 http://www.bpb.de/wissen/2MCCQW.html (10 May 2005).

In a European comparison, the female employment rate in Germany is in the mid-range (59 per cent), along with France (57 per cent) and Austria (63 per cent), but behind Sweden (72 per cent), and ahead of Poland (46 per cent) or Italy (43 per cent) (all figures from 2003; cf. Annex I, "Employment rate women"). It should be noted, however, that the relatively high figure for Germany includes the fact that almost 50 per cent of working women are employed part-time[14].

From the German perspective, the "institution of the life course" contains three dimensions: behavioural regularities, institutional regulations and normative orientation. During the last quarter of the twentieth century, all three became either "de-standardized" (Kohli 1985, 24; Allmendinger 1994, 279) or were subject to processes of "de-institutionalization" (Brose 2003, 600; Sackmann 2003) as a result of the political and economic developments in the country since the 1980s. This created "discontinuous" as well as "non-standard life courses" characterized by "[...] frequent shifts between temporary work, work at an occupation, unemployment, further training, and caring for children [...] not just at the bottom of society but in the middle" (Vester et al. 2001, 83f.). By the 1990s, these "unsteady biographies" had hardened to situations of "precarious prosperity" (Vester ibid.).

With regard to the institutionalization of life courses, this has led to a loosening of the typically close link between individual life phases and certain activities (school, training, career, retirement) so characteristic of Fordism (Vester et al. 2001, 84; Lange 2003, 5). This is also the case for the transition to retirement. In an international comparison, Germany (with the exception of former East Germany, now the eastern states) has had a very low rate of employment for people over sixty years of age (Koller et al. 2003, 24). This is, however, beginning to change. More recent studies indicate signs of "[...] increased insecurity over the timing of one's own transition into retirement" (Engstler 2003, 19f.).

The impact of these changes on the relationship between family/kin and financial or other security, e.g., the "effect of non-standard employment on the ties to family and social networks," has thus far rarely been explored (Diewald and Eberle 2003, 695). Initial findings indicate that "unbounded work" leads to "stressed families" (Voß 2003). The "increased

---

14 http://www.bpb.de/wissen/QCAFMP,,0,Entwicklung_der_Teilzeitbesch%E4ftigung_nach_Geschlecht.html (22 February 2006).

need for coordination and synchronization" has been "largely addressed by women" (Jurczyk 2005, 95f.). Jurczyk predicts that this kind of "unboundedness" demands "a higher degree of self-structuring by the families and their subjects, and calls for new forms of societal support" (id., 90f.).

Residence and household structures

A "[...] decentralized settlement structure, with numerous cities and urban regions more or less evenly distributed across the entire territory [...]" is characteristic of Germany (Gatzweiler and Irmen 1997, 47). Due to a West German policy of subsidizing the acquisition of single-family homes, a large percentage of the population in this part of the country are home owners: it is almost "a central component of the normal biography" for people to have lived in their own house on the outskirts of town (Häußermann and Siebel 2004, 74). In the GDR, and now in the eastern states, comparatively few people own their own homes, and the square footage of residential space available per person is lower (Frick and Lahmann 1996, 252).

Typical of both east and west, however, is the close residential proximity of generations, although households may be separate. This is true for both urban and rural regions. Dubbed "near co-residence" (Kohli et al. 1997, 161, 170), it has been confirmed by more recent studies (Hoff 2003, 5). This close living together of generations is a precondition for the provision of assistance among kin. This German pattern of residential proximity of the generations is similar to that found in Austria or Poland, while the geographical distance between the generations is greater in France, and considerably less in Italy (cf. Annex I, "About how long would it take to get to where your mother lives?").

In analysing the kin/family networks today, the presence of, or work done, by other personnel must also be taken into account. In German migration research, the phrase "private households as a world market" has been used (Gather et al. 2002). Female migrants often live in the private households that provide them with work. They also maintain intense contact with their own families in their countries of origin. Particularly conservative welfare states like Germany, where people-oriented social services (child care, elderly care) are not provided in a comprehensive or universal manner and where the onus is on families and relatives, virtually promote such illegal working arrangements, frequently with exploitative components (Schönwälder et al. 2004; Hess 2005 on child care).

Income and wealth

The prevailing differences between western and eastern German states with regard to income and wealth reflect the disparate paths taken by East and West Germany (Mittelbach 1994, 72; Kohli 2004, 18; Engstler and Menning 2003, 161). One specifically German trait, originating from the 1957 pension reform, is the guaranteed maintenance of living standards after transition to retirement. Despite several changes in pension policy, this goal continues to be met, and in comparison with other countries, means that retirement is not accompanied by a lowering of social status. In 1990, West German pension regulations were adopted in the eastern states, so that the latter's pension generation, particularly in the light of the poor social security provided by the GDR, is now considerably better off. This applies in particular to women. They can expect a higher pension based on continuous full-time employment, whereas women in West Germany are far more likely to have had careers of frequently interrupted part-time employment.

Poverty, on the other hand, is more typical for single parents, who constitute a high percentage of those on social welfare (Mädje and Neusüß 1996; Engstler and Menning 2003, 156). More than 40 per cent of single parents in Germany are described as poor. This should be contrasted with the national average, whereby only one in eight households are defined as such.[15]

The fact that wealth is "far more unequally distributed than income" is another characteristic of Germany (Beckert 2003, 793), and results from a tax system in which "[...] the returns on wealth are privileged as compared to the income from work" (Zacher 2001, 658f.). This unequal distribution of wealth is reproduced and magnified by financial transfers and family/kin inheritances (Kosmann 1998, 50–55; Szydlik 2000, 238; Kohli 2004, 21). Recent studies predict that this will lead to an increase in social inequality (Szydlik 1999, 101; Szydlik and Schupp 2004, 625f.). Key here is the fact that private transfers represented by inheritance between the generations

---

15 http://www.bpb.de/wissen/AAPZ12.html [10 May 2005].

do not complement the public transfers between them – such as through the pension system – but instead reinforce them. (Szydlik and Schupp 2004, 626). Particularly significant for inheritance in Germany is residential property: "[...] nationally, it constitutes the largest proportion of private household wealth, is almost always inherited debt-free, and is sold only in crisis, as when high nursing costs need to be covered" (Braun 2003, 113). Here, too, there is a marked east/west difference, since testators in the east are far less likely to own residential property, reinforcing its significance for inheritance in the west (Frick and Lahmann 1996, 252).

Networks, practices, ideals and ideologies of family/kin

Living in nuclear families

Though frequently assumed otherwise, the nuclear family, consisting of parents (or one parent) with child(ren), has a long tradition, extending into the pre-industrial era (Rosenbaum 1996, 1998). In the second half of the twentieth century, nuclear families became the dominant form, especially during the 1950s and 1960s, the "Golden Age of Marriage" (Nave-Herz 1998, 294). Never before, and never again, did so many marriages take place. This upsurge in "family" and the accompanying "baby boom" was not to endure, however, but had a lasting effect on the awareness of the older generation. It became the touchstone for the evaluation of subsequent birth, marriage and divorce rates, and of cohabitation without a marriage licence. Not unlike the case of skilled workers in the Wilhelmine and Weimar eras, an unemployed wife was proof of respectability during this period, both for the male breadwinner and the particular family in question (Pfau-Effinger 2000, 117).

Gender relations

As a basic structural element, gender relations provide a fundamental dynamic to the relationship between family/kin and social security. The bourgeois ideal of "gender character" has been central to the development of gender relations in Germany since the nineteenth century, and is determined by "a dissociation between professional life and family life" (Hausen

1976). The tasks "appropriate to a woman's nature and interests" were seen in the family and the household; those of a man in employment.

a) An ideology of motherhood

A distinctive aspect of West German cultural ideals with respect to gender is the preference to have children, especially very young children, raised and looked after by the mother. In a comparative European perspective, Letablier and Jönsson (2003, 96) refer to this particular "caring regime" in a comparative European perspective as "child care as the mother's responsibility", a specifically German variant of the motherhood ideology that reaches back to the nineteenth century. In the course of time, it was promoted by various societal groups, and not always under the same political banner; nor was it fostered by men only (Ebbinghaus 1987; Chamberlayne 1990; Chamberlayne 1991; Schenk 1996; Gerhard 1997, Pfau-Effinger 2000).

As a result, the majority view in the western part of the country is still that "[...] child care and child-raising is primarily a family responsibility, particularly of the woman, and [...] having children cared for all day outside the home is not considered desirable [...]"; the employment of mothers is regarded as detrimental to children, in particular to the very young (Pfau-Effinger 2000, 124; Wendt and Maucher 2000, 84; Kolbe 2002, 417f.; Dornseiff and Sackmann 2003, 344; Dorbritz et al. 2005, 11). This fundamental cultural devaluation of out-of-home child care as well as all-day care primarily affects children under three and over six years of age; as a result, both groups are poorly served institutionally (BMFSFJ 2005c).

For pre-school children between the ages of three and six, however, out-of-home child care has been widely accepted; since 1996, half-day kindergarten places can be legally claimed. The rationale behind this move was more a matter of educational policies based on the study of pedagogy than a fundemental shift in the motherhood ideology. Correspondingly, research indicates that there has "[...] thus far – and this speaks for the broad cultural anchoring of this model – been no major political effort to create full-day kindergartens and schools in Germany" (Pfau-Effinger 2000, 134). Comprehensive studies further testify that this orientation was reinforced by the lack of supply (Merkle 1994, 206; Pfau-Effinger 2000, 145; Spieß and Büchel 2002). Thus, efforts to render motherhood and full-time employment compatible, in turn associated with the provision of all-day care, has up to now remained the interest of a minority, and largely been confined to the eastern states.[16]

Since the origins of the motherhood ideology are older than the two German states, its dynamic also affected East Germany. However, because East Germany was forced to strongly advocate female employment for political and economic reasons, the attitude towards child care, in particular that of infants and toddlers, was to undergo radical, comprehesive and permanent change. This occurred in tandem with the massive expansion of child-care facilities that began in the early 1970s (Niebsch 1989, 84). In the final year of the GDR's existence, in fact, the demand for infant and toddler care outside the home exceeded the supply, which was already at a high level (approx. 80 per cent coverage) (Cromm 1998, 421). Research indicates that even today there is still a difference in attitude between mothers in the eastern states and those in the west with regard to the most desirable care options, i.e., the preference of the former for full-day care for children and infants outside the family. This is coupled in part with a positive attitude of mothers towards full-time employment, but is also the outcome of ideas on socialization (Kolinsky 1998, 119; Scheller 2003, 863f.; Dornseiff and Sackmann 2003, 346; Knijn et al. 2003, 179; Dorbritz et al. 2005, 11). Hence, Germany contains two contrasting or co-existent cultural orientations in terms of child care and the employment of mothers.

The fact that mothers in the eastern states still maintain their employment orientation, or rather the notion that mothers can engage in full-time employment, is particularly remarkable. In the process of transforming East Germany, the orientation towards the collective did not survive; instead, there has been a turn towards the family (Scheller 2004, 37f.). Thus, although the concept of family has gained in status, it has not been accompanied by a downgrading of institutionalized, full-day care for (young) children. However, recent qualitative research has indicated a trend in eastern Germany towards the "retraditionalization" of family, gender and

16 The hegemonic nature of the bourgeois or petty bourgeois notions of mother-child relations is also evident in the fact that they were adopted by sections of West German society that were socio-economically organized in a different manner. Thus, farmer families developed a "child-orientation" (Fliege 1998, 182f.) and farmers' wives became "rural housewives and mothers" (Albers 1997, 194; Albers 2001). More recent developments, however, have moved away from this bougeoisification of the peasant family, and now follow neoliberal premises that address women in agriculture as "female agrarian entrepreneurs" (Prugl 2004, 366).

work; this is seen as the effect of a downturn in the labour market (Thelen et al. 2006, 18; Schmidt and Schönberger 1999, 190f.).

With respect to the intersection of family/kin and social security, the cultural ideals of motherhood led to a tendency in the western states to regard child care as the responsibility of the mothers, or at least for child care to be provided by families and relatives. The situation in the eastern states is more difficult to determine, given the deep-seated changes that have taken place in the last fifteen years. The practice of releasing mothers from child-care obligations in favour of employment, especially in the immediate post-war years, was forced through against the interests of the women themselves, who were both exhausted and overburdened (Schneider 2004, 348–351). It was eventually adopted by women as an ideal for their own life courses as well as a form of family organization, an approach that survived the transformation process. However, due to the persistence of a weak labour market in the east, the massive shutdown of child-care facilities and the adoption of the old West German family policy in the eastern states, it could only be realized to a limited degree (Franz and Herlyn 1995, 101; Niephaus 2003, 25).

b) The male-breadwinner marriage as the dominant pattern

The history and current state of family/kin and social security relations in Germany is characterized by the ideal of the male-breadwinner model and its practices. Having emerged in the bourgeois middle class in Germany in the course of industrialization (Rosenbaum 1996), it has since remained the "culturally dominant model" (Pfau-Effinger 2000, 111).

The expansion of part-time employment for mothers during the 1960s, however, did not prompt any change (von Oertzen 1999; Kuller 2004, 74). The constant labour shortage in West Germany, the response to which was not only labour migration (of so-called "guest workers") but also the recruitment of women and mothers into the labour force, provided the setting for this expansion (Kuller 2004, 74). At the same time, however, the ideal and the practice of the male-breadwinner model was maintained, in effect assigning "gender connotations" to part-time employment and ultimately "stabilizing the traditional division of roles in the family" (Kuller 2004, 78; Pfau-Effinger 2000, 124). In more technical terms, we can speak of the "compatibility model of the male-breadwinner marriage" (Pfau-Effinger 2000, 145), of the "modernized housewife family" (Becker 2000,

294) or of the "additional (female) income marriage" model (Engstler and Menning 2003, 113, 124; Dorbritz et al. 2005, 11).

By international comparison, the visible preference on the part of women and mothers for part-time employment is seen as typical for West Germany (Drobnič and Blossfeld 2001, 372). The last decade has seen a trend in the direction of full-time employment, as the desired standard of living can no longer be achieved on one, or even one-and-a-half salaries (Blossfeld et al. 2001, 72; Pfau-Effinger 2000, 122). This shift from the "provider marriage" to the "additional (female) income marriage" can be found throughout Europe (Engstler and Menning 2003, 113, 124).

In the context of gender relations, the relationship between political maxims and legal regulations, on the one hand, and cultural ideals, on the other, set developments in motion that were diametrically opposed in East and West Germany. In the East, the prescribed and legally anchored ideal of the "socialist family" meant deep changes in the hitherto general practice of living in nuclear family units. As noted above, this was particularly evident in the context of female employment. It was "taken for granted" (Ochs 1993, 49) that women "[...] would be employed, would have their own social position, would feel themselves economically independent, and would at the same time raise at least one child" (Winkler 1990, 138). This orientation towards employment on the part of women, mothers and wives has not diminished in the eastern states (Jasper 1993, 109; Spellerberg 1994, 15f.; Nowossadeck 1994, 624; Schmidt and Schönberger 1999, 188), and newer studies indicate that "[...] the model of the economically independent woman has become established in marriage as well" (Konietzka and Kreyenfeld 2005a, 37). This is not necessarily the result, or at least not exclusively, of a new approach favouring full-time employment by wives and mothers, but instead correlates with the "weaker labour market position of men in the east" (Konietzka and Kreyenfeld 2005b, 57). The extent to which this may be responsible for qualitative or quantitative differences in the gendered division of labour within the family, at least in comparison with western German states, has not as yet been clearly established (Gysi 1989, 156–67; Gysi 1990, 36; Dölling 1993, 26f.; Ecarius 1995, 184; Cromm 1998, 413–20; Dennis 1998, 46; Kolinsky 1998, 123).

Overall, however, the dominance of the male-breadwinner model in Germany provoked a situation whereby wives and mothers became the generators of social security within the family and kin, and still are in the present day. This is compatible with the widespread practice on the part of women to engage in part-time employment. The growing tendency to transfer to full-time employment implies a restriction on the time available for the family. The East German example, where women looked after the elderly in addition to full-time employment (see below), suggests that this task does not necessarily imply a trade-off between full-time female employment and care obligations within the family.

Generational relations and networks among family and kin

The structure of networks

Family/kin networks in Germany are "[...] largely intergenerational relationships. Relationships between those of the same generation (such as brother and sister, or brother-in-law and sister-in-law) are of less importance" (Nauck and Kohlmann 1998, 226)[17]. Recent research on networks has revealed that, with the exception of grandparents, family relations play a more vital role in Germany than kin relations, particularly when it comes to support or aid, and that kin relations are mobilized above all by widows and widowers in an effort to create an active network when family members are unavailable (Lang and Schütze 1998, 179; also Diewald 1998, 201; Neef and Schäfer 1996, 82 on East Germany). This is correlated with the demographic development that led to a decline in horizontal and an increase in vertical kin (see above). Nauck and Schwenk (2001, 1871) have also observed a broadening or intensification of relationships with more distant kin, which they interpret as a response to the rollback in welfare benefits. In this respect, it repeats a frequently observed, albeit typical, response to crisis situations: the activation of kin networks (ibid. 1876). It is characteristic of Germany, as distinct from other countries, that "[...] the network of relationships focuses more intensely on the nearest kin, but at the same time extends to include other, non-family persons to whom

17 In contrast, Turkish migrants living in Germany were shown to attribute greater importance to intragenerational family and kinship networks (Nauck and Kohlmann 1998, 226). This does not necessarily derive from culturally different practices, but instead most likely arises from the situation in which migrants find themselves. Intragenerational networks have been shown in historical analyses to be highly significant for Germans who migrate within their own country (Rosenbaum 1992, 140–48).

one relates" (Höllinger 1989, 534).[18] Research has now begun to concentrate on the significance of other networks, i.e., friendship, the workplace, and the neighbourhood, (Höllinger 1989, 534; Schubert 1990; Reichenwallner et al 1991; Harth and Herlyn 1996; Schmidt 2002; Diewald 2003a and 2003b; Diewald and Eberle 2003; Schuster et al. 2003; Haug 2004).

Network research, including recent studies, has more generally affirmed the existence of a "life-long solidarity" principle between the generations (Szydlik 2000, 233f.; Borchers 1997, 168; Dorbritz et al. 2005, 9). Here, women have a "kin-keeper function", while men "generally have less close intergenerational ties" (Szydlik 1997, 191f.). Networks remain stable into old age. However, there is directionality in what is provided between the generations: "[...] private monetary transfers flow from top to bottom, which means from grandparents and parents to children and grandchildren; other kinds of aid and support flow more frequently in the opposite direction, from younger to older generations" (Szydlik 2000, 235).

The support grandparents, and in particular grandmothers, provide by looking after toddlers and children of kindergarten age is crucial given the lack of institutional alternatives and the inflexibility of existent facilities. The likelihood that this care will be offered increases with geographic proximity (Templeton and Bauereiss 1994, 252, 259; Wendt and Maucher 2000, 90). Neighbourly support in the form of care, however, is rarely availed of, except when family members are unable to provide help. This type of assistance is more characteristic of those at the bottom of the social scale and among immigrant groups (Wendt and Maucher 2000, 90f.). In the gender context, women provide far more care in quantitative terms and at the same time contribute a broader qualitative spectrum of support, in informal networks more generally and for family/kin more specifically, than men do (Borchers 1997, 168; Ludwig et al. 2002, 124; von Rosenbladt 2003, 9; BMFSFJ 2005b).

18 With respect to this finding, it should also be noted that due to German research traditions in family sociology, the focus has primarily been on the family; it was only later extended to include kin or relatives (Bruckner 1993; Rosenbaum 1993; Lang and Schütze 1998; Marbach 1998, 91f.; Schütze and Wagner 1998; Wagner 2002; Schuster et al. 2003; Haug 2004). This also means that the significance of kin and the associated practices have hitherto been explored to a minor degree only.

Housing and generational networks in the FRG/in West Germany

Public or political debates on the relationship between the generations frequently speak of the "isolation" or "loneliness" of the elderly in Germany. This is the dominant interpretation since the Second World War and is based on the shrinking size of households, or rather, on the composition of the household in generational terms (Kohli et al. 1997, 157). The household concept used in statistics, however, merely exposes one side inasmuch as it reflects those who actually live together in the household. It does not measure the relationships between households, unlike network research, which can and does indicate close geographic proximity, as well as intensive exchange and aid relationships between the households of different generations (Grunow 1985; Diewald 1989, 192; Marbach 1994, 194).[19] As illustrated above, the fact that generations live in separate households has a long history. It is supported by the individualization that applies to the elderly as well as to the generation of retirees. The fact that households are separated by age cohorts is not a reflection of isolation in old age or lack of relationship between the generations, but rather of a residential form chosen by the retiree generation itself (BMFSFJ 1998, 94f.).

Current research on the transfers provided within families and for family members underscores the close intertwining between the generations, particularly in the care or nursing of older people. The vast majority of those in need[20] are looked after on an outpatient basis or at home, and are taken care of by members of the family.[21] Parents and parents-in-law are the most frequent recipients of unpaid assistance from family/kin, which is primarily provided by those aged between forty and sixty-five (von Rosenbladt 2003, 20). Care or nursing is provided almost exclusively (to 80 per cent) by women (Engstler and Menning 2003, 139), more often than not

19 For this reason, German research on family/kin networks has rejected as inadequate the approach used, for example, by Reher (1998, 227), i.e., "a proxy for loneliness in society is the proportion of single-person households" (Vaskovics et al. 1994, 89).

20 Figures here vary from 67.6 per cent (Hoffmann 2004, for 2003) to 72 per cent (Engstler and Menning 2003, 137, for 1999) or 75 per cent (Bender 1994, 248) to 90 per cent (Schulz 1999, 102).

21 This cannot be assumed to be the result of an attitude that clearly favours family-sponsored aid. Schütze and Wagner (1995, 324) reach the conclusion that "the majority of the children asked provided help independent of their attitude about whether families should do so or not."

by wives and daughters[22] (Bender 1994, 242f.; Maly 2001). This is a visible aspect of the finding that of all family relationships, that of mother and daughter is the closest, and more so in the eastern than the western states (Szydlik 1997, 194). Among the care providers, however, women are those who are "more likely to combine outpatient services with their care work" (Bender 1994, 243; Maly 2001). This means, in turn, that women who provide care play a vital gatekeeper role in arranging, integrating or combining outpatient services and the social security provided by the family and the state. Unlike in the eastern part of Germany, nursing and other forms of care in the western states are characterized by a "home orientation" on the part of caregivers, and are defined by "[...] weak ties outside the home, whether with services, employment, informal networks, or wider family situations" (Chamberlayne 1999, 157, 163).

Key here is the fact that the elderly are not merely recipients of support payments provided by the state or the family. The extensive state coverage of the current generation of retirees in Germany enables them to provide a certain amount of social security and assistance in kinship networks and/or in the sector of voluntary help. This is corroborated by the results of an international study, which indicate that older parents receive most help from younger generations in countries with the most comprehensive welfare support system (Künemund and Rein 1999, 115). The authors argue therefore that Germany has "a pattern of complementarity of state and family", since "the generosity of the state has reinforced family solidarity by promoting a pattern of crowding in" (see also the argument in Reil-Held 2005, 23f.)[23].

This connection between the support provided by the welfare state and by the family impacts on the relationships, since the networks described

22 The nursing care provided by minors in the family has not as yet been investigated or documented statistically in Germany (Dietz and Clasen 1995, 65; Hantrais and Becker 1995, 82). However, here too, care is provided by daughters to an overwhelming degree (Dietz and Clasen 1995, 73).

23 However, Reil-Held (2005, 24) argues there is also a socially differentiated "crowding out", since "the poorer elderly receive less private financial help when the state provides the income for their basic needs." The terms "crowding in" and "crowding out" refer to the relationship between private and public services and financial transfers. Künemund and Rein (1999, 93–102, 115), Brooks (2000, 451f.), Ostner (2004, 78f.), and Reil-Held (2005, 4) use "crowding in" to describe the stimulation and facilitation of private services and transfers through public services. "Crowding out," in contrast, designates the dynamic whereby public services and transfers lead to a reduction in private efforts and transfers.

lead to an increase in family and kin integration (Motel-Klingebiel 2000, 289–292; Szydlik 2000, 244f.). These recent findings of the generally catalysing effects of the welfare stare, and of the German *Sozialstaat* in particular, rest on the fact that aid or support provided by families is not exclusively altruistic in character or oriented solely towards immediate needs. On the contrary, "exchange", "reciprocity", and "affection" play vital roles – albeit the precondition is always the financial security provided to the older generation by the pension system (Künemund and Motel 2000, 124, 126). In addition, increased mobility and the advances in communication technology have the effect of "fostering even closer solidarity" (Bengtson and Martin 2001, 215; Schönberger 2000, 39). This finding of generational solidarity complements the results of various comparative studies that have examined the orientation towards nursing and care across a variety of EU countries (Attias-Donfut 2000, 235; Berger-Schmitt 2003, 2).[24] These studies are consistent in their assertions that family and kinship networks will continue to be significant in Germany (Bender 1994, 224; Bengtson and Martin 2001, 215; Hollstein 2005).

However, the effects of the demographic shift, the changes in the transition to retirement (see above), as well as the ongoing cutbacks in state benefits, with particular reference to the older generation, make it difficult to know for certain. "De-solidarization" within the family networks concerned could be a possible consequence (Künemund and Motel 2000, 135; Motel-Klingebiel 2000, 289f.; Reil-Held 2005, 23f.; Szydlik 2000, 245f.).

Housing and generational networks in the GDR/in East Germany

In the GDR, private networks or those that provided aid and support to family and kin were not politically endorsed, since the socialist regime had a greater interest in mobilizing as many people as possible to join the labour force (Metzig and Pönsch 1989, 160). Nonetheless, there was no apparent decline of elder care within the confines of the family. This was due in part to the fact that both outpatient services and institutional nursing care covered only half the required needs (Angerhausen et al. 1998, 126), leaving them either unmet, or – similar to the FRG – in the hands of the family (Matthesius and Waldschmidt 1989, 145; Scharf 1998, 202; Chamberlayne 1999, 167). Not unlike the situation in the West, older peo-

24 German orientations are thereby closer to those found in southern European countries than in Scandinavia (Berger-Schmitt 2003, 4).

ple in East Germany were not solely aid recipients but played a major role themselves as "the provider generation" (Vaskovics et al. 1994, 144). Because births occurred earlier in life courses in the GDR, grandparents were somewhat younger (and hence physically more robust) than in West Germany. On the other hand, the high female employment rate in the East automatically restricted the amount of help grandmothers were in a position to provide. Similar to the FRG, ideals of individualization were relevant in the GDR, where the older generation also preferred "[...] to live separate from, but in close proximity to their children" (Autorenkollektiv 1983, 72).

The transformations East Germany has undergone since 1989 did not bring about a fundamental change in this practice (Ecarius 1995, 182; Petermann 2002), but instead led to a shift in types of transfer, or rather, in the significance of networks. Networks based on instrumental relations either disappeared or became commodified (Neef and Schäfer 1996, 82; Nauck and Schwenk 2001, 1871, 1876). In contrast, family relationships and other close networks were intensified or emotionalized (Rüschemeyer 1990, 294; Neef and Schäfer 1996, 82; Szydlik 1997, 194f.; Schmidt and Schönberger 1999, 191; Scheller 2004).[25] Care of the elderly within or by the family, in particular, was also facilitated by improved supplies, a better standard of living and increased outpatient services (Scharf 1998, 202). In the eastern states, elder care is guided by an "impulse to 'get out'", implying the propensity of carers for contact outside the home (Chamberlayne 1999, 162).

In an effort to facilitate female employment in the eastern states, relatives are now increasingly relied upon to provide child care. Due to early retirement regulations, however, which can bring active working life to an end by the age of fifty-five (Koller et al. 2003, 24), a shift has taken place in both gender and generational patterns, so that child care is now provided by grandparents, a radical departure from the circumstances that prevailed in former East Germany (Uhlendorff 2003, 215; Thelen 2005). Researchers therefore speak of the "revitalization of familial resources" or of "reactivated family networks" (Schmidt and Schönberger 1999, 190f.).

---

25 In East Germany, kinship relations outside the nuclear family as well as those that exceeded direct relations between the generations were negligible (Diewald 1998, 201) and/or declined even further in the process of transformation (Neef and Schäfer 1996, 82).

Of importance in this arrangement is the fact that the current grandparent generation in the eastern German states are not only in a position but want to be actively engaged. To some extent the result of early retirement provisions and the highly beneficial conversion of accrued pension rights for the present generation of grandparents in eastern Germany, this is also due to the "falling away of social contacts previously provided through work settings" (Schmidt and Schönberger 1999, 191; also Herlyn et al. 1998; Uhlendorff 2003, 216f.). It has been suggested that grandparents are important to the current parent generation because their pensions allow them to give financial support, and at least "... in some families they might be the only ones with a guaranteed income" (Kohli et al. 1997, 162)[26].

Conclusion: "crowding in"

Due to the extensive system of social insurance, or rather, the widespread pattern of different generations living in separate households, Germany is regarded as a "weak-family society" in comparison to other countries (Reher 1998, 210, 217). This assessment overlooks the relevance of family and kin to everyday life in the country in both east and west. Close, even very close, relationships and support among the generations is the norm, where child care, financial support, and care of the elderly and the handicapped are the key realms.

Although familial support is not a substitute here for the absence of state contributions to social security, it is closely related. Contrary to a first, superficial impression, the economic security provided by social insurance systems to members of the older generation is in fact the prerequisite for the extensive support and security they themselves provide for their family and kin. This in turn creates preconditions for the later nursing of the aged by members of the younger generations (Künemund and Rein 1999; Künemund and Motel 2000; Motel-Klingebiel 2000; Szydlik 2000).

26 In addition to the growing needs of the younger generation, this is one of the factors that explains why – despite the weaker economic situation of private households in the eastern states – financial transfers by the very old to their children are far more common in the eastern than the western states (Kohli 2004, 21).

With respect to West Germany, or what are now Germany's western states, the dynamics of generational relations are complex and somewhat contradictory, at least in terms of how family/kin and social security interrelate. The need to provide financial support to the older generation became obsolete with the pension reform of 1957, which at the same time created a "crowding-in" dynamic (see Ostner 2004, 78f.). In other words, the financial independence of the retiree generation enabled them for the first time to be a source of support, i.e., to take care of grandchildren, and to provide emotional support for young families and financial support to their parents, to the point of inheritance. In recent decades, their release from employment as a result of generous early retirement settlements has provided them with more time and thus greater availability, for example, in the area of child care.

The current relationship between family/kin and social security is therefore determined by a stable cultural orientation and a customary daily practice of aid and transfers between and to the benefit of family members or relatives. Of crucial importance, quantitatively and qualitatively, and in the context of combining public, commodified and private goods (aid, transfers, support), is the work carried out by women, both directly and in terms of organizing and combining these forms of social security. Finally, there are indications that private networks are expanding to include friends and neighbours. Whether this is a prompt reaction to demographic change and thus evidence of a persistent cultural orientation towards providing support through private rather than public means remains to be investigated.

However, research has pointed to factors that endanger private networks in general, and family/kin networks in particular. Among them are the structural changes to families and generations as a result of demographic change (an increase in childlessness and a decline in marriage rates), the change in labour conditions and the concomitant "de-standardization" of life courses, and the absence of the catalyst and multiplier effect of the welfare state. Furthermore, endangering the notion and the ideal of social, if not societal, solidarity by dismantling the welfare state is not unimportant.

Last but not least, the dangers that arise from the stopgap networks themselves should be observed and not merely be seen as solidarity efforts by citizens to organize themselves according to the ideals of civil society. Davis (2006, 808) warns against the "glorification" of informal economies.

Studies on poverty areas in Germany (such as those with highrise building complexes in poor neighbourhoods on the margins of several large cities in the eastern states) indicate that people who live there are either thrown back or rely on informal strategies to survive. There is an intrinsic danger that those who do so "will fail to integrate into society" or drift from informal to illegal survival strategies (Keller 2005, 196–201). The recent, more intense research interest in the role voluntary work plays in the informal economy – including work carried out illegally (in the context of the family) – should be placed in this context (Merz and Wolff 1989; Bundesministerium für Bildung und Forschung 2000; Backhaus-Maul et al. 2002; Deutscher Verein/ISIS 2002; Enquete-Kommission 2002, 2003; Engstler u.a. 2004; Hoffmann 2005).

In the light of this historical and sociological evidence, it should be emphasized that far from being a substitute for the lack of state benefits, private networks are in fact strongly dependent on them.

Bibliography

Aglietta, M. (1976), *Régulation et crises du capitalisme: l'expérience des Etats-Unis*, Paris: Calmann-Lévy.

Alber, J. (1982), *Vom Armenhaus zum Wohlfahrtsstaat. Analysen zur Entwicklung der Sozialversicherung in Westeuropa*, Frankfurt/M.: Campus Verlag.

Albers, H. (1997), "Hin zur 'weiblichen Berufung'. Bäuerinnen in Westdeutschland", in G.-F. Budde, (ed.), *Frauen arbeiten. Weibliche Erwerbstätigkeit in Ost- und Westdeutschland nach 1945,* Göttingen: Vandenhoeck & Ruprecht, pp. 157–170.

— (2001), *Zwischen Hof, Haushalt und Familie. Bäuerinnen in Westfalen-Lippe 1920–1960*, Paderborn: Schöningh.

Allmendinger, J. (1994), *Lebensverlauf und Sozialpolitik. Die Ungleichheit zwischen Mann und Frau und ihr öffentlicher Ertrag*, Frankfurt/M. and New York: Campus Verlag.

Alt, C. (2003), "Wandel familialer Lebensverhältnisse minderjähriger Kinder in Zeiten der Pluralisierung", in W. Bien and J. H. Marbach (eds.), *Partnerschaft und Familiengründung. Ergebnisse der dritten Welle des Familien-Survey. Deutsches Jugendinstitut, Familien-Survey, Vol.11*, Opladen: Leske und Budrich, pp. 219–244.

Andreß, H.-J. and T. Seeck (2007), "Ist das Normalarbeitsverhältnis noch armutsvermeidend? Erwerbstätigkeit in Zeiten deregulierter Arbeitsmärkte und des Umbaus sozialer Sicherungssysteme", *Kölner Zeitschrift für Soziologie und Sozialpsychologie* 59(3), pp. 459–492.

Angerhausen, S., H. Backhaus-Maul, C. Offe, T. Olk and M. Schiebel (1998), *Überholen ohne einzuholen. Freie Wohlfahrtspflege in Ostdeutschland.* Opladen: Westdeutscher Verlag.

Attias-Donfut, C. (2000), "Familialer Austausch und soziale Sicherung", in M. Kohli and M. Szydlik, (eds.), *Generationen in Familie und Gesellschaft. Lebenslauf – Alter – Generation, Vol. 3.* Opladen: Leske und Budrich, pp.222–237.

Autorenkollektiv der Karl-Marx-Universität Leipzig (1983), *Gerontologische Forschungsvorhaben im Feierabend- und Pflegeheim "Emma Gerbig" Leipzig*, Ed. by U. J. Schmidt, G. Brüschke, S. Eitner, W. Ries and W. Rühland. Berlin (East).

Backhaus-Maul, H., O. Ebert, G. Jakob and T. Olk (eds.) (2002), *Freiwilliges Engagement in Ostdeutschland*, Opladen: Leske und Budrich.

Bahle, T. and A. Pfenning (2001), *Angebotsformen und Trägerstrukturen sozialer Dienste im europäischen Vergleich*, Mannheimer Zentrum für Europäische Sozialforschung, Working Paper 4, Frankfurt/M.

Becker, A. (2000), *Mutterschaft im Wohlfahrtsstaat. Familienbezogene Sozialpolitik und die Erwerbsintegration von Frauen in Deutschland und Frankreich*, Berlin: wvb.

Beckert, J. (2003), "Lachende Erben? Leistungsprinzip und Erfolgsorientierung am Beispiel der Eigentumsvererbung", in J. Allmendinger (ed.), *Entstaatlichung und soziale Sicherheit. Verhandlungen des 31. Kongresses der Deutschen Gesellschaft für Soziologie in Leipzig 2002, Part 2*, Opladen: Leske und Budrich, pp.792–799.

Bender, D. (1994), "Versorgung von hilfs- und pflegebedürftigen Angehörigen", in W. Bien (ed.), *Eigeninteresse oder Solidarität. Beziehungen in modernen Mehrgenerationenfamilien,* Opladen: Leske und Budrich, pp. 223–248.

Bengtson, V. L. and P. Martin (2001), "Families and intergenerational relationship in aging societies: comparing the United States with German-speaking countries", *Zeitschrift für Gerontologie und Geriatrie* 34(3), pp. 207–217.

Bengtson, V. L. and Y. Schütze (1992), "Altern und Generationsbeziehungen: Aussichten für das kommende Jahrhundert", in P. B. Baltes and J. Mittelstraß (eds.), *Zukunft des Alterns und gesellschaftliche Entwicklung. Akademie der Wissenschaften zu Berlin. Forschungsbericht 5*, Berlin and New York: de Gruyter, pp. 207–217.

Berger-Schmitt, R. (2003), "Betreuung und Pflege alter Menschen in den Ländern der Europäischen Union. Perspektiven zur Rolle familialer Netzwerke", in J. Allmendinger, (ed.), *Entstaatlichung und soziale Sicherheit. Verhandlungen des 31. Kongresses der Deutschen Gesellschaft für Soziologie in Leipzig, Part 1 (CD-Rom),* Opladen: Leske und Budrich.

Bergeron, L. (1981), "Familienstruktur und Industrieunternehmen in Frankreich (18. bis 20. Jahrhundert)", in N. Bulst u.a. (eds.), *Familie zwischen Tradition und Moderne.* Göttingen: Vandenhoeck & Ruprecht.

Blossfeld, H.-P., S. Drobnič and G. Rohwer (2001), "Spouses' Employment Careers in (West) Germany", in H.-P. Blossfeld and S. Drobnič (eds.), *Careers of couples in contemporary societies: a cross-national comparison of the transition from male breadwinner to dual-earner families*, Oxford: University Press, pp. 53–76.

Boldorf, M. (1998), "Sozialfürsorge in der SBZ/DDR 1945–1953. Ursachen, Ausmaß und Bewältigung der Nachkriegsarmut", *Vierteljahresschrift für Sozial- und Wirtschaftsgeschichte No. 138,* Stuttgart: Franz Steiner Verlag.

Borchers, A. (1997), *Die Sandwich-Generation. Ihre zeitlichen und finanziellen Leistungen und Belastungen*, Frankfurt/M.: Campus Verlag.

Borchert, J. (1995), *Die konservative Transformation des Wohlfahrtsstaates. Großbritannien, Kanada, die USA und Deutschland im Vergleich*, Frankfurt/M. and New York: Campus Verlag.

Borscheid, P. (1987), *Geschichte des Alterns, 16.–18. Jahrhundert*, 2nd ed., Münster: Coppenrath.

Bouvier, B. (2002), *Die DDR – ein Sozialstaat? Sozialpolitik in der Ära Honecker*, Bonn: Karl Dietz Verlag.

Boyer, R. (1986), *La théorie de la regulation: une analyse critique*, Paris: La Decouverte.

Braun, R. (2003), "Hat die Erbengeneration ausgespart? Nach der Rentenillusion droht eine Erbschaftsillusion", in F. Lettke, (ed.), *Erben und Vererben. Gestaltung und Regulation von Generationenbeziehungen. Konstanzer Beiträge zur sozialwissenschaftlichen Forschung, Vol. 11.*, Konstanz: UVK Verlagsgesellschaft, pp. 91–114.

Brooks, A. C. (2000), "Public subsidies and charitable giving: crowding out, crowding in, or both?", *Journal of Policy Analysis and Management 19(3)*, pp. 451–464.

Brose, H.-G. (2003), "Die Subversion der Institution – Über Riesters Rente, lebenslanges Lernen und andere Kleinigkeiten", in J. Allmendinger (ed.), *Entstaatlichung und soziale Sicherheit. Verhandlungen des 31. Kongresses der Deutschen Gesellschaft für Soziologie in Leipzig 2002, Part 1,* Opladen: Leske und Budrich, pp. 583–603.

Bruckner, E. (1993), *Zur Bedeutung von Partnerschaft und Verwandtschaft. Ein internationaler Vergleich.* Mannheimer Zentrum für Europäische Sozialforschung. Arbeitspapier Nr. 4.

Brüderl, J. and T. Klein (2003), "Die Pluralisierung partnerschaftlicher Lebensformen in Westdeutschland, 1960–2000. Eine empirische Untersuchung mit dem Familiensurvey 2000", in W. Bien and J. Marbach (eds.), *Partnerschaft und Familiengründung. Ergebnisse der dritten Welle des Familien-Survey. Deutsches Jugendinstitut, Familiensurvey, Vol. 11,* Opladen: Leske und Budrich, pp. 189–217.

Bundesministerium für Bildung und Forschung (ed.) (2000), *Informelle Ökonomie, Schattenwirtschaft und Zivilgesellschaft als Herausforderung für die europäische Sozialforschung. Neue Herausforderungen für Forschung und Politik im Spannungsfeld zwischen Schwarzarbeit, Eigenarbeit, Ehrenamt und drittem Sektor*, Bonn: BMBF, Referat Öffentlichkeitsarbeit.

Bundesministerium für Familie, Senioren, Frauen und Jugend (ed.) (1998), *Zweiter Bericht zur Lage der älteren Generation in der Bundesrepublik Deutschland: Wohnen im Alter*, Bonn: BMFSFJ.

— (2002), *Einnahmeeffekte beim Ausbau von Kindertagesbetreuung. Wesentliche Ergebnisse des Gutachtens des Deutschen Instituts für Wirtschaftsforschung Berlin*, Berlin: BMFSFJ.

— (2005a), *Altenbericht im Dialog. Potenziale des Alters in Wirtschaft und Gesellschaft*, Berlin: BMFSFJ.

— (2005b), *Zwölfter Kinder- und Jugendbericht. Bericht über die Lebenssituation junger Menschen und die Leistungen der Kinder- und Jugendhilfe in Deutschland*, Berlin: BMFSFJ.

— (2005c), *Zukunft: Familie. Ergebnisse aus dem 7. Familienbericht*, Berlin: BMFSFJ.

— (2006), *Familie zwischen Flexibilität und Verlässlichkeit. Perspektiven für eine lebenslaufbezogene Familienpolitik*, Berlin: BMFSFJ.

Chamberlayne, P. (1990), "The 'mothers' manifesto' and the debate over Mütterlichkeit", *Feminist Review 35*, pp. 9–23.

— (1991), "The 'mothers' manifesto' and the concept of Mütterlichkeit", in E. Kolinsky (ed.), *The Federal Republic of Germany: the end of an era*, Oxford: Berg, pp. 199–218.

— (1999), "Cultural analysis of the informal sphere", in P. Chamberlayne, A. Cooper, R. Freeman and M. Rustin (eds.), *Welfare and culture in Europe. Towards a new paradigm in social policy*, London: Kingsley, pp. 151–171.

Chamberlayne, P. and A. King (2000), *Cultures of care. Biographies of carers in Britain and the two Germanies*, Bristol: The Policy Press.

Chorus, S. (2007), "Who cares? Kapitalismus, Geschlechterverhältnisse und Frauenarbeiten. Regulationstheoretische Sehkorrekturen", *Feministische Studien 2*, pp. 202–216.

Conrad, C. (1990), "Gewinner und Verlierer im Wohlfahrtsstaat. Deutsche und internationale Tendenzen im 20. Jahrhundert", *Archiv für Sozialgeschichte 30*, pp. 297–326.

— (1998), "Alterssicherung", in H. G. Hockerts (ed.), *Drei Wege deutscher Sozialstaatlichkeit. NS-Diktatur, Bundesrepublik und DDR im Vergleich, Schriftenreihe der Vierteljahreshefte für Zeitgeschichte, vol. 76*, München: Oldenbourg Verlag, pp. 101–116.

Crew, D. F. (1990), "'Wohlfahrtsbrot ist bitteres Brot': the elderly, the disabled and the local welfare authorities in the Weimar Republic 1924–1933", *Archiv für Sozialgeschichte 30*, pp. 217–245.

Cromm, J. (1998), *Familienbildung in Deutschland. Soziodemographische Prozesse, Theorie, Recht und Politik unter besonderer Berücksichtigung der DDR*, Opladen: Leske und Budrich.

Davis, M. (2006), "Planet der Slums", *Blätter für deutsche und internationale Politik 7*, pp. 805–816.

Dennis, M. (1998), "Family policy and family function in the German Democratic Republic", in E. Kolinsky (ed.), *Social transformation and the family in post-communist Germany*, London: MacMillan, pp. 37–57.

Deutscher Verein für öffentliche und private Fürsorge, ISIS-Sozialforschung (2002), *Recherche zum freiwilligen Engagement von Migrantinnen und Migranten*. Dokumentation im Auftrag des Bundesministeriums für Familie, Senioren, Frauen und Jugend. Frankfurt/M.

Dietz, B. and J. Clasen (1995), "Young carers in Gemany", in S. Becker (ed.), *Young carers in Europe: an exploratory cross-national study in Britain, France, Sweden and Germany,* Leicestershire: Young Carers Research Group, pp. 65–75.

Diewald, M. (1989), "Haushalts- und Familienformen im sozialen Wandel – Entsolidarisierung oder neue Formen der Solidarisierung?", in G. Wagner, N. Ott and H.-J. Hoffmann-Nowotny (eds.), *Familienbildung und Erwerbstätigkeit im demographischen Wandel. Proceedings der 23. Arbeitstagung der Deutschen Gesellschaft für Bevölkerungswissenschaft am 28. Februar – 3. März 1989 in Bad Homburg v.d.H. Berlin*, Berlin and Heidelberg: Springer Verlag, pp. 177–195.

— (1998), "Persönliche Bindung und gesellschaftliche Veränderungen – Zum Wandel von Familien- und Verwandtschaftsbeziehungen in Ostdeutschland nach der Wende", in M. Wagner and Y. Schütze (eds.), *Verwandtschaft. Sozialwissenschaftliche Beiträge zu einem vernachlässigten Thema,* Stuttgart: Enke, pp. 183–202.

Diewald, M. and M. Eberle (2003), "Unsichere Beschäftigung – unsichere Integration? Auswirkungen destandardisierter Beschäftigung auf die Einbindung in Familie und soziale Netzwerke", in J. Allmendinger (ed.), *Entstaatlichung und soziale Sicherheit. Verhandlungen des 31. Kongresses der Deutschen Gesellschaft für Soziologie in Leipzig 2002, Part 2,* Opladen: Leske und Budrich.

Dingeldey, I. (2002), "Das deutsche System der Ehegattenbesteuerung im europäischen Vergleich", *WSI-Mitteilungen Heft 3,* pp. 154–160.

Dölling, I. (1993), Gespaltenes Bewusstsein – Frauen- und Männerbilder in der DDR, in G. Helwig and H. M. Nickel (eds.), *Frauen in Deutschland 1945–1992,* Berlin: Akademie-Verlag GmbH.

Dorbritz, J., A. Lengerer and K. Ruckdeschel (2005), *Einstellungen zu demographischen Trends und zu bevölkerungsrelevanten Politiken. Ergebnisse der Population Policy Acceptance Study*, Schriftenreihe des Bundesinstituts für Bevölkerungsforschung, Sonderheft, Wiesbaden: Bundesinstitut für Bevölkerungsforschung beim Statistischen Bundesamt.

Dornseiff, J.-M. and R. Sackmann (2003), "Familien, Erwerbs- und Fertilitätsdynamiken in Ost- und Westdeutschland", in W. Bien and J. H. Marbach (eds.), *Partnerschaft und Familiengründung. Ergebnisse der dritten Welle des Familien-Surveys.* Opladen: Leske und Budrich, pp. 309–348.

Drobnič, S. and H.-P. Blossfeld (2001), "Careers of couples and trends in inequality", in H.-P. Blossfeld and S. Drobnič (eds.), *Careers of couples in contemporary societies: a cross-national comparison of the transition from male breadwinner to dual-earner families*, Oxford: University Press, pp. 371–386.

Ebbinghaus, A. (1987), "Das Müttermanifest – eine Variante der Bevölkerungspolitik", *Zeitschrift für Sozialgeschichte des 20. und 21. Jahrhunderts Heft 3*, pp. 4–7.

Eberling, M., V. Hielscher, E. Hildebrandt and K. Jürgens (2004), *Prekäre Balancen. Flexible Arbeitszeiten zwischen betrieblicher Regulierung und individuellen Ansprüchen*, Berlin: Edition Sigma.

Ecarius, J. (1995), "Generationenbeziehungen in ostdeutschen Familien. Moderne Familienbeziehungen in drei Generationen", in M. Löw, D. Meister and U.

Sander (eds.), *Pädagogik im Umbruch. Kontinuität und Wandel in den neuen Bundesländern,* Opladen: Leske und Budrich, pp. 171–185.

Ehmer, J. (1990), *Sozialgeschichte des Alters,* Frankfurt/M.: Suhrkamp.

— (2004), *Bevölkerungsgeschichte und historische Demographie 1800–2000,* Enzyklopädie Deutscher Geschichte, Vol. 71, München: Oldenbourg.

Eisen, R. (2001), "Soziale Sicherungssysteme und demographische Herausforderungen. 5 Jahre Gesetzliche Pflegeversicherung. Eine Zwischenbilanz", in W. Schmähl and V. Ulrich (eds.), *Soziale Sicherungssysteme und demographische Herausforderungen,* Tübingen: Mohr Siebeck, pp. 73–94.

Engstler, H. (2003), *Geplantes und realisiertes Austrittsalter aus dem Erwerbsleben. Ergebnisse des Alterssurveys 1996 und 2002. Kurzbericht No. 3,* Berlin: DZA Nr. 41.

Engstler, H. and S. Menning (2003), *Die Familie im Spiegel der amtlichen Statistik. Lebensformen, Familienstrukturen, wirtschaftliche Situation der Familien und familiendemographische Entwicklung in Deutschland,* Erstellt im Auftrag des Bundesministeriums für Familie, Senioren, Frauen und Jugend in Zusammenarbeit mit dem Statistischen Bundesamt. Bonn.

Engstler, H., S. Menning, E. Hoffmann and C. Tesch-Römer (2004), "Die Zeitverwendung älterer Menschen", in Statistisches Bundesamt (ed.), *Alltag in Deutschland – Analysen zur Zeitverwendung. Schriftenreihe Forum der Bundesstatistik, 43,* Stuttgart: Metzler Poeschel, pp. 216–246.

Enquete-Kommission "Zukunft des Bürgerschaftlichen Engagements" Deutscher Bundestag (ed.) (2002), *Bürgerschaftliches Engagement – die lebendige Seite des Sozialstaates,* Opladen: Leske und Budrich.

— (2003), *Bürgerschaftliches Engagement und Sozialstaat,* Opladen: Leske und Budrich.

Erning, G., K. Neumann and J. Reyer (eds.) (1987), *Geschichte des Kindergartens. Vol. I: Entstehung und Entwicklung der öffentlichen Kleinkinderziehung in Deutschland von den Anfängen bis zur Gegenwart,* Freiburg: Lambertus.

Esping-Andersen, G. (1990), *The three worlds of welfare capitalism.* Cambridge: Polity Press.

Farahat, A., S. Janczyk, A. Mängel and B. Schönig (2006), "Exklusive Emanzipation. Zur Frauen- und Familienpolitik der großen Koalition", *Blätter für deutsche und internationale Politik 51 (8),* pp. 985–994.

Fliege, T. (1998), *Bauernfamilien zwischen Tradition und Moderne. Eine Ethnographie bäuerlicher Lebensstile,* Frankfurt/M.: Campus Verlag.

Franz, P. and U. Herlyn (1995), "Familie als Bollwerk oder als Hindernis? Die Rolle der Familienbeziehungen bei der Bewältigung der Vereinigungsfolgen", in B. Nauck, N. F. Schneider and A. Tölke (eds.), *Familie und Lebensverlauf im gesellschaftlichen Umbruch. Der Mensch als personales und soziales Wesen, vol. 12.* Stuttgart: Enke, pp. 90–102.

Frerich, J. and M. Frey (1996a), *Handbuch der Geschichte der Sozialpolitik in Deutschland, Vol. 1: Von der vorindustriellen Zeit bis zum Ende des Dritten Reiches, 2nd ed,* München, Wien: Oldenbourg.

— (1996b), *Handbuch der Geschichte der Sozialpolitik in Deutschland, Vol. 2: Sozialpolitik in der Deutschen Demokratischen Republik, 2nd ed*, München, Wien: Oldenbourg.

— (1996c), *Handbuch der Geschichte der Sozialpolitik in Deutschland, vol. 3: Sozialpolitik in der Bundesrepublik Deutschland bis zur Herstellung der Deutschen Einheit, 2nd ed*, München, Wien: Oldenbourg.

Frick, J. and H. Lahmann (1996), "Verbesserung der Wohnqualität und Entwicklung der Mieten in den neuen Bundesländern seit der Vereinigung", in H. Häußermann and R. Neef (eds.), *Stadtentwicklung in Ostdeutschland. Soziale und räumliche Tendenzen*, Opladen: Westdeutscher Verlag, pp. 249–262.

Gather, C., B. Geissler and M. S. Rerrich (2002), *Weltmarkt Privathaushalt. Bezahlte Hausarbeit im globalen Wandel*, Münster: Westfälisches Dampfboot.

Gatzweiler, H.-P. and E. Irmen (1997), "Die Entwicklung der Regionen in der Bundesrepublik Deutschland", in J. Friedrichs (ed.), *Die Städte in den 90er Jahren. Demographische, ökonomische und soziale Entwicklungen*, Opladen: Westdeutscher Verlag, pp. 37–66.

Gaunt, D. (1982), "Formen der Altersversorgung in Bauernfamilien Nord- und Mitteleuropas", in M. Mitterauer and R. Sieder (eds.), *Historische Familienforschung*, Frankfurt/M.: Suhrkamp, pp. 156–191.

Gerhard, U. (1997), "Die 'langen Wellen' der Frauenbewegung – Traditionslinien und unerledigte Anliegen", in R. Becker-Schmidt and G.-A. Knapp (eds.), *Das Geschlechterverhältnis als Gegenstand der Sozialwissenschaften*, Frankfurt/M.: Campus, pp. 247–278.

Gerhard, U., T. Knijn and A. Weckwert (2003), Einleitung: Sozialpolitik und soziale Praxis, in U. Gerhard, T. Knijn and A. Weckwert (eds.), *Erwerbstätige Mütter. Ein europäischer Vergleich*, München: Beck Verlag, pp. 8–28.

Gottfried, H. and J. O'Reilly (2002), "Reregulating breadwinner models in socially conservative welfare systems: comparing Germany and Japan", *Social Politics. International Studies in Gender, State & Society 9*, pp. 29–59.

Grunow, D. (1985), "Drei-Generationen-Solidarität in der Familie", in K. Weigel (ed.), *Familie und Familienpolitik. Zur Situation der Bundesrepublik Deutschland. Forschungsbericht No. 44*, Melle, pp. 146–155.

Gysi, J. (1989), *Familienleben in der DDR. Zum Alltag von Familien mit Kindern*, Berlin: Akademie Verlag.

— (1990), "Die Zukunft von Familie und Ehe. Familienpolitik und Familienforschung in der DDR", Sozialisation und Sozialismus. Lebensbedingungen in der DDR im Umbruch. *Zeitschrift für Sozialisationsforschung und Erziehungssoziologie*, 1. Beiheft, pp. 33–41.

Hachtmann, R. (1998), "Arbeitsverfassung", in H. G. Hockerts: *Drei Wege deutscher Sozialstaatlichkeit. NS-Diktatur, Bundesrepublik und DDR im Vergleich. Schriftenreihe der Vierteljahreshefte für Zeitgeschichte*, Vol. 76, München: Oldenbourg, pp. 27–54.

Häußermann, H. and W. Siebel (2004), *Stadtsoziologie. Eine Einführung*, Frankfurt/M.: Campus Verlag.

Haines, E. (2000), "Die Familienberichte der Bundesregierung", in W. Bien and R. Rathgeber (eds.), *Die Familie in der Sozialberichterstattung. Ein europäischer Vergleich. Deutsches Jugendinstitut, Familien-Survey,* Vol. 8, Opladen: Leske und Budrich, pp. 49–67.

Hammerschmidt, P. (1999), *Die Wohlfahrtsverbände im NS-Staat. Die NSV und die konfessionellen Verbände Caritas und Innere Mission im Gefüge der Wohlfahrtspflege des Nationalsozialismus*, Opladen: Leske und Budrich.

Hantrais, L. and S. Becker (1995), "Young carers in Europe: a comparative perspective", in S. Becker (ed.), *Young carers in Europe: an exploratory cross-national study in Britain, France, Sweden and Germany,* Leicestershire: Young Carers Research Group 1995, pp. 77–93.

Hattenhauer, H. (ed.) (1994), *Allgemeines Landrecht für die preußischen Staaten von 1794*, 2nd, enlarged edition, Neuwied: Luchterhand.

Haug, S. (2004), "Soziale Integration durch Einbettung in Familie, Verwandtschafts- und Freundesnetzwerke", *Zeitschrift für Bevölkerungswissenschaft* 29, pp. 163–192.

Hausen, K. (1976), "Die Polarisierung der 'Geschlechtscharaktere' – eine Spiegelung der Dissoziation von Erwerbs- und Familienleben", in W. Conze (ed.), *Sozialgeschichte der Familie in der Neuzeit Europas. Neue Forschungen,* Stuttgart: Klett.

Hausen, K. (1997), "Arbeiterinnenschutz, Mutterschutz und gesetzliche Krankenversicherung im Deutschen Kaiserreich und in der Weimarer Republik. Zur Funktion von Arbeits- und Sozialrecht für die Normierung und Stabilisierung der Geschlechterverhältnisse", in U. Gerhard (ed.), *Frauen in der Geschichte des Rechts. Von der frühen Neuzeit bis zur Gegenwart,* München: Beck Verlag, pp. 713–743.

Herlyn, I. et al. (1998), *Großmutterschaft im weiblichen Lebenszusammenhang. Eine Untersuchung zu familialen Generationsbeziehungen aus der Perspektive von Großmüttern*, Pfaffenweiler: Centaurus Verlag.

Hess, S. (2005), *Globalisierte Hausarbeit. Au-pair als Migrationsstrategie von Frauen aus Osteuropa*, Wiesbanden: VS Verlag.

Hettlage, R. (1992), *Familienreport 1992*, München: Beck Verlag.

Hockerts, H. G. (2007), "Vom Problemlöser zum Problemerzeuger? Der Sozialstaat im 20. Jahrhundert", in *Archiv für Sozialgeschichte 47*, pp. 3–29.

Hoecklin, L. M. (1998), "'Equal, but different?' Welfare, gender ideology and a 'mothers' centre' in southern Germany", in I. Edgar and A. Russell (eds.), *The anthropology of welfare*, London and New York: Routledge, pp. 73–97.

— (2002), "Mutterschaft im Vaterland", in T. Hauschild and B. J. Warneken (eds.), *Inspecting Germany. Internationale Deutschland-Ethnographie der Gegenwart. Forum Europäische Ethnologie,* Vol. 1, Münster: LIT Verlag, pp. 74–88.

Hoff, A. (2003), *Die Entwicklung sozialer Beziehungen in der zweiten Lebenshälfte. Ergebnisse des Alterssurveys 2002. Veränderungen im Längsschnitt über einen Zeitraum von sechs Jahren. Kurzbericht an das Bundesministerium für Familie, Senioren, Frauen und Jugend*, Berlin: DZA.

Hoffmann, E. (2004), "Ausgewählte Daten der amtlichen Pflegestatistik Deutschlands", *Informationsdienst Altersfragen*, Heft 05 (Sept./Okt.).
— (2005), "Übergang in den Ruhestand – Zeitstrukturen – Aktivitätsmuster", *Informationsdienst Altersfragen*, Heft 01.
Hollstein, B. (2005), "Reziprozität in familialen Generationenbeziehungen", in F. Adloff and S. Mau (eds.), *Vom Geben und Nehmen. Zur Soziologie der Reziprozität. Theorie und Gesellschaft, Vol. 55*. Frankfurt/M.: Campus Verlag, pp. 187–209.
Homburg, H. (1985), "Vom Arbeitslosen zum Zwangsarbeiter. Arbeitslosenpolitik und Fraktionierung der Arbeiterschaft in Deutschland 1930–1933 am Beispiel der Wohlfahrtserwerbslosen und der kommunalen Wohlfahrtshilfe", *Archiv für Sozialgeschichte XXV*, pp. 251–298.
Imhof, A. (1981), *Die gewonnenen Jahre*, München: Beck Verlag.
Jasper, G. (1993), "Zur Krise der Frauenerwerbstätigkeit in den neuen Bundesländern", in K. Hausen and G. Krell (eds.), *Frauenerwerbsarbeit. Forschungen zu Geschichte und Gegenwart*, München: Hampp, pp. 108–130.
Jurczyk, K. (2005), "Familie – Arbeit – Entgrenzung", *WestEnd. Neue Zeitschrift für Sozialforschung 2(2)*, pp. 90–99.
Kaufmann, F.-X. (1973), *Sicherheit als soziologisches und sozialpolitisches Problem*, Stuttgart: Enke.
— (2003), *Varianten des Wohlfahrtsstaats. Der deutsche Sozialstaat im internationalen Vergleich*, Frankfurt/M.: Suhrkamp.
Keller, C. (2005), *Leben im Plattenbau. Zur Dynamik sozialer Ausgrenzung*, Frankfurt/M.: Campus.
Kind, C. and K. Ronneberger (1996), *Zur Durchsetzung des Fordismus in Deutschland. Literaturstudie für die Stiftung Bauhaus Dessau*, Frankfurt/M.
Klein, T., Y. Niephaus, H. Diefenbach and J. Kopp (1996), "Entwicklungsperspektiven von Elternschaft und ehelicher Stabilität in den neuen Bundesländern seit 1989", in W. Bien (ed.), *Familie an der Schwelle zum neuen Jahrtausend. Wandel und Entwicklung familialer Lebensformen*, Opladen: Leske und Budrich, pp. 60–112.
Knijn, T., I. Jönsson and U. Klammer (2003), "Betreuungspakete schnüren: Zur Alltagsorganisation berufstätiger Mütter", in U. Gerhard, T. Knijn and A. Weckwert (eds.), *Erwerbstätige Mütter. Ein europäischer Vergleich*, München: Beck, pp. 162–251.
König, C. (1988), *Die Frau im Recht des Nationalsozialismus. Eine Analyse ihrer familien-, erb- und arbeitsrechtlichen Stellung*, Frankfurt/Main.
Kohli, M. (1985), "Die Institutionalisierung des Lebenslaufs", *Kölner Zeitschrift für Soziologie und Sozialpsychologie 37*, pp. 1–29.
— (2003), "Der institutionalisierte Lebenslauf: ein Blick zurück und nach vorn", in J. Allmendinger (ed.), *Entstaatlichung und soziale Sicherheit. Verhandlungen des 31. Kongresses der Deutschen Gesellschaft für Soziologie in Leipzig 2002*, Part 1, Opladen: Leske und Budrich, pp. 525–545.

— (2004), "Intergenerational transfers and inheritance: a comparative view", unpublished chapter for M. Silverstein, R. Giarrusso and V. L. Bengtson (eds.), *Intergenerational relations across time and place.*

Kohli, M., H. Künemund, A. Motel and M. Szydlik (1997), "Generationenkonstellationen, Haushaltsstrukturen und Wohnentfernungen in der zweiten Lebenshälfte. Erste Befunde des Alters-Survey", in R. Becker (ed.), *Generation und sozialer Wandel. Generationsdynamik, Generationsbeziehungen und Differenzierung von Generation.* Opladen: Leske und Budrich, pp. 157–175.

Kolbe, W. (2002), "Elternschaft im Wohlfahrtsstaat. Schweden und die Bundesrepublik im Vergleich 1945 – 2000",. *Geschichte und Geschlechter*, Vol. 38, Frankfurt/M. and New York: Campus.

Kolinsky, E. (1998), "Recasting biographies: women and the family", in E. Kolinsky (ed.), *Social transformation and the family in post-communist Germany,* New York: St. Martin's Press, pp. 118–140.

Koller, B., H.-U. Bach and U. Brixy (2003), *Ältere ab 55 Jahren – Erwerbstätigkeit, Arbeitslosigkeit und Leistungen der Bundesanstalt für Arbeit. Institut für Arbeitsmarkt- und Berufsforschung. Werkstattbericht No. 5*, Nürnberg.

Konietzka, D. and M. Kreyenfeld (2005a), "Nichteheliche Mutterschaft und soziale Ungleichheit. Zur sozioökonomischen Differenzierung der Familienformen in Ost- und Westdeutschland", *Max Planck Institut für Demographie. Working Paper 001 (Feb.)*, Rostock.

— (2005b), "Nichteheliche Mutterschaft und soziale Ungleichheit im familialistischen Wohlfahrtsstaat", *Kölner Zeitschrift für Soziologie und Sozialpsychologie 57(1)*, pp. 32–61.

Konrad, F.-M. (2004), *Der Kindergarten. Seine Geschichte von den Anfängen bis in die Gegenwart*, Freiburg i. Br: Lambertus.

Kontos, M. (2005), "Entgrenzte Arbeit in Familienbetrieben von Migranten", *WestEnd. Neue Zeitschrift für Sozialforschung 2(2)*, pp. 100–111.

Kosmann, M. (1998), *Wie Frauen erben. Geschlechterverhältnis und Erbprozess. Geschlecht und Gesellschaft, Vol. 13*, Opladen: Leske und Budrich.

Kratzer, N. and D. Sauer (2007), "Entgrenzte Arbeit – gefährdete Reproduktion. Genderfragen in der Arbeitsforschung", in B. Aulenbacher, M. Funder, H. Jacobsen and S. Völker (eds.), *Arbeit und Geschlecht im Umbruch der modernen Gesellschaft. Geschlecht und Gesellschaft, Vol. 40,* Wiesbaden: VS Verlag, pp. 235–249.

Kreyenfeld, M. (2004), "Fertility decisions in the FRG and GDR: an analysis with data from the German fertility and family survey", *Max Planck Institut für Demographie. Working Paper 008 (Feb.), Rostock.*

Künemund, H. and A. Motel (2000), "Verbreitung, Motivation und Entwicklungsperspektiven privater intergenerationeller Hilfeleistungen und Transfers", in M. Kohli and M. Szydlik (eds.), *Generationen in Familie und Gesellschaft. Lebenslauf – Alter – Generation, Vol. 3,* Opladen: Leske und Budrich, pp. 122–137.

Künemund, H. and M. Rein (1999), "There is more to receiving than needing: theoretical arguments and empirical explorations of crowding in and crowding out", *Ageing and Society 19*, pp. 93–121.

Kuller, C. (2004), *Familienpolitik im föderativen Sozialstaat. Die Formierung eines Politikfeldes in der Bundesrepublik 1949–1975*, München: Oldenbourg.

Lang, F. R. and Y. Schütze (1998), "Verfügbarkeit und Leistungen verwandtschaftlicher Beziehungen im Alter", in M. Wagner and Y. Schütze (eds.), *Verwandtschaft. Sozialwissenschaftliche Beiträge zu einem vernachlässigten Thema,* Stuttgart: Enke, pp. 163–182.

Lange, A. (2003), "Spielen, Lernen, Arbeiten. Thesen zur Destabilisierung des fordistischen Generationentransfers in der Hochmoderne", in J. Allmendinger (ed.), *Verhandlungen des 31. Kongresses der Deutschen Gesellschaft für Soziologie in Leipzig, Part 1. Beiträge aus Arbeitsgruppen, Sektionssitzungen und den Ad-hoc-Gruppen (CD-Rom)*, Opladen: Leske und Budrich.

Leisering, L. (2000), "Wohlfahrtsstaatliche Generationen", in M. Kohli and Marc S. (eds.), *Generationen in Familie und Gesellschaft. Lebenslauf – Alter – Generation, Vol. 3,* Opladen: Leske und Budrich, pp. 59–76.

Letablier, M.-T. and I. Jönsson (2003), "Kinderbetreuung und politische Handlungslogik", in U. Gerhard, T. Knijn and A. Weckwert (eds.), *Erwerbstätige Mütter. Ein europäischer Vergleich*, München: Beck Verlag, pp. 85–109.

Lewis, J. (2003), "Erwerbstätigkeit versus Betreuungsarbeit", in U. Gerhard, T. Knijn and A. Weckwert (eds.), *Erwerbstätige Mütter. Ein europäischer Vergleich,* München: Beck Verlag, pp. 29–52.

Lindenberger, T. (2005), "'Asoziale Lebensweise', Herrschaftslegitimation, Sozialdisziplinierung und die Konstruktion eines 'negativen Milieus' in der SED-Diktatur", *Geschichte und Gesellschaft. Zeitschrift für Historische Sozialwissenschaft 31(2)*, pp. 227–254.

Lipietz, A. (1985), *Mirages et miracles: problèmes de l'industrialisation dans le tiers monde,* Paris: Éd. La Découverte.

Lipp, C. (1982), "Dörfliche Formen generativer und sozialer Reproduktion", in W. Kaschuba and C. Lipp (eds.), *Dörfliches Überleben,* Tübingen: Tübinger Vereinigung für Volkskunde.

— (2006), "Verwandtschaft – ein negiertes Element in der politischen Kultur des 19. Jahrhunderts", *Historische Zeitschrift 283(1)*, pp. 31–77.

Ludwig, I., V. Schlevogt, U. Klammer and U. Gerhard (2002), *Managerinnen des Alltags. Strategien erwerbstätiger Mütter in Ost- und Westdeutschland. Forschung aus der Hans-Böckler-Stiftung, 43*, Berlin: Edition Sigma.

Lutz, B. (1984), *Der kurze Traum immerwährender Prosperität,* Frankfurt/M.: Campus.

Mädje, E. and C. Neusüß (1996), *Frauen im Sozialstaat. Zur Lebenssituation alleinerziehender Sozialhilfeempfängerinnen*, Frankfurt/M.: Campus.

Maly, N. (2001), *Töchter, die ihre Mütter pflegen. Eine Analyse ihrer Lebenssituation. Dortmunder Beiträge zur Sozial- und Gesellschaftspolitik, Vol. 34*, Münster, Hamburg and London: LIT Verlag.

Marbach, J. H. (1994), "Tauschbeziehungen zwischen Generationen. Kommunikation, Dienstleistungen und finanzielle Unterstützung in Dreigenerationenfamilien", in W. Bien (ed.), *Eigeninteresse oder Solidarität. Beziehungen in modernen Mehrgenerationenfamilien,* Opladen: Leske und Budrich, pp. 163–196.

— (1998), "Verwandtschaftsbeziehungen und Abstammung – Eine Prüfung soziobiologischer und ethnologischer Thesen mit Hilfe familiensoziologischer Daten", in M. Wagner and Y. Schütze (eds.), *Verwandtschaft. Sozialwissenschaftliche Beiträge zu einem vernachlässigten Thema. Der Mensch als soziales und personales Wesen, Vol. 14,* Stuttgart: Enke, pp. 91–126.

— (2003), "Familiale Lebensformen im Wandel", in W. Bien and J. H. Marbach (eds.), Partnerschaft und Familiengründung. Ergebnisse der dritten Welle des Familien-Survey. Deutsches Jugendinstitut, Familien-Survey, Vol. 11, Opladen: Leske und Budrich, pp. 141–187.

Marschalck, P. (1984), *Bevölkerungsgeschichte Deutschlands im 19. und 20. Jahrhundert,* Frankfurt/M.: Suhrkamp.

Matthesius, R. and S. Waldschmidt (1989), "Zu Ausgangspunkten und aktuellen Aspekten der medizinischen und sozialen Betreuung älterer Bürger", in A., P. Peuker and O. Weiss et al. (eds.), *Medizinische und soziale Betreuung im Territorium. Ausgewählte Probleme der Leitung, Planung und Organisation,* Berlin: Verlag Volk und Wissen, pp. 134–148.

Merkle, L. E. (1994), *Frauenerwerbstätigkeit und Kinderbetreuung. Eine theoretische und empirische Analyse für die Bundesrepublik Deutschland. Wirtschaftswissenschaftliche Beiträge, Vol. 103,* Heidelberg: Physica Verlag.

Merz, J. and K. Wolff (1989), "Schwarzarbeit und Eigenarbeit – Informelle familiale Versorgungsstrategien", in G. Wagner, N. Ott and H.-J. Hoffmann-Nowotny (eds.), *Familienbildung und Erwerbstätigkeit im demographischen Wandel. Proceedings der 23. Arbeitstagung der Deutschen Gesellschaft für Bevölkerungswissenschaft am 28. Februar – 3. März 1989 in Bad Homburg v.d.H.* Berlin: Springer Verlag, pp. 196–219.

Metzig, H. and D. Pönisch (1989), "Der Bedürfniswandel bei sozialer Betreuung von Bürgern im höheren Lebensalter", in Alfred Keck, P. Peuker and O. Weiss et al. (eds.), *Medizinische und soziale Betreuung im Territorium. Ausgewählte Probleme der Leitung, Planung und Organisation,* Berlin: Verlag Volk und Wissen, pp. 154–161.

Meulders-Klein, M.-T. and I. Théry (eds.) (1998), *Fortsetzungsfamilien. Neue familiale Lebensformen in pluridisziplinärer Betrachtung,* Konstanz: Universitätsverlag Konstanz.

Mittelbach, H. (1994), "Familienpolitik und Lage der Familien in den neuen Bundesländern", in J. Zerche (ed.), *Vom sozialistischen Versorgungsstaat zum Sozialstaat Bundesrepublik. Ausbau oder Abbau der sozialen Lage in den neuen Bundesländern? Kölner Schriften zur Sozial- und Wirtschaftspolitik,* Vol. 25, Regensburg: Transfer Verlag, pp. 55–95.

Mitterauer, M. (1977), "Der Mythos von der vorindustriellen Großfamilie", in M. Mitterauer and R. Sieder (eds.), *Vom Patriarchat zur Partnerschaft*, München: Beck, pp. 94–119.

Moeller, R. G. (1989), "Reconstructing the family in reconstructing Germany: women and social policy in the Federal Republic, 1949–1955", *Feminist Studies 15(1)*, pp. 137–169.

Morgan, K. J. and K. Zippel (2003), "Paid to care: the origins and effects of care leave policies in western Europe", *Social Politics. International Studies in Gender, State & Society 10*, pp. 49–85.

Motel-Klingebiel, A. (2000), *Alter und Generationenvertrag im Wandel des Sozialstaats. Alterssicherung und private Generationenbeziehungen in der zweiten Lebenshälfte. Beiträge zur Alterns- und Lebenslaufforschung*, Vol. 2, Berlin: Weißensee Verlag.

Münch, U. (1990), *Familienpolitik in der Bundesrepublik. Maßnahmen, Defizite, Organisation familienpolitischer Staatstätigkeit*, Freiburg: Lambertus Verlag.

Napp-Peters, A. (1985), *Ein-Elternteil-Familien. Soziale Randgruppe oder neues familiales Selbstverständnis?*, Weinheim: Juventa.

Nauck, B. and A. Kohlmann (1998), "Verwandtschaft als soziales Kapital. Netzwerkbeziehungen in türkischen Migrantenfamilien", in M. Wagner and Y. Schütze (eds.), *Verwandtschaft. Sozialwissenschaftliche Beiträge zu einem vernachlässigten Thema*, Stuttgart: Enke, pp. 203–235.

Nauck, B. and O. G. Schwenk (2001), "Did societal transformation destroy the social networks of families in East Germany?", *American Behavioral Scientist 44(11) (July)*, pp. 1864–1878.

Nave-Herz, R. (1998), "Die These über den 'Zerfall der Familie'", in J. Friedrichs, R. M. Lepsius and K. U. Mayer (eds.), *Die Diagnosefähigkeit der Soziologie. Kölner Zeitschrift für Soziologie und Sozialpsychologie, Sonderheft 38*, Opladen: Westdeutscher Verlag, pp. 286–315.

Neef, R. and U. Schäfer (1996), "Zusammenleben und Auseinanderleben. Veränderungen sozialer Lagen und Beziehungen in Ostdeutschland", in H. Häußermann and R. Neef (eds.), *Stadtentwicklung in Ostdeutschland. Soziale und räumliche Tendenzen*, Opladen: Westdeutscher Verlag, pp. 49–86.

Niebsch, G. (1989), "Umfassende Betreuung der Kinder in Kinderkrippen", in A. Keck, P. Peucker and O. Weiss (eds.), *Medizinische und soziale Betreuung im Territorium. Ausgewählte Probleme der Leitung, Planung und Organisation*, Berlin: Verlag Volk und Wissen, pp. 83–90.

Niehuss, M. (2001), *Familie, Frau und Gesellschaft. Studien zur Strukturgeschichte der Familie in Westdeutschland 1945–1960*, Göttingen: Vandenhoeck & Ruprecht.

Niephaus, Y. (2003), *Der Geburteneinbruch in Ostdeutschland nach 1990. Staatliche Regulierung generativen Handelns. Forschung Soziologie, Vol. 16*, Opladen: Leske und Budrich.

Nowossadeck, S. (1994), "Paradigmenwechsel beim Rollenverständnis ostdeutscher Frauen? Eine Auswertung empirischer Untersuchungen", in P. Beckmann and G. Engelbrecht (eds.), *Arbeitsmarkt für Frauen 2000 – Ein Schritt vor oder ein Schritt zurück? Kompendium zur Erwerbstätigkeit von Frauen. Beiträge zur Arbeitsmarkt- und Berufsforschung 179,* Nürnberg, pp 615–627.

Ostner, I. (2004), "Familiale Solidarität", in J. Beckert, J. Eckert, M. Kohli and W. Streeck (eds.), *Transnationale Solidarität. Chancen und Grenzen,* Frankfurt/M.: Campus, pp. 78–94.

Pabst, S. and H. Rothgang (2000), "Reformfähigkeit und Reformblockaden: Kontinuität und Wandel bei Einführung der Pflegeversicherung", in S. Leibfried and U. Wagschal (eds.), *Der deutsche Sozialstaat. Bilanzen – Reformen – Perspektiven,* Frankfurt/M.: Campus, pp. 340–377.

Petermann, S. (2002), *Persönliche Netzwerke in Stadt und Land. Siedlungsstruktur und soziale Unterstützungsnetzwerke im Raum Halle/Saale,* Wiesbaden: Westdeutscher Verlag.

Pfau-Effinger, B. (2000), *Kultur und Frauenerwerbstätigkeit in Europa. Theorie und Empirie des internationalen Vergleichs,* Opladen: Leske und Budrich.

Prugl, E. (2004), "Gender orders in German agriculture: from the patriarchal welfare state to liberal environmentalism", *Sociologia Ruralis 44(4) (Oct.),* pp. 349–372.

Rauchfleisch, U. (1997), *Alternative Familienformen: Eineltern, gleichgeschlechtliche Paare, Hausmänner,* Göttingen: Vandenhoeck & Ruprecht.

Reher, D. S. (1998), "Family ties in western Europe: persistent contrasts", *Population and Development Review 24(2) (June),* pp. 203–234.

Reif, H. (1982), "Soziale Lage und Erfahrungen des alternden Fabrikarbeiters in der Schwerindustrie des westlichen Ruhrgebiets während der Hochindustrialisierung", *Archiv für Sozialgeschichte 22,* pp. 1–94.

Reil-Held, A. (2005), "Crowding out or crowding in? Public and private transfers in Germany", *Sonderforschungsbereich 504, Discussion Paper 72.*

Ritter, G. A. (1998), *Soziale Frage und Sozialpolitik in Deutschland seit Beginn des 19. Jahrhunderts,* Opladen: Leske und Budrich.

Rosenbaum, H. (1992), *Proletarische Familien. Arbeiterfamilien und Arbeiterväter im frühen 20. Jahrhundert zwischen traditioneller, sozialdemokratischer und kleinbürgerlicher Orientierung,* Frankfurt/M.: Suhrkamp.

— (1993), "Vaterlose Familien. Zur Bedeutung von Verwandtschaftsbeziehungen in der Arbeiterschaft des frühen 20. Jahrhunderts – am Beispiel der Industriestadt Linden bei Hannover", in J. Schlumbohm (ed.), *Familie und Familienlosigkeit. Fallstudien aus Niedersachsen und Bremen vom 15. bis 20. Jahrhundert,* Hannover: Verlag Hahnsche Buchhandlung, pp. 235–242.

— (1996), *Formen der Familie. Untersuchungen zum Zusammenhang von Familienverhältnissen, Sozialstruktur und sozialem Wandel in der deutschen Gesellschaft des 19. Jahrhunderts. 7th edition,* Frankfurt/M.: Suhrkamp.

— (1998), "Verwandtschaft in historischer Perspektive", in M. Wagner and Y. Schütze (eds.), *Verwandtschaft. Sozialwissenschaftliche Beiträge zu einem vernachlässigten Thema,* Stuttgart: Enke, pp. 17–33.

Rosenbaum, H. and E. Timm (2008), *Familie, Verwandtschaft und soziale Sicherheit im Deutschland des 20. Jahrhunderts*, Konstanz: Universitätsverlag Konstanz.

Rosenbladt, B. von (ed.) (2003), *Freiwilliges Engagement in Deutschland. Ergebnisse der Repräsentativerhebung zu Ehrenamt, Freiwilligenarbeit und bürgerschaftlichem Engagement. Vol. 1: Gesamtbericht. Schriftenreihe des Bundesministeriums für Familie, Senioren, Frauen und Jugend*, Vol. 194, 1, Stuttgart, Berlin and Köln: Verlag Kohlhammer.

Rudloff, W. (1998), "Öffentliche Fürsorge", in H. G. Hockerts (ed.), Drei Wege deutscher Sozialstaatlichkeit. NS-Diktatur, Bundesrepublik und DDR im Vergleich. Schriftenreihe der Vierteljahreshefte für Zeitgeschichte, Vol. 76, München: Oldenbourg, pp 191–229.

Rüschemeyer, M. (1990), "Entwicklungen der Familienstruktur in einer staatssozialistischen Gesellschaft: Die Deutsche Demokratische Republik", in K. Lüscher, F. Schultheis and M. Wehrspaun (eds.), *Die "postmoderne" Familie. Familiale Strategien und Familienpolitik in einer Übergangszeit. Konstanzer Beiträge zur sozialwissenschaftlichen Forschung, Vol. 3. 2nd, unmodified edition,* Konstanz: Universitätsverlag Konstanz, pp. 282–443.

Ruhl, K.-J. (1991), "Die NS-Familienpolitik (1933–1945), Ideologie, Maßnahmen, Bilanz", *Geschichte in Wissenschaft und Unterricht 42*, pp. 479–488.

Sabean, D. W. (1998), *Kinship in Neckarhausen,* Cambridge: Cambridge University Press.

Sachße, C. and F. Tennstedt (1980), *Geschichte der Armenfürsorge in Deutschland, Bd. 1: Vom Spätmittelalter bis zum Ersten Weltkrieg*, Stuttgart, Berlin.

— (1992), *Geschichte der Armenfürsorge. Bd. 3: Der Wohlfahrtsstaat im Nationalsozialismus*, Stuttgart and Berlin: Kohlhammer Verlag.

Sackmann, R. (2003), "Institutionalisierte Lebensläufe in der Krise", in J. Allmendinger (ed.), *Verhandlungen des 31. Kongresses der Deutschen Gesellschaft für Soziologie in Leipzig 2002, Part 1,* Opladen: Leske und Budrich, pp. 565–582.

Schäfgen, K. and A. Spellerberg (1998), "Kulturelle Leitbilder und institutionelle Regelungen für Frauen in der USA, in West- und Ostdeutschland", *Berliner Journal für Soziologie I*, pp. 73–90.

Scharf, T. (1998), "Family support of older people in post-communist Germany", in E. Kolinsky (ed.), *Social transformation and the family in post-communist Germany,* London: MacMillan, pp. 184–206.

Scheiwe, K. (1994), "Wer wird unterstützt? Die Absicherung von Familien mit Kindern zwischen Sozial- und Privatrecht in Belgien, Deutschland und dem Vereinigten Königreich", *Internationale Revue für soziale Sicherheit 47(3–4)*, pp. 53–75.

Scheller, G. (2003), "Ostdeutsche Ehen und Familien im Spannungsfeld zwischen Entstaatlichung, neuen Aufgaben und Abhängigkeiten", in J. Allmendinger (ed.), *Entstaatlichung und soziale Sicherheit. Verhandlungen des 31. Kongresses der Deutschen Gesellschaft für Soziologie in Leipzig 2002, Part 2,* Opladen: Leske und Budrich, pp. 852–868 .

— (2004), "Partner- und Eltern-Kind-Beziehung in der DDR und nach der Wende", *Aus Politik und Zeitgeschichte B 19*, pp. 33–38.

Schelsky, H. (1953/1967), *Wandlungen der deutschen Familie in der Gegenwart*, 5th ed. Stuttgart: Enke.

— (1954/1967), "Der Irrtum eines Familienministers", in H. Schelsky (ed.), *Wandlungen der deutschen Familie in der Gegenwart. 5th edition.* Stuttgart: Enke, pp. 376–389.

Schenk, H. (1996), *Wieviel Mutter braucht der Mensch? Der Mythos von der guten Mutter*, Köln: Rowohlt.

Schlumbohm, J. (1994), *Lebensläufe, Familien, Höfe,* Göttingen: Vandenhoeck und Ruprecht.

Schmid, J. (2002), *Wohlfahrtsstaaten im Vergleich. Soziale Sicherung in Europa: Organisation, Finanzierung, Leistungen und Probleme*, 2nd, completely revised and extended edition, Opladen: Leske und Budrich.

Schmidt, M. G. (2000), "Reformen der Sozialpolitik in Deutschland: Lehren des historischen und internationalen Vergleichs", in S. Leibfried and U. Wagschal (eds.), *Der deutsche Sozialstaat. Bilanzen – Reformen – Perspektiven,* Frankfurt/M.: Campus, pp. 153–170.

— (2001), "Grundlagen der Sozialpolitik in der Deutschen Demokratischen Republik", in Bundesministerium für Arbeit und Sozialordnung und Bundesarchiv (ed.), *Geschichte der Sozialpolitik in Deutschland seit 1945. Vol. 1: Grundlagen der Sozialpolitik,* Baden-Baden: Nomos Verlag, pp. 685–798.

Schmidt, U. (2002), *Deutsche Familiensoziologie. Entwicklung nach dem Zweiten Weltkrieg*, Wiesbaden: Westdeutscher Verlag.

Schmidt, W. and K. Schönberger (1999), *"Jeder hat jetzt mit sich selbst zu tun." Arbeit, Freizeit und politische Orientierungen in Ostdeutschland*, Konstanz: Universitätsverlag Konstanz.

Schneider, N. F. and K. Ruckdeschel (2003), "Partnerschaften mit zwei Haushalten. Eine moderne Lebensform zwischen Partnerschaftsideal und beruflichen Erfordernissen", in W. Bien and J. H. Marbach (ed.), *Partnerschaft und Familiengründung. Ergebnisse der dritten Welle des Familien-Surveys,* Opladen: Leske und Budrich, pp. 245–258.

Schneider, U. (2004), *Hausväteridylle oder sozialistische Utopie? Die Familie im Recht der DDR*, Köln u.a.: Böhlau Verlag.

Schönberger, K. (2000), "Internet und Netzkommunikation im sozialen Nahbereich. Anmerkungen zum langen Arm des 'real life'", *forum medienethik 2*, pp. 33–42.

Schönwälder, K., D. Vogel and G. Sciortino (2004), "Migration und Illegalität in Deutschland. Forschungsbilanz I der Arbeitsstelle Interkulturelle Konflikte und gesellschaftliche Integration (AKI), Wissenschaftszentrum Berlin für Sozialforschung (WZB)", http://www.wz-berlin.de/zkd/aki/files/aki_illegalitaetsbericht.pdf [22.2.2006].

Schütze, Y. and M. Wagner (1995), "Familiale Solidarität in den späten Phasen des Familienverlaufs", in B. Nauck and C. Onnen-Isemann (eds.), *Familie im Brennpunkt von Wissenschaft und Forschung,* Neuwied: Luchterhand, pp. 307–327.

— (1998), "Verwandtschaft – Begriff und Tendenzen der Forschung", in Y. Schütze and M. Wagner (eds.), *Verwandtschaft. Sozialwissenschaftliche Beiträge zu einem vernachlässigten Thema,* Stuttgart: Enke, pp. 7–16.

Schulz, E. (1999), "Demographische Alterung und Entwicklung der Familienerwerbsbeteiligung", in E. Grünheid and C. Höhn (eds.), *Demographische Alterung und Wirtschaftswachstum. Seminar des Bundesinstituts für Bevölkerungsforschung 1998 in Bingen,* Opladen: Leske und Budrich, pp. 89–107.

Schumann, E. (1998), *Die nichteheliche Familie. Reformvorschläge für das Familienrecht mit einer Darstellung der geschichtlichen Entwicklung und unter Berücksichtigung des Völker- und Verfassungsrechts,* München: Beck.

Schuster, P., R. Stichweh and G. Schlee (2003), "Freundschaft und Verwandtschaft als Gegenstand interdisziplinärer Forschung. Einleitung zum Themenschwerpunkt", *Sozialer Sinn. Zeitschrift für hermeneutische Forschung, Heft 1,* pp. 3–20.

Spellerberg, A. (1994), Wissenschaftszentrum Berlin für Sozialforschung (WZB), Arbeitsgruppe Sozialberichterstattung (ed.), *Alltagskultur in Ost- und Westdeutschland. Unterschiede und Gemeinsamkeiten,* Berlin.

Spieß, K. C. and F. Büchel (2002), *Form der Kinderbetreuung und Arbeitsmarktverhalten von Müttern in West- und Ostdeutschland.* Schriftenreihe des Bundesministeriums für Familie, Senioren, Frauen, und Jugend, Vol. 220. Stuttgart: Kohlhammer Verlag.

Statistisches Bundesamt (ed.) (2004), *Bevölkerung und Erwerbstätigkeit. Natürliche Bevölkerungsbewegung 2000–2002. Tabellenteil (Fachserie 1/Reihe 1.1.),* Wiesbaden.

Szydlik, M. (1997), "Zur Qualität von Filiationsbeziehungen – ein Vergleich von Ostdeutschen und Westdeutschen", in R. Becker (ed.), *Generationen und sozialer Wandel. Generationsdynamik, Generationenbeziehungen und Differenzierung von Generationen,* Opladen: Leske und Budrich, pp. 177–198..

— (1999), "Erben in der Bundesrepublik Deutschland: Zum Verhältnis von familialer Solidarität und sozialer Ungleichheit", *Kölner Zeitschrift für Soziologie und Sozialpsychologie,* pp. 80–104.

— (2000), *Lebenslange Solidarität? Generationenbeziehungen zwischen erwachsenen Kindern und Eltern. Lebenslauf – Alter – Generation,* Vol. 2, Opladen: Leske und Budrich.

— (2007) (ed.), *Flexibilisierung. Folgen für Arbeit und Familie,* Opladen: Leske und Budrich.

Szydlik, M. and J. Schupp (2004), "Wer erbt mehr? Erbschaften, Sozialstruktur und Alterssicherung", *Kölner Zeitschrift für Soziologie und Sozialpsychologie 56,* pp. 609–629.

Templeton, R. and R. Bauereiss (1994), "Kinderbetreuung zwischen den Generationen", in W. Bien (ed.), *Eigeninteresse oder Solidarität. Beziehungen in modernen Mehrgenerationenfamilien. Deutsches Jugendinstitut, Familien-Survey, Vol. 3,* Opladen: Leske und Budrich, pp. 249–266.

Teppe, K. (1977), "Zur Sozialpolitik des Dritten Reiches am Beispiel der Sozialversicherung", *Archiv für Sozialgeschichte 17*, pp. 195–250.

Thelen, T. (2005), "Caring grandfathers: changes in support between generations in East Germany", in H. Haukanes and F. Pine (eds.), *Generations, kinship and care: gendered provisions of social security in central eastern Europe*, Bergen: Univ. of Bergen, pp. 163–188.

Thelen, T., A. Baerwolf and T. Grätz (2006), *Ambivalenzen der Flexibilisierung: Traditionalisierung in Familien- und Geschlechterbeziehungen in Ostberlin und Brandenburg.* Max Planck Institute for Social Anthropology, Working Papers No. 89. Halle/Saale.

Uhlendorff, H. (2003), "Family and family orientation in East Germany", in E. Kolinsky and H. M. Nickel (eds.), *Reinventing gender: women in eastern Germany since unification,* London and Portland: Frank Cass, pp. 209–228.

Usborne, C. (1994), Frauenkörper – Volkskörper: Geburtenkontrolle und Bevölkerungspolitik in der Weimarer Republik. *Theorie und Geschichte der bürgerlichen Gesellschaft 7*, Münster.

Vaskovics, L. A. et al. (1994), *Familien- und Haushaltsstrukturen in der ehemaligen DDR und in der Bundesrepublik Deutschland von 1980 bis 1989. Ein Vergleich. Materialien zur Bevölkerungswissenschaft, Sonderheft 24*, Wiesbaden.

Vaskovics, L. A. and H. Rost (1999), *Väter und Erziehungsurlaub*, Stuttgart: Kohlhammer Verlag.

Vester, M. et al. (2001), *Soziale Milieus im gesellschaftlichen Strukturwandel. Zwischen Integration und Ausgrenzung*, Frankfurt/M.: Suhrkamp.

Vollmer, F. (2004), "Das Ehegattensplitting ist antastbar", *Gewerkschaftliche Monatshefte 55*, pp. 427–430.

Voß, G. G. (2003), "Entgrenzte Arbeit – gestresste Familien", Zeitschrift für Familienforschung. *Beiträge zu Haushalt, Verwandtschaft und Lebenslauf*, pp. 329–336.

Wagner, M. (2002), "Familie und soziales Netzwerk", in R. Nave-Herz (ed.), *Kontinuität und Wandel der Familie in Deutschland. Eine zeitgeschichtliche Analyse,* Stuttgart: Lucius & Lucius, pp. 227–251.

Wegener, A. (2005), "Regenbogenfamilien. Lesbische und schwule Elternschaft zwischen Heteronormativität und Anerkennung als Familienform", *Feministische Studien – Zeitschrift für interdisziplinäre Frauen- und Geschlechterforschung 23(1)*, pp. 53–67.

Welzk, S. (2006), "Die 'Alterskatastrophe' und der Absturz der Renten", *Blätter für deutsche und internationale Politik 51(6)*, pp. 707–721.

Wendt, C. and M. Maucher (2000), *Mütter zwischen Kinderbetreuung und Erwerbstätigkeit. Institutionelle Hilfen und Hürden bei einem beruflichen Wiedereinstieg nach einer Kinderpause*, Mannheimer Zentrum für Europäische Sozialforschung. Arbeitspapier 18.

Wendt, H. (1993), "Geburtenhäufigkeit in beiden deutschen Staaten – zwischen Konvergenz und Divergenz", *Zeitschrift für Bevölkerungswissenschaft 17(3)*, pp. 251–280.

Wendt, W. R. (1995), *Geschichte der Sozialen Arbeit*, 4th, revised edition, Stuttgart: Kohlhammer Verlag.

Willekens, H. (2003), "Is contemporary western family law historically unique?", *Journal of Family History 28(1)*, pp. 70–107.

Willms, A. (1980), "Grundzüge der Entwicklung der Frauenarbeit von 1880 bis 1980", in W. Müller, A. Willms and J. Handl (eds.), Strukturwandel der Frauenarbeit 1880–1980, Frankfurt/M. and New York: Campus, pp. 25–54.

Winkler, G. (1990) (ed.), *Frauenreport '90*, Berlin: Verlag der Wirtschaft.

Zacher, H. F. (2001), "Grundlagen der Sozialpolitik in der Bundesrepublik Deutschland", in Bundesministerium für Arbeit und Sozialordnung, Bundesarchiv (ed.), *Geschichte der Sozialpolitik in Deutschland seit 1945. Vol. 1: Grundlagen der Sozialpolitik*, Baden-Baden: Nomos, pp. 333–684.

French individualism and kinship ties

Georges Augustins and Martine Segalen

Ever since the Code Civil was promulgated by Napoleon in 1804, the family has been a subject of concern in France, expressed in ideologies, policies and social movements. By enacting the equality of children in regard to family inheritance, the Code was said to have deprived fathers of their fundamental rights. Louis de Bonald, a conservative, claimed that this would lead to "deconstitution" of the family. But as the battle was waged to extend equality and citizenship to all Frenchmen, "family disorganization" sprang from another site. The consequences of the industrial revolution focused the family question on social classes and the threat of the working class. At the same time, demography became a national cause, as the French population declined in relation to that of other European countries, namely, Germany. For this reason, family became another matter of national concern.

France's recent family history (since the 1970s) has been characterized by three traits:

- important shifts in family policies and laws; in this last regard, the patriarchal structure of the Code Civil has been totally dismantled over the last thirty years to yield an equal place to men and women within the family,
- deep changes in the family structure have occurred, as evaluated through socio-demographic indexes and
- changes in family values have mainly concerned the question of "gender"; besides, contrary to other European states, such as Poland, Austria or Croatia, France is now considered "sortie de la religion", to have quit religion, which has a minimal influence.

More recently, the rhetoric of the family crisis has now moved towards the problem of culture shocks between the occidental family model and that of the migrants, whose Muslim culture clashes mainly on the grounds of the contemporary status of women in society.

Family policies: from familialism to individualism

The origins of family policy date back to the end of the nineteenth century if we admit that the law limiting the rights of fathers ("puissance parentale") over their children marks the first step to intervention of the state in private family matters.

The very first social protection measure was developed by the French Navy in 1854 in the interests of its sailors; other measures followed for railroad workers or civil servants. Between the two World Wars, a number of social provisions were extended to the workers by the company, under the impetus of the Catholic movements and Jacques Bertillon's natalist movement of the Alliance nationale contre la dépopulation (founded in 1896). Resistance to these provisions came from familist movements like the Société d'Etudes Sociales created by Fredéric Le Play, who tried to stop the state from invading the family, for example with the compulsory retirement plan project. As Emile Cheysson, a follower of Le Play, claimed:

> "[...] the burden is shared between the state, the worker and the boss. But the son disappears from the law; it is as if, once detached from his family, he has no further duties and is delivered from the obligation of obeying the great principle that is the very basis of society: 'Honour your father and your mother'. He is dispensed of this sacred duty by a law on retirement pensions, which takes over in his stead" (Cheysson 1901).

From the law of 1938 to the 1970s

With the introduction of the first law (November 1938) to create family allowances independent of salaries and firms, and the Code de la famille promulgated in July 1939, the way was paved for the development of the family policies that social movements had been advocating for years. Based on the male-breadwinner model, it was to last until the 1970s. The provisions, inspired both by familism and natalism, aimed at sustaining fertility and compensating for the cost of raising children; they focused on the protection of both mother and child, and the improvement of their health. Institutionally speaking, this characterizes the "familialisme à la française" that targeted the family and not the individual.

"The end of the last World War and the Liberation period represent a break with the anterior context. The definitive transition to compulsory law logic, deprived of discrimination due to universal criteria, departs from the employer liberalities logic that had previously prevailed. Financial considerations, based on a certain vision of equity (horizontal redistribution), override more normative preoccupations about the institution of family. This does not mean that political motivation becomes devoid of ideological positions, nor that underlying model references aimed at favouring this or that type of family cannot be found. However, such considerations no longer hold the central place they had in the previous period. Behind the large consensus that accompanies the implementation of this policy of financial support to families, a more neutral family policy is developing" (Commaille 1994, 18).

In 1942, special status was awarded to family associations and enacted in March 1945 as a result of the importance given to UNAF (Union nationale des associations familiales). These trends and provisions were confirmed after the war in December 1945 with fiscal provisions, "quotient familial" and, in the course of twenty years, with a variety of allowances (starting with the second child, for maternity leave, housing, orphans, handicapped children and child care) and loans for young couples (1972). In the 1950s, 40 per cent of social security expenses were devoted to the "family branch" (as against 9.9 per cent in 2000, whereas the share of social security expenses in the GNP has tripled from ten per cent to 30 per cent).

The shift in policies

In the 1970s, two factors linked to the long period of economic growth brought about a change: on the one hand, a fairly affluent middle-class sector had emerged, deeming it necessary to provide more help for those in need; on the other hand, the new status acquired by women in society and the family made it difficult to continue with collective provisions for couples, and not individuals. Under the impetus of Pierre Laroque, a promoter of the social security system after the war, a shift took place in family policies. As of that time, the focus was to be on "socially handicapped families" and, in an attempt to fight inequality, most provisions were to be granted to the less prosperous only. A host of provisions were voted on by the Parliament in the 1970s and 1980s in relation to housing, single parents (API), young children, working mothers who leave their jobs to educate their children (APE), and at-home child care for working mothers (AGED). These measures were developed under the presidency of François Mitterrand, despite the fact that in France the left had always been distrustful of family policies.

Reforms have accelerated since 1997, regarding both social security provisions and the civil rights of the family, thereby acknowledging the relative change in the position of women and men.

Although highly developed, policies dealing with child care for working mothers have shifted from support for collective structures to help with home care, either at the childminder's home (300 000 "assistantes maternelles" take care of 740 000 children under three years of age) or the child's own home. Paternity leave was established in 2002; various measures target working mothers, offering either assistance with child care or the opportunity to stay at home (Complément de libre choix d'activité), which effectively means that this allowance encourages women to leave the job market.

In 2006, a long complex story can be summarized by stressing the shift in family policy from supporting families in the form of compensation for the cost of raising children to helping those in dire need (very often single mothers, the unemployed and migrants). However, its publicized axis of action is "conciliation between family and work", with women as the main target: development of child-care provisions and the possibility for women to suspend employment and return after a given period. A second goal is to compensate for the break-up of family ties with the use of mediation and to help parents with violent and delinquent children.

The question of ageing

In the past, old age was associated with an image of dependence and decrepitude. Since the 1970s, however, revalorization of retirement pensions has caused our society to develop a new relationship with the elderly and to reinvent grandparenting. What is known as "the ageing process" of the French population is made clear by the following statistics: the proportion of people aged sixty and over was approximately 14 per cent in 1920, 16 per cent in 1950, 18 per cent in 1970 and 20.5 per cent in 2000. With the constant increase in life expectancy, the elderly now go through two stages in life: the so-called "third" age (fifty-five to seventy-five) and the fourth age (seventy-five and over). The former are generally people who have retired and enjoy good health. Three-quarters of them live as couples. Increasing the financial autonomy of retirees has strongly contributed to reducing recourse to their children and deeply changes kinship relationships.

The fourth age, on the contrary, is often characterized by dependence, disabilities, chronic disease and the degeneration of essential functions. Nevertheless, some people dissociate the seventy-five to eighty-four bracket from the eighty-five-year-olds and over. In the seventy-five to eight-four age group, couples are still a minority: one woman out of two lives alone and women are twice as numerous as men. However, there has been a 25 to 35 per cent increase in the number of couples since the end of the 1960s, while the progression in the number of singles is even more rapid: 30 per cent were single in 1962 and 45 per cent in 1990. A rapid decline in the number of people accommodated by a close relative has also been observed, as the seventy-five to eighty-four age group have more physical, intellectual and financial autonomy than in the past. In 1962, almost 50 per cent of people aged eighty-five and over co-resided with kin, as against less than 20 per cent today. The desire for residential independence is now valued both by the young and the old; the latter benefit from public allowances, enabling them to be taken care of in their homes.

Similar to elsewhere in Europe, the ageing of the population has led to a new problem in French society: the dependence of old people. Dependent are those who need help from another person to accomplish elementary tasks such as getting dressed, washing, eating or moving about, or to carry out domestic tasks that allow them to live on their own (e.g., housework, shopping, cooking). A survey entitled HID (handicap-incapacité-dépendance) indicates a decline in the physically incapacitated dependent population since the beginning of the 1990s.

"243,000 old people not confined to bed or to an armchair only need help with washing themselves (211,000 of whom are at home), and 130,000 (103,000 of whom are at home) only need help only in getting dressed, for instance putting on a coat [...] The most significant proportion (79%) of physically incapacitated dependent residents are in long-term hospital care" (*Etudes et résultats*, issue 94, December 2000, 3).

In 1990, there were almost two million people aged eighty and over, of whom 20 per cent were dependent and 40 per cent semi-dependent. According to INSEE (Institut national des Statistiques et des Etudes économiques), the number of people aged eighty and over in France will have reached almost four million by 2020, that is, 1.8 times more than in 2000. By 2040, France could have almost seven million people aged eighty and over, that is, 3.2 times more than in 2000.

The welfare state system did not originally provide for the elderly. Death occurred quite shortly after retirement and the financial cost of age was low, whereas today and for the near future, it has become a key sector of public expenditure. A number of provisions were extended to the elderly in an effort to provide as much care within the home as possible: domestic services were created in 1962, developed further in the 1980s, and are now available in almost every town council (non-profit local associations organize care with gratuitous participation and/or town council agreement). In 1995, 600 000 people aged sixty-five were beneficiaries (twice as many as in 1980). The financial costs are appropriated to the income of the elderly, and complemented by the pension or social care.

"Home care", a service created as an experiment in 1977, is available on a medical prescription, as are "auxiliaires de vie" (1981) to help dependent people who have returned home after a stay in hospital. Alongside the public services, the private sector has developed a new market with small hotels and family boarding houses for the elderly. Finally, as of 1989, the law authorizes placement of the elderly in families other than their own. Whatever the importance of the services provided by the public sector, in the expanding domain of elderly care, it is families that predominate when it comes to assisting, coordinating the various public interventions and supervising the care of ageing parents. This constitutes a key area in kin relationships.

The emergence of new family values

While the state as a provider of social welfare has shifted its policies to respond to the needs of the poorest sections of the population (single mothers, ageing dependents), as a provider of a normative frame, it has also followed cultural changes within the family. In the Napoleonic Code of 1804, the family did not exist outside marriage. Throughout the nineteenth century, the husband remained the household head and could freely dispose of his wife's wealth. Marriage was conceived of as an institution to assemble two lines and two patrimonies. With the exception of the working classes, where marriage was built on personal attraction and the salaried couple was the basic unit of survival and organization, both bourgeois and peasant weddings had always separated love from marriage. The power of love slowly entered the marriage picture in the course of the nineteenth century, and the image of the "couple" emerged from that of the larger kin group. Once admitted into the marriage picture, love swept young couples off their feet and arranged marriages disappeared. In the 1950s, mutual love and free choice of partners had legal marriage as the horizon to start a family.

Due to a number of economic and cultural changes regarding values and the place of women in society, the patriarchal construction of the family was dismantled by a series of laws that tended to acknowledge diverse family forms. The Act of 13 July 1965 reformed the matrimonial rules in order to ensure equality between spouses. In 1970, the law substituted the notion of "puissance paternelle" with that of "autorité parentale" and the title of "household head" vanished. The push towards more autonomy led to an increase in the number of divorces, which were still regulated by the law of 1884 that authorized fault divorce. Revisions of the law, granting more and more freedom to divorce, first took place with the Act of 11 July 1975, which, although maintening fault divorce, established divorce by mutual consent. In 1995, however, 43.3 per cent of divorces were still fault divorces, 42 per cent by joint request. In 26 May 2004, a new law authorized divorce after separation of de facto two years. The defender cannot oppose it, and the petitioner cannot be penalized. Marriage has now become a union that is in principle no longer indissoluble. No fault is required and it is sufficient to state that one of the partners rejects sharing a common life.

The spread of cohabitation without marriage and the increase in the number of children born outside wedlock gave the impulse to legally acknowledge private life without state intervention. Sharing life in an initmate relationship with a common residence has gradually been legally recognized with the institution of the PACS (Pacte civil de solidarité) in 15 November 1999. Initially the intention of this law was to protect the rights of the surviving partner of a homosexual couple, where one of the cohabiting partners had died of AIDS. It was extended to include heterosexuals and dissociates sharing a common life from procreation – a general trend since the development of chemical contraception. Thus concubinage entered the Code Civil, granting fiscal, social and civil rights. However, the question of children has not been solved and the push to authorize adoption or extend marriage to homosexuals with full rights to filiation is still hotly contested, in spite of a strong and active lobby in the French Parliament.

Having acknowledged the diversity of family structures (unmarried couples, monoparental families, blended families, homosexual couples), the law has striven to continue enforcing two principles: the protection of children and the equality of men and women. It is only recently that equality in filiation has been acknowledged independent of whether children are born in or out of wedlock, and in the case of adultery. The law of 2002 asserts "co-parentality" in all cases. In March 2005, the distinction between "natural" and "legitimate" filiation was abolished, which means that only unmarried fathers have to recognize their child. A new law – signed in January 2006 – establishes eighteen as the minimum marriage age for both sexes (instead of the previous fifteen for girls) in order to prevent forced marriages of young girls, especially among the immigrant population.

The price of freedom of choice is strict control by the judicial institution via the family courts that judge "in the best interest of the child", thus subjecting parental agreements (e.g., alternate residence, visits, alimony) to their authority. It is hard to believe that "desinstitutionnalisation" of the family, as the proposition goes, has taken place; social control has moved from marriage and civil law to the judicial realm (Segalen 2006).

From the nuclear to the "unclear" family

Family and inheritance customs

The history of the transformation of family forms in France during the modern period can be described as the interplay between three variables: law, the economy and family ethics.

Law historians (Klimrath 1843; Yver 1966) were the first social scientists to insist on the striking differences in the local inheritance customs that existed in France at the beginning of the nineteenth century, despite the promulgation of the Civil Code (1804). According to their findings, it is possible to draw a curved line that corresponds more or less to the Loire river and divides the country horizontally into two parts of approximately equal size. The southern part is known as *pays de droit écrit* and the northern part *pays de droit coutumier.*

The southern part had long been influenced by Roman law, which authorized the will and made it possible to advantage an heir and even introduce the right of primogeniture. Conversely, the northern part had come under the influence of the Germanic customs that promoted partible inheritance, allowing all siblings to receive an equal share of the inheritance.

Furthermore, local customs in the southern part varied according to the degree of freedom given to the testator. In most cases, however, goods were considered to be tightly linked to the estate and placed in the hands of an owner who could transmit them to the heir of his choice.

In the northern part of the country the situation was more complicated still. Jean Yver cleverly analysed its customs in the best scholarly manner, emphasizing the fact that differences in local devolution customs were linked to various forms of family organization. The analysis of the uses (usages) prevailing in the different regions indicated that two opposing principles seem to have dominated in northern France: either the entire estate of the parents (including what had already been given to some of the children) had to be re-divided equally after their death, or, conversely, only what had not already been given to the children upon their marriage. The first was the expression, as Jean Yver demonstrated, of a lineage principle (the goods belonged to the lineage and as such were to be equally divided between its members), the second principle expressed the permanence of the married couple (goods given to a couple must remain within their household to guarantee its survival).

In summary, up to the beginning of the nineteenth century each region of ancient France possessed a parliament that enacted its own private laws, the result of which was a wide variety of customs related to the perpetuation of the family. Three major categories emerged from this great diversity:

- The house-oriented system whereby property was unified into an estate to be transmitted intact to the next generation through a main heir chosen by the head of the household, a substitute for the Roman paterfamilias. This type of system could be found in various forms in the southern part of the country.
- The lineage- or parentela-oriented system, in which the kin network became the real unit of familial life (patrilineal kin in the case of a line-

age and cognatic kin in the case of a parentela). This system held that all goods were to be divided equally among the heirs, a situation that prevailed in the most northern and eastern parts of the country for the patrilineal-oriented systems, and in the west for those of the parantela.

– The married couple-oriented system, where continuity of the family, more or less associated with a household, became the dominant principle. Widespread in urban areas only, this became the dominant type in the twentieth century due to a combination of factors: on the one hand, rural emigration and the dispersal of kin, and on the other, the growth of individualism and independence from parents.

Strangely enough these differences survived the introduction of the Civil Code in 1804, the intention of which was to unify practices and hence promote equal treatment of children. To achieve this end the Code stipulated dividing the majority of the property equally among the heirs, while permitting withdrawal of a quarter of the total to be disposed freely by the testator. Numerous studies have shown that the activity of the *notaires* in rural France was – and still is – mostly devoted to rendering ancient local customs, still frequently perceived as valid, compatible with modern law.

Thus, either the family was – and to a large extent still is – conceived as a residential unit, or, conversely, as a network of consanguineal kin. The implications of these differences cannot be overestimated since they made a decisive contribution to defining the forms of assistance and solidarity that derive from kinship and family organization.

In order to clarify the interrelation between customary conceptions of the family, the economy and law, we will now present a detailed account of specific cases.

The house-oriented system

The most salient characteristic of the house-oriented system is, as previously stated, the association between an estate and a house, both of which are transmitted to a sole heir. This system specifies that the family group is limited to the household; more fundamentally, the family is conceived of as the group of people associated both in the past and the present with one house, the rule of composition of this domestic group being largely determined by the order of birth. The first-born child remains in the house and marries, while the other children remain bachelors at home or leave. Those who leave either marry into another house or emigrate and lose contact with the house.

Membership of a given house is expressed in ordinary life by bearing the name of the house to the exclusion of any other name (except for administrative purposes, which require the use of the patronymic); at least this is true in areas where the house-oriented system still exists in its pure form (i.e., mostly in the Pyrenees). An unmistakeable implication of this family system is the fact that kinship in the general sense is rarely involved in the construction of mutual support, since kinship almost ceases to exist outside the house. Mutual assistance networks are those that unite neighbours, who in most cases are not kin at all.

Three major factors influenced the transformation of this type of family system in the course of the nineteenth and twentieth centuries: the enforcement of the Code Civil promulgated in 1804, demographic growth and the development of industry in the surrounding world.

It is perfectly obvious that a house-oriented system is highly dependent on the stability of the household composition, i.e., on the rule of marriage of the main inheritor and the departure of the remaining children, with the possible exception of one son, who remains a bachelor at home and performs the task of shepherd half the year round. According to tradition, when the main heir married, his siblings were supposed to relinquish all claims to further inheritance; sisters later received a dowry and brothers were given compensation, a sum that often remained purely virtual and was never paid if they emigrated. Under these circumstances modifying the law of inheritance and, more particularly, the obligation to divide the majority of the estate equally between the children, was in complete contradiction with the local custom and the stem-family system. Furthermore, demographic growth, which began at the end of the eighteenth century, was, at the same time, a major threat to the traditional rule of the single heir. Thus, during the nineteenth century, two forces contributed to undermining the house-oriented system: legal transformation and the demographic growth that gave it a particular force while augmenting the number of potential inheritors who would previously have been discarded by the traditional custom.

Strangely enough the development of industry and the growth of towns did not at that time suffice to initiate significant emigration: some cadets joined the army or the administration, as was customary among cadets at any time. It was only during the last quarter of the nineteenth century that emigration became a significant factor and took the direction of America. The movement gained considerable momentum at the beginning of the twentieth century, only to be stopped temporarily by the First World War.

The parentela-oriented system

Contrary to the system described above, the parentela-oriented system is not based on co-residence but on the sharing of common blood. The idea of consanguinity is central. Widespread in the northern half of France, this type of system conformed strongly with the Code Civil and was promulgated, since the rule of inheritance based on equal shares had always prevailed. The inheritance was divided equally among the children, whether male or female From this point of view parentela societies differ from lineage societies, where only men are supposed to transmit blood and property.

The key factor for survival was therefore not transmission of the estate, but the allocation to each child of advantages that would be of benefit in terms of marriage or livelihood. Personal mobility in a kinship network that could provide assistance in everyday life as well as in exceptional circumstances was crucial to social life. Stability in this context was not and could not be a characteristic of social life. Farmers who rented their farms from a rich landowner were dependent on contract renewal, peasants who owned their land were dependent on family partitions, while everyone else depended on the availability of paid employment. These constraints imply two different types of mobility:

- A mobility determined by the life cycle, where the young had to look for employment or a farm to rent;
- A mobility determined by the need to find a house in the vicinity of the land inherited on both sides, i.e., of the husband and of the wife.

Another consequence is that marriage tends to be contracted between people of equal social status, i.e., in a position to receive approximately equal shares in the process of further inheritance. The result of these interrelated factors is that marriage frequently takes place at a comparatively early age (between twenty and twenty-five for both sexes) between kin (not close kin such as first cousins, but kin nevertheless) who possess property rights over adjacent plots of land. All of these kin members form a large family, which is alluded to by the use of the patronymic of one salient ancestor in the cognatic line. This family group can be technically referred to by the term parentela.

The system remains viable as long as the mechanisms of the matrimonial alliance allow the redistribution of land rights among kinsmen, but becomes highly unstable when land partitioned by inheritance is no longer compensated for by such redistribution, an observation implying that marriage alliances do not unite cousins. When emigration begins to take place, the cycles of marriage are disturbed and partition impossible to avoid or compensate. On the other hand, the network of kin can remain active in terms of the family and indeed social life. It is well known, for instance, that kinship networks were highly active in facilitating immigration to the Parisian districts frequented by Bretons and even contributed to transforming the area around the Gare Montparnasse (where the trains arrive from Brittany) into a Breton quarter.

Family systems and social change

The most striking factor is the persistence of different family models despite an overall change in French society: economic constraints, changes in family law (with serious consequences for inheritance patterns) and modifications in the conception of spouse status (increase in divorce rates) did not substantially modify the old provincial family patterns. Furthermore, the notion that the institution of family constituted the key factor in human well-being was paradoxically reinforced. This particular French cultural trait can be seen as both an advantage and an inconvenience.

There is an obvious advantage from the social solidarity point of view, since family networks are still considered a valuable source of support in crisis situations arising from personal circumstances or old age, and supply emotional and financial assistance. However, it can also be interpreted as an inconvenience; the notion of living far from their family cradle would be a cause of insecurity for most people and make them feel deprived of the very source of their identity. Jean-François Gossiaux (1992), for instance, exemplified this situation in the case of the Ardennes (eastern France), where young people are not prepared to move despite massive unemployment, a circumstance that could be attenuated if they were willing to transfer to another region. This reluctance to move can be interpreted as a remnant of the importance of inclusion in a local kinship network, a prerequisite for obtaining social status.

A new life cycle

The years after the Second World War can be characterized as the golden age of nuptiality in France, the period referring to the ideology of the "traditional" family. It has already been shown that the 1950–1975 model was merely transitional, previously non-existent, and to be challenged thereafter.

Historians have shown that throughout the nineteenth century, married couples became more and more private, unlike before, where they were subjected to the scrutiny of their kin, their neighbours, and the community. The notion of a "couple" on its own was simply non-existent; it came along with the decline in the number of children and the growing value of love. A lesser number of children, albeit better taken care of and more educated, gradually emerged as individuals. Legitimizing love as the basis of forming a couple began to take root in bourgeois families. The Talcott Parsons model – with the husband as breadwinner and the wife as homemaker – held sway between 1950 and 1970, a period marked by a high nuptiality rate, a low age at marriage, and a low divorce rate. Women, who had been a key factor in the labour force during the initial stages of industrialization, returned to take care of their homes, their husbands and their children. Patriarchal authority prevailed. Unions were stable and based on the gender division of roles; the nuclear family, which implies living separately from the older generation, was widely implemented through the expansion of housing. Public subsidies supplied the high-rise apartment blocks that today are accused of being the root of all social ills and hence demolished wherever possible. Seen through the eyes of demographic change, the perturbation of the family began at the turn of the seventies, and was accompanied by a change in statistics: a decline in nuptiality and fertility rates, and an increase in cohabitation without marriage and the number of divorces.

As a result of the decline in the number of children born, the size of households decreased; cohabitation between generations vanished almost completely. In the 1970s, sociologists began to focus on the structure of families with children after divorce and coined the term "monoparental" families. If unmarried mothers had been considered marginal in the former model, due to the extension of divorce after the 1970s, mothers with children were now reintegrated into the category of "family". In the past, most of them had been widows with children, but from then on, divorced mothers (1.6 million in 2000 or 16 per cent of all households) formed the majority. Sociological literature has stressed the correlation between this new family structure and the increase in poverty: new housing had to be found, fathers failed to pay alimony, and women dropped into the lower strata of society, finding only poorly paid part-time jobs.

A new model emerged and was referred to as "blended families". This model generally implied a woman with children who remarried or resettled with a new partner (who may also have been divorced). Again, remarriage was a frequent occurrence in the past, following the death of one of the spouses; the norm was to substitute a new parent for the deceased in order to erase the former union, which represented the old model of a unique marriage. Today, various blended family models have developed. The "traditional" idea of one marriage only is prevalent among the more modest social groups, and if the biological father has vanished, the new husband replaces him, often to the extent of adopting his wife's children. In more affluent sections of the population, the model whereby the biological father holds his position and the social father is recognized as a new member of the kinship network is more widespread.

The number of children living in this type of family has increased greatly; the social status of the original and the new partners, their residential patterns, all concur to produce different types of blended families. Discussions are ongoing as to whether social status should be conferred on the mother's new partner, who sometimes shares the residence of his wife's children and hence develops domestic ties of filiation. However, the law has not yet made provisions for legal status of this relationship. Legally speaking, there is no consanguinity among the various children of blended families. Nonetheless, sharing a common apartment or house stirs a quasi-filial relationship, and an affair, if it were to develop, would conjure up a feeling of incest. In other words, consanguinity is fabricated where there is none. Approximately one million blended families exist; they are fragile structures and the children of such families may have to experience a further break-up.

Although the family is now "unclear" (Simpson 1994), or at least highly diverse in structure, it is still a family, and as we know from several surveys, the goal of becoming a stable couple is still at the top of the value charts among the younger generations.

Since the 1980s, a series of significant changes has occurred regarding the life cycle. The characteristics of adulthood that once coincided – access to sexuality, marriage, employment, separate housing – have now been split. First sexual intercourse for boys and girls, for example, takes place earlier than it did in the 1960s; forming a couple no longer coincides with economic independence; entering a stable job can be delayed until the age of at least thirty. The age of youth has been rejuvenated, on the one hand, and prolonged, on the other. All this is due to a number of complex economic and cultural factors: scarcity of jobs is not favourable to couple stability; the female revolution has made young girls more independent than their mothers were, while the former have at the same time become the first victims of unemployment. The age at leaving home has increased, although it has not reached the level of Spain or Italy. The current model for young people is one of "back and forth" from the parental home (referred to as "boomerang kids" in the United States) and can continue until they have reached their thirties. These changes have not strained family relationships, since in France, parents are willing to help their children as young adults until such time as they are independent. Yet support from parents depends on income, and is more crucial at the top of the ladder. Nonetheless, even parents in the more modest social groups support their children who study at university, provided the latter can benefit from public scholarships.

Given the difficulties of the job market, a new characteristic of the life cycle appears to be the late age at mothering, which has surpassed the high ages observed in the eighteenth century. In France, women tend to have children in their thirties in order to gain a foothold in their first paid position, occasionally even in their forties if a new family structure has been formed after divorce and the new couple wants to have a child over and above the children they already have from other partnerships.

At the other end of the life cycle, the prinicipal change is related to the extraordinary increase in life expectancy and has led to a new generation known in French as "les seniors", i.e., people between fifty-five and seventy who are in good health, have a reasonable retirement pension, and lead an active life. This latest generation in our society, as a result of better living and health conditions, has now become providers for and helpers of the family. A fresh generation of women has emerged, referred to as the "pivot generation", and takes care both of ageing parents and young grandchildren. They are also the first generation of active women who retire and enjoy a pension. It should be stressed, however, that this situation will not be replicated by forthcoming generations, since those who have now reached the age of sixty are the baby-boom children. They enjoyed better living conditions, improved education and a favourable labour market; their pension standard is high. Twenty-five years from now, this equilibrium will be shattered, as social contributions dwindle due to late entry into the labour market; although the number of young people has declined, they will have to provide for a greater number of people with a longer life span; the age of retirement will most likely be pushed back again, endangering the possibility of family support and exchanges.

New gender relationships

Henri Mendras has dubbed the rapid modernization of the habitat the "seconde révolution française" (1994), with its construction of the then acclaimed social housing and the development of communication means, be it telephone, highways or modern domestic appliances, the fruits of the economic boom that succeeded World War Two. All of this benefited a large section of the population, which evolved into a prosperous, if not affluent, middle class, without, however, erasing the social differences of class and patrimony. Women, who emerged in society as public actors, were undoubtedly the chief beneficiaries. They had worked on the farms, in the workshops and in planting but the wages they brought home were merely considered "additional" earnings, and would be superflous as soon as men's salaries increased. The bourgeois women of the nineteenth century had also retired to their homes, supervising the education of their children and working their social networks. Ever since the end of the nineteenth century, medical progress has mainly benefited children (a decrease in infant and child mortality) and women (medically controlled pregnancies and deliveries). Freed from what had looked like a Judaeo-Christian malediction on their bodies, women entered school and university after 1945, where they quickly found themselves on a par with men. The importance of schooling in the achievement of gender equality cannot be emphasized enough.

"In a country where as early as the 1960s, owing to the remarkable development of education, the quasi-totality of children – boys and girls – went to school after their fourth birthday and remained until they were about fifteen, the influence of the school lever was central. Girls and boys were placed as equals on the same school benches; above all, school set them free, encouraging aspirations of autonomy from the family and motivated personal development in work; it also opened up opportunities for girls to take alternative paths to the millenary function of being a parent" (Chesnais 1988, 197).

In the 1960s and 1970s, school results were upgraded for both sexes. Access to university provided women with opportunities to take up a career. However, girls and boys continued to take different paths, with a large number of girls, for example, choosing social diplomas that would lead to jobs related to care. On the other hand, schools participated in the women's emancipation movement throughout the twentieth century; the development of education favoured and explains the fall in fertility rates and the expansion of salaried female activity.

During the period of economic growth, a host of new jobs that seemed to correspond particularly with female qualities were opened in the tertiary sector, e.g., teaching, social work, health, and tourism. Economic progress was immediately visible in the home, which was now equipped with modern electric appliances to facilitate domestic work, first and foremost the washing machines that were to rescue women from the chores of the boiler. Less time was required for homemaking. Women entered the job market at a rapid pace and the Parsonian family model was shaken by the new status women had gained within a short space of time.

The feminist movement, which was never as strong as in the United States, was nevertheless highly influential in its cry for freedom in the wake of the student movement of 1968. Freedom from marriage (in the feminist argument, husbands exploited their wives with domestic work), freedom from unwanted pregnancies, freedom for themselves. New methods of contraception were developed, which, for the first time in the history of mankind, placed the decision of when and with whom they would have children entirely in the hands of the women themselves. Along with the important body of new laws establishing equality among the couple, a law was passed on freedom of contraception (lois Neuwirth 1967, 1974) and subsequently on freedom of abortion (loi Veil 1975). New patterns of family formation emerged, accompanied by the new values of individualism and self-fulfilment.

Both laws gave new powers and autonomy to women, who could now decide alone when they wanted to procreate or to abort, without informing the father. The shift from "maternity under constraint" to "chosen maternity" brought with it a new definition of parental and gender roles. The diffusion of chemical contraception allowed for the dissociation of sex from procreation and a decision on the desired number of children. It also liberated women from the fear of unwanted pregnancy, thereby creating better sexual relations. Women were thus at the centre of the decision-making process, while men saw their control over the production of their offspring reduced. Owing to the generalization of contraceptive practices, unwanted births are now more rare. Modern contraception is therefore "a factor in the nuptiality decline because sexuality and child conception are easily separated" (Daguet 1995, 9). Contraception or fertility control makes it possible to eliminate risk in prenuptial sex. Cohabitation before marriage no longer implies unwanted pregnancy. Sex and procreation have become separate issues, enabling a discussion on "free love for women" – women who can lead a "boy's life" (Knibielher 1991, 81–82).

However, contrary to certain feminist ideas, mainly those of Simone de Beauvoir, who considered that maternity was a constraint on female freedom, French women continue to combine having children with employment. In contrast to other European states, there is very little childlessness in France. The parallel between the extension of contraception and of female employment we have witnessed comes as no surprise. Women's return to the job market is inscribed in a context of changing fertility behaviour – late and less numerous births that occupy a shorter sequence in the life cycle, and leave room for salaried activity.

The upturn in cultural values regarding the "working mother" has been quite striking. In the 1960s, having one's child taken care of in a "crèche" was considered detrimental to the child, who was seen as abandoned; the mother was pitied because poverty had forced her to work; the word "crèche" carried a distinct connotation of charity. Twenty years later, women were desperately looking for more openings in child-care institutions, convinced that the child's socialization would benefit from this collective structure. In France, a working mother is not considered a bad mother, although working women always bear some sort of guilt, which is one explanation for their secondary employment positions and salaries compared to men. Today, the working mother is a "normal" model.

The French labour market is characterized by the presence of mothers of young children: in 2003, more than 80 per cent of women with a child under three, for example, were working. In 1982, for the first time, the number of double-income couples was far more significant than the number of couples where only the husband worked. The expansion of the bi-active couple has several consequences for the family and the public sphere. The temporalities between work and family have shifted, for example, and any free time after work, in the evenings or on holidays is devoted to children (Thery 1998, 45).

The high female activity rate indicates a change in the familial model.

> "From now on, the dominant model was neither one of choice (work or family), nor of alternation (to work – to stop – to go back to work), but a combination of both. Besides, it is this change in the social norms of familial activity that has allowed the growth of a totally active population: in the last thirty years, the only category in France to show an increase in activity rates is the current twenty-five to forty-nine-year-old female category" (Maruani 1996, 231).

This growing participation of women in the labour market is partly the result of a family policy development that began in the 1970s and integrated the model of the working mother (essentially in the context of child care for young children). Besides, the educational policy provides schooling for all children aged three in kindergartens. The idea that policies in support of working mothers are the best method of promoting fertility has now been widely accepted.

Although the cultural changes with regard to women in the private and public domain are striking and are accompanied by a shift in the position of the fathers, who are now closer to their children than was the case in the patriarchal model, it is obvious, as sociologist William Goode stated a long time ago, that "men resist" (1981). This resistance is revealed in the organization of large competitive private companies, where working hours extend far beyond the time when children return from school, and is one reason why educated professional women hit the "glass ceiling" and cannot reach higher paid jobs. At home, things are not much better. All surveys show that, contrary to what the feminist movement had striven for and expected in the 1970s, men do not perform a great deal more domestic tasks, leaving their wives to manage the double life of working and mothering.

The new cultural values that have developed in France concern first and foremost the status of women within the family and society. They clash with the family values of the most recent waves of Muslim immigrants, where the position of women is secondary to that of men. The recent eruption of violence in the French suburbs of our cities has once again brought to the forefront the question of the "family crisis". The mix of poverty and disacculturation, the shock between the western Judaeo-Christian family culture and that of the Maghrebians or Africans has been identified as one of the causes of this violence.

Family and kinship

Discovering family networks

In the past, the family was the only recourse for its most vulnerable members, i.e., children, the elderly and the infirm. With the extension of state provisions, it was believed that the welfare state was there to provide for social needs, substituting former family relations. Up to the 1990s, sociology focused on the change in family structures and cultures, leaving aside the question of family ties. Anthropologists discussed kinship at length but the concept seemed, in so-called modern countries, to be irrelevant. Not only was the thesis of the nuclear family undisputed, but in a context of freedom and individualism it seemed improper to discuss assistance from the family, since everyone was deemed to be independent. However, research devoted to housing proved, as a side effect, the vitality of family ties in the 1950s, when a vast number of married parents and children were forced to share an apartment due to a shortage of housing. The importance of kinship, as demonstrated by anthropology in its diverse models (see supra) became visible and ideologically acceptable, with the set-back of Marxism.

The 1960s and 1970s brought a shift in the relative situation of the generations. Due to retirement pensions, and family and housing allowances, the elderly were no longer dependent on their children in old age and were even able to help them, a new situation that considerably modified the context of kinship and mutual support. Several pioneer works, notably by Louis Roussel (1976), began to demonstrate the importance of exchanges between the generations, discussing new forms of help given to children. Although the family had undergone radical change and each partner earned a salary, parental solidarity was strong, despite new-found residential independence. Dowries were no longer bestowed at marriage (especially since children were under no obligation to marry), but throughout the life cycle, money was given to children and help provided at various life stages (moving out, becoming a couple, possibly getting married, having children). The survey carried out in 1970 indicated that geographic propinquity was still significant: 75 per cent of all children's households are no further than twenty kilometres away from those of their parents. This is a key factor in explaining the density of exchanges and is a direct consequence of the strategies of married children to reside close to their parents. The survey concentrated on frequency of meeting and contact, and endeavoured to evaluate the importance of descending financial flows.

A subsequent survey by Agnès Pitrou (1977) stressed the different uses of family contact in the various social groups; in the higher social strata contacts are a means of promoting children ("aide de promotion"), whereas in the lower strata, they rather serve to "maintain" ("aide de subsistence") them. These differences have been confirmed by more recent surveys.

Pioneer works of this kind stated for the first time what has since been repeatedly observed, i.e., when young couples are independent, frequent contact and exchanges are deliberate. Sociologists stress that autonomy is at the risk of being sacrificed when gifts in the form of money or goods are accepted from parents who attempt to hold on to their children and nurture possessive afterthoughts. However, given the stability of kin relationship patterns, each generation seems to have learnt to keep to its boundaries. Today the model is that of "distant solidarity" which, without co-residence, enables numerous exchanges and services.

In the 1980s, the trend of research devoted to KASS, opened by Roussel, Pitrou and several others, remained without successors, while sociologists dealt at length with the changes taking place in marriage, divorce, companionship or fertility. They furthermore explored the effects of individualism, which were measured along with the growing independence of women: prolific research focused on women at work, leaving the kindred out of the picture. It was not until the end of the 1990s, with the threat of diminishing pensions and the doom of ageing populations, that work on KASS began to flourish.

Research has shown that family ties become more close-knit when families can rely on public resources, which are in turn refuelled on the family circuit. This explains why millions of people take to the streets when governments change the rules for pension systems or medical care.

A survey conducted in two steps, 1992 (quantitative) and 1995 (qualitative), based on three-generational families pointed to the importance of transfers between generations and the links between private and public solidarities (Attias-Donfut and Segalen 1998). It was demonstrated that money gifts flow downwards, whereas services are granted equally between the three generations. Among the most vital services produced among kin are those for the old generation. Fifty per cent of this generation receive some form of regular help from someone in their family. However, eighty-four per cent of them suffer from impaired health and thus cannot carry out life's daily chores.

Family solidarity intervenes in periods where dependence risks are greatest, i.e., entry into adult life and in the course of old age. Intergenerational exchanges can occur over three, or even four, generations.

Up to the 1960s, generations succeeded one another, whereas today they overlap. The coexistence of successive generations is accompanied by a greater intensity of exchanges, long underestimated, but now rediscovered. All surveys underline that intergenerational exchanges and solidarity are firstly vertical, concern blood relations, are matrilineal, and polarized over the middle generation. The most striking social phenomenon is thus the emergence of this "pivot" generation, which is intermediary to the younger and the older generations. Thirty-two per cent of the pivot generation (6.6 per cent of the young) provide support for the elderly in their family who are handicapped to a certain degree. Half of the men and women over seventy benefit from support that comes from the family circle: 21.6 per cent of men resort to their spouses, and 27 per cent to their offspring; 6.7 per cent of women are looked after by their spouses, and 40 per cent by their offspring. In three-quarters of the cases, it is women who provide care: a daughter (63 per cent of cases) or a daughter-in-law (nine per cent).

Catherine Bonvalet has coined the word "famille-entourage" (2003) to describe the fact that, in 30 per cent of all households, couples living in the same city as one of their parents have contact with them at least once a week and frequent service exchanges; however, 17 per cent of households who do not reside in close proximity still maintain strong relationships. It is as though several residences become akin to what is known in West Africa, for instance, as a "compound".

Marriage break-ups impact on intergenerational relations, e.g., when couples separate. Unlike on the mother's side in the case of separation, the relationship of the father is less intense with the children than when parents are still married. Relations with parents, children and grandchildren tend to become weaker when separation or divorce is followed by a new union than when this does not occur (women who are divorced or separated are more involved with the children of their previous union than men). Kin relationships frequently play the role of safety net after a young couple separate. Contrary to the ideology associated with the emergence of the "individual" and its seeming opposition to kinship ties, it is precisely the strength of these ties that permits individualism.

Help with housing

Help can also be related to house purchasing and intergenerational support plays a significant role in the development of home ownership. Claudine Attias-Donfut states that:

> "The observation of this support, generation after generation, shows that it is not new, since 43% of the older generation benefited from a family contribution and, if we only consider home owners [...], 80% received family help in purchasing their property, which essentially came from the ascendants in the form of direct help, donations or inheritance [...] Pivots personally contributed more to the purchase of their property than the other two generations. 50% of owners did not receive help from their family. The development of property in the pivot generation was encouraged by credit facilities, inflation and several public measures. Among young people, 76% of owners benefited from family allowances, for the most part from ascendant generations, especially parents or parents-in-law, followed by grandparents. Families not only help in the case of home ownership. Numerous gifts are made to non-owners, such as accommodation, housing at their disposal or help with the rent. Young people are huge beneficiaries. 34% of tenants have been helped in one way or another, 4% occupy a house owned by their parents. In total, 44% of young people who left home have benefited from some sort of support" (Attias-Donfut 1995, 75–76).

These varied contributions to housing are complemented by inheritances and donations that help the younger generation to access home ownership.

Monetary exchanges

Money flows downwards, from pivots to young people, or, skipping a generation, from the oldest to the youngest, whereby the stronger the ties, the more frequent the financial gifts. In 1990, 70 per cent of French people said they had been financially supported by their parents. The increase in retirement pensions improved the status of the elderly within the family, and was subsequently expressed in the form of valuable gifts to their children and grandchildren:

> "Private transfers between generations circulate in the opposite direction to public transfers orchestrated by the pension system. The initial hypothesis of the presence of a circular mecanism between these two circuits is at the same time confirmed by the financial flows between elderly retirees and their children and, skipping a generation, between grandparents and adult grandchildren involved in the working world. Savings owned by the elderly as a result of retirement pensions situates them in the position of suppliers to their children and their grandchildren, even when their incomes are low" (Attias-Donfut 1995, 79).

The elderly give money most often to the young with very low incomes (students or young people out of work); the frequency of these gifts is independent of the recipients' needs. On the whole, the propensity to give money does not vary according to income, since the gift itself is a practice unrelated to income (with the exception of those whose income is below the old-age minimum, preventing them from giving more often). Gifts extended to pivots, however, are more dependent on income. The circulation of money takes place among the more privileged when the oldest generation makes a gift to the pivot generation. Here when pivots give money to young people, on the other hand, the contribution has a more utilitarian value. Beneficiaries are often unemployed or have very low incomes. Irène Théry has remarked that a good relationship between young people and their parents is crucial (Théry 1998). Young people who do not get on with their parents are helped less often during the year of their departure from home: among young men without a stable job, 54 per cent of whose who do not get on well with their parents and 68 per cent of those who do, receive financial support from their parents (52 per cent and 74 per cent respectively for young women).

It should be noted that when parents have a house and a vegetable garden, the produce becomes the object of numerous gifts to their children; in this form of family solidarity, the family network takes on the guise of an underground economy. Finally, family networks also come into play in the working world, where many young people find their first jobs as a result of the network of kinship ties.

The consequences of increased life expectancy and the overlapping of generations has radically altered the nature of inheritance, as described earlier, which no longer occurs at a given time, as in the past, i.e., after the parents' death; nowadays, it is distributed along the life cycle, e.g., to finance university studies, to provide support when a couple marry or cohabit or on the occasion of births. Families now generally inherit from their parents at an age close to retirement and at a time when their own children are settling down.

Grandparenting

At the macro-economic level, compensatory transfers between generations are an expression of family support. Since the elderly have become financially independent, their children do not have to support or accommodate them. Contrary to their dependent status in the past, grandparents have now become the suppliers of their descendants. For the latter, involved in professional life, the pension system represents a twofold gain: they do not have to worry about their own old age or that of their parents, since they are protected by retirement provisions. The economic effort can then be concentrated on helping their children and/or the constitution of a patrimony they can transmit.

> "Retirement has thus favoured the reorientation of family solidarities towards young people, acting indirectly in the same way as family allowances, explicitly intended for children [...] Public and obligatory provisions produce a social link between generations. Their complementarity with private solidarities reinforces their function of redistribution and of social cohesion within family lines" (Attias-Donfut and Segalen 1998).

Parents support their adult children in the domestic, social, professional and economic fields: they make gifts in kind or in cash, provide several services, or help them finance their housing. However, once children become parents, they call on their own parents less often, receive less gifts, money and services in the domestic field, and, conversely, young parents provide less services to "pivots". However, the involvement of parents with married children does not weaken, but instead takes the form of grandparenting.

People now enter old age in stages. As mentioned earlier, a novel generation emerged in the 1980s, i.e., the "seniors", whose members are characterized by their vitality, financial stability and good health. A contemporary social person was born, active and rich in resources for the latest generations, first and foremost their performance in the grandparent role. They can be seen accompanying their grandchildren to public gardens, to the cinema, to leisure parks or to school. In 1999, France had 12.4 million grandparents, including two million great-grandparents, with an average of four grandchildren. The distinguishing feature of these grandparents is an infinitely greater participation in the lives of their families than was the case in previous generations, and the devotion of more time and money to their grandchildren. These new intergenerational ties have never been so strong. Claudine Attias-Donfut underlines the impact of higher pensions on the status of the elderly:

> "The increase in retirement pensions has revalorized the status of the elderly in the family, which finds its expression in valuable gifts to children and grandchildren, which in turn sustain the cycle of reciprocity. Today, the intrafamilial redistribution of public benefits is an integral part of the exchange dynamics between the generations and in family relationships" (Attias-Donfut 1995, 23).

These powerful new bonds with grandparents ensued for the most part from the recent valorization of affective ties in our society. The strong emotional links that exist today between grandparents and their grandchildren are at the heart of intergenerational relations. The parent-child link is composed of mutual rights and duties, while the grandparent/grandchild link is free of such obligations. Young grandparents (especially grandmothers) have a closer bond with their children than their parents, and contrary to the latter in their time, have adopted a more liberal attitude towards their children. The reflux of permissive models from the 1960s, the difficulties of the economic context and the necessary constraints imposed on children when parents want to obtain school results all define the relations between parents and children differently. Our time is characterized by the existence of a vigorous intergenerational link that contrasts with the frailty of the union.

Care of grandchildren is a vital service parents provide to their children. It is inscribed in a wider scope of intergenerational solidarities but is also one of the care solutions that parents resort to in association with other social forms. Despite the importance of public child care, child care provided by grandparents is highly developed. Grandparents do not take care of their children's offspring on a daily basis, but rather at weekends, during the holidays or in the case of a family crisis (e.g., illness, divorce). Almost one out of every two in the pivot generation takes care of grandchildren at weekends or in the holidays. If we exclude cases where grandchildren are still too young to be taken care of by grandparents, 74 per cent of grandparents are host to a grandchild during the holidays, 68 per cent outside the holidays and, in sum, 82 per cent take care of them on a daily basis or during the holidays. 37.5 per cent would like to be involved more often.

Elderly care

When the public care system and the medicalization of old age were in the process of development, health-related services within the family were overlooked, depriving families and individuals of the opportunity to acquire disease management skills. "This amplification has led to a form of 'hospital-centrism', the immediate consequence of which was the denial of family competences regarding health, even in the less significant and non-technical acts of daily hygiene" (Bungener 1993, 29–30).

Since the 1980s, with the growth of the economic crisis and evidence of the ageing process, family care in relation to services provided by the state has been rehabilitated: there was a shift from hospital to home care. Family solidarities were thus publicly revalorized in the context of difficult financial circumstances and the criticism of hospital-centrism. Allowances for the elderly are now considered normal. Public solidarity has not generated the disappearance of private mutual aid, but complements it instead, and care of grandchildren has not made elderly care superfluous. For instance, 47 per cent of those who take care of their grandchildren every week are also involved in looking after parents.

The macro-economy of KASS

On the European scene, French families stand out with several specificities, as mentioned above: very little childlessness, a working mother model sustained by strong policies, and competition between informal unions and marriage. These characteristics can easily be measured statistically, unlike the case of family ties, which are less simple to express in figures.

The availability of the family seems to be universal in France, albeit in relation to the income level of the family members prepared to help, i.e., the central couple (referred to as "pivots" in a three-generational survey). An assessment of the importance of kin networks in all social categories shows considerable diversity. For the wealthiest, independence is the rule, and exchanges and support sustain the goal of social reproduction; for the poorest, help takes shape within the extended family so that services and help can be exchanged on a much more frequent basis. Even individuals who benefit from RMI (Revenu minimum d'insertion allocated to resourceless persons) are caught in this network, where gifts in money are infrequent, but those in the form of goods (food, clothes) are a staple. In the modest social groups, the availabilility of family is directly associated with residential propinquity and surveys have shown that most families develop strategies to remain close to parents, even in urban environments such as Besançon and Nanterre (see Volume II).

The stability of family and kin will be looked at in the following in relation to habitat and housing strategies. When divorce was limited, the regular family trajectory was to start by renting an apartment, the ultimate goal being to attain ownership of a house, which symbolized family stability and material success. Fifty-seven percent of French households now live in privately owned houses, either suburban houses, or houses located in recently built private housing developments. The tight link between privately owned houses and nuclear families has been constantly supported by public policies. A stable model, it has been seriously challenged by new family forms that include living as solitaries who rent small apartments, monoparental families that turn to social housing and blended families that juggle with living space depending on the number of offspring. Family instability is reflected in the instability of residential trajectories. Coupled with job insecurity, this situation draws up a new map in relation to housing. Access to property is more expensive, on the one hand, and is not secure for the rest of people's lives, given family reconfigurations. Inasmuch as habitat reflects family practices, it is obvious that we are far from the stable model of the 1960s: the new model requires more fluidity on the housing market, and a larger number of apartments to rent.

It has been shown, and our ethnographic data confirms this result (see Augustins and Sourdril, Chevalier and Amiotte-Suchet, Segalen and Manceron, forthcoming), that family and kin stability revolves around the secondary homes that are characteristic of the French housing situation. This is where grandparenting comes in, 38 per cent of couples with grandchildren, as against 33 per cent of those without, own such a house, a meeting point for parents, grandparents and grandchildren. It is this house that plays a key role in creating kinship network ties, constructing common memories among cousins. At the macro-economic level, however, this service exchange and financial support has no redistributive effect, which means that it does not further social equity. It has a compensatory effect within the lines, digging distance between the well-off and the less well-off, without compensating for the differences.

Moreover, some recent ethnographic observations seem to show that, as previously stated, the traditional organization of the family in rural areas still has a bearing on the forms of mutual support undertaken by the networks. More precisely, it can be argued that, in areas where the stem family prevailed, networks were mostly organized on the principle of reciprocal help between neighbours, whereas in areas with the parentela system the same networks tended to select relations within the kinship. What seems to be at stake in all cases is the local conception of reliability, more precisely those who can be relied upon are those who were traditionally thought of as close: first neighbours in the house-oriented system (as exemplified in the case of the South-West France, see Volume II), cousins in the parentela system.

Nevertheless, the rediscovery of kinship and kinship ties has nothing to do with "tradition" or "traditional society". They are a strong component of twenty-first century society and a sound basis for stability, an aspect that becomes all the more obvious against the backdrop of the negative consequences involved for those deprived of them (SDF [sans domicile fixe], or children of broken migrant families). Public and private support appear inseparable and not mutually exclusive. To reduce public allowances would lead to a weakening of private support and make families more dependent, while the transfer of expenses to families in order to solve social and financial problems is pure illusion.

Bibliography

Attias-Donfut, C. (ed.) (1995), *Les solidarités entre générations: Vieillesse, famille*, Etat, Paris: Nathan.

Attias-Donfut, C. and M. Segalen (1998), *Grands-parents. La famille à travers les générations*, Paris: Odile Jacob.

Bonvalet, C. (2003), "La famille-entourage locale", *Population*, pp. 9–44.

Bungener, M. (1993), "France. Familles et alternative à l'hospitalisation", in F. Lesemann and M. Claude (eds.), *Les personnes âgées*, Paris: La documentation française, pp. 27–51.

Chesnais, J.-C. (1988), "La politique de population française depuis 1914", *Histoire de la population française. 4, De 1914 à nos jours, Paris, PUF*, pp. 181–228.

Cheysson, C. (2003), "La famille devant la loi et les mœurs", discours prononcé le 11 janvier 1901 à la Société d'Economie Sociale, in Rémi Lenoir, *Généalogie de la morale familiale*, Paris: Seuil, p. 74.

Commaille, J. (1994), "France: d'une politique de la famille à des politiques envers la famille", in W. Dumon (ed.), *Evolution des politiques familiales dans les états membres de l'Union Européenne.*

Daguet, F. (1995), *Un siècle de démographie française. Structure et évolution de la population de 1901 à 1993*, INSEE.

Goode, W. (1981), "Why men resist", in B. Thorne and Marilyn Yalom (eds.), *Rethinking the family*, New York: Longman, pp. 131–150.

Gossiaux, J.-F. (1992), *Avoir seize ans dans les Ardennes*, Paris: Editions du CTHS.

Klimrath, H. (1843), *Travaux sur l'histoire du droit français Paris*, Joubert, Strasbourg: Levrault.

Knibielher, Y. (1991), "Le célibat. Approche historique", in F. de Singly (ed.), *La famille, l'état des savoirs*, Paris: La Découverte, pp. 81–82.

Maruani, M. (1996), "Anciens clivages, nouveaux partages", in F. de Singly et al., *La famille en question*, Paris: Syros.

Mendras, H. (1994), *La seconde révolution française 1965–1984*, Paris: Gallimard.

Pitrou, A. (1977), "Le soutien familial dans la société urbaine", *Revue française de sociologie, XVIII*, pp. 47–84.

Roussel, L. (1976), *La famille après le mariage des enfants, Travaux et documents*, Cahier n. 78, Paris: Presses Universitaires de France.

Segalen, M. (2006), *Sociologie de la famille, 6e édition*, Paris: Armand Colin.

Simpson, B. (1994), Bringing "unclear" family into focus: divorce and re-marriage in contemporary Britain, *Journal of the Royal Anthropological Institute 29*, pp. 831–851.

Thery, I. (1998), *Couple, filiation et parenté. Le droit face aux mutations de la famille et de la vie privée*, Paris: Odile Jacob-La documentation française.

Yver, J. (1966), Egalité entre héritiers et exclusion des enfants dotés; essai de géographie coutumière, Paris: Sirey.

Filling gaps in social security: family and kinship ties in Austria

Johannes Pflegerl and Christine Geserick

Chronology of the welfare state

The following analysis will shed light on the key welfare state developments and their effects on the embedding of family and kin in a social insurance system. The chronology is segmented into eleven phases (see figure 6.1) that describe the emergence of the welfare state in the 1860s up until the situation at the end of the twentieth century.

Figure 6.1: Chronology of the welfare state – eleven phases

Source: Pflegerl and Geserick 2007, 115

The development of the Welfare State in Austria from the 1860s to 1945

The first Austrian social policy measures were introduced between 1860 and 1880 (Reichsgemeindegesetz 1862 and Reichsheimatgesetz 1863), imposing the obligation on the municipality to provide poor relief to people in distress, although the intention behind it was to prevent revolts rather than to fight poverty. Relief was organized along the lines of subsidiarity, i.e., the municipality took over responsibility when no family members, relatives, other persons or private organizations were available to intercede. These first steps were significant for Austria insofar as they laid the foundation for a second safety net ("social assistance"), which is still in place today and based on the principle of subsidiarity. It is notable that to this day, social security is granted only after it has been identified that assistance from existing family or kinship resources is not forthcoming.

Towards the end of the nineteenth century, several pivotal steps (introduction of accident insurance in 1887 and obligatory health insurance in 1888) were undertaken towards establishing Austria as a welfare state, in a period often referred to as its "take-off phase" (Tálos 1981, 14). For the first time, these measures provided state protection in the case of accident or illness for certain sections of the population, specifically the growing number of wage earners, regardless of whether they had access to family or kinship resources. Features that were to emerge later in the welfare state concerned benefits organized along the compulsory insurance principle, with entitlements linked to gainful employment. Hence benefits were financed by the contributions of the insured and their employers. In this sense Austria chose a regime that would fundamentally shape its long-term character, i.e., a social security scheme for the gainfully employed linked to status and its preservation rather than a system that provided basic social security (Tálos and Wörister 1994, 16). The nature of the Austrian welfare state, later described as "corporatist" by Esping-Anderson (1990) in his comparative analysis of industrial welfare states, was already visible in these origins.

Welfare benefits expanded rapidly from the end of the First World War to the early 1920s, allowing us to speak of the "first expansion of the welfare state". In the social insurance sector, the establishment of an unemployment insurance scheme in 1920 is among the key achievements of this period. Furthermore, the health insurance scheme extended to all those in an employment relationship and their families. In the late 1920s, when a weak economy led to mounting unemployment, the social security system began to deteriorate into a crisis. This caused the authoritarian Austrofascist regime that had come to power in the 1930s to make massive cuts in welfare benefits. As a result, many were forced to resort to family and kin resources, and to subsistence traditions in order to cope with the distress. Family and kin once again stepped in to fill the gap left by the withdrawal of the state from the delivery of already established social security. Ancient forms of survival were revived, such as cultivating gardens and fields, keeping cattle even in the immediate surroundings of the cities and selling homegrown products or, for example, second-hand clothes, furniture or tools. Here, all the members of the family were integrated in accordance with their age-dependent capacities. Kin networks were crucial in the search for short-term casual labour (Sieder 1987, 226).

When the National Socialists took over in 1938, they aimed to improve these circumstances with targeted economic and social policy measures. Benefits curtailed during the Austrofascist period were for the most part re-extended. The ulterior motive was to mobilize the labour so urgently needed to boost productivity in the armaments industry. Growing social security and the availability of a wider range of consumer goods appear to have relieved, at least in the short term, some of the burden of social protection placed on family and kin, and to have stabilized family life. With the war, however, measures to exploit the labour force were intensified; the drive was on to achieve "total deployment" and social policy measures were markedly curtailed once again. More and more, families were to suffer the consequences of war.

The post-war reconstruction, golden age and final expansion of the welfare state (1945–1983)

Immediately after the Second World War, in the mid- and late 1940s, social policy measures focused on provision for the victims of war and of Nazi persecution. Family measures concentrated on post-war reconstruction in the form of allowances and tax breaks on subsistence provision. Hence in the 1950s, family policies took a different direction. The compensation policy in favour of the poorer sections of the population was replaced by a concept of overall burden equalization at societal level, in line with population, family and social policy objectives:

- Parents were to be enabled to meet their maintenance obligation vis-à-vis their children (maintenance argument)
- The distress caused by the need to meet maintenance obligations for children was to be alleviated (socio-political argument)
- Wages were to be set to account for families, calculated not on performance alone but also on the workers' social situation (family policy argument)

– Maintenance and increase of population figures was to be encouraged at the material level (see also Münz 1985, 175)

The period between 1955 and 1970 could be characterized as the "golden age" of the Austrian welfare state (Tálos and Wörister 1994). Measures for its expansion were intensified as a result of positive economic developments. Enlargement and expansion characterized the relevant sectors of social policy; particularly the social insurance system, which obtained its growth momentum from the General Social Insurance Act adopted in 1955, was to undergo constant expansion in the succeeding decades.

A key factor was the continuous expansion of compulsory insurance coverage in all sectors, the aim of which was to encompass all of the gainfully employed, including the self-employed, farmers, and freelance professionals. In a slow process that reached into the 1970s, each of these groups was drawn into the health, accident and old-age pension insurance systems. With this, the goal of extending social security to the gainfully employed was to a great extent achieved. At the same time, the number of people covered indirectly, specifically including family members with no insurance coverage of their own and entitled survivors, increased parallel. On the other hand, this development made it possible at a structural level to gradually (but never fully) relieve the family and kin of the burden of providing social protection against the risks of old age, unemployment, disability, illness and accidents. This type of health insurance permitted universal coverage by including family members, beneficiaries of old-age pensions and social assistance, and the unemployed. Nevertheless, no effort was made to provide a comprehensive basic insurance that would have relieved the family completely of social security responsibilities: social insurance measures continued to be tied to gainful employment. At the same time, the underlying nature of the social security system as one tied to status and its preservation and set out in its first phase of expansion, remained intact, as did the principle of subsidiarity with regard to state benefits. Thus the family continued to play a key role when it came to minimum protection, and remained principally responsible for child and elder care (Tálos and Wörister 1994, 243). In the 1970s, when the Social Democratic Party came into power, welfare state benefits were broadened for the last time, now in line with the principles of Social Democratic politics, so that this phase can be labelled the final expansion of the welfare state.

Consolidation and makeover of the welfare state (1983–today)

In the course of the 1980s, the economic setting of the welfare state gradually, albeit noticeably, shifted away from the conditions that prevailed in the post-war decades. Unemployment soared as a result of a prolonged cyclical downturn, eroding standard jobs in the process. The attendant shortfall in contributors and a growing number of retirees generated financial problems in the social insurance system, especially in the old-age pension sector. As a result, benefits were cut for the first time since World War II. The sole area exempt from this contraction was long-term care, for which a tax-financed benefit was introduced.

The trend accelerated in the 1990s, fuelled by globalization and the pressure of increased competion. The welfare state was confronted with the stark dilemma of having to cope with growing problems and declining resources. The gap between revenues from contributions and expenditures widened, and financial problems not only arose in old-age pension insurance but also in the health insurance. The response with regard to social policy was to step up adjustments. Since 2000, a wave of change has swept through all social policy sectors, in the face of stiff resistance from certain sections of the public. Pensions, unemployment benefits and health insurance experienced (in part massive) cutbacks. Family policy, on the other hand, ran counter to the previous trend by introducing child-care benefits, which constituted a substantial extension of family policy benefits. This new trend increasingly cut into the dominance of risk coverage traditionally provided by the state and questioned the status-securing principle of social welfare measures. Today, it appears that private provision and the need to draw on family resources, factors that had been of only minor importance in Austria since World War II, have once again come to the fore as instruments to be used in covering social risk. It appears to be the current objective to convert the risk-balancing welfare state into a more liberal version, where risk-sharing based on solidarity in the case of illness, old age, unemployment and accident does not extend to the entire population of the gainfully employed. Instead, state subsidies are to specifically target the deserving needy and disadvantaged (Rosenberger and Schmid 2003). In structural terms, this development aims at the privatization and individualization of social security.

Chronology of family change

Family formation in Austria in historical perspective

Up to the beginning of the twentieth century, most of the Austrian regions were shaped by agriculture. Rural structures had a considerable impact on family formation, which was specifically characterized by late marriage. In the inner alpine regions stretching from the south of lower and upper Austria to Vorarlberg in the far west of Austria in particular, only a certain section of the male population was married at the turn of the twentieth century (Ehmer 1991; Ortmayr 1995). Even in the Austrian regions north, south and east of the Alps, the number of single males exceeded that of other European regions. These trends can be explained primarily by the specific structure of property ownership and the organization of labour. In this context Mitterauer (1986) distinguished for Austria four different rural milieus that shape the process of family formation and the development of family structures: the inner alpine regions dominated by cattle breeding, the lowland regions dominated by grain cultivation, regions at the foothills of the Alps in the east, northeast and southeast of Austria dominated by vine-growing, and the regions in the far west and the north of Austria characterized by early forms of the housing industry. Despite the apparent differences between these regions, the opportunity to marry was mostly confined to that part of the population in possession of property in the form of farms, for example, and small rural estates and vineyards. There was a heavy demand for labour in the inner alpine regions in particular, since the labour required for specific forms of cattle-breeding exceeded the capacity of the family. It was therefore necessary to affiliate servants, who played a significant role in the domain of husbandry in this area. They were not allowed to marry before acquiring property of their own. Because farms in these regions were passed on in their entirety to a single heir, the remaining children in the family were obliged to move to other farms and work there as servants, the majority for the rest of their lives. As a result, they remained single. This practice led in turn to a large number of illegitimate births in these regions. In contrast, the lowland regions, which were characterized by grain cultivation, did not require servants to the same extent, as small farms were the dominant feature, with the exception of several big farms in some of the regions in the northern foothills of the Alps. Since rural property was more equally diversified, opportunities for family formation were less confined than in the alpine regions (Grandits 2007).

On the other hand, most of the non-farming population was made up of people in trade and small businesses. Workers tended to be apprentices and journeymen who lived in their masters' households and were thus precluded from marrying and establishing a household of their own. The situation for industrial workers was quite different, where marriage and setting up household was a defining moment. Nevertheless, at the dawn of the industrial age, early marriage was rare, not least as a result of migration, the high mobility of workers and the shortage of women in the new industrial centres. It was only when industrialization was at its peak and wage-based industrial work had become widespread that the marriage rate among workers began to rise. Skilled workers occupied in the innovative toolmaking and engineering sectors were the first to experience improved opportunities to marry and start a family (Ehmer 1980, 177f.; Ehmer 1991, 121f.).

On the whole, the process of industrialization had a profound impact on family formation in Austria. With the increase in life expectancy and the gradual abolition of economic, social and legal barriers to marriage, more and more people got married and raised children – a reversal of the earlier situation described above. Social change and the modernization of family relationships were mainly driven by the diminishing numbers of self-sufficient farm households and small trades. Countless farmers, (maid)servants, companions and homeworkers became wage earners, and with their new status saw the opportunity to marry and have children (see Münz 1985, 4ff.).

Household structure

Looking at the twentieth century from a longitudinal angle, we see that the number of private households has exploded while at the same time the average household size is in decline. The shift in household structures, especially after 1945, is due among other things to changing age structures. More and more people are getting older and, once their children have moved out, experience a longer phase of life as couples or, after the death of a partner, as singles. Another reason for the contraction of the household size, which has progressed even more rapidly since the 1970s, is the result of changes in family formation and processes of dissolution. Particularly among younger adults, we find a noticeable reduction in household sizes, and households get markedly smaller during the post-adolescent and young adult stages. Apart from smaller families after the baby boom of the 1960s, this can be explained by the severing of the link with the parental home and moving in with a partner, as well as in the growing instability of relationships. Added to this is the marked reduction in the number of more complex family households frequently found in the farming and small commercial context in earlier periods, and which today make up a minuscule percentage of households. Nevertheless, there is still an unmistakable divide between urban and rural life. Complex households are still found more often in rural, heavily farmed regions than in cities, where they have virtually disappeared. One factor in this development is the distinct decline in the number of households that includes a parent of the older generation. Occupational groups similarly show some obvious differences: almost 30 per cent of all civil servants and those working in the services sector are meanwhile living in one-person households, a household category that is still rare in the farming and forestry environment. Conversely, almost a quarter of the latter group still live in households of six or more persons. Altogether, household structures in Austria show a distinct change, which extends to all sections of the population. Despite the few residual incidences of more complex household types in the rural areas, the trend towards reduced household sizes has now begun to spread to these pockets.

Changes in life courses and the sequence of key events

In the course of the twentieth century, pivotal changes took place in several key events, such as the age of first marriage, the duration of marriage and the age of widowhood. Looking at "the big picture", it can be stated that the 1970s mark a peak and transition period for the changing of life-course events. These central changes will be analysed in the following, based on the generational mortality charts for men and women born between 1870 and 1948 (Bundeskanzleramt 1979).

The multigenerational family was already a widespread phenomenon in the 1970s. Never before had so many generations lived at the same time as during this period. A woman could expect not merely to see her daughter get married, but perhaps even to survive until her great-grandchild's first year at school. The principal reason for this was the decline in secular mortality. The reduction in the actual reproductive period up to the first years of marriage and the low age of first marriage, on the other hand, played only a minor role (Bundeskanzleramt 1979, 79). Concrete statistics indicate, e.g., that the duration of marriages was now longer. Men born in 1870 and women born in 1873 could be expected to be married for an average of twenty-three years; for men born in 1946 and women born in 1948, this value almost doubled, to an average of forty-three years. At the same time the mean age for widowers rose from just under fifty-seven to sixty-eight in men born in 1870 and 1946 respectively, with figures for women rising from fifty-six (for those born in 1873) to sixty-five (women born in 1948). At the same time, the mean age of first marriage among these two cohorts fell by six years: from thirty to twenty-four years of age among men, and from twenty-eight to twenty-two among women. Furthermore, life expectancy on becoming a widow/er rose substantially – for men who survive their wives, from seventy-four to almost eighty years of age, and for women who survive their husbands from seventy-six to eighty-three (Gisser et al. 1990, 91f.)

From the 1970s onwards, however, both the age of first marriage as well as the age at which mothers first give birth took an upward curve again, thereby counteracting the former trend. Calculations for the year 2000 clearly point to a decline in the probability that several generations will live together for a longer period, the result of an increase in the age of first marriage and first birth. If current birthing behaviour is projected, today's generations are, at least in theory, still likely to see the birth of their first great-grandchild, but somewhat less likely to survive until the marriage of their first granddaughter (Bundeskanzleramt 1979, 79).

Intergenerational relations

Due to the ambiguity of the generational notion (Rosenmayr 2000), it should be noted that the following examination of intergenerational relations is based first and foremost on the generational notion of filiation. The discussion elucidates economic-emotional exchange processes, cooperation and strained relationships affecting grandparents, parents and children within the family (ibid.). Secondly, we will refer to Dilthey's generational notion (1875), which has a more cultural imprint and perceives generations as socio-related opponents, e.g., in terms of the "intergenerational conflict".

The first half of the twentieth century

The early twentieth century was characterized by a spatially close, but emotionally somewhat distant relationship between parents and their children. Spatial proximity primarily affected working-class families, where, as a result of unaffordable housing, parents and children were frequently obliged to share a bedroom; in numerous cases, even non-family subtenants – bed-renting lodgers ("Schlafburschen", "Bettgeher" and "Aftermieter") – slept in the same room (Sieder 1987, 199). By sharing their bed, children experienced a positive physicality with their parents, but the situation also confined the latter's sexuality. Sieder rejects the assumption that spatial restriction led to a lifting of the taboo on sexuality, i.e., that the workers acted out their sexuality freely in front of the children. On the contrary, he asserts that shame and embarrassment levels were raised precisely because of spatial proximity, and children were left on their own to deal with inevitable observations that frequently unsettled them: "Their involuntary voyeurism did not lead to open-mindedness, but rather to distorted, frequently scary images, with their father in the role of the aggressor who threatened their mother" (ibid., 200). Involuntary multigenerational spatial proximity also existed in working-class families between young couples and parents-in-law. As a rule, these three-generational families were hardship-induced communities. In the first years of their relationship, young couples were frequently impecunious and depended on the social and material support of their parents; until such time as they were able to afford their first apartment, many couples lived with their in-laws and paid for board and lodging (ibid., 209). The policies of the first Austrian Republic (1918–1933) were characterized by a focus on the "modernization of family life", with the "emotionalization of parent-child relationships" as a crucial component. With juvenile delinquency on the rise and large numbers of uncared-for children ("street children"), families were confronted with the normative request to take better care of their children (ibid., 220). Working-class women were offered courses to enlarge their skills, e.g., care of newborn babies and infants, as well as child-raising skills. However, this reform policy failed to a large extent due to working-class opposition. The growth of Austrofascism, and later National Socialism, during the 1930s and 1940s has often been explained by its ability to successfully exploit intergenerational tension as a means of winning people over, primarily adolescents who had problems coming to terms with their fathers' authority (e.g., Sieder 1987, 229; Loewenberg 1985). The Fascist/National Socialist youth groups passively undermined the authoritarian image of the father; young people had an opportunity to distinguish themselves in a non-family framework (e.g., sports groups) and experience an increase in status. Albeit in a paramilitary context, they became acquainted with egalitarian structures that stood out from their typically authoritarian family structures at home (Sieder 1987, 229ff.). During the post-war period, multigenerational cohabitation in nuclear families was substantially affected by the reintegration of homecoming fathers into everyday family life. In the latter's absence, children – in particular the younger ones – were forced to grow up without a father, and now had to get used to the presence of a father they could not even remember. Older children – mostly sons – had more often than not taken over the function of the mother's confidant, a status they now had to relinquish (Sieder 1987, 238). A further problem was the use of violence by fathers as a child-raising tool, which should be seen in relation to their experience of war (ibid.). During the 1968 Student Movement, anti-authoritarian educational patterns became the new ideal of its representatives. In 1969, the first anti-authoritarian kindergarten was established. The trend towards a less authoritarian education was also reflected in the new Federal Act of 1977, which does not expressly state a child's duty of obedience; the law prohibiting the physical castigation of children and youths (Youth Welfare Act), however, was adopted only in the 1990s.

The second half of the twentieth century

As mentioned above, from a demographical point of view, the situation that emerged in the second half of the twentieth century constituted a historical break. Several generations were alive at the same time; many elderly people got to know their great-grandchildren, even great-great-grandchildren. This had a major impact on intergenerational relations at the socio-cultural level. Despite the fact that each generation i.e., of one age cohort, is shaped by specific cultural biographic experiences, the second half of the twentieth century developed a "hitherto unknown cumulation of simultaneousness and non-simultaneousness' (Rosenmayr 2000,

236). Rosenmayr observes that in Austria (as well as in Germany), temporal non-simultaneousness of generations was typically enhanced by the refusal of the younger generation to accept the older as a cultural intermediary. This cultural drifting apart was historically founded, since the older generation was perceived by the younger as having rigid or wavering political value attitudes (e.g., before and after the Nazi period), so that their opinion-forming processes were influenced by politics and the media rather than by the older generations. Rosenmayr contrasts this with France and Italy, where national feeling was far less fractious due to different cultural and political developments (Rosenmayr 2000, 238). Exploring the current situation with regard to the transfer of cultural values, Majce (1998) surveyed the extent of concurrent opinions among parents and children on different subjects. He found considerable concurrence in value attitudes, primarily in

> "[…] areas commonly considered to be conflict topics of materialism and post-materialism: the correct behaviour towards other people, attitudes concerning diligence, punctuality, orderliness, etc., the attitude towards work, job, career; handling money and the attitude towards thriftiness and incurring debts; and with regard to the value of the family, the attitude towards divorce and new types of cohabitation" (Majce 1998, 15).

Areas characterized by more encompassing developments in the course of the twentieth century, such as gender equality, politics and recreational activities, showed the most diverging attitudes. With respect to the age category, it was found that across all issues, parents are more likely to concur with their children than vice versa.[1] With regard to mentioning conflict, the outcome was similar, i.e., parents refer to them less often than children, a phenomenon that is habitually explained as the "harmonistic bias" of parents towards their children, since it is assumed that the parent generation is more closely attached to the children than vice versa (Majce 1998, 14).

In the structural context (household structure), intergenerational relations today tend to be two-generational in the nuclear family (parents with school-going children) and only a minority of families practise three-generational cohabitation. Altogether, intergenerational mutual support within the household and outside is quite stable, with the mother as the

1 Since the respondents were not related, findings should not be seen as intrafamilial, i.e., "from both sides"; the statements were made by those who had a mother, a father or a child.

strong integrative figure who gives and receives a large amount of support; it was also made clear that the older generation provides far more help and support in emotional and financial areas than is generally assumed. To give an outline of the relation between household structures and underlying societal value attitudes, we will select two issues for closer analysis of the Austrian status quo:

- the late age of children leaving the parental home and
- cohabitation with the ancestral generation in times of need

The late age of children leaving the parental home: not unlike most EU countries, quite a large number of grown-up children live in their parents' households. For the most part this is due to extended secondary education, a later age of marriage or the economic needs of youth faced with a high unemployment risk. The emergence of this post-adolescent stage is also visible in Austria, where young adults remain longer in a state of economic dependence and only establish their full social status in their early or mid-thirties, having long since accomplished other youth-specific development tasks related to partnership, sexuality, friendship and value attitudes. For Austria, the census data of 2001 shows that of those aged between twenty-five and twenty-nine, more than every fourth person (28 per cent) still lives with their parents. One generation earlier (in 1971), this figure was only half this amount, with 15 per cent of children between twenty-five and twenty-nine still living at home (Statistische Nachrichten 2003). Similar to other European countries, there is a patent gender difference, with women leaving the parental home earlier than men. For the twenty-five to twenty-nine age group more than a third (37 per cent) of males live with their parents, compared to only 19 per cent of females. Although these figures seem inflated, Austria ranges in the middle field compared to other countries, and with its geographical position in central Europe supports the thesis of a North-South divide. Whereas in Austria 39 per cent have left home by the age of twenty-five, in Denmark it is 75 per cent but only seven per cent in Italy (Richter 2004, 46). Among university students – typically quoted as the group still living at home – we find approximately 31 per cent of the twenty-one-year-old students living at home rather than in their own flat or a student residence hall (HIS 2005, 74). Compared with the other selected European countries[2], this figure was lower only in Ger-

2 The countries represented in the Eurostudent 2005 study are Austria, Germany, Spain, Finland, France, Ireland, Latvia, the Netherlands, Portugal and the United Kingdom.

many (30 per cent) and Finland (seven per cent). In the Mediterranean countries in particular, we see figures up to 79 per cent (Italy) and Spain (71 per cent). A possible reason for the comparatively low percentage of students living with their parents in Austria is the average monthly cost of accommodation, which is quite low, making it simply more affordable for an Austrian student to live in a private flat than an Irish, French or Dutch student. In addition, the Eurostudent study suggests that Austrian students are less satisfied as a result of living at home with their parents. Although two thirds were satisfied with their accommodation in the parental home, the satisfaction of students living alone was higher. In other words, students prefer their own lodgings, a trend indicating their desire to gain spatial independence from their mothers and fathers, one that is only seen in a similar pattern in Germany and Finland (ibid., 80f.). This pattern of proximity between parents and adult children, accompanied by the desire of the economically dependent child (student) to escape from this situation, is reflected in later years, when the older generation becomes dependent on adult children.

Cohabitation with the ancestral generation in times of need: the Population Policy Acceptance Survey (Gisser 2003) has shown for Austria that relations between grown-up children and their parents are characterized by close proximity. Should they need help, the older generation can rely on support from their children. This is shown in 68 per cent of adult children, who agree with the statement that they would ask their parents to live with them if the latter needed help. If assistance is not an immediate necessity, however, far more Austrians (41 per cent) disagree with the statement that they would "like (their) elderly parents to live with (them)". It is evident that willingness to cohabit strongly depends on whether elderly parents are in need of support (Gisser 2003, 46f.). On the parents' part, however, we find more misgivings about moving in with their children, possibly for reasons of consideration, i.e., "not wanting to be a burden". Asked about their preferred form of living in the case of support in old age, 69 per cent say they would prefer to continue living at home and receive help from a third party. The second option is the home for the elderly (11 per cent); a mere three per cent can imagine living with one of their children (Gisser 2003, 48). Current statistics for household structures with regard to caregiving, however, show that 40 per cent of caregivers live in the household of those who require help or care, and 55 per cent under one roof, i.e., in close spatial propinquity. These comparatively high figures suggest that intergenerational social cohesion is strong when the older generation needs help. On the other hand, and possibly out of consideration, older people who are not yet dependent on support are a priori prone to saying no to the notion of living with their children. Surprisingly, we also find a rather large number of potential caregivers who reject their caregiving obligation: in comparison with other KASS countries (specifically France, Germany, Italy, Poland and Russia), the societal rejection (i.e., by non-affected persons, quasi a priori) of the statement that grown-up children should take care of their aged parents, is higher in Austria than in any other country; almost 30 per cent reject this obligation "pro forma" (ISSP 2001). It can be assumed that societal opinion also deviates from the actual response, since social support in the case of an "emergency is strong. The younger generation want to have their own living quarters but are prepared to compromise if their parents need support. Sieder (1987) depicts a similar situation for Germany, where he found that older people expressed a desire to live with their children under one roof only when they had lost their partner. He infers that the desire for cohabitation stems primarily from economic necessity or the need to receive care (Sieder 1987, 253).

Cultural background and gender

When it comes to social security in a family and societal context, the gender issue is crucial to explaining many of the structural and individual changes that occurred during the twentieth century. Following Beck's individualization thesis, late-industrial society was particularly affected by the gender issue, which became relevant after the de-traditionalization of the social classes in pre-industrial society (Beck 1986, 177). Reduced to a time denominator, "in the nineteenth century, people defined themselves through class affiliation, in the twentieth century – through gender affiliation" (Hoffmann 1994, 47). The twentieth century saw the emergence of multi-faceted social currents that spurred on equal treatment of the sexes, such as in education and the labour force participation of women or the involvement of men/fathers in parenting and household chores. However, the "Project of Modernity" is yet awaiting successful completion, since tradition in many spheres of life still holds sway over gender relations. The retrospect below traces its development in Austria.

When speaking of Austrian culture today, we understand twentieth-century Austria as an ethnically and culturally homogeneous nation state, especially in comparison with the multi-ethnic population of the Dual Monarchy that ended in 1918. Today, approximately 92 per cent of the population are German-speaking and about 75 per cent are Catholic. A closer look, however, reveals that Austria's population is not as homogeneous as it seems. It is divided into those who live in rural, often alpine, areas with strong (Catholic) traditions and those in smaller towns and cities or the capital, Vienna. A total of two million Austrians live in Vienna and its surroundings, representing almost a quarter of the Austrian population (8.2 million). In everyday language, Austrians speak of "Vienna" and the "Bundesländer", ignoring the fact that Vienna is itself one of those nine states, thereby pointing to the difference between the capital and "the others".

The first half of the twentieth century

At the beginning of the twentieth century male dominance had long been tradition in Austria. Patriarchal structures were clearly visible in family life, where the male acted as head of the family. However, such patriarchal structures did not derive from patrilineal traditions as in the case of Southern Europe, where male ancestors and living fathers held a strong position over the big family. Male-dominated structures in Austria were more an evolution in practice than rooted in religious traditions of patriarchy. Biologistic beliefs on gender-specific capacities led to a functional division of labour, whereby female-specific labour was rated of less value than that of the male contribution.

The early twentieth century was primarily characterized by the alignment of women's political and social opportunities to participate in public life on an equal footing with men. Universal suffrage was introduced on 16 February 1919, thus according political *sui juris* status to women. In a European comparison, Austria holds the middle position with this date, on a par with Sweden, Czechoslovakia and Poland, where universal suffrage was introduced in the same year. Up to then (from the 1848 Revolution), suffrage had been linked to gender and property, so that only men with property were privileged to vote (ibid.). Obtaining female suffrage is closely linked to the first wave of the women's movement in Austria, whose founder and leader is generally considered to be Marianne Hainisch (1839–1936). At the end of the nineteenth century, she demanded that women be granted access to university education. Similar to other European countries, this first wave aimed at equal legal and social treatment of women on a par with men, in terms of aligning their rights with those hitherto exclusively accorded to men. However, the Austrian women's movement is characterized by a diversity of movements that pursued different political goals and strategies. In the years of the First Republic (1918–1933), Vienna was renowned as the first metropolis under socialist rule, making history as "Red Vienna" (Czeike 1962). The predominantly traditional family and gender image contrasted vividly with the status quo, which showed the growing participation of women in the labour force, even in traditionally male occupations. During the First World War, women had begun to enter the typically male professional domain. The economic distress in the wake of the war further necessitated their contribution to the labour force. The growing strength of women was also boosted by the emancipation movement of Social Democratic women's associations and functionaries (Czeike 1962, 69). The interwar years were also defined by economic crisis. Women's economic position deteriorated with the end of the war: married women were denied the right to paid employment, and men returning from the war thronged back into their jobs, which had in the meantime been taken over by women. (Reinfeldt 1993, 71). Sadly, these developments were also linked to the health risk suffered by women as a result of inappropriately performed pregnancy terminations. Lower-class couples, in particular, could not afford to have more children. Since government and church policies served to prevent the propagation of contraceptives, they were expensive and hence available to the upper classes only. Many women died from self-abortions or the dubious methods used by quacks (Sieder 1987, 210). The period of Austrofascism (1933–1938) was one of special significance for women- and gender-related issues, as it linked the ideological transfiguration of the maternal image to the structural discrimination of women. Austrofascism saw the family as the wellspring of society, a notion that originates from the Roman Catholic image of women. Women were accorded the role of bearing and raising new members of society, a function sanctified by the biologistic view of a role assignment decreed by nature and by God.

On the other hand, motherhood propaganda was accompanied by discriminatory political measures directed against sexual equality. This was reflected in the statutory inequality of the sexes in the May Constitution of 1934, under which, for "pertinent" reasons, civil equality of the sexes could be shifted to benefit men (Ennsmann 1993, 11). Other provisions included celibacy for women in the public service and the restriction of higher education for girls by acting against coeducation and cutting subsidies for private girls' schools. Maternity benefits were also reduced, e.g., with a cutback of the sickness benefit, which included maternity aid (Ennsmann 1993, 3ff.). The "Anschluss" to the German Reich (1938) heralded the seamless transition to Austrian National Socialism, which continued to propagandize the image of women as mothers and homemakers, and their crucial role in mothering the future generation, which is why abortion was forbidden on penalty of death (Geiger and Hacker 1989). Since fathers and sons were in the war, however, the labour shortage meant that in real life women were not needed simply to bear and raise children, but as industrial workers in the war industries, or, in its most "brutal form", for military service (Sieder 1987, 233f.). The blatant contradiction between the housewife image and the factory worker was resolved by the glib NS propaganda argument that "women are especially suited for assembly-line work, because the monotonous work allows them to focus their minds on their housewifely and maternal duties" (Sieder 1987, 233). In reality, women in NS times were confronted with the double burden of having to juggle both family and paid employment, while the ideology stressed their role as mothers and homemakers. The participation of women in the labour force seemed adjustable; depending on the economic situation, women were admitted to the job market or sent back to their domestic spheres (Sieder 1987, 235). The post-war period (from 1945) was a difficult time of "clearing up" and had its impact on gender relations. During the war years, countless women had gained self-confidence as the sole head of the family. Hence they had trouble dealing with their husbands who, now returned from the war, reclaimed their position (Sieder 1987, 237). The alienation of many married couples due to separate experiences (the male war experience, the exhausting female work situation, in some cases even rape at the hands of members of the occupying forces) led to intra-familial tension between the sexes. In the 1950s, "tranquility" returned to marital relations: the emancipatory elements in the lives of women who had become independent receded into the background; family life became more intimate, gender relations more traditional. Before the war, only middle-class families had been able to afford the nuclear-family model, quasi as a "privilege"; it now became the standard (Sieder 1987, 240f.).

The second half of the twentieth century

The year 1968 and the Student Movement in Austria represented less of a cultural break than it had in other states. Although occasionally described as lacking the "political acumen" of Germany and France and the "breadth" typical of Italy, it was characterized by a wide variety of currents (Reitter 2002, 47). Undoubtedly, Austria also experienced a cultural turnaround. In terms of family and gender roles, this development was reflected in the gradual petering out of the predominant model of the 1950s of a "hegemony of the Catholic-inspired, monogamous, heterosexual marriage/family that insisted on men's authoritarian structures vis-à-vis women and children" (Schwendter 1995, 171). The turnaround in the 1960s paved the way for the reform era of the Socialist[3] government under Bruno Kreisky (1970–1983) (Schwendter 1995, 171). A key cultural current of the time was the emergence of the politically or artistically motivated commune culture. On the one hand, it can be perceived as a new form of cohabitation, aloof from the middle-class nuclear family. Even more so, however, the commune is regarded as a place of joint activity in opposition to traditional norms in the private sphere. Another significant factor was the development towards a freer sexuality and, with the introduction in the 1960s of biochemical contraceptives (the Pill) on the Austrian market, an opportunity for self-determined female sexuality. The opening up of the middle and higher education system to women in the 1970s was a milestone in the struggle for equal opportunities for men and women. Tendencies towards individualization involved "collectively more" education and a broader labour force participation of all strata in society. Prepared in the 1950s, this came to the fore in the 1970s (Beck 1986, 122). For women, it implied increased participation in educational institutions and aspirations on the job market. While in 1951, a total of two per cent of women completed their higher education, the figures had risen to three per cent by

3 The SPÖ, founded in 1945 as the "Sozialistische Partei Österreichs" (Austrian Socialist Party), was renamed "Sozialdemokratische Partei Österreichs" (Austrian Social Democratic Party) in 1991. The historical retrospect uses the term "Socialist" or "Social Democrat", depending on the respective period.

1971 and to four per cent by 1981. This trend manifested itself even more clearly in the field of university education: in 1951, women accounted for 15 per cent of university graduations, a figure that had risen to 24.4 per cent by 1971 and to 35.5 per cent ten years later (Statistik Austria 2002, 31f.). Education gave women the opportunity of entering spheres that had hitherto been typical male domains and from which they had been excluded. In the 1970s, equal rights for women received a significant boost in both political and ideological terms, although social reality, principally with respect to paid employment, was still far from representing equality. On the one hand, endorsement of the traditional family model was reflected in an unprecedented marriage rate, and some 80 per cent of Austrians lived in nuclear families (Fischer-Kowalski 1995, 201). However, the Austrian Socialist Party had traditionally viewed marriage and family with "mixed feelings" (ibid.), since they forced women into the domestic sphere of household and family, which was seen as socially inferior, thus depriving them of their independence, not least with regard to sexuality. The political response was to indtroduce concrete political measures aimed at promoting women's right to self-determination. Financial support was granted in the form of marriage and maternity benefits, the divorce law was relaxed, sexual deviance was de-criminalized, the abortion law and the right to birth control were liberalized, and the legal status of children born out of wedlock was improved. The establishment of the Secretariat of State for Women's Affairs (1979) was another major step. Johanna Dohnal, head of the Secretariat, carried out a strident campaign against the discrimination of women; later on (1990), Dohnal became the first Federal Minister for Women's Affairs (Fischer-Kowalski 1995, 201). All of these developments were intertwined with the second wave of the women's movement, whose beginnings can be traced back to the early 1970s. Shortly afterwards, men responded to the women's movement by creating their own movement. Feminist discussion on traditional gender roles increased the pressure on men to come to terms with their male role. While the men's movement was marginal in comparison with that of women, the 1980s did see the emergence of numerous groups, workshops and centres offering professional counselling for men (Männerberatungsstellen). As the 1980s progressed, however, the male discussion shifted its focus back to the private sphere (Foltin 2003, 52). The 1970s brought fundamental structural changes to the participation of women in the labour force: rather than work as family members, e.g., in the agricultural field, they now tended to enter the labour market as salaried employees. With a 30 per cent lower hourly rate, however, their status was usually below that of their male colleagues (Feigl 1985, 43). Female participation in the political arena of the 1970s was similarly marginal, with some six per cent of women in the federal and regional (Länder) governments (Fischer-Kowalski 1995, 205).

What is the state of gender relations in Austria today? With the transition to the twenty-first century, we are witnessing a retrospective discussion on the change from pre-modern to modern and possibly post-modern family structures, and on the areas affected by these developments. Two current gender discussion issues are presented below:

- the intrafamilial division of labour among the sexes (status quo and attitudes), also seen under the aspect of male participation in parenting and child care (paternity leave)
- gender-specific participation in the educational and income-earning sector

A survey carried out in 2001 (Gisser 2003) shows that the traditional division of labour still meets with a fairly high degree of acceptance: a total of almost 38 per cent of respondents agreed with the following statement: "The role of men is to earn money; women are responsible for the household and the family." Broken down by gender, more men tend to favour this concept: 41 per cent agree with and 37 per cent reject the traditional division of labour. The women's group indicates the contrary: the majority of women (44 per cent) reject the statement, while 37 per cent agree with it. Moreover, role appreciation was found to be a generational matter: while almost a third of the over-sixties agreed with this gendered division, only 11.5 per cent of young adults (aged between twenty and twenty-four) did so. By EU comparison, too, Austrians display a highly traditional understanding of gender roles. The Austrian Family Report (Österreichischer Familienbericht/BMSG 1999) compares Austria with Belgium, Germany, Italy and Norway, and reveals that Austrians tend to agree with the following statements more often than citizens of the other countries: "Being a housewife is just as fulfilling as earning an income" (63.7 per cent) or "Most women want a home and children" (61.7 per cent) (BMSG 1999, 79). The actual division of household and family chores also reflects the traditional image. As shown by the ISSP 2002, 58 per cent of women in Austria spend 11–20 hours a week on household chores, as opposed to none to 10 hours spent by 80 per cent of men.

Recent developments are distinguished by a growing societal and individual trend, whereby fathers take an equal part in the care and upbringing of their children. The introduction of paternity leave in 1991 is a sign of the political efforts aimed at enabling fathers to share child-care duties. By comparison, the first paternity-leave model was introduced in Sweden as early as 1974. Experience has shown that very few Austrian fathers avail themselves of this opportunity, with the rate of paternity leave amounting to a mere two per cent, as compared to 16 per cent in Sweden (Dörfler 2005, 179). The objective of the child-care benefit introduced in 2002 is to increase the proportion of fathers engaging in child care, but no such trend has been observed so far (ibid.). While paternity leave is common in several countries, Austria has not yet introduced this type of explicit paternity leave (Dörfler 2004, 235). However, the low rate of participation by fathers cannot be explained exclusively by the value attitudes of women and men, since the paternity leave option meets with fairly widespread acceptance, i.e., 70 per cent are in favour of paternity leave and a mere 17 per cent more or less against it, with women showing a more positive attitude than men (Gisser 2003, 40). It stands to reason that the imbalance between male and female incomes is a crucial aspect when it comes to paternal leave and explains why so few men are prepared to claim this benefit. In the context of education, gender-specific differences are in decline, but continue to persist. Educational expansion in the last three decades has ensured an increase in the higher qualification rates of the entire population, particularly with regard to women. In relation to the total population, the rate of higher education since 1961 has tripled (between 1951 and 2000, from five to 15 per cent), with the proportion of girls in higher education increasing as much as fourfold (from 4 to 16 per cent). Among Austrian students enrolled in regular studies, the proportion of women has grown from ten to 31 per cent since the 1970s (Statistik Austria 2002, 31f.).

Gender-specific labour force participation rates in Austria indicate a constant increase of women on the labour market since 1951. In 1951 itself, the female labour force participation rate was 48.7 per cent and by 2002, had reached 63.5 per cent. Over the same period, the male participation in the labour force fell from 91 per cent to 79.1 per cent, i.e., a distinct shift towards more gender balance has taken place.[4] However, it should be mentioned that there is a tenfold proportion of women in part-time em-

4 Data: Statistik Austria, calculations by OIF.

ployment as compared to men, suggesting that from a working hour perspective, female presence on the job market is still somewhat below the male rate. Female integration also differs along the various economic sectors: from 1971 to 1997, the distribution of income-earning women shifted towards the service sector. A careful analysis shows that the proportion of women still tapers off with the rising status of job positions.

Since the beginning of the 1990s, the tendency for childbirth to have less and less impact on women's decision to work than in previous decades has been observed. The rate of working mothers between the ages of fifteen and fifty-nine increased from 52 per cent in 1986 to 71 per cent in 2001, although many work only part-time. [5]

Although women's employment biographies ensure their independence from men, Austrian societal assessment of the labour force participation of mothers has up to now remained somewhat traditional. By comparison with other KASS countries (here: Sweden, Germany, Italy, Poland, Russia), the ISSP 1994 found that Austrians have the most traditional attitude towards working mothers. They make up the largest group of respondents endorsing the statement "A pre-school child is likely to suffer if his or her mother works", i.e., 37 per cent. In Sweden, e.g., only seven per cent agreed with this statement. Eight years on (ISSP 2002), there is little change in how people see labour force participation of mothers in Austria. Almost a third of the Austrian population still agrees strongly with the statement that children suffer if their mothers are working, thereby ranking the Austrian position as the most traditional in comparison with other countries.

The effects of this attitude can also be seen in the attendance of out-of-home child care institutions in Austria. Since the extension of child-care facilities in Austria after World War II, it is characteristic that only a minority of children – currently about ten per cent under the age of three – attends an out-of-home child-care institution. In contrast, 73 per cent of all children aged between three and six years attend an out-of-home care facility (Statistik Austria and BMSG 2003, 40).

These differences could be due to the fact that out-of-home child care in the public debate has always been seen as positioned in an area of conflict between care and provision, on the one hand, and education, on the other. A great majority of Austrians is still convinced that the provision of

---

5 Data: Statistik Austria, calculations by OIF.

care for children, especially for those under the age of three, is a central task of the family itself (Kränzl-Nagl 2000, 87). This is evident in the fact that additional provision is currently in demand for a mere 7.5 per cent of children under the age of three who do not attend an out-of-home child-care facility. Child care is in fact carried out by mothers, supported for the most part by other female members of the family. Nevertheless, in the last decade an increase in the attendance of out-of-home care institutions for this age group has been observed (Statistik Austria and BMSG 2003, 38–40).

The child-care situation is different for children between between the ages of three and six. For this age group, out-of-home care is accepted to a large extent as an educational measure to promote child development. Therefore child-care provision for this age group is much greater and most children attend institutions that provide half-day care. This accords with an increased social acceptance of part-time work for mothers with children over three years of age (Kränzl-Nagl 2000, 87–88; Statistik Austria and BMSG 2003, 38–40).

Networks

As seen above, the nineteenth century saw the rapid dissolution of the House, which had supplied minimum social protection to much of the rural population. From now on, the state was to gain importance in the delivery of social security. By introducing the General Insurance Act after World War II in particular and expanding the scope of benefits, the state became a key agent in this area. However, the social reality is that informal networks of family and kin as well as extrafamilial support have played a major role throughout the twentieth century and still do. The following passage highlights several historical issues and some relevant data from recent studies.

Demographic aspects of kin availability

In exploring social support networks, we first need to explore the availibilty of potential social exchange and support, whereby the demographic aspects of living kin (time aspect) and geographical proximity play significant roles.

The "myth" of the three-generational family is a key feature in examining the availability of family networks revolving around the generation aspect. Up to the 1970s, Durkheim's contraction thesis dominated the landscape of historical family research, and it was widely believed that industrialization and urbanization had led to a transition from the pre-industrial three-generational extended family to the "famille conjugale", the nuclear family, destroying the typical cohabitation of extended families in the process (Durkheim 1921). In the meantime, this interpretation has been proved unfounded. The three-generational family existed for a short time only, which in Austria covered the period of transition from the nineteenth to the twentieth century, when, in the course of the agricultural revolution and industrialization, "for the first time, life expectancy was sufficiently high and the marrying age had dropped" (Sieder 1987, 252). Especially for Southern and Eastern Europe (Russia), the common dwelling of three generations was more prevalent. For Austria, Sieder claims that in farmer families with three generations alive at the same time the picture was not one of harmony (frequently portrayed as such by Le Play). On the contrary, special contracts to regulate the handing-over of property were sufficient proof that conflicts were an issue (Sieder 1997, 227).

Still, the (at least) geographical proximity was – and still is – more widespread in rural than in urban areas. Taking recent quantitative data into account, the microcensus study (2001) shows a relational network of close relatives composed of seven persons on average. It clearly indicates that networks are substantially bigger in rural than in urban regions. Large-scale relational networks are mostly found in remote rural regions, where 19 per cent of men and 24 per cent of women boast ten or more living relatives, compared to Vienna, where the corresponding figure is eight per cent for men and ten per cent for women (Statistische Nachrichten 2003, 236). Looking at the generational aspect, almost 46 per cent of the overall population in 2001 lived under the same roof as their physical parents, with major differences in age. Again, in terms of distance to parents, there are strong distinctions between urban and rural districts, with almost 70 per cent living with or in close proximity to their parents in extremely remote rural areas. This applies to only 43 per cent of the people living in Vienna. With regard to grandparents, there are strong regional differences. Almost

45 per cent of the population in rural regions live with or close to a grandparent, as against a mere 15 per cent of the Viennese (ibid., 72ff.).

With regard to the (life) time aspect, which is the availability of living family and kin, the increase in life expectancy has undoubtedly influenced availability in a positive way, since more generations now live concurrently. Three out of four people have living relatives from at least two other generations, and for 20 per cent, this extends to three generations. Once again, urban and rural areas diverge. Only four per cent of Austrians have no living relative from a previous or succeeding generation, significantly more in towns and cities than in rural areas with a high farming rate. Both children and the very old tend to live in families combining four or more generations. More concretely: 42 per cent of the 0 to 4-year-olds and 39 per cent of eighty-five-year-olds and older (Statistische Nachrichten 2003, 239).

Availability of networks and social support

The concrete availability of a particular social network is registered as a matter of course when people are confronted with dire circumstances, whether the result of an individual or a nationwide crisis. In the latter case, strong networks became apparent in the mid-1940s. The situation after World War II was one of vast distress for the entire Austrian nation, and exemplifies the kinship ties between families living in rural and urban areas. Sieder points out the unusually strong and reliable ties that allowed urban families who had lost their homes through bombs to avail of sharing a dwelling with their relatives in the countryside. When the state suffered economic and governmental chaos, it was kin who filled the gap (Sieder 1997, 224). It seems, however, that kinship ties were also visible in economically more stable periods, as witnessed in the 1950s and 1960s, when more favourable economic conditions did not lead to a loosening of ties between the generations. These years have often been quoted as the period when young couples emancipated themselves from the immediate influence of the parent generation and used their economic freedom to move away from home, either within the neighbourhood or to the cities. Despite geographical distance, the relationship between the younger and the parent generation was becoming more emotional; Rosenmayr uses the term "intimacy at bay" (Rosenmayr 1958). Sieder describes the strong bond between three generations, where grandparents helped out by taking care of their grandchildren and Christmas was not celebrated in the small "new" households but in the company of parents and in-laws (Sieder 1997, 225). It is becomes obvious here that census data does not suffice to portray kinship ties, e.g., household size is not appropriate to convey a genuine picture of the so-called "modified extended familiy" (Litwak 1965). Sieder briefly mentions that for the new middle class the cohesion of generations might also have to be seen in the light of growing economic wealth and a new quality of what was there to inherit. Terms such as "family cutlery" and "family jewellery" began to evolve, and a helping hand from the younger generation may have influenced the decisions of those who pass on these precious goods (Sieder 1997, 238). On the other hand, Sieder emphasizes that help was often provided by the older to the younger generation; thus, contact or support that is purely calculating from the younger generation upwards is to be rejected out of hand.

Furthermore, contact to the elderly or grantparent generation seems stable today and of an emotional nature. With regard to current support networks along generational lines, we outlined above that the child and parent generations are reliable sources of both top-down and bottom-up support, which comes into place when actual help is required. When it comes to a common dwelling because the younger generation need accommodation until they finish their education or find work, or because the elderly generation is in need of home care, there is particular evidence of strong generational ties in Austria. The grandparent-including model of the "modified extended family" mentioned above still seems to exist today and we can even assume that the elderly generation is of major importance when it comes to child care or flexible babysitting hours. Care of grandchildren is often welcomed in families where both parents are employed and institutional child care is not at hand, or where grandparents are simply the preferred option to institutional care. Also, when we look into the pluralization of family forms, including the evolvement of more one-parent and patchwork families, grandparents frequently provide a back-up for the remaining parent. With the trend towards more divorce today and thus a more liberal understanding of it – at least in general – grandparents could remain valuable family members for their grandchildren even when their son or daughter has left the family.

If we take a more statistical viewpoint and look for quantitative data on networks, help and support in emergencies today, a survey by Majce (1998) provides important results for Austria. Overall, in terms of contact or networks available and as yet not focused on whom they would ask for help in times of need, three-quarters of those surveyed have a female or male friend. Ranked behind them are aunts, sisters, mothers and nephews (all approx. 60 per cent); only 45 per cent of those polled have a living father. The survey found no one unable to name at least one person as a relative or friend (ibid., 4). As for help and support in major or minor emergencies, the study then asked whom they would turn to in a case of need[6] (see figure 6.2) and distinguished between different kinds of help. It showed that in both minor (e.g., to obtain care for children ad hoc) and major emergencies (to look after children or a flat in the event of a two-week illness), the mother was mostly relied upon for help. Sisters and female friends played a major role in minor emergencies, which renders the distinct gender difference visible, i.e., that the help expected derives mostly from women. Even among neighbours, more trust is placed in females. We also see that if the emergency involves financial help, the potential support is concentrated within rather than outside the family. Moreover, males are frequently named in this context. If people needed money, they would turn to male rather than female friends. In line with the traditional role model, but possibly reflecting real income distribution, men rather than women are perceived as owners and distributors of capital. Help required immediately usually comes by way of emotional support or assistance in a small emergency. The type of support most called for is "heart-to-heart talks" (51 per cent), followed by work in the house/flat, such as repair jobs (43 per cent) and short-term nursing (39 per cent). In general, this help comes from among the generations, within the core family, and shows gender-specific tendencies: household help is provided for the most part by mothers and daughters; heart-to-heart talks mostly involve mothers, female friends, sisters or daughters. Long-term nursing care is primarily carried out by mothers and daughters. Male support is then relevant when it comes to household jobs (repairs and moving furniture), where assistance is primarily given by sons and fathers. It is also given in a financial or material emergency; although it is mothers who provide first-line help, fathers and male friends rank immediately behind (Majce 1998).

6 The study focused primarily on the hypothetical support potential: people were asked to state whom they trust and would turn to; the question did not (initially) concern support actually obtained.

Figure 6.2: Who helps out in emergencies? (Austria 1998)

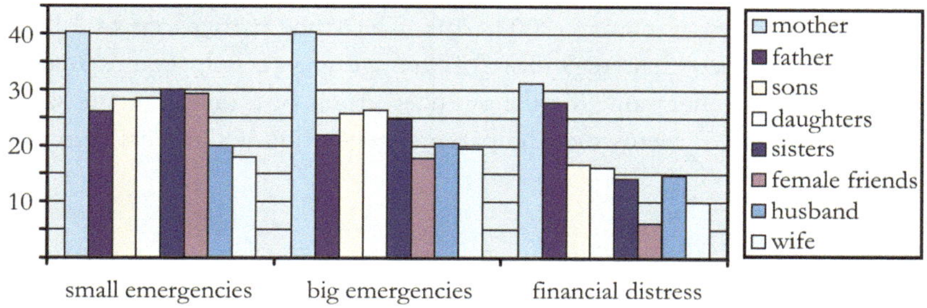

Source: Majce 1998, 5–7, N= 1.000

If we furthermore include data from the microcensus 2002 on long-term care and summarize the findings on gender and age, we see that support is mostly female. The mother is the core figure with regard to maintaining and rendering social support; other providers of assistance tend to be female as well, especially where emotional or nursing help is concerned. Of those who provide long-term nursing care, two thirds are female, while those who receive this help are mostly mothers, partners or mothers-in-law[7]. In the context of long-term nursing, it is notable that the fifty to sixty-four year olds are those who carry most of the care burden, although they themselves are in the second half of their life. It is also conspicuous that more than half (55 per cent) of care recipients live under the same roof as the person who provides care, and 40 per cent live in the household of their care provider; 15 per cent live in the same house but in a separate housing unit (Kytir and Schrittwieser 2003, 106ff.). However, from a general point of view and combining the different types of support, it seems that intergenerational support transfers usually occur "from the top to the bottom", i.e., from the original family to their descendants, especially in terms of financial assistance (Majce 1998, 11). This may be due to the fact that today's older generation is comparatively well-off, an aspect that will no longer be true for future generations (Rosenmayr 2000). Reciprocity among the generations is not merely lacking in financial terms, but also with regard to services and help. Schmatz (2000) used indicators based on data from the Family and Fertility Survey FFS 1996 for services and

7 6.7 per cent of Austrian residents over the age of eighteen nurse relatives or friends in need of long-term assistance (Microcensus 2002).

help rendered and received to demonstrate that with increasing age the gap between services received and rendered becomes wider – to the disadvantage of the elderly (Schmatz 2000, 20)[8]. The study carried out by Majce (1998)[9] confirmed that, regardless of the age group, help comes mainly from an older generation (for the younger group or a group of the same age). Altogether, it seems that the parental generation is the great provider of help and support.

Ideas on the importance of kinship

The previous sections have outlined the embedding of family and kin in the Austrian social insurance system, as it evolved in the course of the twentieth century. In this last section we will try to "bundle" those developments and principles, and to draw a complete picture of the ideas on the importance of kinship that circulated in the twentieth century as cultural, collective representations.

Taking the meaning of family and kinship relations in a longitudinal view allows us to see that in the twentieth century these relations had always carried significant weight in the macro-economy of everyday life, despite changes in the frame of reference over time.

At the beginning of the century the role of family and kin as a key guarantor for at least minimum protection was the dominant notion, since the welfare state was in its infancy at that time. Family and kinship relations, however, were also crucial to child care and care of the elderly, as well as to social circumstances that required mutual assistance and exchange in the context of work. The extension of welfare benefits since the middle of the 1950s strongly relieved family and kinship networks of their duties to provide basic protection against social risks. This was highly relevant to family and kinship networks, which had a limited capacity to provide adequate economic support in the case of old age, unemployment, disability, illness or accidents, circumstances that brought forth mounting poverty at the beginning of the twentieth century. In accordance with their capacities,

8 It should, however, be noted that those polled were between the ages of twenty and fifty-four, i.e., it was not possible to calculate an indicator that would consider people of a more advanced age.

9 People of sixty-one years of age and over were polled in this study.

however, family and kinship networks incurred these duties constantly. This became apparent in the 1930s, for instance, when the state left a gap in social security by introducing massive cuts in welfare benefits established only a decade before. Family and kin stepped in to fill the gap. The above-mentioned release from the duty to provide protection against social risks coupled with improved economic circumstances did not alter the strength of family and kinship ties. Instead, changes in the characteristics of these relations were observed in the macro-economy of everyday life. The general economic and welfare enhancement allowed family and kinship relations, especially those between close kin, to become more emotional. Support networks between the child and the parent generation developed into a reliable and stable source of emotional and material help in the second half of the twentieth century. The elderly generation was of crucial importance when it came to child care or babysitting. The younger generation – predominantly the females – became key providers of care, especially where emotional and nursing support for their parents or parents-in-law was concerned.

Current socio-economic developments and structural changes in family forms lead us to anticipate that family and kinship relations will continue to gain in significance. This may, for example, be the case if actual trends on the labour market continue to increase the need for families to live on double incomes. Coupled with these circumstances, the general increase in female labour market participation and the abiding progress in the transition to flexible employment will require the additional support of affordable child care in Austria, frequently available only from close members of the family. Further disintegration of traditional nuclear families with children will also call for new forms of child care that need to be supported by informal help from family members. Vice versa, the number of elderly people in need of support and care is mounting steadily. There are also clear indications that social policy in Austria will further aim to individualize and privatize social security. These developments clearly privilege those in a position to rely on family and kinship resources.

These changes, however, are taking place against a background of socio-demographic trends and social policy developments that counteract these necessities. Declining birth and marriage rates, accompanied by an increase in the divorce rate, promote the singling of living arrangements, a trend that inevitably implicates a structural downsizing of future family and kinship networks. Due to demographic change it is furthermore accompanied by political strategies that demand extending employment to a more advanced age than is the case today. This will obviously complicate meeting demands for support, in particular with regard to child care and care of the elderly, as well as other forms of informal assistance within family and kinship networks. The latter will undoubtedly continue to provide mutual support in the future and make an effort to fill gaps left by the state, but again, their capacities are likely to be more limited than in times of economic growth and extended welfare provision, such as between the mid-1950s and late 1980s.

Bibliography

Beck, U. (1986), *Risikogesellschaft. Auf dem Weg in eine andere Moderne*, Frankfurt am Main: Suhrkamp.

BMSG (Bundesministerium für soziale Sicherheit und Generationen) (1999), *Österreichischer Familienbericht 1999*, Vienna: BMSG.

Bundeskanzleramt (1979), *Bericht über die Lage der Familien in Österreich. Familienbericht 1979*, Vol. 1, Wien: Bundeskanzleramt.

Czeike, Felix (1962), *Liberale, christlichsoziale und sozialdemokratische Kommunalpolitik (1861–1934)*, Vienna: Verlag für Geschichte und Politik.

Dilthey, W. (1875), *Über das Studium der Geschichte der Wissenschaften vom Menschen, der Gesellschaft und dem Staat. Gesammelte Schriften*, Stuttgart, pp. 31–89.

Dörfler, S. (2004), "Elternurlaub im Vergleich. Eine Gegenüberstellung der Regelungen in Frankreich, Norwegen, Österreich und Schweden", in B. Cizek (ed.), *Familienforschung in Österreich. Markierungen, Ergebnisse, Perspektiven*, Wien: Österreichisches Institut für Familienforschung, pp. 229–246.

— (2005), "Väterkarenz in Österreich und Schweden – Hindernisse, Motivationen und Rahmenbedingungen", in H. Krall (ed.), *Jungen- und Männerarbeit*, Wiesbaden: VS Verlag, pp. 178–189.

Durkheim, E. (1921), "La famille conjugale. Conclusion du cours sur la famille", *Revue Philosophique, 90*, pp. 2–14.

Ehmer, J. (1980), *Familienstruktur und Arbeitsorganisation im frühindustriellen Wien*, Wien: Verlag für Geschichte und Politik.

— (1991), *Heiratsverhalten, Sozialstruktur, ökonomischer Wandel England und Mitteleuropa in der Formationsperiode des Kapitalismus*, Göttingen: Vandenhoeck and Ruprecht.

Ennsmann, B. (1993), *Frauenpolitik und Frauenarbeit im Austrofaschismus*, Wien: Universität Wien, Diplomarbeit.

Esping-Andersen, G. (1990), *The three worlds of welfare capitalism*, Princeton and New Jersey: Princeton University Press.

Feigl, S. (1985), *Frauen in Österreich 1975–1985,* Wien: Staatssekretariat für allgemeine Frauenfragen im Bundeskanzleramt.

Fischer-Kowalksi, M. (1995), "Sozialer Wandel in den 1970er Jahren", in R. Sieder, H. Steinert and E. Tálos (eds.), *Österreich 1945–1995. Gesellschaft, Politik, Kultur*, Wien: Verlag für Gesellschaftskritik.

Foltin, R. (2003), "Soziale Bewegungen in Österreich: Differenzierung der Szenen", *Zeitschrift für linke Theorie and Debatte, 8*, pp. 46–58.

Geiger, B. and H. Hacker (1989), *Donauwalzer Damenwahl. Frauenbewegte Zusammenhänge in Österreich*, Wien: Promedia.

Gisser, R. (2003), *Population policy acceptance survey 2001. Familie, Geschlechterverhältnis, Alter und Migration: Wissen, Einstellungen und Wünsche der Österreicherinnen und Österreicher*, Wien: Institut für Demographie.

Gisser, R. et al. (1990), "Familiale Wirklichkeit aus demographischer und soziologischer Sicht", in R. Gisser, et al. (eds.), *Lebenswelt Familie*, Wien: IEF, pp. 57–98.

Grandits, H. (2007), "Ländliches und städtisches Familienleben im Wandel: die Habsburgermonarchie zwischen 1848 und 1918", in *Die Habsburgermonarchie 1848–1918. Vol. IX. Sozialgeschichte,* Wien: Akademie der Wissenschaften (forthcoming).

HIS-Hochschulinformationssystem Hannover (2005), "Eurostudent Report 2005", www.his.de/Eurostudent/report2005.pdf.

Hoffmann, B. (1994), *Geschlechterpädagogik*, Münster: Votum Verlag.

ISSP (International Social Survey Programme) (2001), 'Social relations and support systems', GESIS Data Archive (http://www.issp.org/data.shtml).

— (2002), 'Family and changing gender roles II', GESIS Data Archive (http://www.issp.org/data.shtml).

Kränzl-Nagl, R. (2000), "Außerfamiliale Angebote der Kinderbetreuung", in Bundesministerium für Umwelt, Jugend und Familie, *4. Österreichischer Familienbericht. Familie zwischen Anspruch und Alltag. Familien und Arbeitswelt*, Wien, pp. 85–101.

Kytir, J. and K. Schrittwieser (2003), *Haushaltsführung, Kinderbetreuung, Pflege. Ergebnisse des Mikrozensus September 2002*, Wien: BMSG.

Litwak, E. (1965), "Extended kin relations in an industrial democratic society", in E. Shanas and G. F. Strieb (eds.), *Social structure and the family: generational relations*, Englewood Cliffs, 1965, pp. 290–223.

Loewenberg, P. (1985), *Decoding the past: the psychohistorical approach*, Berkeley: University of California Press.

Majce, G. (1998), *Generationenbeziehungen in Österreich. Erste Studienergebnisse*, Vienna: BM für Umwelt, Jugend und Familie.

Mitterauer, M. (1986), "Formen ländlicher Familienwirtschaft. Historische Ökotypen und familiale Arbeitsorganisation im österreichischen Raum", in J. Ehmer and M. Mitterauer (eds.), *Familienstruktur und Arbeitsorganisation in ländlichen Gesellschaften*, Wien: Böhlau, pp. 185–324.

Münz, R. (1985), *Soziologische Aspekte der Familienentwicklung und der Instrumente ihrer Beeinflussung*, Habilitation, Universität Wien.

Ortmayr, N. (1995), "Late marriages: causes and consequences of the Austrian alpine marriage pattern", in R. L. Rudolph (ed.), *The European peasant family and society*, Liverpool: Liverpool University Press, pp. 49–63.

Pflegerl, J. and C. Geserick (2007), *Kinship and social security in Austria. A social history for the 20th century. ÖIF Schriftenreihe*, Vol. 17, Innsbruck: Studienverlag.

Reinfeldt, H. (1993), *Familienpolitik im Roten Wien: 1919 – 1934. Exkursion auf der Eisbergspitze*, Wien: Universität Wien, Diplomarbeit.

Reitter, K. (2002), "Die 68er Bewegung – Versuch einer Darstellung Teil 2", in *Grundrisse. Zeitschrift für linke Theorie und Debatte, Vol. 4*, pp. 42–52.

Richter, R. (2004), "General monitoring report Austria 2004 Austria", in Brigitte Cizek and Rudolf Richter (eds.), *Families in the EU 15: policies, challenges and opportunities, ÖIF Materialiensammlung, Vol. 23*, pp. 45–56.

Rosenberger, S. and M. G. Schmid (2003), "Treffsicher. Sozialpolitik zwischen 2000 und 2002", in S. Rosenberger and E. Tálos (eds.), *Sozialstaat. Probleme, Herausforderungen, Perspektiven*, Wien: Mandelbaum, pp. 96–120.

Rosenmayr, L. (1958), "Der alte Mensch in der sozialen Umwelt von heute", *Kölner Zeitschrift für Soziologie und Sozialpsychologie, Bd. 10, 1958*, pp. 642–657.

— (2000), "Neue Daten und Thesen zur Generationenfrage. Österreichische und europäische Befunde", *SWS-Rundschau, 3*, pp. 229–248.

Schmatz, T. (2000), *Familiale Netzwerk. Eine Untersuchung auf Basis des Österreichischen Familien- und Fertilitätssurveys 1996*, Wien: Sozial- und Wirtschaftswissenschaftliche Fakultät Universität Wien.

Schwendter, R. (1995), "Das Jahr 1968. War es eine kulturelle Zäsur?", in R. Sieder, H. Steinert and E. Tálos (eds.), *Österreich 1945–1995. Gesellschaft, Politik, Kultur*, Wien: Verlag für Gesellschaftskritik, pp. 166–175.

Sieder, R. (1987), *Sozialgeschichte der Familie*, Frankfurt: Suhrkamp.

— (1997), "Besitz und Begehren, Erbe und Elternglück. Familien in Deutschland und Österreich", in A. Burguière, C. Klapisch-Zuber, M. Segalen and F. Zonabend (eds.), *Geschichte der Familie. 20. Jahrhundert*, Darmstadt: Wissenschaftliche Buchgesellschaft, pp. 211–284.

Statistik Austria and Bundesministerium für soziale Sicherheit, Generationen und Konsumentenschutz (BMSG) (2003), *Haushaltsführung, Kinderbetreuung, Pflege. Ergebnisse des Mikrozensus 2002*, Wien: BMSG.

Statistik Austria (2002), "Geschlechtsspezifische Disparitäten", in Bundesministerium für Wissenschaft und Kultur (bmbwk) and Bundesministerium für Bildung und Bundesministerium für soziale Sicherheit und Generationen (BMSG) (ed.), *Geschlechtsspezifische Disparitäten*, Wien: Weitzer & Partner GmbH.

Statistische Nachrichten (2002), *11/2002*, Wien: Statistik Austria.

— (2003), *9/2003, Familienstrukturen in Österreich. Ergebnisse der Volkszählungen 1961–2001*, Wien: Statistik Austria.

Tálos, E. (1981), *Staatliche Sozialpolitik in Österreich. Rekonstruktion und Analyse*, Wien: Verlag für Gesellschaftskritik.

Tálos, E. and K. Wörister (1994), *Soziale Sicherung im Sozialstaat Österreich. Entwicklung –Herausforderungen – Strukturen*, Baden-Baden: Nomos.

Kinship and the welfare state in twentieth-century Croatian transitions

Hannes Grandits

Family and kin were crucial factors in political legitimization discourse in Croatia even before the last century. Lawyers, social reformers and intellectuals began to engage in the second half of the nineteenth century in heated debates about the future of the then defined "zadrugas" – the occasionally large patrilineal family households, the members of which collectively owned and worked the family farms. In the wake of the late nineteenth-century "agrarian crisis" provoked by an increase in global capitalist market processes, some wanted to see this rural family arrangement legally protected. Others were in favour of imposing legislation that would help to "overcome" it as soon as possible in the interests of "social progress". Later, in the interwar period, the Croatian Peasant Party, the leading political force in the Croatian lands of that time, idealized this "harmonious" rural family household, fabricating a model of society around it. Even the socialist ideologists who came to power after the Second World War – as a rule somewhat less sympathetic to what they considered "outdated" rural social relations – were involved in the "zadruga" discussion. They stressed that this family model (already on the wane at that time) would serve to demonstrate the original "collectivist" nature of the country's rural population.

Up to the present day family and kin have remained emotionally charged topics in public and private discourse in Croatia. Family solidarity and the awareness of kin roots seem to be important tropes in defining the position of the individual in society, although Croatians have been aware for some time of the discourse on the precarious situation of the family. As elsewhere, the specific regional history of social and political developments has heavily influenced how people envisage the "ideal family" in Croatia. What is sometimes less present in the public consciousness in Croatia, however, is the fact that "lived" family realities throughout the last century became increasingly interlinked with the development of the welfare state –

its early implementation and limited growth over a long period, as well as its expansion under socialism and subsequent redefinition.

Chronology of the welfare state

Early development of the welfare system up to the Second World War

Welfare state policy initially took place within the framework of the Austrian-Hungarian Empire, to which the Croatian lands belonged until 1918. In a European comparison the Hapsburg Empire was among the pioneers in the field of state-driven welfare legislation (Alber 1987, 24–29). The goal of Austria's welfare take-off phase was a policy of social stabilization "from above", ideologically rooted in a socio-political conservative Catholicism (Schmidt 1988, 117–123; Tálos and Wörister 1994, 13–18).

The Croatian lands belonged to both parts of the Austrian-Hungarian dual monarchy. Dalmatia was part of the Austrian side of the Empire and Croatia-Slavonia of the Hungarian side. This had consequences for the introduction of the first welfare legislation. Compulsory accident insurance was introduced in Dalmatia in 1887 and compulsory health insurance in 1888; both insurance schemes were initially confined to workers in factories and large companies; health insurance also encompassed workers in trades and small-scale industry (Tálos and Wörister 1994, 17–18). Equivalent legislation was adopted in Croatia-Slavonia in 1891 and 1907 respectively (Czúcz 1991, 330–331).

Old-age pension insurance evolved in very few sectors of professional life. Similar to accident and health insurance, it was organized in compliance with a corporatist ideology and according to profession. Civil servants were privileged in this respect. They had already enjoyed – not unlike military personnel – inclusion in pension schemes since the middle of the nineteenth century. The same was true for state railway staff. Several mining unions also introduced their own pension systems, which were legally supervised by the state. Furthermore, white-collar workers in Dalmatia had been covered by a newly established pension scheme since 1909 (Zavod za mirovinsko osiguranje 2002, 11–12; Baryli 1977).

In 1918, the Croatian regions became part of the Kingdom of Serbs, Croats and Slovenes (renamed Yugoslavia in 1929), but the basic principles of the social insurance schemes in place remained for the most part in operation up to the Second World War. This applied primarily to the various regulations in the professional sectors, which were legally adapted step by step and expanded to form new regulations, e.g., for civil servants in 1931, for various (white-collar) professional groups in 1926 and 1931, for craftsmen and merchants in 1931, and for the military in 1934. All of these groups developed their own institutions for accident, health and, gradually, for old-age insurance (Vizjak 1937).

The new regime made efforts to expand the welfare system to include the working class. Crucial in this regard was the "Law on Workers' Insurance" (Zakon o osiguranju radnika – ZOR) from May 1922, which represented a uniform social insurance scheme valid for all (blue-collar) workers and also provided for the family members of those insured. Furthermore, the law provided for the introduction of an old-age pension system for the working class. As a result of prolonged conflict concerning the financial basis of the system, it was not until 1937 that workers were legally entitled to old-age pensions. Since the retirement age was laid down at seventy years of age, very few workers became old-age pensioners prior to the Second World War (Zavod za mirovinsko osiguranje 2002, 12–21).

In effect the system of social welfare provided by the state had created a first social security net. However, welfare targeted only a certain section of the population, which was very limited up to the Second World War. The vast majority of rural agricultural families – in the late 1940s, the percentage of those who lived on agriculture was still high at 62.4 per cent – were only marginally eligible for state benefits or not at all (the Croatian Peasant Party (HSS), a powerful force in Croatian village life at the time, did attempt to organize some form of insurance). Risk coverage for many of the proletarian or "low-income" families was minimal, and often consisted of scant financial contributions in times of need. Only certain segments of the professional work force could expect old-age pensions that would guarantee some form of social independence. Hence from a pragmatic point of view, the welfare state was of little benefit to the majority of rural families, or indeed to a large number of those in the urban centres. In large pockets of society up to the middle of the twentieth century, despite the enlargement of state benefits, there was no real evidence of kinship being "crowded out" by the state system of social security.

Socialist welfare expansion (1945–1990)

The Second World War was the caesura after which a far-reaching and accelerated process of social transformation was launched. The consequences of the Second World War were disastrous. According to reliable estimates, up to 300,000 people were killed (i.e., soldiers in the military formations of the fascist Ustaša government or those in the communist-dominated partisan movement, albeit the overwhelming majority of war victims were civilians). In short, almost nine per cent (!) of the total population of Croatia died in the catastrophic years between 1941, when Yugoslavia was attacked and occupied by the German Wehrmacht and its allies, and 1945, when the war came to an end. There was hardly a single family that had not been affected by a tragic loss in the closer or wider kinship group (Gelo 1987; Puljiz and Zrinščak 2004).

In 1945, the communist-dominated partisan movement that won the war immediately began to take over all governmental and administrative institutions in the country. Yugoslavia was transformed into a socialist state. Croatia became one of the six federal republics of socialist Yugoslavia. In the coming four-and-a-half decades, socialist ideology was to form the background of state policy (see, for instance, Zukin 1975).

In the initial period after 1945, social rights guaranteed by the state had two basic functions: to ease the massive difficulties caused by the Second World War and to build a "socialist society". The group focused upon from the outset was the so-called "working class" (Bošnjak 1973; Allcock 1980; Grandits 2002; Puljiz 2004). The explicit state goal of transforming a "traditional" society into a "modern socialist" state was likewise clearly formulated for family relations. The notion of transforming women into "working women" was officially promoted as the key to "emancipation" and a means of introducing change to existing "patriarchal family relations". Female employment became a priority in official policy and by the late 1980s women made up approximately 45 per cent of the total labour force. Official rhetoric conjured up the "modern" two-breadwinner family with children as the ideal form of family life (Barbič 1984; Andrić 1980; First-Dilić 1984; Kerovec 1990).

Notwithstanding this rhetoric, welfare state measures that concerned family life and child care were not a priority of socialist policy (in contrast to the expansion of the school infrastructure, which was made available to all children). During and immediately after the Second World War, the socialist government concentrated first of all on the care of countless war orphans and children who were socially "vulnerable". Almost one hundred homes for children in this category were established on the territory of the Socialist Republic of Croatia. The number of homes was gradually reduced in the course of the next decades (Ban 1984). The general system of public care for pre-school children (nurseries, day care, kindergartens), however, remained underdeveloped. Despite growing female employment rates and the ideal of the "two-breadwinner family", the infrastructure required to implement this model was not handled with great enthusiasm (Puljiz and Zrinščak 2004; Iris 1984).

Seen chronologically, the efficiency of the old-age social security system, – and this is also very true for other welfare spheres, such as health insurance – went through several phases of development (Puljiz 1996). In a first phase extending from 1945 to the late 1950s, social policy tended to focus solely on employees in socialist companies and the public sector. This initially small group and their families were incorporated into a comprehensive system of social security and became entitled to state pensions (in addition, many veterans and war victims of the ruling communist partisans began to enjoy privileged pension arrangements) (Piškulić 1957).

In a second phase lasting from the 1960s to the beginning of the 1970s, the system expanded but began to experience financial difficulties. The socialist economy faced the enormous pressure of having to employ a constantly growing workforce that had abandoned agriculture to seek employment in industry or the public services (Puljiz 1996, 277). During this period the quite generous criteria for pension entitlement (in the 1950s, women could retire at the age of fifty, men at fifty-five) were made more restrictive (Zavod za mirovinsko osiguranje 2002, 40; Cota 1973).

In a third phase, which took place from 1973/1974 until 1990, the pension system was forced to respond to a massive increase in the number of pensioners. By 1990, pensioners already constituted 13.2 per cent of the total population. This inflation in the number of retirees was partly due to the fact that pension schemes were now established for professional and social groups that had not been included in the system up to then: in 1965 private craftsmen became part of the compulsory pension insurance scheme and 1980 saw the introduction of a pension insurance for farmers. However, the increase in the number of pensioners was also a consequence of the reality that growing numbers of workers and employees in the socialist economy and public sector had reached a pensionable age (Zavod za mirovinsko osiguranje 2002; Divjak et al. 1987).

In the early stages of this third phase, the entire welfare system was to undergo a process of significant reorganization. New financial procedures were introduced and the obligations of socialist companies to participate in the financing of welfare programmes increased dramatically (in 1990, socialist companies, for instance, paid 27 per cent of all pension contributions). Initially this had positive effects on the capacity of the welfare state. In the course of the 1980s, however, when an economic crisis began to severely burden the economy, the welfare system ran into deep trouble (Škrbić et al. 1984; Puljiz and Zrinščak 2004).

The post-socialist and transition period (1995–2006)

In 1991, Croatia became an independent state and was faced with a dramatic situation in its first years of existence. The war of 1991/1995 left huge social problems in its wake. In late 1991, when the war began to escalate, about 400,000 citizens became displaced persons or refugees; more than 20,000 people were killed (Živić 1999; Akrap and Živić 2001; Akrap et al. 2003; Gelo 2003). In addition, the post-socialist transition of the 1990s led to high social differentiation. As a result of the war, the employment slump in the socialist sector, inflation, and increasing economic differentiation, many people lost their homes, their workplace or their entire savings. There is also a pronounced regional differentiation in terms of economic development, a consequence of both socialist industrialization and urbanization, and the impact of the 1990s war. One could even speak of "two Croatias": one, visible in some of the larger urban centres (especially in the Zagreb region), that is quite prosperous, and the other, including most of the war-affected areas, characterized by difficult perspectives for future economic development (Bošnjak et al. 2002; Leutloff-Grandits 2006).

Despite this social and regional polarization, Croatia's macro-economic trends have taken an increasingly positive turn since the late 1990s, a process acknowledged by the EU in its "Avis", which paved the way for Croatia's integration into the EU (Commission of the EC 2004; Grandits 2004).

However, these trends have not solved the problems of "underemployment". The number of new jobs has not matched the loss caused by widespread "rationalization" in the early stages of transition (Balaband 1997; Kerovec 2003; Crnković-Pozaić 2004). More than one hundred thousand employees were forced into early retirement, adding to the already high number of pensioners. Figure 7.1 shows the dramatic change in the ratio between the economically active (socially insured) and the retired population during this period.

Figure 7.1: Insured and economically active population in comparision to pensioners, Croatia 1985–2003

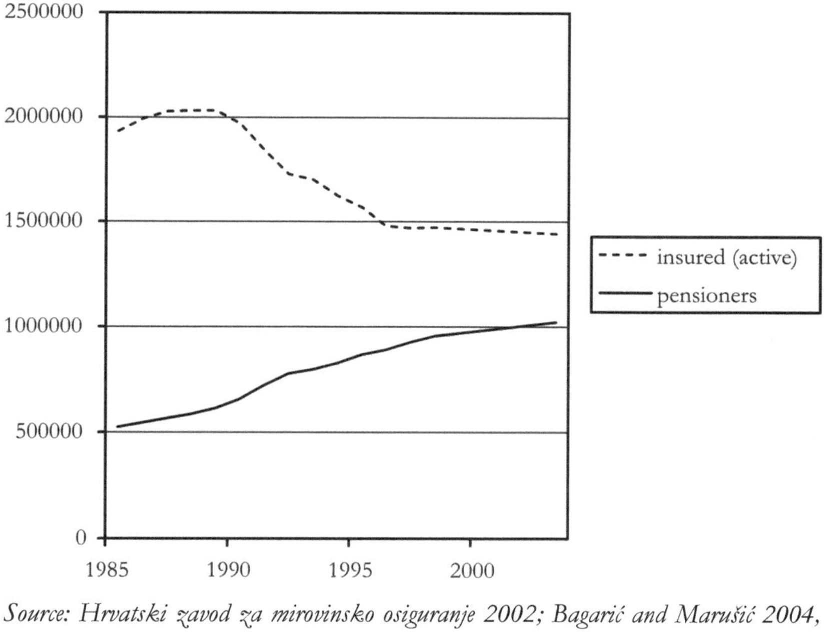

Source: Hrvatski zavod za mirovinsko osiguranje 2002; Bagarić and Marušić 2004, 53–59

While at the end of the 1980s more than two million socially insured were looking at approximately 600,000 pensioners, by 2003 the number of active/socially insured had plummeted to 1.44 million, while the number of pensioners had soared to more than a million (i.e., almost a fifth of Croatia's current population of 4.5 million people). In 2003, the ratio of the active/socially insured to pensioners was 1.37 to 1 (!) (Zrinščak 2000, 238; Bagarić and Marušić 2004, 39–61). Financing the pension scheme soon became the biggest stumbling block in Croatia's welfare system. In 1999, more than 13 per cent of Croatia's GNP went into financing existing pensions – by far the largest aspect of public social security payments (Potočnjak 2000, 1–18).

The efforts of Croatian government policy to reduce the role of the state in the welfare sphere was a response to the fear of overburdening its financial capacities. A series of laws were put in force, replacing the earlier principles of the socialist period. "Subsidiarity" became the leading principle in most social and family legislation projects. Responsibility was to be transferred to the individual citizen, to family and kin, to the local communities, to associations of civil society or to the market (see also Puljiz 2004, 3–20).

Legislation in the field of family relations ("Family law" of 1998) brought more strongly accentuated legal protection to the institution of family in society. The "National programme of demographic development" (1996) introduced a series of legal measures aimed at drawing a halt to the decline in Croatia's birth rate. With its approach to motherhood and gender roles this law could be described as extremely conservative in terms of the family. After several refinements, a new "Family law" was legislated in the summer of 2003. It modified certain aspects of the law passed in 1998, which in many respects stood for the dominant nationalist and Catholic orientations of government policy in the 1990s. These recent family policy reforms have translated into less financial support for families. This was explained by the fact that the generous financial transfers to large families in the 1990s had no effect on the ongoing low birth rate in the country (Puljiz 1999, 21–33; Puljiz and Zrinščak 2002; Milas 2003, 47–53).

During the so-called post-socialist "transition", Croatia's family policy was, as we have seen, embedded in a welfare state that was to undergo far-reaching reformulation. Possibly one of the most vital aspects in the last fifteen years has been its response to continuously low birth rates. Under socialism (and even prior to this) state welfare policy made repeated efforts to respond to ongoing changes in family life and life-course developments. The following section will briefly discuss some of the dominant family tendencies and life-course changes in Croatian society. We will first describe several pre-socialist family characteristics and go on to focus on selected life-course changes and continuities during and after the socialist period up until the present day.

Chronology of family change

Rural and urban family backgrounds prior to socialism

Extended or complex families with co-resident family members in a joint household (which could have up to twenty or even more family members), as mentioned earlier, were historically quite common in many rural regions of the Croatian lands (coastal Dalmatia and the island were usually not among them). But in village life small family households had always existed parallel. In earlier times, as a rule, due to the more or less regular division of households, the number of smaller households even greatly exceeded them in many regions. When the division of households was carried out in a kind of "mass movement" in the late nineteenth century and the "dissolution" of the traditional "zadruga" family regime hotly debated by contemporaries, small family households gradually became the dominant model in rural family life (Utješenović 1859; Bogišić 1874; Pavličević 1989; Čapo 1991; Kaser 1996). This development took regionally diverse courses and typically went hand in hand with massive land fragmentation (as a result of the predominant male-centred norms of equal inheritance). In some instances, complex family constellations remained a factor of social organization almost up to the second half of the twentieth century (Erlich 1964; Grandits 2002; Leček 2003).

Urban family life in cities like Zagreb, Rijeka or Split (as well as other towns) should be seen in quite different social, economic and cultural contexts. Zagreb, for instance, was historically an administrative centre and a hub of bourgeois culture. Small trade and small-scale industry formed the economic basis for the majority of the population. Domestic service was a characteristic feature of bourgeois family lifestyle, and journeymen and apprentices an integral part of the traditional small-trade and craftsmen households (Gross and Szabo 1985). The growing population influx that had accelerated in the second half of the nineteenth century, however, now brought forth a new urban majority, i.e., the proletarian classes. The "new" working-class families endeavoured to cope with unaccustomed urban milieus, and while they adopted in part the values of the dominant petty-bourgeois family regimes, they were also influenced by their own rural backgrounds (Kolar-Dimitrijević 1973).

Sequencing of life-course events during and after socialism

A common feature of both rural and urban family life was the fact that marriage at an early age was not merely a phenomenon of the "baby-boom" decades following the Second World War, as in many other European countries, but should be seen as a time-honoured tradition (especially in rural life). During the socialist era, marriages still took place at an early age (with a more pronounced tendency in the urban areas). From 1983 to 1985, for instance, 25 per cent of all women who married did so before their twentieth birthday; 86 per cent of marriageable women were married in their late twenties. Men also married quite early. In the first half of the 1980s, 77.7 per cent of all marriageable men were married before they were thirty years old (Akrap et al. 2003, 127).

A key characteristic of family life in Croatia in the twentieth century (and prior to it) was the fact that children were still predominately born in wedlock, one that remained almost unchanged both during and after the socialist era. In the 1980s, for instance, over 95 per cent of all children were born in wedlock and in the early 2000s, over 92 per cent. (Wertheimer-Baletić 2003, 26–31; Akrap et al. 2003, 128).

Under socialism, marrying and having children at a young age was linked to a certain extent to the housing policy of the time ("socially owned" housing became the norm in the course of massive urbanization). Despite endemic housing shortages in the rapidly growing cities and towns, married partners with children still had a good chance of being allocated a flat or a housing loan that was virtually interest-free. Couples with a child, and particularly those with several children, constituted a priority group. After the demise of socialism, the tie-in between families with children and the allocation of housing disappeared. In the early stages of the 1990s, the new Croatian democratic government privatized the socially owned housing sector. "Socially owned" flats were privatized via a complicated system of price reductions and primarily bought by the former tenants. Hence in terms of housing Croatia became a society of "owners": 83 per cent of flats and housing space is now privately owned (of the remaining 17 per cent, only seven per cent of flats are "free" to be placed on the housing market as rented accommodation). This vast change in the housing sector has not necessarily meant an improvement for young couples. Housing shortages in large cities are rampant and, where rented accommodation is concerned, frequently expensive (Bežovan 1987; Bežovan 2004, 97; Bežovan 2005,

27–31). Today, the difficulty of finding a flat, or indeed being able to pay for it, is one of the decisive reasons why young couples opt to postpone marriage.

Availability of kin

A current tendency in the sphere of family formation in Croatia is the decline in the marriage rate. In recent years, in particular, the issue of "less marriages" has been a topic of wide public debate, and been addressed with emotion by the Catholic Church. Up until the 1980s, the marriage rate was stable (between 1961 and 1983 the total number of marriages remained constant between 36,634 and 33,135) but has since fallen, especially during the 1990s, by more than a third to 22,806 marriages in 2002 (Akrap and Živić 2001, 645; Akrap 2003, 123).

Does this mean that a steadily growing percentage of the population is no longer interested in marriage? To a certain extent, the answer to this question is yes. Marriage has lost its earlier "universality" in the life course, above all since the 1990s. In the urban areas, an increased pluralization of lifestyles and family forms has gradually come to the fore. Nevertheless, the drop in the number of marriages is still largely the result of developments that are closely interlinked. The first of these is related to the 1991–1995 war and the concomitant large-scale migration. According to demographic calculations, the migration processes of the 1990s and early 2000s led to the permanent emigration of more than 200,000 – primarily young – people from Croatia (many of them Croatian Serbs). Since the overwhelming majority of these emigrants were of "marriageable age", it is not surprising that marriage rates have plummeted. The second factor involves the general ageing of Croatia's population. This process was accelerated by an earlier "wave" of emigration to Western Europe in the mid-1960s and 1970s (in the course of which almost 200,000 young Croats left Croatia to live and work permanently in Western Europe). It is also a consequence of the baby-boom generation's "departure" from the age of marriage (Akrap 2003, 129–132). The decline in Croatian marriage rates is almost certainly due in greater measure to this background of migration and demographic change than to the fact that marriage as an "institution" is being questioned. Despite (urban) trends towards alternative living patterns, marriage has remained a crucial element in the life course for the absolute majority of young people.

This also holds true with regard to having children. When women marry, they eventually have children. If change has occurred over time, it is imperceptible. When we look, for instance, at the percentage of women in the thirty-five to thirty-nine age group, who bore children between 1983 and 1985, and again the percentage in 2001, the figures are almost identical, i.e., 87.7 per cent between 1983 and 1985, and 86.9 in 2001. Interestingly, these figures give no indication of the presence of yet another trend (and one that is more hotly contested in Croatian society than the marriage issue): the comparative reduction in the number of children.

Significant changes had already set in during the socialist decades, in the course of which the reproduction rate fell from an average 2.9 children per woman in the first decade after 1945 to 1.6 at the end of the socialist period. Hence Croatia developed from being a country with a high birth rate and substantial natural population growth to a society with a low birth rate and almost no natural growth in the population (natural growth came to 0.7 in 1990) (Gelo 1987; Wertheimer-Baletić 1996; Akrap and Živić 2001; Wertheimer-Baletić 2003). This development was to continue in the decade from 1991 to 2001. Up until now there has been no evidence of improvement in the natural growth rate and for the last fifteen years an extremely low birth rate, with an average of less than 1.3 births per woman, has remained a characteristic of Croatia (Wertheimer-Baletić 1996; Živić 2003; Gelo 2003).

Low birth rates will eventually lead to shrinking kinship networks. Coupled with the long-term consequences of the above-mentioned migrations, this can mean a limited "availability" of kin in the future. Even today, massive rural-urban migration during the socialist periods of industrialization and urbanization, and several waves of "Gastarbeiter" emigration have led to a situation in which many of the younger generation now live at a great distance from their parental generation (First-Dilić 1977).

Stability of family and kin

One approach to familial stability is to look at the divorce rates in a given society. Socialist policies and legislation introduced divorce into family law in the second half of the 1940s. In the course of the 1950s, divorce had already become a familiar aspect of family life in socialist Croatia, albeit divorce rates were always low. There has been little change from the 1960s up to the present. Annual divorce rates (number of divorces in relation to every 100 marriages) indicate a seesaw movement, oscillating between 13.8 and 18.5 per cent from 1961 to 1989, and between 14.7 and 22.6 per cent from 1990 to 2002 (the post-war years of the 1990s were "exceptional" in terms of frequency of divorce) (Akrap 2003, 123). In short, socialist rule had made divorce "acceptable". In a European comparison, however, divorce in Croatia has hitherto kept a low profile with regard to structuring family situations (while other "transitional" countries such as the Czech Republic or Hungary had rates of 67.5 and 46.1 respectively in 1996, and Austria's divorce rate for the same year was 42.7, Croatia still had a divorce rate of only 14.7; Grozdanić 2000, 169–181). This corresponds with the almost negligible increase in the percentage of one-parent families with children from 11.2 to 15.9 per cent between 1971 and 2001 (Živić 2003, 66).

The considerations of this section have indicated the fact that, despite far-reaching social transformation, marriage and the family have maintained an impressive position in Croatian society up to now. This could be explained by the universally strong cultural convictions that guide family concepts and gender relations. It is, however, no easy task to classify this "value sphere" in social life. In the following section we will explore some of the characteristics of family, gender and kin values in Croatian society. This takes the form of a three step-approach that combines two long-term – seemingly "contradictory" – historical processes with the findings of several contemporary surveys.

Gender relations and family values

Socialism versus and with patriarchy

The Croatian fascist Ustaša movement, which had been installed by the Third Reich during the Second World War to rule the short-lived "Independent State of Croatia" (1941–1945), aimed at implementing policies inspired by those of the Nazi regime in Germany. The patriarchal notions contained in their family ideology were closely linked to a totalitarian concept of society based on nationalism. Women were praised for their role of giving birth to the children of an "expanding" nationalist society. The vigourous attempts of the Ustašas to involve the Catholic Church in its concept of society furthered a new expansion of religious symbolism in the images of the family propagated by the state (Jelić-Butić 1977; Sundhaussen 1983).

When the communist-led partisans took power in 1944/1945, "fascist" rule and consequently its family ideology were condemned as having been disastrous for the social development of Croatia. In addition, the new communist propaganda left little room for the "bourgeois" family values of the "capitalist elite" and urban petty bourgeoisie, rejecting their ideology out of hand. The same was true for the "patriarchy" of rural family life, which was stigmatized as "backward" and to be overcome in the process of socialism (Šuvar 1988).

Propaganda efforts to implement a socialist way of family life were particularly intense in the early phase of socialist rule. Private agriculture was depicted as being hand in glove with "ancient" patriarchal relations. The striving for private land was termed "peasant idiotism" and the "bourgeoisie" ideals of private life deemed anti-socialist. As already discussed in previous sections, the goal of employing women in the labour force was seen as crucial to realizing a progressive socialist family model (from the very beginning of socialist rule, the constitution guaranteed women full equality rights). Youth education was another important aspect. Discussions in schools about family and the village in the past were contrasted with socialist visions of a "modern future". Here, families no longer had several children; two children was the norm, with both parents working and – interestingly – close relations between children, parents and grandparents. Socialism was presented as a new linkage between the generations (Grandits 2002).

In the latter period of socialism, the praises of the "modern socialist family" were sung less aggressively. From the 1960s and 1970s on, sociological research began to evaluate how far society had progressed in its efforts at modernization. Public discourse was beginning to deal with the problems that arise on the path to a classless society. Furthermore, the Yugoslav approach of an independent path to socialism, which combined the "workers' self-administration" with the incorporation of "Western" market principles into the socialist economy, had implications for family life. Not unlike the economy, the social areas of daily life in Croatia became increasingly open to "Western" lifestyle trends (ranging from consumer goods to films, and from fashion trends to shopping tourism). This "westernization" impacted on several spheres of ordinary life. However, something else seems to have been even more characteristic of family life and gender relations, i.e., the fusion of patriarchal values and socialist role expectations.

This interpretation seems a fair assumption when reflecting on the sociological and ethnological literature that deals in particular with the (late-) socialist transformations of family life (both rural and urban). It should be noted here that between 1945 and the 1980s, the rural population of Croatia dropped from 80 per cent to 50 per cent (and the number of people who lived on agriculture fell from 65 per cent to little more than ten per cent). The social landscape of the rural areas became more "complex". De-agrarianization had increased the number of non-agricultural households and part-time farmers to such an extent that full-time peasant families had become a village minority towards the end of the socialist era. Stressing in particular the trends that evolved as a consequence of social transformation under socialism, R. First-Dilić summed up "continuity and change" in rural family life in Croatia in the early 1980s as follows:

- a growing appraisal of individual labour
- a change of attitude to patrimony and to the land, which had ranked highest in the value scale in the past (and a trend to invest in a house rather than land)
- increasing independence of the individual from family, kin, neighbourhood and village community
- a decline in the number of children desired and born, and a decline in the number of co-residing generations coupled with a strong trend towards two-generational households
- a decline in the authority of the father and the husband

R. First-Dilić identified degrees of "more" or "less" in the abovementioned trends, pointing to the fact that change was long-term rather than "revolutionary". This perspective is maintained in the résumé of altered gender relations, which graduated "from patricentricity to equality", albeit it was "more aspired to than the real order of behaviour" (First-Dilić 1981, 140).

Other research has dealt with the close relation between the rural and the urban as a result of mass migration from rural villages to towns and cities. Interpretations centred on the "ruralization" of many spheres of urban life, implying once again a "fusion" of rural (former "agriculturally based") patriarchy with socialist family and gender ideals of growing importance (e.g., Štambuk 1990, 74).

Stimulating research has been carried out on socialist urban family life without referring to "rural patriarchy", although patriarchal tendencies are addressed. The ethnologist D. Rihtman-Auguštin dealt comprehensively with transformation in socialist urban life in Croatia. On the one hand, she appreciated the enormous ideological value that official socialist policy attributed to gender "emancipation" (in contrast to the preceding historic periods, where "patriarchy was part of the ideology of the state and the ruling religion") and stressed the fact that accelerated female employment had shattered the "exclusion of women from the public sphere". On the other hand, she by no means idealized the situation. In particular she pointed out two characteristic tendencies: firstly, the fact that most female employees worked in low-wage sectors of the socialist industry (e.g., 70 per cent of female industrial workers in the 1980s worked in the textile, leather or dry goods industries, which were known as the "cheapest" industrial sectors) and that women were rarely visible in the upper echelons of management, politics or science. Secondly, despite changes in the lifestyle of working women, strong elements of "traditionalism" remained firmly anchored in the family domain. "Patriarchy" was still manifest in the deep-rooted classical differentiation of gender roles. The realm of child care and the home persisted almost exclusively as a female "obligation". Despite publicly propagated feminist orientations and the socialist rhetoric of emancipation, the stereotype of the wife as responsible for the members of the family, i.e., husband and children, and a "perfectly" maintained household, continued to prevail. Hence two different styles of behaviour were characteristic of urban family life. D. Rihtman-Auguštin described this vividly as follows:

> "The father, of course, can read the newspaper and watch TV, while the mother cooks or does the washing or irons the laundry. The problem is that in 44 per cent of all Yugoslav households the mother can only turn to household chores after a full day at her workplace. As a matter of interest, no different to the father" (Rihtman-Auguštin 1988, 201).

These reflections clearly demonstrate that in terms of family, care was seen primarily as a female task. Women were held responsible for the household, their husbands and their children. Looking at the sphere of intergenerational help, research has shown that the differentiation was less explicit.

Socialist modernization has led to a greater convergence of the gender specifics involved in the intergenerational contact between grown-up children and their elderly parents. A study carried out in the late 1970s dealing with support given to rural families by their children who had left the village indicates that almost 60 per cent of the parents interviewed confirmed that they had received support from their children. The tendency to help was higher among sons than daughters (although the kind/quality of help could vary). Respondents frequently pointed out that daughters were too busy looking after their own family and children, and that sons had more time at their disposal (and, in the case of financial assistance, that sons were in a better position). Nonetheless, female support in this context was also substantial. Interpreted in restrospect, it is still a matter for dispute in socio-ethnological discourse as to whether this convergence of gender-specific generational support in Croatian rural life became more common as a result of "socialist equality" policies or whether it should be seen as "tradition" in the daughter-mother relationship (First-Dilić 1977, 75–85).

Nationalism, Catholicism and post-modernity

At the beginning of the 1990s and amidst the savagery of war, Croatia established a multi-party democracy. Public (political) discourse in subsequent years was largely overshadowed by nationalist rhetoric. During the first decade of independence, Croatian policy was dominated by the nationalist HDZ movement (and since the year 2000 by various coalition governments). Programmatically the HDZ firmed as a movement to overcome socialist one-party repression and mismanagement, and to build up western-oriented capitalist market democracy. It might be appropriate in scrutinizing the ideological positions of this popular movement on family values to take note of several ambiguities in its dominant rhetoric. The same holds true for public discourse in the 1990s.

Two core trends that were to become highly significant can be identified: nationalism laced with patriarchal connotations and the revival of religion as a key factor in society. Moreover, nationalism and a patriarchal approach to family – typically almost inseparable – were closely linked in the Croatia of the 1990s. The image of the national leader who attends to the "well-being of the nation" was presented primarily as that of a father taking care of his family. The archaic term "hearth" (ognjište) began to enter political rhetoric as an equivalent for family or household and referred symbolically to the old family traditions of peasant life. A mythological "natural order" of the past, where family harmony went hand in hand with the traditional roles of mothers and fathers, and wives and husbands, was slowly becoming implicit.

Parallel to this nationalist boom, religion re-emerged as a dominant aspect of public and political life. Both the Catholic and the Orthodox Churches in Croatia had suffered oppression under socialism. The aim of atheist socialist policy was to devaluate popular religiosity (via the media, the educational system, and propaganda on an anti-religious way of life), a policy that became more moderate in the latter stages of socialist rule. The 1990s saw an unmistakeable renaissance of the church/religion in political and social life (Vrcan 2001). Church rituals once again became increasingly prominent among both Catholic and Orthodox populations. The destruction of churches during the war of the 1990s was an attempt to symbolically damage the other's nation/religion. After the exodus of the Serbian population following the military breakdown of their secessionist movement in the summer of 1995, Catholicism became the sole and omnipresent state religion of Croatia. Official celebrations without the attendance of a Catholic priest or higher church officials were rare. Studies on the development of religiosity in Croatia in the initial post-communist decade showed that between 1989 and 1996, the percentage of devout believers, based on self-assessment, more than doubled from 15 to 36 per cent, and that for the same period the percentage of atheists fell dramatically from 34 to 11 per cent (Marinović-Jerolimović and Skledar 1997, 185).

The Catholic Church has obviously become (again) a significant factor in public life in Croatia (and about 80 per cent of the population declare themselves Roman Catholics). Family plays a vital role in the religious reflections of the Catholic Church. Despite the fact that religiosity has been given a strong impetus (which has become less pronounced in the last few years), however, the consequences for family life should not be overestimated. According to a survey that compared the significance of religiosity in Croatia, Poland and Austria, religious positions seem to be of extreme importance to only a limited group of staunch believers. The latter made up little more than ten per cent of those interviewed, who claimed that Catholic positions on the family were valid for their own family lives as well. A large majority of those who professed to be "religious" stated that although religiosity played a role in their lives it did not function as a shaping model for their approach to the family. This was exemplified, for instance, by the highly controversial issue of abortion, where the position of the Church was passionately discussed. Women had been granted a constitutional right to abortion during the socialist era. The survey indicated that the majority of respondents did not question this right and that the opinion prevailed, even among many of the "religious", that abortion should remain a constitutional right. (Leutar 2001, 85–107). Maintaining the right to abortion, which the HDZ government of the 1990s attempted to restrict, is one illustrative example that the revival of nationalism and of religion may only have a temporary effect on the realities of ordinary family life in the long term. In the end, lack of popular support for this issue led to the withdrawal of a legal initiative on the abortion question during the 1990s (Puljiz 2001, 171). Due also to a general tail off in popular support, the nationalist government lost power in early 2000.

What followed, and has never really been absent in recent decades, was the increasing importance of approaches to family, in which global consumer trends were integrated (or not) with existing patriarchal paradigms and/or socialist values on family and gender relations. Still, social stratification and the above-mentioned regionally very diverse economic and social situation do not make this ongoing change a uniform process in Croatian society.

Contemporary survey results

In the last fifteen years numerous studies have been carried out on family values and interfamilial relations in "transitional" Croatia. Against the backdrop of developments discussed above, it might be helpful to learn what is currently considered "characteristic" in the various spheres of Croatian society with regard to the frame of family and gender values.

A topic frequently discussed in surveys is the persistence of "patriarchal attitudes" in familial and social relations. In a large study carried out in 1999, the great majority of those surveyed accepted or even affirmed patriarchal principles in family life (with a slight difference in emphasis on gender, educational and rural-urban categories). This acceptance of patriarchy in the midst of a "crisis of values and ideologies" (e.g., the collapse of socialism) and an atmosphere of social uncertainty and massive unemployment has been interpreted as the "dream of a lost past", where despite the absence of equality, people were happy and secure. In this sense, patriarchy seemed to represent an ideal society that not only functioned but gave prominence to the value of caring (about the family, about society). However, the same study stressed that, on the contrary, patriarchy was no longer a "homogeneous" phenomenon. Patriarchal values were often accepted in discourse only under the condition that the "liberal" standards of ordinary family life achieved under socialism were not abandoned, as, for instance, the equal right to decision-making of both married partners (Kodrnja 2002, 155–180).

Research based on the European Value Study project (EVS) for Croatia indicates in the context of male and female role expectations – and despite the above-mentioned "patriarchal" trends and distinct family orientation – that social value standards are undergoing even greater change. These studies emphasize the process of "individualization" that has currently taken hold of Croatian society in various dynamics and levels of intensity and is most evident among women between the ages of eighteen and twenty-four. The young women of this age group were quite vehement in their criticism of "traditional" gender role expectations in society. Men across all age groups were more strongly influenced than women by the traditional view of gender roles. In addition, EVS results illustrated that certain attitudes, which to some extent are highly disputed in Western Europe, are rarely questioned in post-socialist Croatia. This applies particularly to the position on female employment – a legacy of the socialist period. 73.6 per cent of all respondents in the study agreed or strongly agreed with the opinion that "employment is the best way for a woman to realize independence". In the eighteen to twent-four age bracket, 87 per cent of women agreed with this position, a view that was only slightly less agreed to by older women. Women over the age of fifty-five agreed to 84.2 per cent. Agreement with the statement was furthermore quite high among the male population. Interestingly, it was higher for the older than the younger age group: 76.6 per cent of men over fifty-five agreed with the position as against 66.3 per cent of young men between eighteen and twenty-four (Črpić and Biščan 2000, 421–442).

Notwithstanding the trends observed in the direction of "individualization" and the growing criticism of the traditional gender role expectations voiced by younger women, a further study based on the EVS project (and an additional survey) indicates that one aspect of the value system has remained "stable", i.e., the extremely positive attitude towards marriage, starting a family and having children. Only 1.5 per cent of those interviewed had no desire to have children, whereas more than 77 per cent claimed they would even like to have two or three children. The authors of the study concluded that in accordance with the answers to questions dealing with the desire to have children "Croatia would in the near future predominantly have families with two or three children" (Črpić and Koračević 2000, 343–357). Taking demographic developments into account, on the other hand, and the conspicuous drop in the birth rate during the 1990s, it is obvious that the reality of everyday life is quite a different matter (Živić 2003, 66).

All of the studies reviewed make manifest that the dominant values in society and the socio-economic realities of family life have to be brought to terms. For many in present-day (post-) "transitional" Croatia, achieving this goal is not an easy task. Key issues here seem to be reconciling family and female employment, and the social reality of care. The following section will give some understanding of the relevant strategies pursued within the current framework of the Croatian welfare state.

Public and private sides to care

Female employment and child care

The development of female employment in Croatia was, as mentioned earlier, one of the most "revolutionary" advancements of the socialist era (and definitely one that had a substantial impact on the changes in the life courses and generational relations in recent decades). During the 1990s, the high percentage of female employees in the total workforce has remained stable. By 2001, it had even risen slightly to 45.5 per cent. However, the figures for women actually employed went through a series of significant disruptions. During the war and in the course of economic reforms countless women left the labour market, many of whom became unemployed (see figure 7.2). By the end of 2001, more than 20 per cent of working women were registered as unemployed (Kerovec 2003, 342).

Figure 7.2: Total number of unemployed and female unemployment, Croatia 1985–2001

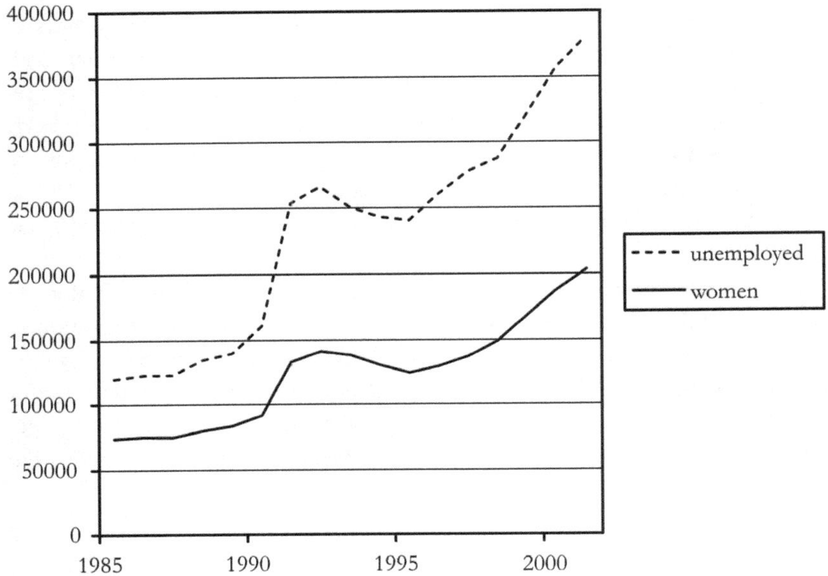

Source: Kerovec 2003, 342

Despite the problem of unemployment, wage work has remained an integral part of the female life course in Croatian society. In 2000, 56 per cent of women between the ages of fifteen and sixty-four participated in the labour market, a far higher rate, for instance, than in EU countries such as Italy (39.6 per cent) or Spain (40.3 per cent), but lower than in several northern European countries, e.g., Sweden (71 per cent). This should also be seen against the background that part-time employment – in many European countries the principal "job reality" for women with (small) children (77 per cent of women in the Netherlands work part-time; 36 per cent in Sweden) – in Croatia does not carry much weight. In the year 2000, only two per cent of female employees in Croatia worked part-time (Kerovec 2003, 330; European Commission 2001, 69).

During the socialist era, the advanced form of state-sponsored day care for pre-school children in many socialist countries enabled women to work outside the home, thereby increasing the percentage of women in the labour force. As mentioned earlier, this was not really the case in the republics of former Yugoslavia. In 1989, less than a third of children aged between three and six (29.4 per cent) attended kindergarten in socialist Croatia. This changed little during the first decade of transition. In 2000, the percentage of children betwenn three and six years of age who went to kindergarten increased only slightly to 36.3 per cent. In other words, almost two thirds of pre-school children of kindergarten age did not attend this institution. Looking at the enrolment rate of children between one and three years of age, the percentage of children in public day-care institutions is even smaller. Only 15 per cent of children in this age group attended public care institutions in 2000. In an international comparative study that dealt with fifteen European so-called transition countries, Croatia ranked almost last in terms of enrolment of pre-school children in public day care (Raboteg-Šarić 2004, 547; Stropnik 2003, 559–596).

Three reasons can be identified for the relatively low rate of public child care despite the pronounced female employment rates previously discussed. Firstly, socialist policy did not put a great deal of effort into building up a public day-care system for pre-school children in the 1970s and 1980s (when this sector expanded Europe-wide). Secondly, the war period during the 1990s caused massive destruction of public infrastructure (UNICEF 1998). After the war, the lion's share of state investment therefore went first of all into the repairs and reconstruction of damaged buildings and only very rarely into expanding or improving the quality of the public child-care system. Thirdly, and probably most importantly, the particularly high value that Croatian citizens put on family obligations in child care must be taken into consideration. The attitude that children should be with their families as long as possible during their early years is dominant in large parts of society. It is frequently combined with the conviction that child care in existing public institutions is of a comparatively "bad quality" (Raboteg-Šarić 2004, 549).

Due to lack of research, it is difficult to assess how child care is organized in families of working parents with children who do not send their pre-school children to public day-care institutions or do so for a short time only. One study based on interviews with 1,500 young families has shown that some basic trends seem characteristic: in many Croatian families, grandparents assume a significant role in child care. They sometimes live with the young couple in a multigenerational household or, more often, in separate households close by (grandparents seem to provide most of the support to parents with small children, although brothers, sisters, friends and neighbours participate to a remarkable extent). Parents who do not have close relatives – and not only these – are forced to develop excellent "organizing" skills (e.g., parents adjust their work shifts so that one of them is available when their children come home). The findings of the study quoted here have further shown that 68 per cent of fathers and 39 per cent of mothers spend more than eight hours daily at work, and that only 28 per cent of working mothers spend less than eight hours at work. It is quite evident from these figures that reconciling work and child care in "transitional" Croatia without family help or institutional support is virtually impossible (Milanović et al. 2000; Raboteg-Šarić 2004, 563).

There are, however, deficits in institutional support. Parents in many communities have difficulty in finding suitable places for their children (with particular reference to nurseries) (Raboteg-Šarić 2004, 547). For many low-income families, public day care seems comparatively expensive. A study conducted in 2002, in which 812 parents were interviewed, indicated that 34 per cent of the interviewed couples with children and 45 per cent of the single parents stated that the cost of public day care was "high" or "too high" for their pockets (Raboteg-Šarić and Josipović 2003). The private child-care institutions, playhouses or baby-sitting services, that have mushroomed in many urban contexts in recent years are even more expensive (Raboteg-Šarić 2004, 548).

We have, however, not yet touched on the most relevant options: mothers decide to interrupt or give up their employment in order to make their wish to have children a reality. Many of the 44 per cent of all women in Croatia between fifteen and sixty-four years of age who are not employed gave up work when they became mothers. Bearing in mind the severe problem of unemployment and the insecurity of existing jobs, women having children also has the unintended effect of leaving the labour market for an indeterminate period or even permanently. Consequently many couples "postpone" having children. As already discussed above, Croatia has one of the lowest birth rates in Europe. The uneven tenor of the economic sphere and the inherent difficulty of combining female employment, particularly that of mothers, with family "obligations" is undoubtedly one crucial explanation for the low birth rate.

Retirement arrangements

The life-course characteristics of the elderly in Croatian society must be seen against an economic and social backdrop that has undergone radical change since the middle of the twentieth century. At the beginning of the socialist period, Croatia was a predominantly agricultural rural society with quite a "young" population and relatively few old people. Of the 110,660 pensioners (or 2.7 per cent of the total population) in 1953, only 28,489 were old-age pensioners (41,938 were invalid pensioners and 40,233 family pensioners). Towards the end of the socialist era Croatia became an industrialized country with a large urban population. In 1991, 17.5 per cent of the population was over sixty years of age, a figure that increased to 21.5 per cent by 2001. (Živić 2003, 64; Zavod za mirovinsko osiguranje 2002, 40, 92)

In the early stages of socialism, those who lived on private agriculture could not expect a state pension. They were obliged in old age to live off the land they owned and from the help and solidarity of their children and their relatives. The situation of the employed in the expanding socialist economy was a different matter. In the 1950s, this "working class" was able to retire quite early and enjoy a pension that amounted to a large percentage of the wages they had earned in their active professional life. "Socialist pensioners" were subsequently regarded as a particularly privileged social group.

In the last two decades this has changed radically. The difficulties associated with social security in old age have already been mentioned in the course of the above observations.

The pension reforms carried out in 1998 and 1999 had a significant social and economic impact on the pension system (Potočnjak 2000, 1–18). All in all, these reforms were regarded as indispensable to preventing the financial breakdown of the system. It became apparent, however, that the issue of numerous pensioners having to survive on very low pensions had not been tackled adequately (Bagarić and Marušić 2004, 39–61). According to the Central Bureau of Statistics (2004), 32 per cent of the elderly in Croatia (with either a very low pension or none at all) were registered as poor, i.e., were living on an income below the official "poverty threshold".

It was characteristic of the socialist era in Croatia that elderly care had not been "institutionalized" to the extent of establishing a large infrastructure of homes for the elderly. By the end of the socialist period, only 7,629 of the approximately 600,000 pensioners were living in homes of this kind, i.e., only 1.3 per cent of all pensioners (and 2.9 per cent of old-age pensioners) (Zavod za mirovinsko osiguranje 2002, 60). With the almost doubling of the total number of pensioners during the 1990s, the percentage is now probably even smaller than it was fifteen years ago.

The extremely low rate of old-age care in specialized institutions (which, without going into further detail about the system of public home care at this point, only gradually began to expand in the final stages of the socialist period) shows that family and kin – when available – must have had a key function in (dependent) elderly care. As current research has indicated, close ties between grown-up children and older parents have always been a priority in Croatian society (Črpić 2003, 170). Social expectations with regard to care of needy elderly parents by their children and family are certainly high (as was the case in socialist times, First-Dilić 1977, 74–85). The placement of an elderly father or mother in a home for the elderly is still largely perceived as neglect on the part of their children. Still, expectations are frequently not met. The problem of elderly people being "abandoned" as a result of rural emigration was already a vital issue in socialist sociology (Šuvar 1988; Livada 1970, 1983; Puljiz 1984). The war and migrations of the 1990s, and severe economic problems (low pensions, high unemployment) have made elderly care in an even greater number of cases a heavy burden for the younger generations.

Social care and support for the poor and the handicapped

When war cast a shadow over social life from 1991 to 1995, Croatia's welfare system was severely tried. Care of the masses of displaced persons and refugees – at times more than 15 per cent of the total population – was organized within the framework of special governmental programmes. Here, international organizations such as UNHCR or those financed by the EU and several countries outside of Europe, played an important role. Furthermore, both newly established NGOs and those that had already been in operation under socialism became engaged in various fields of humanitarian and social aid in war-torn Croatia. In the years after the war, international humanitarian aid, which had hitherto been distributed via the national networks of Croatian NGOs, was gradually cut back. Due to demobilization of the military and the strong increase in unemployment, many people became dependent on social assistance. Refugee families who had returned to their homes in the heavily destroyed war zones found themselves in this situation for a long period. Apart from supporting socially vulnerable groups, i.e., the unemployed and the elderly/pensioners, the welfare system was faced with the massive problems of displaced persons and returnees, as well as other victims of war (Šućur 2000, 257–258; Leutloff-Grandits 2005). Significant sections of the population in many of the former war zones still live more or less exclusively on social welfare. In Šibenik-Knin county, for instance, almost 12 per cent of the population survives on benefit payments, and in five other badly affected counties approximately five per cent of the total population lives on welfare (Šućur 2004, 27).

As a consequence of the war, both state and non-state infrastructure in the field of social care has developed dense networks. The state-sponsored network of "Social care centres", which were established in the 1950s, have remained crucial to the organization and distribution of social care and social assistance. However, many other institutions in the communities also became active during and after the war. The authors of a study on social care in present-day Croatia concluded that restrictions on public care and support for the needy is not so much due to a lack of organizational potential. On the contrary, as a result of massive efforts to deal with serious wartime situations, organizations have gained substantial experience in this field. What the study criticizes is the now dwindling amount of funds available to the social care sector. The absence of funds not only limits the activities of existing institutions, but at the same time restrains their ability to cope with current demands (Havelka et al. 2000, 26).

The crisis of the 1990s and the subsequent transition was a particularly hard blow to the handicapped, their families and their position in society. In the year 2000, the author of a study on the handicapped in transitional Croatia summarizes their situation as follows: "The handicapped are often the last to obtain work and among the first to lose it, which isolates them socially and "condemns" them to languishing at home with their families and on the periphery of society, and thus become a target of social welfare" (Zovko 2000, 286). The study is highly critical of the poor integration of the handicapped in society, thereby rendering them either dependent on their families or on public welfare. The reality of the social system for the handicapped in Croatia is characterized to some degree by a structural contrast. On the one hand, the system of public care for the handicapped is underdeveloped, i.e., the number of people (or their families) eligible for state support, such as financial assistance for private care, home care or access to care in specific institutions does not exceed 0.7 per cent of the total population (this percentage is up to ten times higher in many EU-countries). On the other hand, the number of invalid pensioners in Croatia is extremely high. By the end of the socialist period in 1990, invalid pensioners numbered 163,309. This figure rose to even more than 200,000 in the course of the next decade and a half (Zovko 2000, 278; Zavod za mirovinsko osiguranje 2002, 57, 92).

Conclusion

After the collapse of the socialist system in Croatia, the war of the 1990s and the subsequent radical change in the socio-economic landscape, a new approach to social security became vital. It defined the commitments of the state differently to those prevailing under socialism. The state was to become one of several major factors in the field of social security. In particular, family and kin, the market (e.g., private insurance or services) and civil society institutions were to assume responsibilities and contribute to the establishment of a so-called "mixed system". The idea was to prevent the state from being financially overburdened and render the social security system more efficient.

The answer to the question of whether state policy intended to "crowd in" family and kin – a major aspect of our research – into social security arrangements is a definitive yes! Although the state has remained a key actor in the sphere of social security, it has withdrawn from several areas. An unmistakeable trend has been observed over the last fifteen years: the state is reducing its involvement (e.g., in the field of unemployment insurance), hoping that other "actors" in the mixed system will take over some of the responsibility.

During the (repeatedly crisis-ridden) socialist welfare expansion, public and kinship-based social security increasingly complemented each other. And "intensive" family and kin relations have remained an important value up to the present. However, despite the prominent significance still given to family and kin, and their various functions in providing social security (in making things work: from reconciling employment with family to supporting dependent elderly people), the impact of the dramatic scaling-down of the welfare state was soon to become evident: a vast increase in the social stratification of society accompanied by alarming pauperization in certain sections (usually among the most vulnerable with very little material resources or kin networks, i.e., among pensioners, single mothers, the unemployed or returnees to war-torn regions).

In addition, the remarkably low birth rates in Croatia are in all likelihood strongly related to a welfare system that is not sufficiently supportive of working women and young mothers in an otherwise general atmosphere of economic liberalization.

Bibliography

Akrap, A. (2003), "Promjene u strukturama fertilnoga kontingenta u Hrvatskoj 1971–2001", *Zbornik ekonomskog fakulteta u Zagreb,* Br. 1, pp. 105–128.

Akrap, A. and D. Živić (2001), "Demografske odrednice i obilježja obiteljske strukture stanovništva Hrvatske", *Društvena istraživanja*, god. 10., br. 54/55, pp. 621–653.

Akrap, A., I. Čipin, N. Pokos, T. Ridzak, and D. Živić (2003), *Činitelji demografskih kretanja u Republici Hrvatskoj. državni zavod za zaštitu obitelji, materinstva i mladeži*, Zagreb.

Alber, J. (1987), *Vom Armenhaus zum Wohlfahrtsstaat. Analysen zur Entwicklung der Sozialversicherung in Westeuropa*, (2), Frankfurt/New York: Campus.

Allcock, J. B. (1980), "The socialist transformation of the village: Yugoslav agricultural policy since 1945", in R. A. Francisco, B. A. Laird and R. D. Laird (eds.), *Agricultural policies in the USSR and eastern Europe*, Boulder: Westview Press, pp. 199–216.

Andrić, N. (1980), "Društveno-ekonomski razvoj i planiranje položaja žene i porodice", *Žena, 38 (3)*, pp. 43–50.

Bagarić, N. and L. Marušić (2004), "Pristup socijalnim pravima u Hrvatskoj: mirovinsko osiguranje", *Revija za socijalnu politiku*, God. 11, br. 1, pp. 39–61.

Balaband, A. (1997), "Socijalna skrb i nezaposlenost u Hrvatskoj", *Revija za socijalnu politiku*, God. IV. br. 3, pp. 253–264.

Ban, B. (1984), "Domovi za djecu i omladinum", in Mirna Škrbić et al. (eds.), *Socijalna zaštita u Sociajističkoj Republici Hrvatskoj. Razvoj, stanje, perspektive*, Zagreb: Jugoslavenska Medicinska naklada, pp. 390–394.

Barbič, A. (1984), "Seoske žene zaposlene izvan gospodarstva", *Sociologija sela*, pp. 83–86.

Baryli, A. (1977), *Die Sonder-Sozialversicherung der Angestellten in Österreich bis 1938*, 2, Wien: (Diss. Univ. Wien).

Bežovan, G. (1987), *Stanovanje i stambena kriza*, Zagreb: CDD.

— (2004), "Stambena prava u Hrvatskoj i problemi njihova ostvarenja", *Revija za socijalnu politiku*, God. 11. br. 1, pp. 89–106.

— (2005), "Kroatien: Improvisationen in der Wohnungspolitik", *Ost-West Gegeninformationen*, 17(1), pp. 27–31.

Bogišić, B. (1874), *Zbornik sadašnih pravnih običaja u Južnih Slovena*, Zagreb.

Bošnjak, V. (1973), "Razvoj socijalne zaštite od 1945–1965. godine", *Socijalni rad 3–4*, pp. 5–10.

Bošnjak, V., J. Mimica, V. Puljiz, T. Radočaj, P. Stubbs and S. Zrinščak (2002), *Social policies and welfare in Croatia: an assessment review for UNICEF*, Zagreb.

Commission of the European Communities (2004), *Communication from the commission. Opinion on Croatia's application for membership of the European Union*, Brussels.

Cota, Z. (1973), *Mirovinsko i invalidsko osiguranje (zbirka propisa i objašnjenjima)*, Zagreb: Narodne novine.

Crnković-Pozaić, S. (2004), "Pravo na rad: od obveze države do osobne odgovornosti", *Revija za socijalnu politiku*, God. 11. br. 1, pp.79–87.

Czúcz, O. (1991), "Ungarn: Die doppelte Krise eines einhundertjährigen Sozialversicherungssystems", *Zeitschrift für ausländisches und internationales Arbeits- und Sozialrecht (ZIAS)*, 5, pp. 326–351.

Čapo, J. (1991), *Vlastenlinstvo Cernik. Gospodarstvene i demografske promjene na hrvatskom selu u kasnome feudalizmu*, Zagreb: Institut za etnologiju i folkloristiku,.

Črpić, G. and Ž. Bišćan (2000), "Muško i žensko između uloge i osobe: ispitivanje promjene uloge spolova u hrvatskom društvu", *Bogoslovska smotra*, 70 (2), pp. 421–442.

Črpić, G. and K. Kovačević (2000), "Stavovi hrvatskih građana prema djeci", in *Bogoslovska smotra*, 70 (2), pp. 343–357.

Črpić, G. (2003), "Obrisi hrvatske demografske implozije", in Dražen Živić, Nenad Pokos and Anka Mišetić (eds.), *Stanovništvo Hrvatske – Dosadašnji razvoj i perspektive*, Zagreb: Institut društvenih znanosti Ivo Pilar, pp. 161–176.

Divjak, B. et al. (1987), *Mirovinsko i invalidsko osiguranje (zbirka propisa i objašnjenjima)*, Zagreb: Narodne novine.

Erlich, V. (1964), *Porodica u transformaciji. Studija u tri stotine jugoslavenskih sela*, Zagreb: Liber, Izdanja Instituta za Znanost o Knjizevnosti.

European Commission (2001), *Employment in EUROPE 2000*, n.p.

First-Dilić, R. (1977), "Međugeneracijsko ispomaganje u seoskoj porodici", *Sociologija sela*, 55–56, god. 15, siječanj-lipanj: pp. 75–85.

— (1981), *Seoska porodica danas: kontinuitet ili promjene*, Zagreb: Institut za društvena istraživanja Sveučilišta.

— (1984), "Changing economic role of rural women in SFR Yugoslavia", in *Social classes, social change and economic development in the Mediterranean:* international conference of the Foundation for Mediterranean Studies, Athens, pp. 247–274.

Gelo, J. (1987), *Demografske promjene u Hrvatskoj od 1780 do. 1981*, Zagreb: Globus.

— (2003), "Demografske promjene u Hrvatskoj kao osnova Nacionalne obiteljske politike", in V. Puljiz and D. Bouillet (eds.), *Nacionalna obiteljska politika. Drugo prošireno izdanje*, Zagreb: Državni zavod za zaštitu obitelji, materinstva imladeži, pp. 73–101.

Grandits, H. (2002), *Familie und sozialer Wandel im ländlichen Kroatien (18.–20. Jahrhundert)*, Wien, Köln, Weimar: Böhlau.

— (2004), "Kroatien: EU-Euphorie als Mittel zu innenpolitischer Besonnenheit", *Ost-West Gegeninformationen*, 16(1), pp. 40–44.

Gross, M. and A. Szabo (1985), "Die Stadt Zagreb an der Wende vom 19. zum 20. Jahrhundert. Der Fall eines Nachholprozesses", in M. Glettler et al. (eds.), *Zentrale Städte und ihr Umland. Wechselwirkungen während der Industrialisierungsperiode in Mitteleuropa*, St. Katharinen: Scripta Mercaturae Verlag, pp. 246–271.

Grozdanić, S. (2000), *Kvaliteta odnosa medu članovima jednoroditeljskih obitelji: magistarski rad*, Zagreb.

Havelka, M., J. Despot-Lučanin and D. Lučanin (2000), "Potrebe starijih osoba za cjelovitim uslugama skrbi u lokalnoj zajednici", *Revija za socijalnu politiku*, (1), pp. 19–27.

Iris, G. (1984), "Društvena briga o djeci predškolskog uzrasta", in Milan Škrbić, et al. (eds.), *Socijalna zaštita u Sociajističkoj Republici Hrvatskoj. Razvoj, stanje, perspektive*, Zagreb: Jugoslavenska Medicinska naklada, pp. 318–325.

Jelić-Butić, F. (1977), *Ustaše i Nezavisna Država Hrvatske*, Zagreb: Školska knjiga.

Kaser, K. (1996), "Household and family contexts in the Balkans", *The History of the Family. An International Quarterly*, Vol. 1/4. 1996, pp. 375–387.

Kerovec, N. (1990), "Položaj žene u zapošljavanju", *Žena 48* (1–2) 1990, pp. 87–97.

— (2003), "Položaj žena na hrvatskom tržištu rada", in V. Puljiz and D. Bouillet, (eds.), *Nacionalna obiteljska politika. 2. prošireno izdanje*, Zagreb: Državni zavod za zaštitu obitelji, materinstva i mladeži, pp. 323–355.

Kodrnja, J. (2002), "Patrijarhalnost u hrvatskoj obitelji: briga ili dominacija", *Sociologija sela*, God. 40, 1/2 (155/156). Zagreb: siječanj-lipanj, pp. 155–180.

Kolar-Dimitrijević, M. (1973), *Radni slojevi Zagreba od 1918 do 1931*, Zagreb: Institut za radničkog pokreta Hrvatske.

Leček, S. (2003), *Seljačka obitelj u sjeverozapadnoj Hrvatskoj 1918–1941*, Zagreb: Srednja Europa.

Leutar, Z. (2001), "Religioznost obitelji u Hrvatskoj, Austriji i Poljskoj", *Bogoslovna smotra*, LXXI/1., pp. 85–107.

Leutloff-Grandits, C. (2005), "Return as a strategy of social security? Generational and family based approaches to return of Serbian war-refugees to Croatia", in H. Haukanes and F. Pine (eds.), *Generations, kinship and care: gendered provisions of social security in central eastern Europe*, Bergen: Univ. of Bergen, pp. 207–229.

— (2006), *Claiming ownership in post-war Croatia: the dynamics of property relations and ethnic conflict*, Berlin: LIT.

Livada, S. (1970), "Stari ljudi – sve teži problem našeg sela", *Naše teme,* (10–11) 14/1970, pp. 1901–1918.

Marinović-Jerolimović, D. and N. Skledar (1997), "Uloga religije i religioznosti u integracijskim procesima u Hrvatskoj", *Politička misao,* Br. 2/1997: pp. 177–190.

Milanović, M. I. Sričević, D. Maleš and A. Sekulić-Majurec (2000), *Early childhood and care in the Republic of Croatia,* Zagreb: Targa.

Milas, I. (2003), "Koje promjene donosi Obiteljski zakon", *Pravo i porezi: časopis za pravnu i ekonomsku teoriju i praksu,* God. 12. 11/2003: pp. 47–53.

Pavličević, D. (1989) *Hrvatske kućne zadruge I,* Zagreb.

Piškulić, K. (1957), *Socijalno osiguranje rezultat borbe radničke klase,* Zagreb: Mladost.

Potočnjak, Ž. (2000), "Nove mirovinske formule mirovinskog osiguranja generacijske solidarnosti", *Revija za socijalnu politiku,* God. 7, br. 1/2000: pp. 1–18.

Puljiz, V. (1984), "Deagrarizacija", in M. Škrbić et al. (eds.), *Socijalna zaštita u Sociajističkoj Republici Hrvatskoj. Razvoj, stanje, perspektive,* Zagreb: Savez samoupravnih interesnih zajednica socijalne zaštite Socijalističke Republike Hrvatske, pp. 86–90.

— (1996), "Trendovi u socijalnoj politici Hrvatske", *Revija za socijalnu politiku,* God. III. 3–4/1996: pp. 273–284.

— (1999), "Profili obiteljske politike", *Revija za socijalnu politiku,* God. VI. br. 1, pp. 21–33.

— (2001), "Reforme sustava socijalne politike u Hrvatskoj", *Revija za socijalnu politiku,* God. VIII. br. 2, pp. 159–176.

— (2004), "Socijalna prava i socijalni razvoj Republike Hrvatske", *Revija za socijalnu politiku,* God. 11. br. 1, pp. 3–20.

Puljiz, V. and S. Zrinščak (2004), *Demografska kretanja i obiteljska politika Republike Hrvatske* (Manuscript for publ. in Japan), pp. 1–33.

Raboteg-Šarić, Z. and V. Josipović (2003), "Obitelj, rad i skrb o djec'i" in Z. Raboteg-Šarić et al. (eds.), *Jednoroditeljske obitelji: osobni doživljaj i stavovi okoline,* Zagreb: Državni zavod za zaštitu obitelji, materinstva i mladeži., pp. 109–120.

Raboteg-Šarić, Z. (2004), "Children's welfare in the context of social and economic changes in Croatia", in A.-M. Jensen et al. (eds.), *Children's welfare in ageing Europe. Vol. II. Norwegian Centre for Child Research,* Trondheim: Tartu University Press.

Rihtman-Auguštin, D. (1988), *Etnologija naše svakodnevnice,* Zagreb: Školska knjiga.

Schmidt, M. G. (1998), *Sozialpolitik in Deutschland. Historische Entwicklung und internationaler Vergleich,* Opladen: Leske & Budrich.

Sundhaussen, H. (1983), *Wirtschaftsgeschichte Kroatiens im nationalsozialistischem Großraum 1941–45. Das Scheitern einer Ausbeutungsstrategie,* Stuttgart: Deutsche Verlags-Anstalt.

Škrbić, M., S. Šuvar and B. Popović (1984), "Socijalna politika i socijalna zaštita u funkciji udruženog rada", in M. Škrbić et al. (eds.), *Socijalna zaštita u Sociajističkoj Republici Hrvatskoj. Razvoj, stanje, perspektive,* Zagreb: Savez samoupravnih interesnih zajednica socijalne zaštite Socijalističke Republike Hrvatske, pp. 52–65.

Štambuk, M. (1990), "Stanovništvo i domaćinstva gradskih i seoskih naselja", *Sociologija sela*, 107–108, god. 28, siječanj-lipanj, pp. 63–76.

Stropnik, N. (2003), "Impact of transition on family policy", in I. E. Kotowska and J. Jozwiak (eds.), *Population of central and eastern Europe: challenges and opportunities*, Warsaw: Statistical Publishing Establishment, pp. 559–596.

Šućur, Z. (2000), "Socijalna pomoć u Hrvatskoj: budući pravci razvoja", *Revija za socijalnu politiku,* God. 7. br. 3–4, pp. 257–271.

— (2004), "Pristup pravima opće socijalne pomoći", *Revija za socijalnu politiku,* God. 11. br. 1, pp. 21–38.

Šuvar, S. (1988), *Sociologija sela,* Zagreb: Školska knjiga.

Tálos, E. and K. Wörister (1994), *Soziale Sicherung im Sozialstaat Österreich. Entwicklung – Herausforderungen – Strukturen*, Baden-Baden: Nomos.

UNICEF (1998), *Children and women in the Republic of Croatia: summary of the situation analysis*, Zagreb: UNICEF Office.

Utiešenović, O. (1859), *Hauskommunionen der Südslaven. Eine Denkschrift zur Beleuchtung der volkstümlichen Acker- und Familienverfassung des serbischen und kroatischen Volkes*, Wien: F. Manz & Compagnie.

Vizjak, A. (1937), *Penziono osiguranje službenika: sistem,* Beograd: vlast. nakl.

Vrcan, S. (2001), *Vjera u vrtlozima tranzicije,* Split: Glas Dalmacije – revija Dalmatinske akcije.

Wertheimer-Baletić, A. (1996), Demoreprodukcijski procesi u Hrvatskoj, in *Rad Hrvatske akademije znanosti i umjetnosti,* Knjiga XXXIV. Zagreb: HAZU, pp. 114–140.

— (2003), "Determinante reprodukcije stanovništva Hrvatske u drugoj polovici 20. stoljeća", in D. Živić, N. Pokos and A. Mišetić (eds.), *Stanovništvo Hrvatske – Dosadašnji razvoj i perspektive,* Zagreb: Institut društvenih znanosti Ivo Pilar, pp. 9–37.

Zavod za Mirovinsko Osiguranje (2002), *80 godina mirovinskog osiguranja u Hrvatskoj 1922–2002*, Zagreb: Hrvatski zavod za mirovinsko osiguranje.

Zovko, G. (2000), "Socijalna skrb o invalidima u Republici Hrvatskoj", *Revija za socijalnu politiku,* God. 7. br. 3–4, pp. 273–287.

Zrinjščak, S. (2000), "Skile i haridbe socijalne sigurnosti", *Revija za socijalnu politiku,* God. 7. br. 3–4, pp. 229–243.

Zukin, S. (1975), *Beyond Marx and Tito: theory and practice in Yugoslav Socialism*, Cambridge: Cambridge University Press.

Živić, D. (1999), "Promjene u dinamici i razmještaju prognaničko-izbjegličkog kontingenta u Republici Hrvatskoj od sredine 1991. do sredine 1998. godine", *Društvena istraživanja 8*, (5–6), pp. 767–791.

— (2003), "Demografski okvir i razvoj obiteljske strukture stanovništva Hrvatske 1971–2001", *Revija za sociologiju.* Vol. XXXIV. No. 1–2, pp. 57–73.

Family and state in twentieth-century Poland

Leon Dyczewski

The historical context of family and kinship in Poland

During the Partitions of Poland, when the country was under foreign domination, family and kinship systems were effectively the only source of support for individuals, social activities and Polish culture until such time as Poland regained its independence in 1918. After independence, these systems were key factors in shaping social life, firmly anchored in society and supported by the state. Yet this was to last for only one generation. In 1945, in the aftermath of the Second World War, the Soviet Union imposed a Marxist-Leninist ideology and socialist government on Polish society. Social life was constructed on the following principles: a) priority of the state over the individual and the family; b) the rejection of cultural heritage based on Christian values and of relations with Western culture; this new culture was to be secular and based on cooperation with the Soviet Union; c) adults were obliged to work, including wives/mothers; d) struggle is the principle of life and a crucial factor in social development; e) the means of production belong to the state and state property takes precedence over private property (established centuries ago, this principle undermined the law of inheritance, on which intergenerational family relationships were based to a large extent).

These principles did not conform to what had constituted Polish culture up to that time. Their implementation in the socialist context threatened the intergenerational bonds of family and kinship relations.

The socialist government created new social structures and popularized a new culture. The Polish family accepted many elements of the former or adjusted their lives accordingly. Its attitude to the new socialist culture, however, was either defensive or passive, and in its place a symbolic culture circulated inofficially via family relationships and family friends. Thus changes to the social structure were not correlated with those of the symbolic culture or of mutual assistance. These two social domains remained unconnected – both in terms of family life and of social life in general – and frequently functioned independent of each other. This is largely responsible for the somewhat tentative change in Polish family circumstances in comparison to Western countries, where family life has undergone a far-reaching transformation. The dissimilarity between Polish families and those of Western societies manifested itself, for example, in the number of children; the upholding of strong links between the generations; a lower divorce rate; a deep sense of religion and close relations with its institution, the Catholic Church, and a strong tendency to preserve family traditions. The family, which sustained cultural sovereignty, became the underlying support for the cultural continuation of Polish society and the stabilizing factor in social life.

The model of the family promoted during the Polish People's Republic was far from stable. Its different elements were accentuated by social change and the changes in social policy. In the initial post-war decade, state policy promoted a family model with numerous children, which it supported with added social benefits. With the introduction of the abortion law in 1956, political policies promoted the reverse, i.e., a family model with less children, gradually cutting back benefits for large families. In the 1970s and 1980s of the twentieth century the state clearly advertised a family model with not more than two children. After the transformation of the social system (after 1989), when social policy was dominated by liberal tendencies, no stipulations were made as to how many children a family should have. State policy accepted that having children was a matter for the couple concerned and thus gradually began to reduce family benefits. During the Polish People's Republic, state policy strongly underlined the need for the formal contraction of marriage and made concubinage illegal. Informal marriages are currently tolerated by law and even promoted by the mass media. The popularization of partnership between conjoints and the independence of generations was common at the time of the Polish People's Republic and has now regained popularity in the Third Republic of Poland. Socialist propaganda conveyed an ideology that stressed the superiority of the younger generation over that of the parent and, even more so, of the grandparent generation. Today, liberal propaganda is repeating the process. The leading social and liberal political groups in both periods perform actions that weaken family ties, popularize liberalization in the sexual domain, and opt for divorce, contraception, abortion and fertilization in vitro. Liberalism has a more far-reaching effect in these domains than was the case in the period of the Polish People's Republic. The phenomena that existed in the Polish People's Republic have now been added to by homosexual relationships, which at that time were completely invisible and condemned.

As already mentioned, during the Polish People's Republic, the Polish family put up strong resistance to socio-cultural change. Currently, we can observe an acceleration in the pace of these changes – for many both strange and surprising. The extent of these changes and their consequences are still hard to discern and would require long-term multi-aspectual research. Here I will merely discuss what is clearly visible.

With the reverse of the political system in 1989, Polish society clearly accepted a Western orientation. This led to the following phenomena: a) moral views on marriage and the family became more liberal; b) the authority of religion and the clergy in shaping marriage/family life was weakened; c) hitherto unambiguous ideas of marriage and family became blurred; d) living standards differ greatly and have deteriorated for families with children; e) a trend towards tailing off family support on the part of the state.

Factors unpropitious to the family

Instability of the human factor

Between 1918 and 1939, the population of Poland showed a rapid increase from 25.2 million in 1900, to 27.4 in 1921 and 35.1 in 1939 (GUS 1939, 10). As a result of World War II, Poland was to lose more than 14.9 million citizens between 1939 and 1950 (GUS 1994, 199). Over the next two generations (1946–2004) the number of Polish citizens increased by 14.5 million (from 23.6 to 38.2 million)[1]. The Polish people became geographically and socially more mobile after the Second World War. Three factors were instrumental to this mobility: the changeover in the political system, displacement due to the alteration of state borders, and the process of extensive urbanization and industrialization.

1 According to the National Census, Poland had 32,348,000 inhabitants in 1931, 35,100,000 in 1939, and 23,767,000 in 1946 (GUS 1939, 34; GUS 2000, 95, table 3).

The reversal of the political system elevated thousands of people from the lower strata to leading social positions; countless others were downgraded. The new power shaped its own social elite. Unknown figures filled prominent positions in all areas of life. The scale of social promotion in Polish society after the Second World War becomes apparent, for example, on hearing that 48 per cent of adult Poles in October 1999 claimed that their own social position was higher than that of their parents, and 59 per cent that it was higher than that of their grandparents; only 11 per cent claimed that their social position was lower than that of their parents and 9 per cent that it was lower than that of their grandparents (CBOS 2000a, 23).

The development of urbanization and industrialization over two generations has altered the urban and rural proportions of the population. In 2004 the urban population constituted almost the same percentage (61.8 per cent) of the entire population of Poland as the rural population after the Second World War (66 per cent in 1946) (GUS: Rocznik Statystyczny 1960–2005). People moved en masse from rural villages to existing or newly built towns and cities, thereby rapidly swelling their populations.

Changes in the political system and the shifting of the Polish borders to the west caused a genuine "migration of nations". Millions of people from the central region of Poland and the eastern territory that had been annexed by the Soviet Union migrated to the western and northern areas adjoined to Poland. A vast number of Polish citizens left the country. From 1952, when the Polish western border was closed, until 1999, 1.3 million people emigrated, especially the young, who were either single or had small children (GUS: Rocznik Statystyczny 1960–2005).

The instability of the human factor, clearly indicated by the phenomena described above, was not favourable to maintaining intergenerational family bonds, since generations were separated both socially and geographically. Moreover, major differences arose between them with regard to political ideas and world views. The older generations were strongly attached to the Christian religion, in particular to the Catholic Church that predominated in Poland, and politically inclined towards democracy. The younger generations were educated in various state institutions with a non-religious ideology or one hostile to religion, and with political views imposed by the Soviet Union. After the collapse of the socialist system, the younger generation was in turn drawn to the political and ethical ideas and world views found in Western societies.

The ideologizing of the younger generation

The new socialist system in Poland explicitly benefited the younger generation. The desire of the Polish United Workers Party to control and have the younger generation at its disposal induced it to develop an ideology of youth.

Young people had priority and were counted upon, in the hope that they would accept the values introduced by the new socio-political system and build a socialist Poland. Among other things, young people were provided with free education from primary to university level and guaranteed a job after schooling; the government built recreation and vacation centres, which were available free of charge.

The young were granted a series of privileges, while older generations were encouraged to make sacrifices. The latter's old-age pensions and disability payments were barely enough to survive on, not to mention any further personal progress. After the youth rebellions of the 1960s and 1970s, state policy switched to favouring the middle generation, i.e, to promoting idealized role models, such as teachers, officers, engineers, workers or farmers.

The changeover of the political system in Poland at the end of the 1980s once again created an advantageous situation for the younger generation. The young have once more taken centre stage and are now relied upon. They were previously required to accept the ideology and politics of the Polish United Workers Party. Today, however, the principal advantages of young people are their knowledge of new technologies, their familiarity with new electronic devices, their command of foreign languages and a willingness to take risks, all highly useful features in a liberal market economy.

The ideologizing and privileging of the younger generation, both during the Polish People's Republic and today, quite often leads to the ignoring of or even disdain for the older generations' experience of life. The privileged position of the younger and neglect of the older generations is evidenced in the extremely low pensions that most of the elderly receive. The differences between the generations were accompanied by a specific youth cult that came to Poland from West European countries and was strongly popularized by the mass media. Overall, these circumstances were not conducive to promoting intergenerational family bonds.

Pluralism of values with regard to marriage and family life

In recent years pluralism has become a highly esteemed value – everything must contain pluralism. This trend aims at a more individualistic, and at the same time more relativistic, interpretation of values and moral norms with regard to marriage and the family, and particularly sexuality, conception, and the durability of marriage. The approach of the younger generation to these issues is more liberal than that of the parent, not to mention the grandparent generation. This has been confirmed by a variety of research findings. For example, of 1,500 students from thirteen Polish universities, 38.9 per cent declared they had intercourse on a regular basis and 27.1 per cent on an irregular basis; 17.3 per cent had not had intercourse, while 16.7 per cent gave no answer (Slany 2002, 223). The overwhelming majority of young people between the ages of eighteen and twenty-eight were in favour of divorce in serious cases (76.2 per cent) and of abortion after rape and in the case of the mother's illness (56.9 per cent) or material hardship (5.1 percent). A substantial number of young people opted for equating married and unmarried couples (36.2 per cent), and were in favour of homosexual marriages (22.8 per cent)[2]. A liberalization of the approach to Catholic marriage/family ethics is visible in the younger and middle generations. According to research carried out in the Bug region in 1996, 58.2 per cent of respondents allowed sexual relations before marriage; 48.5 per cent allowed the dissolution of marriage; 33.7 per cent allowed abortion (Dyczewski 1997, 186–193).

Decreasing state interest in the family

In post-socialist Poland many of the political parties have begun to openly treat the issue of family as a private matter. Thus, the number of children,

2 Research carried out by the author in 2005–2006 in several provinces, using a sample of 2,351 persons, mostly pupils in their final years at high school and university students. Results not yet published.

the standard of education and health care are to be considered a family concern. On the other hand, in the modern society the young people are incorporated into institutional activities from early childhood and hence pulled out of the family environment. In turn, the family has less and less influence on the process of socialization and personality formation. The numerous activities prevent parents and children from spending time together, so that they seldom communicate with each other. Thus, while primary socialization is weakened, the importance of secondary socialization, i.e., outside the family, is on the increase. Children become independent very quickly. Although less visible in Poland than in America or other countries of the European Union, it is intensifying.

The phenomena presented above create a specific context for but are not conducive to marriage/family life. Although new to Polish society, they are currently enjoying increased popularity.

Factors propitious to the family

A strong sense of community and belonging to the family

Although the circle of relatives with whom close contact is maintained has diminished, it is still quite comprehensive. Close contact is first and foremost maintained with relatives who live within proximity, with whom interpersonal communication is uncomplicated, and who have common interests or hobbies. Contact with other relatives tends to be sporadic, and is usually determined by family occasions such as weddings, funerals and, less frequently, christenings. At name days and birthday parties people from outside the family gather together – a circle of friends. In contrast, the entire extended family assembles at weddings and funerals, sometimes over a hundred people. It is a deeply internalized duty to invite all the members of the family to such events, even those with whom contact is more intermittent, e.g., via correspondence.

The family bond embraces both the living and the dead. A vast number of Poles visit the graves of their relatives. On All Saints Day trains are overcrowded and roads packed, as people travel to visit the graves of their loved ones.

The oldest generation plays a key role in keeping family contacts alive. It preserves numerous family customs and habits, even when the latter are not wholly intelligible to the youngest generation. Although grandparents, and nowadays more frequently great-grandparents, have lost much of their former power over adult children and grandchildren, and their traditional authority has weakened, they still incorporate an eminent moral authority. A special bond links grandparents and grandchildren. The intergenerational span is quite a common phenomenon, i.e., the relationship children have with their grandparents is often stronger than that with their own parents (Dyczewski 1981, 1984).

The high value of marriage and family in Polish society

Despite the myriad changes in Polish society, marriage and family remain the most desirable values and play a major role in people's lives. The younger generation of Poles still associate their future with marriage and a family. This attitude is independent of whether they come from a prosperous or less prosperous family (Dyczewski 1980; 1998; 2005; Dyczewski et al. 2006; Doniec 2001, 119–132; CBOS 1999). Almost a third (30 per cent) of the people between eighteen and forty-four who were asked in a representative survey about family values believes that family life has a greater significance today, while 42 per cent declared there was no change (OBOP 1998). Young people between eighteen and twenty-six have a similar approach to family life, children and the home (table 8.1). Life without a family is considered unthinkable. Polish society does not promote the model of single life. At the end of the twentieth century, only 3.3 per cent of men and 5.3 per cent of woman in their sixties or older were single.

Table 8.1: Values, life goals and life principles youth desire for their future.

Values, life goals and life principles youth desire for their future	Scale from 6 to 1 6 = very important – 1= not important 6	5	4	3	2	1	aver-age	Total
To have a good relationship with children	61.0	28.0	7.4	1.8	0.4	1.4	5.43	2295-100,0
To have my own house or apartment	50.6	31.2	12.2	4.0	0.9	1.1	5.23	2297-100,0
To have children	54.5	24.9	10.5	4.5	2.4	3.2	5.14	2291-100,0
To be married	53.2	24.9	11.3	4.7	1.9	4.0	5.10	2293-100,0
To have a lot of friends	41.8	34.0	17.4	4.8	1.1	0.8	5.08	2289-100,0
To have a good relationship with parents	41.2	30.7	17.8	6.7	1.6	1.9	4.97	2287-100,0
Well informed, well travelled, experienced	31.0	31.8	22.3	9.8	3.0	2.1	4.71	2288-100,0
To concentrate on a professional career	6.1	17.2	37.6	23.8	10.2	5.1	3.69	2272-100,0
To have grandchildren	15.9	15.2	19.5	17.5	13.9	17.9	3.48	2251-100,0
To live (or live again) in the same place	9.4	10.2	21.6	20.2	12.5	26.2	3.05	2232-100,0
To live with a partner unmarried	6.4	7.2	16.0	14.5	12.6	43.4	2.50	2125-100,0

Source: Own research in 2005–2006 using a sample of 2,351 people between 18 and 26 years of age

The specificity of the "Polish home"

The pattern of Polish homes emerged gradually and was fixed in the practices of people from various social strata. It was described vividly by representatives of the nobility, who were numerous in Poland compared to other European countries and constituted 14 per cent (according to some historians even 20 per cent) of the population before the partition of Poland. The houses of the nobility (manor houses), built in either wood or stone, and the homes created there were imitated by other social strata and influenced the homes of the intelligentsia, the peasantry and later the working class. In literature and memoirs, the home is described as a family nest that unites the living relatives of all generations, cultivates traditions and religion, a place that is hospitable, warm and safe.

The image of the home was a frequent topic in literature. It has become a reality, dreamt of and desired by all, a place to turn to at any time in life, especially in moments of chaos and anxiety, or of personal disaster or separation. Home was considered the most stable element in life. The folk poet Bronisława Fastowiec summarizes its essence in the following words: "Home – it is joy and sorrow, a fortress and support" (Fastowiec 1996, 21).

The Polish home is linked steadfastly to the nation. This bond was deepened and enriched during partition, subsequently during the German and later Russian occupation, and finally under the communist regime. In the Polish consciousness, home was seen as a form of asylum, a safe place, where mutual assistance and rest prevailed. Piotr Łukasiewicz stresses that during the German occupation several extended communities were created on the basis of kinship and friendship. Services and production were organized on a family/house basis, both for their own people as well as for strangers. Łukasiewicz writes: "In a situation when almost all public institutions, including the national state, were destroyed or suspended, the home – exclusively by the power of its existence – seemed to confirm the continuance of social life […] At home life pre-occupational normality of everyday life could survive" (Łukasiewicz 1989, 81). At home the transmission of national and religious traditions continued to take place.

Under the communist regime, the home played a similar role, albeit in a slightly different manner. Home and strong family ties were the major reasons why Polish society did not submit to the regime. In fact, two spheres of life prevailed. On the one hand, the official sphere, based on structures imposed by the socialist state and, on the other, an inoffical sphere based on the family and the Polish home. A knowledge of these family bonds and the Polish home contributes to understanding that in a society where inofficial associations or organizations were forbidden, the list of political organizations in *The Lexicon of Political Opposition 1976–1989* is eight pages long (Ceduła 1989). The still vibrant family ties and specificity of the Polish home are now fostering the development of a variety of family associations and organizations.

The fact that the current high rate of unemployment in Poland (approx. 14 per cent in 2006) has not had such dramatic consequences is due to the ideal of the Polish home and the numerous values it cultivates.

Religiosity and festive traditions

Family life and relations between the generations in Poland have been shaped for centuries primarily by the Catholic and Orthodox Churches and by Judaism. In 1931, Catholics constituted 75.1 per cent of Polish society, Orthodox Christians 11.8 per cent, and people of Jewish faith 9.8 per cent (GUS 1939, 27, table 22). As a result of the Holocaust and the border alterations decided upon by Józef Stalin, Franklin D. Roosevelt and Winston Churchill, Poland became an almost exclusively Catholic country after the Second World War. According to research conducted in 1998–1999, 93.9 per cent of the population identifies with the Catholic Church as a religious organization (Zembrzuski 2000).

Both the Catholic and Orthodox Churches, and the Jewish religion emphasize the character of the family as a community, thereby shaping strong family ties between the generations. The commandments contained in the Bible oblige parents to look after their children, even when they are grown up; they also oblige children to take care of their aging parents.

This promotion of the family in the teachings of the Catholic Church manifests itself among other things in the traditional family manner in which religious feasts are celebrated, e.g., Christmas, Easter, All Saints Day, weddings, christenings, First Holy Communion, and funerals. Close relatives gather on these occasions, and those living nearby are obliged to pay a visit, a custom that is still very much alive in Poland. The family character of these celebrations is reinforced by the joint participation in religious acts. The comparatively recent non-religious family feasts, such as Mother's Day, Children's Day, Father's Day, Grandmother's and Grandfather's day became popular quite rapidly. Here the family assembles for dinner, for example, and all are expected to present the person concerned with a gift.

The awareness of belonging to the family is highly esteemed in Polish culture. The attachment to home, to the close relatives people grew up with and to family memories, the nostalgia for the warmth and charm of childhood are still felt strongly among the young, despite their sense of autonomy and independence. Even after members of the younger generation have started their own families, the close relationship to their families of origin remains.

It is not to institutions specialized in various types of assistance that people turn for help in crucial situations but to the family. Ahead of any other institution, the family is the instance that helps to find a new job, a new apartment or a change of social environment.

The strong and active family bond that extends beyond parents and children is responsible for the fact that the nuclear family model (small isolated family) has not established itself in Polish society to any major degree. The extended family is practiced in Poland more often than in West European countries and occurs in two forms: a) a multigenerational family living together, where adult generations maintain either common or separate households; b) a multigenerational family where adult children live separately but in the vicinity, remain in close contact, visit each other frequently, and help one another both spiritually and financially (Dyczewski 1972, 1976; Turowski 1977).

Multiplication of forms of family life

A married couple with children – the predominant form of family life

Families with children based on marriage predominate in Polish society. The percentage of such families, however, decreased from 63.5 per cent in 1978 to 61.8 per cent in 1988, and from 59.6 per cent in 1995 to 56 percent in 2002. This decline occurred in both urban and rural areas. (GUS 1996, 94–96; GUS 2003, 28). The decline in the number of marriages with children in the 1990s was a direct result of demographic change and the subsequent decline in the number of marriages involving those of suitable age to start a family. In recent years a trend not to get married has been observed. This is due to unemployment (particularly high in the relevant age group), the uncertainty of continued employment and low salaries. For the same reasons, the percentage of marriages without children has grown in the last few years. The number of single-parent families increased dynamically and was especially visible in 2004, when the government cut back the benefits for families with children and increased it for single-parent families with a single breadwinner.

The growth of the single-parent family

Table 8.2: Single-parent families among the total number of families

Year	Total number of families	Number of single-parent families		Percentage of single-parent families	Growth dynamic of single-parent families
1970	8,196,624	1,249,235		12.7%	X
1978				13.4%	142,3
1988	10,226,191	1,574,000		15.4%	179,3
		Mothers with children	Fathers with children		
		1, 396,000	178,000		
1995	10,533,428	1,772,578		16.8%	199,0
		Mothers with children	Fathers with children		
		1,580,000	192,000		
2002	10,457,600	2,030,100		19.4%	x
		Mothers with children	Fathers with children		
		1,798,300	231,800		

Sources: GUS 1981, p.3; GUS 1990, 99; GUS 1996, 94; GUS 2003, 28; GUS Rocznik statystyczny 1998, 93, table 9 (122)

The number and percentage of single-parent families indicates a systematic increase in Polish society. Of the total number of families in Poland in 1970, those with children and one parent constituted 12.7 per cent; in 1988 they made up 15.4 per cent, while in 2002 this type of family had already formed 19.4 per cent of all families in the country (GUS 2003, 28). Single-parent families have the highest growth rate of all family types (see table 8.2). They emerge more frequently in the urban environment and are primarily characteristic of large urban agglomerations. In 2002, of the total number of families living in cities, 21.1 per cent were single-parent families, whereas only 16.4 per cent belonged to this category in the rural areas.

The most interesting group in terms of social policy are the single-parent families with dependent children up to the age of twenty-four. In 2002, there were 1,125,500 of these families. This figure had increased since 1988 by 224,900 (GUS 2003, 31).

Single-parent families usually originate as a result of the death of a spouse or of divorce, and more and more frequently the birth of a child outside marriage. In 1980, the number of children born outside marriage constituted 4.7 per cent of all children born alive, increased in 1990 to 6.7 per cent, and in 2001 reached 13.1 per cent (GUS: Rocznik Statystyczny 1990, GUS: Demograficzny Rocznik Statystyczny 2002).

In 2002, 1,660,900 dependent children up to the age of twenty-four were raised in single-parent families, i.e., 15.4 per cent of the total number of children in this category (1,173,000 in urban centres and 487,800 in the countryside). In comparison to the year 1988, the number of children in single-parent family increased by 320,000, i.e., 207,000 in cities, and 112,700 in the rural areas (Balcerzak-Paradowska 2004, 125).

As a rule, the absence of one of the parents is detrimental to family life. In the case of families with single mothers, which are the most common, women typically have lower salaries than men. The material situation of these families is critical when the single parent is unemployed or on a pension. In 2002, almost every fifth parent with a dependent child up to the age of twenty-four was unemployed, and every third was professionally passive (i.e., unemployed or on a pension) (Balcerzak-Paradowska 2004, 125).

Married couples without children

The percentage of marriages without children remained stable for a long time. In 1988 they constituted 22.8 per cent of all families, and in 2002, 22.7 per cent (GUS 2003, 28). Childless marriages include those of young people who do not yet have children as well as the marriages of older people whose children have left home. More and more marriages are childless due to an inability to conceive or to carry a child to term. Various studies on marital infertility have shown that approx. 15 per cent of childless marriages are due to the aforementioned reasons. Over and above, the inability to carry a child to term constitutes more than 20 per cent of all pregnancies (Wierzchosławski 1991, 46). There is now an increase in marriages where the couple postpones having children until later; many of these marriages remain childless.

Cohabitation

The cohabitation of heterosexual couples without a formal marriage (civil or religious) ceremony is not as popular in Poland as it is in Western countries. However, it is becoming more widespread, particularly in the urban environment, and among students. This type of union was registered for the first time in the National Census of 2002 and entitled "partner relationship". At the time, approximately 197,400 such partnerships existed altogether, 148,000 in cities, 49,400 in villages. This number has now increased. Of the total number of families of this type 110,700 had children (GUS 2003, 33).

A further form of family life, on which its supporters are attempting to confer the status of marriage/family life, is the homosexual relationship. Whereas knowledge of this type of relationship originally shocked Polish society, it is now gradually becoming accustomed to it.

The forms of family life presented above were also common in the past, albeit with one fundamental difference. In the past, marriages that included children (the full family) were habitually regarded as "normal", i.e., were generally approved and universally desired, while other family forms were either considered departures from the cultural pattern (the norm) or transitional. Social opinion now attributes an aspect of normality to all of these family forms. Researchers on the family regard popularizing the existence of several forms of family life and their treatment by social opinion as one of the most significant transformations in the last few decades. This tendency seems to be an expression of the key transformations in contemporary symbolic culture and social structure, above all the expansion of freedom, subjectivism, individualism, the ideology of personal happiness and success, secularization of awareness, an absence of involvement, an increase in the complexity of life, and openness.

Several researchers perceive a process of de-institutionalization of the family in the acceptance of multiple forms of family life (Tyrell 1988). However, this claim does not appear justified, since certain features of these new forms of family life are institutional in nature, albeit unlike those of old family forms. The predominant feature is impermanence, whereas the old institutional family form was characterized by permanence, to the extent that individuals often sacrificed their personal happiness for the sake of maintaining the family. This trend now seems to have been reversed. Today the institution of the family is subordinated to individual personal happiness. When people come to the conclusion that their personal happiness cannot be achieved in a given family, they abandon it and find a new one (Dyczewski 1999).

Children as a social value, the fertility decline and the ageing of society

A child is the most precious value in Poland, and only a small number of families are without children. No more than ten per cent of Polish people have no children by the age of forty, whereas this is the case for 23 per cent in Germany, 21 per cent in Switzerland and 20 per cent in the Netherlands (Jagiełło 2000). Asked about how many children they would like to have, the great majority of respondents replied that they would like to have two, three or more children, but rarely only one child. The declarations of men and women with regard to this issue are almost identical (cf. table 8.3). The more engaged the Polish are in religious practices, the higher they evaluate their economic situation, and the more conservative their political views, the more likely they are to adhere to the idea of large families. The preferred family model is one of slightly extended reproduction[3]. Yet, the decrease in the number of births tends to indicate diminished reproduction. All the indices characterizing the demographic situation of Polish society indicate a decrease in fertility.

3 The responses to the question "How many children should an average family have in your view" were as follows: one – 3 per cent; two – 62 per cent; three – 30 per cent; four, five, six, and more – 3 per cent; I do not know, it is difficult to say – 2 per cent. See: OBOP 2000, 2–3.

Table 8.3: The number of children desired in the family

The number of children	Answers of respondents		
	Answers of respondents between 18 and 44 (in percentage) September 1996	Answers of respondents between 18 and 44 (in percentage) February – March 2000	Answers of respondents between 18 and 26 (in percentage) 2006
None	1	2	–
One	9	12	4.7
Two	58	57	55.7
Three	20	20	21.2
Four	3	3	4.0
Five or more	2	3	1.2
Open for any number of children	5	0	–
Difficult to say, no answer	2	2	13.2

Sources: CBOS, 2000b; own research

The total fertility rate of women between the ages of fifteen and forty-nine indicates a dramatic decline since the 1950s. In 1950, the fertility rate was 3.7; in 1970, 2.2; in 1990, 2.0; in 2000, 1.37, and in 2004, 1.22 (GUS: Rocznik Statystyczny 1960–2005).

In 1985, (i.e., under the socialist system) the overall net rate of reproduction in Poland was 1.1; in 1990, 0.97 (0.84 for cities and 1.18 for villages), while in 2004, the fertility rate dropped to 0.59 for the whole country (0.54 for cities and 0.67 for villages) (GUS: Demograficzny Rocznik Statystyczny 1998–2005).

In recent years Polish society has succeeded from somewhat extended to slightly narrowed reproduction. If this process continues, future mothers born today will not replace the number of current mothers.

In the aftermath of the Second World War, two processes made rapid progress in Polish society. At least three reasons were responsible: a) a decline in the birth rate; b) extension of the life span; c) permanent emigration (this last reason is of less significance).

The percentage of people aged sixty or over in the Polish population increased from 8.3 per cent to 17.1 per cent between 1950 and 2004. Of the total number of elderly in the population, the percentage of the oldest old, i.e., seventy-five years of age and over, increased rapidly. In 1950, they constituted 19.8 per cent of the total number of elderly. By 1997, this figure had reached 24.5 per cent (GUS 1999, 14–15). Within the next twenty years the number of elderly will have increased by 40 per cent. In 2020, the elderly will constitute 22.4 per cent of the Polish population (GUS 1999, 29). This data clearly demonstrates that the younger generation in Poland will decrease and the demographic situation will be similar to that of Germany or Greece.

Those asked in opinion polls about reasons for limiting the number of children in Polish families typically alluded to poor living conditions, the housing shortage, a sense of being let down by the state, fear of losing jobs, growing unemployment, and the likelihood of a decline in living standards. The social policy strategy introduced by the government in 2004 did not take these arguments into account. Family benefits were generally scaled down, and only one-parent families benefited. This strategy could therefore be called an anti-family strategy. Current government policy aims at greater support for the family; however, the state budget appears to be unable to put this into practice.

In the period analysed, Poland pursued a highly inconsistent demographic policy: 1945–1955: significant population growth, pronatalist policy; 1956–1970: decrease in the birthrate, anti-natalist policy; 1971–1981: further decrease in the birthrate, pronatalist policy; 1980s: stabilization of the birth level, neutral policy; 1990s: decrease in the birthrate, pronatalist policy; 2000s: decrease in the birthrate, neutral policy.

Families in difficult material/financial circumstances

Families with one member unemployed

The changeover of the political system in Poland brought a massive increase in unemployment. In 1998, 764,000 (12 per cent) of the total number of families with dependent children up to twenty-four years of age had at least one parent who was unemployed. In 2002, this figure increased to 1,230,000 (21.6 per cent) (Balcerzak-Paradowska 2004, 110). Unemployment is one of the key factors thrusting families into poverty. Income generated by employment, today the universal basis for livelihood and development, has been replaced by benefits in the form of unemployment benefit paid periodically. When the latter expires (regulated by law), social welfare, a somewhat paltry sum, becomes the sole source of income.

Families with numerous children

Up to the 1970s, large families (three or more children) were a common phenomenon in Polish society. The National Census of 1988, however, registered a decline in their number. Among the families with dependent children up to the age of twenty-four, 1,166,200 (18.8 per cent) were large families. In 2002, this figure dropped to 1,024,000 (16.9 per cent) (GUS 2003, 32–33). Admittedly the number of families with several children decreased, yet the number of large families with four or more children increased (from 29 to 30 per cent). In 2002, 355,000 children were raised in large families, i.e., every third child of the total number of dependent children up to the age of twenty-four was raised in such a family (Balcerzak-Paradowska 1999, 129). For a long time large families were more common in rural than in urban areas, and in the lower rather than the upper social classes. As of the 1980s, families with serveral children became more evident in the urban areas and had a relatively high standard of education. The number of large families in rural areas decreased for economic reasons, while families in urban areas deliberately adopted the family model with several children as a result of their religion and their world views.

Families in underdeveloped regions

Rural areas and small towns in Poland are still coping with an underdeveloped network of social services. Children and youth have less opportunity of satisfying their educational and cultural needs than their contemporaries in the urban centres. Family policy has up to now not been able to prevent the social inequality that accompanies underdevelopment in certain regions.

Development of partnership relations in the family

Today young people generally opt for the equal division of household duties. Recent research has proved to a great extent the strengthening of the partnership model in families (CBOS 1997; Balcerzak-Paradowska 2003). In the context of mutual relations in everyday family life, however, it is not only the young who emphasize features such as mutual love, understanding, positive communicativeness, equal division of household tasks, empathy, personal development, and a sense of satisfaction and happiness that stems from marriage/family life. With regard to the household division of labour, a pattern has emerged of so-called partnership relations between spouses and generations.

Research on family life in Poland has indicated that several factors hamper realization of the so-called partnership pattern of marriage/family relations. Taking these factors into consideration they identify "partnership not entirely fulfilled" and "postponed partnership" (Warzywoda-Kruszyńska and Krzyszkowski 1990, 104–106; Dyczewski 1999, 103–132).

"Partnership not entirely fulfilled" occurs when spouses do not participate equally in all domains of life, i.e., routine housekeeping, child care, recreation and repose. Men participate less in housekeeping and child care as a rule, and have more time for recreation and repose than women. This is either due to an insufficient awareness of the issue or to personality, on the one hand, or external conditions created by the workplace and the general infrastructure of family life, on the other.

"Postponed partnership" prevails when spouses fully accept the partnership relation in the family, are ready to put it into practice, but fail to do so as a result of external obstacles. In this case they wait for a change in the situation, e.g., they do not have adequate housing, one of the partners is unemployed or they do not have enough money, has changed.

The model of partnership relations in marriage/family life is commonly accepted among the younger generation. Failure to realize the model in the long term, however, can lead to frustration and dissatisfaction with married/family life and the respective partner, and ultimately to the disintegration of the family.

From community to proximity

The tendency in Poland to separate the nuclear family (consisting of parents and children) from the traditional extended family, both in terms of dwelling and of maintaining the household, was already visible after the First World War (Thomas and Znaniecki 1974; Chałasiński 1938; Mysłakowski 1931; Dobrowolski 1966; Wójcicki 1922). This process – although diverse in nature, as it took a different course in the rural and the urban areas – embraced the whole state and developed so quickly that in the years prior to and immediately after the Second World War, the small extended family had already dominated in the rural areas (Dodziuk and Markowska 1967; Markowska 1964).

The development of this phenomenon was fostered by the agrarian politics of the time, and was also a result of the accelerated industrialization and urbanization of society. A major factor here was geographical, professional and social mobility. These factors were even more effective after the Second World War and led to a decline in the percentage of multigenerational families. The findings of a research project carried out in 1962 indicated that among the 15,649 households investigated in a representative sampling, three-generational families living together constituted only 16,8 per cent of the households, in urban areas approx. 14 per cent (Dodziuk-Lityńska and Markowska 1972, 9 and 16).

In 1995, multigenerational family households made up 11.8 per cent of the 12,500,802 households in Poland (formed by people who lived together and shared a household). They are found three times more often, i.e, 20.3 per cent (16.8 per cent in the 1960s), in rural than in urban areas, i.e., 7.2 per cent (7.7 per cent in the 1960s) (see table 8.4). In relation to the 1960s, the frequency of multigenerational families in the rural areas with a common household increased by 3.5 per cent, and decreased by almost half (from 14 to 7.7 percent) in the urban centres. The most marked difference between villages and cities are the living conditions. Apartments in urban centres are typically designed for one family. More than one family in such an apartment is an indication of the difficulty of young families to find a suitable apartment of their own. Houses in the countryside are designed to allow space for children and their future families, and are hence planned as multi-family buildings from the outset.

Table 8.4: Household members according to age – 1995

Households and families	Age						
	Exclusively			Young and middle-aged	With elderly persons		
	Young 0–29 years	Middle-aged 30–59 years	Elderly 60 years and over		Young	Middle-aged	Young and middle-aged
Total in Poland	6.9%	12.7%	18.4%	41.8%	2.6%	8.3%	9.3%
Family households	6.5%	6.6%	9.4%	52.9%	2.5%	10.3%	11,.8%
				URBAN AREAS			
Total	7.7%	14.8%	18.5%	43.5%	2.4%	7.6%	5.5%
Family households	7.2%	7.9%	9.3%	56.7%	2.1%	9.6%	7.2%
				RURAL AREAS			
Total	5.4%	8.2%	18.3%	38.3%	3.0%	9.8%	17.0%
Family households	5.5%	4.2%	9.7%	45.6%	3.3%	11.4%	20.3%

Source: GUS 1996, 89–91

The frequent occurrence of multigenerational households found in censuses has been confirmed by sample surveys carried out on adult Poles. A survey conducted in December 1997 showed that almost a third of respondents (31 per cent) had lived with their grandparents during their childhood. This phenomenon occurred more frequently in rural areas (38 per cent) than in cities with more than 500 000 inhabitants (28 per cent), and far less frequently in small and medium-sized towns (21–22 per cent) (CBOS 1998a, 13). Respondents from the rural areas confirmed that to almost the same extent (37 per cent) as in their own childhood (38 per cent) children lived with their parents/grandparents or the parents/grandparents of their spouses. Nevertheless, multigenerational family communities are currently less frequent in cities with 100–500 000 inhabitants (16 per cent) and more than 500 000 (19 per cent). On the other hand, in small and medium-sized towns every fourth or fifth adult Pole lives with his/her own parents/grandparents or with the parents/grandparents of a spouse (CBOS 1998a, 13).

The same results are obtained when the phenomenon of the multigenerational family is analysed from the perspective of the total population of elderly people. Polish research on the living conditions of people at the age of sixty-five and over carried out in the 1960s indicated that 65 per cent of those who had children lived with them. This was more often the case with elderly farmers (76 per cent) than those with other occupations (57 per cent). More than every third person of sixty-five years of age and over (36 per cent) lived in a household consisting of three or four generations, a more frequent occurrence in the agricultural sector (46 per cent) than elsewhere (27 per cent)[4]. Today 76 per cent of the elderly in the rural areas live with their children, whereas only about 50 per cent do so in urban areas (Łobożewicz 1994, 163). The rest either live alone or with their spouses.

Shared adult generational households occur when:

- young people come to live permanent with one set of parents after their marriage;
- young people who intend to live temporarily with their parents after marriage find themselves doing so for many years due to lack of alternative housing;
- one or both parents who have become grandparents come to live with their adult children in order to assist in raising children, i.e., their grandchildren;
- one or both parents come to live with their adult children because permanent health care is necessary.

The first two cases occur more often in rural than in urban areas. In the 1970s, two-thirds of elderly men in the agricultural sector provided living space for their children. Outside of this sector, a little more than a third of those interviewed on the issue claimed this was the case (Piotrowski 1971, 119). In 1989, every fifth older person provided housing for their children. On the other hand, one out of every ten moved into their children's home, twice as many of whom were women. The number of parents who live

4 This research was carried out by the Department of Work Sociology of the Instytut Gospodarstwa Społecznego between 1964–1968 and directed by J. Piotrowski. It covered 43 towns and 125 villages in 42 administrative districts. In all, 2,714 full-length and 131 partial interviews (questionnaires) were conducted. Cf. Piotrowski 1973, 178, 185–186.

with their children increases as the former advance in age (Szatur-Jaworska 1999, 35).

Relations between the generations can be deep-rooted and all-embracing; there are multiple advantages to be gained by living together, such as a reduction in the cost of living, a facilitating of mutual assistance, and a lessening of the widespread phenomenon of isolation and loneliness among the elderly. Yet, a large percentage of young people and their parents and grandparents prefer to live close to each other but separately. This solution is acceptable both to those who did not display a strong pro-family attitude as well as those (and to no small degree) who did.

In the 1960s, the majority of the elderly and their children were in favour of living separately but in close proximity. Almost half of the married women belonging to the middle generation (54 per cent) did not want to live with their own mothers, while the rest entertained this idea for the sole purpose that the latter could assist in maintaining the household and raising the children (Piotrowski 1971, 121–122). According to the results of research on families in Puławy, the tendency to live close but separately occurred in all generations. However, it was strongest among representatives of the middle generation (59.1 per cent) and less strong among the oldest (47.8 per cent) and youngest (45.4 per cent) generations (Dyczewski 1976, 106). This attitude is based on a desire to be independent and self-sufficient as well as on experience leading to the conviction that if three generations live together, conflict will arise. Conflict and tension are primarily the result of differences in opinion, behaviour, and life style, and of ambitions to control family life and subordinate the younger to the older generation or vice versa. Confined space and an overburdening of duties can also lead to tension, from which the oldest generation is not exempt. In the case of a working mother with two or three children, the retired grandmother who takes on the role of household manager is often physically more tired and mentally more exhausted than she was during her professional life.

Nevertheless, conflict and tension between generations that live together should not be magnified. A study of research data shows that relations between the elderly, their children and grandchildren are predominantly cordial and not clouded by an atmosphere of bias and quarrel. A substantial majority of those who are sixty-five and over (80 per cent) assessed their cohabitation with their children as good or very good. Relations were occasionally described as "bad" or "various", and applied to a son or daughter in a shared household (in 15 per cent of cases) or more frequently with a daughter-in-law or a son-in-law (in 25 per cent of cases). Cohabitation was less harmonious in the case of elderly women than men, and in farmer families than in working-class families (Piotrowski 1971, 121).

It should be stressed that although the tendency for generations to live separately takes priority over acceptance of cohabitation, it is by no means universal. In the above-mentioned research on intergenerational families bonds in Puławy, 50 per cent of the elderly, 35.6 per cent of those in the middle generation and 37.2 per cent of young respondents declared their readiness to live together, albeit with separate rooms for members of the oldest generation (Dyczewski 1976, 106).

Overall, generations prefer to live close to each other but separately. This tendency is best expressed by the term "distant intimacy". Most Poles (70 per cent) have a sense of territorial proximity to the members of their close family who live separately (parents, parents-in-law, grown-up children, siblings, grandparents and grandchildren). The family of almost every fourth Pole (23 per cent) is scattered throughout the country and every sixteenth (6 per cent) all over the world. One per cent claims to have no family at all. (CBOS 2004).

A strong intergenerational bond

Despite the prevailing differences in many domains, strong bonds exist between the generations in Polish families. This is manifested in mutual visits, as well as in mutual material and spiritual assistance. At least once a week, Poles meet their parents (72 per cent), grandchildren (62 per cent) or children who live separately (60 per cent). Quite frequently they visit their parents-in-law (47 per cent) and siblings (44 per cent). Celebrating Christmas with the family (92 per cent), Easter (91 per cent) and All Saints Day (90 per cent) is also widespread. People spend New Year's Day (63 per cent) or New Year's Eve (50 per cent) with their families to a lesser extent and rarer still, spend national holidays together (18 per cent). Most of those surveyed claim they keep in touch with relatives on weekdays (76 per cent) or Saturdays and Sundays (71 per cent), but spend long weekends or vacations less often with their families (60 per cent) (CBOS 2004).

The different generations in the family help each other in a variety of ways. Assistance is voluntary and based on strong emotional ties. The direction of help is twofold: parents even help their children and grandchildren who are independent, and in turn themselves mostly receive the help they require (see table 8.5).

In Poland at the end of the 1990s, 24.1 per cent of pensioner households received constant help from their families and 26.3 per cent occasional assistance. It is more rare for pensioners to avail of social welfare: 20.6 per cent of households do so regularly and 15.9 per cent of households occasionally (Balcerzak-Paradowska 1999, 68).

Thus in Poland private transfers within the family flow in the opposite direction to that of public transfers. In the first case, they flow from older to younger generations, in the second, the younger generation transfers part of their income to the older generations.

Table 8.5: Frequency of help according to type and source in percentage – 1995

Specification	Kind of help*			
	Financial	Material	Services	Child Care
Households using help (Total households** = 100)	13.2	17.8	6.8	14.9
Source of help***: (Households using help of a given kind = 100)				
Parents	56.7	59.9	91.7	16.5
Adult children	10.5	15.9	61.2	–
Relatives living in Poland	8.9	20.9	18.1	12.6
Friends living in Poland	1.0	9.2	9.3	6.7
Communal authorities	21.5	6.1	3.1	0.3

* Financial help for housing is omitted. ** The number of interviewed households in general: 3844; the percentage with regard to child care in relation to the total number of households with children (2190). *** Some rarely indicated sources, such as charity and religious organizations, the Church and parishes, friends and relatives from abroad, and several others are omitted.

Source: NDP: Poziom zaspokojenia potrzeb rodzin w 1995 r., 1999, 81

The type and extent of intergenerational mutual assistance is influenced by the type of dwelling involved. Generations who live in a household-economic community have numerous occasions for contact and cooperation. Hence help can be given/received more often and in greater variety than if they lived separately.

However, in all types of families there are several forms of permanent or occasional cooperation between the elderly, their children and their grandchildren. Providing mutual assistance in the form of material support and services is usually governed by the strict rule of reciprocity, but also by the principle of what and how much each of the parties believes is needed and fair to be given. On the whole parents give more, particularly in the initial years of their childrens' marriage. This is because they are still full of life and professionally active. Generations not only support each other but believe that they should do so rather than involve other people or institutions. This conviction was expressed by almost 100 per cent of the respondents who came from three-generational families in Puławy. Almost everyone claimed that children are obliged to support the elderly in need. In reply to the question "If your parents or parents-in-law had no financial means or were so ill (disabled) that they could not cope with everyday life, what would you do?" 91.4 per cent of the respondents in the middle generation and 86.9 per cent in the younger generation stated that they would certainly take them into their home. The rest would look for a place in a nursing home (in sequence: 1.6 per cent, 3 per cent) or employ a carer and then visit their parents (6.2 per cent; 8.5 per cent). None of the respondents displayed a lack of interest in the lot of their parents. (Dyczewski 1976, 88). Recent research has also confirmed this attitude of the younger generations towards the older. Parents expect help first and foremost from their family.

Yet, parents claim that they would help their children even when they came of age and were independent. More than half (59 per cent) of the respondents believe that children always need help from parents. This opinion prevails in all social groups. It is least asserted by people with higher education, who frequently advocate the idea of disinterested aid for children (48 per cent), as well as cancelling of assistance when a child becomes financially independent (41 per cent) (CBOS 1998b).

The result of research conducted by the Polish Gerontology Society in the year 2000 indicates that should they be in need, people of sixty-five and over would principally ask the family for help, first and foremost a daughter (45.8 per cent) or son (37.7 per cent), then a husband/wife (35.1 per cent), and much later a son/daughter-in-law (10.5 per cent), other members of the family (6.0 per cent), brother/sister (4.6 per cent) or neighbours (4.6 per cent) (Czekanowski 2002, 168). The poll carried out by CBOS in the year 2000 confirmed this expectation, showing that the elderly in need obtain help mostly from their family, primarily from children (78 per cent) and grandchildren (47 per cent) (CBOS 2000c). Support from neighbours, acquaintances and friends occurs to a much smaller – albeit significant – degree; specialists and volunteers participate marginally in helping the elderly. This proves the strength of family solidarity in Poland and reveals at the same time the weakness of social services.

Mutual assistance between generations in the form of material support and services now clearly focuses on the youngest generation. This feature occurs in all types of families. In the past, the mutual intergenerational help in farmer and craftsmen families often concentrated on production/consumption activities and only later on nurturing and educational tasks. Today the situation is completely the opposite. Intergenerational mutual assistance is first of all directed at nurturing the younger generation, with household activities coming second[5]. This shift is clearly visible in the quality of interpersonal relations, where the load is more of a personal than an objective nature.

Contact and assistance between the generations is not burdened with the same urgency as in the past. Pensions have made it possible in most cases for the elderly in all types of families to be financially independent of their children, an aspect that brings about considerable freedom in intergenerational contacts. There have been cases in the past in both working-class and farming families of exploitation of parents or parents-in-law by their children. There are still some instances of this today (Warunki 1929; Turowski 1972), but as a rule the attitude of adult children is far from exploitative of parents or parents-in-law, e.g., treating them as domestic help. Intergenerational mutual assistance in the form of services and material support is currently practised on a voluntary basis and given according to the genuine ability of each generation.

5 According to poll data gathered in 1927 in Warsaw, Łódź and Zagłębie Dąbrowskie, of 331 families, parents of either the wife or the husband, older siblings, relatives and strangers helped to nurture children in 44 (13.2 per cent) cases (Warunki 1929, p. 231). Having examined 869 working women with children in Warsaw, Katowice and Zabrze in the 1960s, H. Strzemińska claimed that more than 20 per cent of the women took advantage of some help from their mothers and mothers-in-law (Strzemińska 1966, pp. 205, 213.

Both intergenerational mutual aid and the willingness to provide it prove that there is not only a strong sense of family solidarity but that the function of the family as social security – despite the introduction of social insurances – is deeply rooted in the consciousness of Polish society.

Research shows a certain cultural continuation but at the same time differentiation of generations within the family. The generations are linked by key values, such as common care of the family and its individual members. The scope of the cultural heritage passed on depends on the intensity of intergenerational contact. Adult Poles who were raised and educated by their grandparents for the most part believe that they owe them their moral principles (90 per cent); a sense of being loved (92 per cent); faith (88 per cent); acquaintance with the history of the family (84 per cent); virtues such as dutifulness, diligence, self-discipline and will power (81 per cent); love of their country (78 per cent); knowledge of historical events (78 per cent), and specific skills (68 per cent) (CBOS 2001). Intergenerational cultural communication is weaker in families where grandparents do not have close contact with the youngest generation, which usually obtains while nurturing and educating children.

The place and role of the older generation in the family is currently determined by: 1. financial independence, 2. strong interpersonal bonds, 3. mutual aid in various forms.

Family policy

Family policy in Poland was shaped at the very beginning of the welfare state. During the Partition of Poland prior to the First World War, however, it took a different form in each region. Family policy in the area ruled by Prussia was quite remarkable. Social insurance against health risks at work came into operation in the German Reich in 1883, while in 1889 early forms of old-age and disability insurance were introduced. Although crucial to the workers and their families, these forms of insurance were established to counteract their dissatisfaction rather than serve their benefit. Initial forms of vacation and maternity leave also came into being. The workers gradually gained some protection with regard to working conditions, e.g., shorter working hours, which was in turn advantageous to family life. In the Polish regions that belonged to the Hapsburg Empire, family policy developed less rapidly, and was slowest in the area belonging to Russia.

Family policy in Poland 1918–1939

It is possible to speak of family policy in Poland only after the First World War, when Poland regained independence. In the first year of Polish political independence (1918), women were enfranchized (with passive and active voting rights), thereby reinforcing their position in relation to men, both in society and in the family. Family policy was based on the following articles from the Constitution of the Republic of Poland of 17 March 1921[6]:

> "Art. 103: Children without sufficient parental care or neglected with respect to education, have the right to state care and support within the limits to be determined by statute. Parents may not be deprived of authority over their children except by judicial decision. Special statutes determine the protection of motherhood. Children under fifteen years of age may not be wage-earners; neither may they be employed at night, or young labourers employed in industries detrimental to their health."

The family was considered an independent unit and the basic environment for child development. Out of concern for mother and child, maternity leave and maternity benefits were introduced in 1924.

In 1933, a social insurance bill was passed. The latter was modelled on German legislation, implying that the social strategies accepted in the bill were by no means inferior to those of other European countries, and succeeded by disability and old-age pensions. The bill regarded people over sixty-five years of age (steelworkers at sixty) unemployable. However, it did not take into consideration individual farmers, who were the most numerous group in the Polish population.

Various organizations, religious associations and above all social housing played a supporting role in the upbringing and education of children.

6 http://www-personal.engin.umich.edu:80/~zbigniew/Constitutions/k1921.E.html

Nationalized social policy (1945–1989)

In the aftermath of the Second World War, Poland came under the control of the USSR, and Soviet state policy imposed a socialist system on Poland with a centrally planned economy. Social insurance and family care were an integral part of the social policy introduced by the government. The socialist authorities needed to win social support and therefore generally pursued family-friendly social strategies. Two goals were to be accomplished: a) to assist the family in fulfilling its basic functions, since the family was (and still is) key in the value system of Polish society across all social strata, and b) to facilitate the employment of women/mothers, since this was a political system that expected every employable adult to work, including mothers. In the socialist system, those who were employed were awarded social benefits and insurances, gained in social status and were seen as valuable members of society. Hence the socialist system assumed (and followed this assumption) that all women/mothers would work, which they did en masse.

This pro-family social policy in the Polish People's Republic was based on the following Article in the Constitution of the People's Republic of Poland of 22 July 1952[7]:

> "Article 79: (1) Marriage, motherhood and family shall be safeguarded and protected by the Republic of Poland. The State shall extend special protection to families with many children. /.../.
>
> (3) The Republic of Poland shall ensure the implementation of rights and obligations in respect of alimony./.../.
>
> (5) The Republic of Poland, being mindful of the interests of the family, shall strive to improve housing conditions, and, in co-operation with citizens, shall develop and promote various forms of residential construction, especially those promoted by co-operative societies, and shall show care in the proper management of housing resources."

Of considerable importance for the organization of family policy was the Family and Welfare Code enacted in 1964 (which came into force on 10 January 1965). It was based on four assumptions: durability of marriage, equality of spouses' rights, child protection, and mutual support of conjoints. Much attention (in the third section of the Code) is paid to children without adequate parental care and wardship anticipated for incapacitated family members. In addition, the Juvenile Act of 1982 and the Act of 26

7 http://www.oefre.unibe.ch/law/icl/pl01000_.html

October 1982 on upbringing in sobriety and the prevention of alcoholism were also of consequence.

In accordance with the principles of the above act, so crucial to family policy, diverse measures to support families became a priority. Many of these steps had already been introduced in the inter-war period, and later confirmed or modified. The following are the most important:

- Family benefits for children and spouses: the unemployed handicapped, women over fifty and men over sixty-five, disabled members of the family (introduced in 1947). The goal of family benefits was to provide some form of equality in standards of living and development opportunities for children. The amount involved in and conditions for obtaining benefits changed constantly.
- Leave and child sickness benefits (1954): in the case of a child's illness, up to sixty days a year; in the case of illness of another member of the family, up to fourteen days.
- One-year parental leave (unpaid) was introduced in 1969 and extended in 1975 to four years. This legally guaranteed the stability of employment relations, permitted a return to the workplace and added the period of leave to the total period of employment.
- Childbirth allowance (1974) for female workers and unemployed wives of workers.
- An alimony fund (1974) for those who were not able to pay alimony ordered by the court.
- Nursing benefits (1974) for children in need of medical care, for the disabled and for people over seventy-five years of age.
- Child-care benefit (1981).

Maternity benefits were extended and in the 1970s encompassed medical advice during pregnancy, obstetric assistance in hospital or at home, medical care for mother and child after birth, milk rations and layettes (Piotrowski 1966, 102).

Confirmed and extended were:

- Dependent pensions for all family members who had been supported by a now deceased breadwinner.
- A one-time financial benefit by death of the breadwinner, granted to the strictly defined circle of relatives of the deceased.
- Death gratuity.

In the Polish People's Republic, families were well served with day nurseries, kindergartens and common rooms. The family received additional support from organizations such as The Family Council, The National Child Committee, and those of the Catholic Church. In cases where families did not fulfil their function satisfactorily, guardianship of children and youth was taken over by specialized institutions such as substitute families, orphanages, single-mother houses or the children's village.

Family policy after 1989

When the political order in Poland changed from a socialist to a democratic system with a free market economy, family policy took shape in a new political, economic and cultural context. The Constitution of the Third Republic of Poland from 2 April 1997 established the following directives for this policy[8]:

"Article 18:

Marriage, being a union of a man and a woman, as well as the family, motherhood and parenthood, shall be placed under the protection and care of the Republic of Poland.

Article 71:

The State, in its social and economic policy, shall take into account the good of the family. Families finding themselves in difficult material and social circumstances – particularly those with many children or a single parent – shall have the right to special assistance from public authorities.

A mother, before and after birth, shall have the right to special assistance from public authorities, to the extent specified by statute.

Article 72:

The Republic of Poland shall ensure protection of the rights of the child. Everyone shall have the right to demand of organs of public authority that they defend children against violence, cruelty, exploitation and actions which undermine their moral sense.

A child deprived of parental care shall have the right to care and assistance provided by public authorities."

The above directives are supplemented by ratified international documents that postulate various forms of family support, especially the European Social Charter and the European Charter of Children's Rights.

8 http://www.sejm.gov.pl/prawo/konst/angielski/kon1.htm

Accordingly the following principles have been accepted with regard to family policy:

- subject character of the family, i.e., the family is first and foremost responsible for its own destiny, and for child care, upbringing and education;
- subsidiarity, i.e., the principle that postulates decentralization of state entitlements in terms of running and financing most social services, e.g., those of self-governing bodies and local governments;
- plurality of family support, i.e., the state does not have a monopoly on family policies; the law and public bodies support initiatives by self-governing bodies in the interests of the family; private institutions and non-governmental organizations that supervise the upbringing and education of children and youth have emerged;
- marketization of social services (including family services).

During the transformation of the political system, the government and society as a whole became more interested in the conditions under which families lived and the problems of those concerned. The celebration of the International Year of the Family (1994) contributed to this phenomenon to a certain extent. More significant causes, however, were the worsening in the material circumstances of the average family; a decline in the birthrate and the emergence of several pathological phenomena in society, or at least their disclosure in the mass media. In 1989, family policy became a feature of political party programmes. Proposals for particular measures in relation to this policy were a permanent bone of contention in the struggle for political power. This had a negative effect on family policy, as it caused an incoherence of particular decisions and disrupted the continuity of family-related programmes. On the whole, the principal goal of family policy after 1989 was to secure the survival of families in difficult circumstances, i.e., those who were poorest. In accordance with the criterion that priority must be given to those who have least, financial support was offered first and foremost, above all family benefits; men and women were equally entitled to these benefits and pronatalist actions were reinforced (Balcerzak-Paradowska 2004, 121–122). The following were the most significant decisions on family policy after 1989:

- In 1990, the introduction of permanent benefits for qualified people who are unemployed or leave their job to raise a child that requires constant care. In 2003, this form of benefit was replaced by nursing benefits.

- In 1993, the introduction of benefits for women who are pregnant and bringing up children. The terms under which these benefits were granted and the amount paid were modified, however, in 1994 (twice: in March and October), 1999, and 2001.

Guaranteed temporary benefits for those no longer on unemployment benefit and who were raising their children (up to the age of fifteen) on their own were introduced in 1997. The terms under which these benefits could be granted were modified in 2003.

The terms of the following benefits were modified: family benefits (1992, 1993, 1994, 1997, 2001, 2003); childbirth allowance (1991, 1995, 2003); nursing benefits (1991, 2003), care benefits (1995), alimony fund benefits (1989, 1990, 1999, 2003); maternity leave was extended and the amount of maternity benefit increased (1998); the terms for granting parental leave and parental benefits were also modified (1996, 1999).

Social policy in the context of family benefits is based on family income and standard of living, analysis of social and family life, and observations on demographical phenomena and trends. The extent and type of family support is adjusted to the respective family needs. The main purpose of this assistance is: 1) to secure basic needs and help to satisfy personal development needs, i.e., equal opportunities for the development of both children and adults; 2) to increase the material and cultural standard of family life; 3) to rectify the distribution of the national income; 4) to realize the principle of social solidarity.

Seen in general, numerous organizations act on behalf of the family, youth and young children. In 1997, this was the case with every fourth non-governmental organization in Poland. Reseach on the NGO sector indicates that there were approximately 900 organizations of this type (Głosz 1997). They provide families and children with material support (food, clothing, house appliances, hygiene and cleaning materials, and textbooks) and services, and to a lesser degree with financial support.

Conclusion

Confirmed by substantial research in recent decades, I consider the following to be the most essential and most visible changes in Polish family life:

- the spreading of different forms of family life;
- changes in the arrangement of family bonds, i.e., domination of the personal bonds;
- changes of position and authority in the family, i.e., development of partnership relations between spouses and generations;
- changes in the structure of the family;
- demographic changes, i.e., a decline in the number of children in the family;
- differentiation of family support, i.e., improved adjustment to the needs of specific family categories.

Bibliography

Balcerzak-Paradowska, B. (1999), "Transfery w zakresie różnych form pomocy", in D. Graniewska (ed.) *Warunki życia emerytów i rencistów*, Warszawa: IPiSS.

— (ed.) (2003), *Praca kobiet w sektorze prywatnym. Szanse i bariery*, „Studia i Monografie", Warszawa: IPiSS.

— (2004), *Rodzina i polityka rodzinna na przełomie wieków. Przemiany, zagrożenia, potrzeba działań*, Warszawa: IPiSS 2004.

CBOS. (1997), *Kobiety o podziale obowiązków domowych w rodzinie. Komunikat z badań*, Warszawa.

— (1998a), *Dom rodzinny w pamięci Polaków. Komunikat z badań*, Warszawa.

— (1998b), *Zbiorowa aktywność społeczna Polaków*, Warszawa.

— (1999), *Plany, dążenia i aspiracje życiowe młodzieży. Komunikat z badań. Warszawa, czerwiec. Sondaż przeprowadzony 1–13.12.1998, losowa ogólnopolska próba młodzieży ostatnich klas szkół ponadpodstawowych*, N= 1316.

— (2000a), *Dzieje rodziny w naszej pamięci. Komunikat z badań*, Warszawa: styczeń.

— (2000b), *Sytuacja Polskich rodzin. Komunikat z badań*, Warszawa: marzec.

— (2000c), *Polacy wobec ludzi starych i własnej starości. Komunikat z badań*, Warszawa: grudzień.

— (2001), *Co zawdzięczamy swoim babciom i dziadkom. Komunikat z badań*, Warszawa: styczeń.

— (2004), *W kręgu rodziny i przyjaciół. Komunikat z badań*, Warszawa: styczeń.

Ceduła, D. (1989), *Leksykon opozycji politycznej 1976–1989*, Warszawa: TRUST.

Chałasiński, J. (1938), *Młode pokolenie chłopów*, Warszawa: Ludowa Spółdzielnia Wydawnicza.

Czekanowski, P. (2002), "Rodzina w życiu osób starszych i osoby starsze w rodzinie", in B. Synak (ed.), *Polska starość*, Gdańsk: Wydawnictwo Uniwersytetu Gdańskiego.

Dobrowolski, K. (1966), *Studia nad życiem społecznym i kulturą*, Wrocław: Ossolineum.

Dodziuk, A. and D. Markowska (1967), "Wiejska starość", *Wieś Współczesna*, No. 12.

Dodziuk-Lityńska, A. and D. Markowska (1972), "Środowiskowe odmiany rodziny wielopokoleniowej w Polsce", *Problemy Rodziny*, No. 1.

Doniec, R. (2001), *Rodzina wielkiego miasta*, Kraków: Wydawnictwo Uniwersytetu Jagiellońskiego.

Dyczewski, L. (1972), "Problem rodziny nuklearnej i rodziny szerokiej we współczesnym społeczeństwie", *Roczniki Filozoficzne*, No. 2.

— (1976), *Więź pokoleń w rodzinie*, Warszawa: ODISS.

— (1980), "System wartości w świadomości młodego pokolenia", *Roczniki Nauk Społecznych,*, No. 8.

— (1981), "Rodzice jako dziadkowie", in F. Adamski (ed.), *Miłość, małżeństwo, rodzina*, Kraków: Wydaw, Apostolstwa Modlitwy.

— (1984), "Konflikt kulturowy czy kulturowa kontynuacja pokoleń w rodzinie miejskiej", in T. Kukołowicz (ed.) *Z badań nad rodziną*, Lublin: Redakcja Wydawnictw KUL.

— (1997), *Społeczno-kulturowe czynniki rozwoju regionu środkowo-wschodniej Polski i Euroregionu Bug*, Lublin: Norbertinum.

— (1998), "Wartości dorastającego pokolenia Polaków w okresie transformacji systemowej", in T. Sołtysia and I. Łabuć-Kryski (eds.), *Trudne problemy dorastającego pokolenia*, Bydgoszcz: Wydaw, WSP.

— (1999), *The Family in a transforming society*, Lublin: The Learned Society of the Catholic University of Lublin.

— (2005), "Familialer Wandel in Polen", in F. W. Busch and R. Nave-Herz (eds.), *Familie und Gesellschaft. Beiträge zur Familienforschung*, Oldenburg: Bibliotheks- und Informationssystem der Universität Oldenburg, pp. 317–338.

Dyczewski, L. and D. Wadowski (1999), *Przezwyciężanie ubóstwa i przeciwdziałanie bezrobociu,* Lublin: Program Narodów Zjednoczonych do Spraw Rozwoju w Polsce, IPiSS, KUL.

Dyczewski, L., T. Biernat, P. Sobierajski and J. Szulich-Kałuża (2006), "Familienvorstellungen Jugendlicher in Polen", in F. W. Busch, W. Schulz (eds.), *Familienvorstellungen zwischen Fortschrittlichkeit und Beharrung. Ergebnisse einer Untersuchung von Ehe- und Familienvorstellungen Jugendlicher im internationalen Vergleich*, Wuerzburg: Ergon pp. 137–182.

Fastowiec, B. (1996), *Mój dom ze zbioru wierszy pt. „Ścieżek złoty piach"*, Chełm: Fastowiec.

Głosz, D. (1997), "Organizacje pozarządowe partnerem rodziny", in Raport IPiSS, *Partnerstwo w rodzinie i na rzecz rodziny*, Warszawa: IPiSS.

GUS (1939), *Mały Rocznik Statystyczny*, Warszawa.

— (1960–2005), *Rocznik Statystyczny*, Warszawa.

— (1973–2005), *Demograficzny Rocznik Statystyczny*, Warszawa.

— (1981), "Narodowy spis powszechny", *Rodzina z dnia 17.12.1978*, Warszawa.

— (1990), *Gospodarstwa domowe i rodziny. Narodowy Spis Powszechny*. Warszawa.

— (1994), *Historia Polski w liczbach. Ludność, terytorium*. Warszawa.

— (1996), *Gospodarstwa domowe i rodziny. Spis ludności mieszkań metodą reprezentacyjną 1995*, Warszawa.

— (1999), *Seniorzy w polskim społeczeństwie* (Elderly in Polish society). Warszawa.

— (2003), *Gospodarstwa domowe i rodziny. Narodowy spis powszechny ludności i mieszkań*. Warszawa.

Jagiełło, K. (2000), "Niemcy na kocią łapę", *Życie 8–9*. IV.

Łobożewicz, T. (1994), "Rekreacja i turystyka dziadków z wnukami", in M. Dzięgielewska and B. Butrymowicz (eds.), *Międzynarodowa konferencja „Ludzie starsi na rzecz rodziny"*, Łódź: PTG, UŁ.

Łukasiewicz, P. (1989), "Funkcje domu w okresie okupacji niemieckiej", *Kultura i Społeczeństwo*, No 2.

Markowska, D. (1964), "Kierunki przeobrażeń współczesnej rodziny wiejskiej", *Roczniki Socjologii Wsi*, No. 2.

Mysłakowski, Z. (1931), *Rodzina wiejska jako środowisko wychowawcze*, Warszawa: Książnica-Atlas.

NDP (1999), *Poziom zaspokojenia potrzeb rodzin w 1995 r.*, Warszawa: NDP.

OBOP (1998), *Małżeństwo i życie rodzinne w opinii Polaków*, Warszawa: luty.

Piotrowski, J. (1966), *Zabezpieczenie społeczne. Problematyka i metody*, Warszawa: Książka i Wiedza.

— (1971), "Starość w Polsce. Przyczynek do pojęcia starości", *Przegląd Socjologiczny*, Vol. 24.

— (1973), *Miejsce człowieka starego w rodzinie i społeczeństwie*, Warszawa: PWN.

Slany, K. (2002), *Alternatywne formy życia małżeńsko-rodzinnego w ponowoczesnym świecie*, Kraków: NOMOS.

Strzemińska, H. (1966), "Budżet czasu wolnego urzędniczek i ekspedientek", in M. Sokołowska (ed.), *Kobieta współczesna*, Warszawa.

Szatur-Jaworska, B. (1999), "Życie rodzinne ludzi starszych w Polsce", *Polityka Społeczna*, No. 9.

Thomas, W. I. and F. Znaniecki (1974), *The polish peasant in Europe and America*, New York: Octagon Books.

Turowski, J. (1972), "Stosunki społeczne rodzin w wielkim mieście (teorie, wyniki badań, wnioski)", in A. Kwilecki (ed.), *Teoria i badania socjologiczne a praktyka społeczna*. Warszawa: PWN.

— (1977), "Inadequacy of the theory of the nuclear family: the Polish experience", in L. Lenero-Otero (ed.), *Beyond the nuclear family model: cross cultural perspectives*, Beverly Hills: Sage Publications Ltd.

Tyrell, H. (1988), "Ehe und Familie – Institutionalisierung und Deinstitutionalisierung", in K. Luescher, F. Schultheis and M. Wehrspaun (eds.), *Die "postmoderne" Familie*, Konstanz: Universitätsverlag Konstanz.

Warunki życia robotniczego w Warszawie (1929), *Łodzi i Zagłębiu Dąbrowskim w świetle ankiet 1927 roku.*, Warszawa.

Warzywoda-Kruszyńska, W. and J. Krzyszkowski (1990), *Młode małżeństwa w wielkim mieście*, Łódź: Instytut Socjologii Uniwersytetu Łódzkiego.

Wierzchosławski, S. (1991), "Przemiany rodziny polskiej w aspekcie demograficznym", in Z. Tyszka (ed.), *Stan i przeobrażenia współczesnych rodzin polskich*, Poznań: Centralny Program Badań Podstawowych.

Wóycicki, A. (1922), *Robotnik polski w życiu rodzinnym*, Monografia społeczna. Warszawa.

Zembrzuski, T. (2000), "Podsumowanie", in W. Zdaniewicz and T. Zembrzuski (eds.), *Kościół i religijność Polaków 1945–1999*, Warszawa: Instytut Statystyki Kościoła Katolickiego SAC.

Statistical Appendix

Table 8.6: Population, Marriage, Divorce, Reproduction rate

Year	Total population in thous.	Contracted marriages in thous.	Contracted marriages per 1000 of population	Divorces per 1000 of population	Births per 1000 of population	Reproduction rate Total fertility rate	Net reproduction rate
1921	27 200	317	11,7		32,8		
1931	32 100	271	8,5		30,2		
1938	34 900	279	8,1		24,6		
1946	23 640	281,9	11,9	0,3	26,2		
1950	25 035	267,1	10,8	0,4	30,7	3,705	
1960	29 795	244,2	8,2	0,5	22,6	2,980	
1970	32 658	280 311	8,5	1,1	16,8	2,200	1,011
1980	35 735	307 373	8,6	1,1	19,5	2,276	1,073
1985	37 341	266 816	7,2	1,3	18,2	2,329	1,100
1990	38 183	255 369	6,7	1,1	14,3	2,039	0,967
1995	38 609	207 081	5,4	1,0	11,2	1,611	0,765
2000	38 644	211,2	5,5	1,1	9,9	1,367	0,653
2004	38 180	192,0	5,0	1,3	9,3	1,227	0,590

Sources: GUS, Mały Rocznik Statystyczny 1939; Rocznik Statystyczny 1960–2005; Demograficzny Rocznik Statystyczny 1973–2004

Table 8.7: Families (in thous.)

Specification	Families					Cohabiting couples	Children	
		marriages			fathers with children			with dependants up to age 24
	total	without children	with children	mothers with children			total	
1988	10,226	2,329	6,323	1,396	178	–	14650	11593
1995	10,533	2,483	6,278	1,580	192	–	14995	11793
2002	10,458	2,370	5,860	1,798	232	197	14,245	10,809
Households:								
One-family	9,205,2	1,994,2	5,344,1	1,479,7	204,1	183,1	12,889,8	9,740,4
Two-family	1,173,0	354,9	484,7	294,2	26,0	13,3	1,268,1	995,0
Three-family and more	79,4	20,7	31,5	24,5	1,7	1,0	87,1	73,3

Sources: GUS 1996; Rocznik Statystyczny 2005, 200–201

Table 8.8: Number of children in single-parent families

Year	Average number of children in the family	One child	Two children	Three or more children
1995	1,52	62.5%	27.4%	10.1%
2002	1,45	67,3%	24,4%	8,4%

Sources: GUS 1996, 110–120, table 19; GUS 2003, 33

Table 8.9: Persons living self-contained

Age of persons	Total 2 468 297 = 6,5% of Polish population 38 230 956	Men 892 636 = 4,80% of 18 586 401	Women 1 575 661= 8,02% of 19 644 555
19 years old and younger	15 989 = 0,04	7 967 = 0,04	8 022 = 0,04
20–24	96 652 = 0,25	50 664 = 0,27	44 988 = 0,22
25–29	102 706 = 0,27	66 479 = 0,35	36 227 = 0,18
30–34	101 878 = 0,26	68 650 = 0,36	33 228 = 0,16
35–39	135 440 = 0,35	96 501 = 0,51	38 939 = 0,19
40–44	152 350 = 0,39	100 299 = 0,53	52 951 = 0,26
45–49	162 188 = 0,42	91 068 = 0,48	71 120 = 0,36
50–54	145 320 = 0,38	66 114 = 0,35	79 206 = 0,40
55–59	206 055 = 0,53	75 540 = 0,40	130 515 = 0,66
60–64	268 056 = 0,70	71 545 = 0,38	196 511 = 1,00
65 and over	1 079 549 = 2,80	196 403 = 1,05	883 146 = 4,49

Source: GUS 1996

Kinship ties and family support in twentieth-century Russia

Irina Trotsuk and Alexander Nikulin

Introduction

Throughout history, poor rural households facing endemic risks and lacking insurance and credit markets have come together in social, ethnic and occupational groups to provide mutual economic assistance. In many instances, group members related by birth, marriage, and/or ethnicity formed the "extended family system" ("kin system"). The kin system has been described by Charles Wolf (1955) as "a system of shared rights and obligations encompassing a large number of near and distant relatives". In other words, the kin system is a social contract of mutual assistance among members of an extended family. In rural, predominantly non-market, economies the kin system is a valuable institution that provides vital community goods and insurance services in the absence of their market or public provision.

Kinship relations are typically understood today as a network of family ties and links with friends that provides the individual with a set of norms and behavioural patterns to regulate their private life. Kinship can be interpreted as a hierarchy of involvement patterns creating a common bond that develops along a certain trajectory in the life course. What is the basis of the phenomenon of kinship ties and family support? The chief components of the traditional (most widely spread) family model are blood kinship (e.g., parents and children, brothers and sisters) and legal kinship (marriage). However, understanding kinship from a traditional perspective is not enough, since over and above its legal registration, even marriage – as an integral part of the relations between men and women – presupposes the psychological and social transformation of a "stranger" into "one's own", establishing him or her as a "relative" of the social group in general and of the husband and wife's families in particular (Vorontsov 2004).

Throughout the twentieth century, the concrete forms of family support and its basic components in Russian society have undergone a series of changes, all of which have been explored in the Russian analytical tradition in studies on exchange networks and the family. The first branch of studies on kinship ties is characterized by clichéd phrases according to which "the family is the basic unit of society" (Shmeleva 1997; Rimashevskaya et al. 1999) and reflects either the essence of current change in society as a whole (Zdravomyslova and Arutyunyan 1999) or, on the contrary, is seen as "an island of stability", protecting its "population" from the influence of "external" social transformations (Rimashevskaya 1997; Vassilenko and Ivanenko 1999).

The logic of family functioning is tied in with the functioning of other institutions, which allows for the classification of Russian family studies into several groups (Ushakin 2004). In recent decades, the monopoly of the "production" approach (family as the social institution of societal reproduction [Antonov and Borissov 1990; Antonov and Medkov 1987]) has been undermined by other approaches (in particular, the evolutionary), which stresses, with the help of comparative analysis, the transitory and historically determined nature of family types. With the evolutionary approach, for instance, S.I. Golod identifies three "historically ideal family types" (1995, 1996): (1) the traditional patriarchal form of "family dependence of the wife on the husband, and of children on their parents" that gradually gave way to (2) the "child-centred"/"modern" family, characterized by excessive attention to private life in general and the emotional element of parenthood in particular; (3) the "matrimonial"/"post-modern" family type based on the "symmetry of the rights and responsibilities of both spouses" that began to evolve in recent decades.

In the traditional complex village family, immense authority was ascribed not only to the "bolshak" (the head of the family), but also to the mother-in-law, in strict command of several daughters-in-law. The bolshak took charge of the purse (especially in a case of departure), while the mother-in-law guarded the oven and the table: this rivalry for power in the home created tension in the family and made adult sons and their wives think about moving out of the household. When we speak today of the family crisis, we mean precisely this patriarchal model, which has gradually been eroded since the turn of the twentieth century by such developments as women's emancipation, the change in matrimonial behaviour, and the growing number of divorces and liaisons. The initial decades of the twentieth century saw the formation of a new type of monogamy – marriage and family that was child-centred, based on personal choice, and highlighted the intimacy of private life and the value of children. The triumph of the "child-centred" over the patriarchal family type is usually explained by the mass shift that took place at the turn of the twentieth century in marriage contracting, i.e., from "match-making" (a custom) to courting (individual free will). This led to children becoming more independent of their parents' permanent care and wives emancipated from their husbands, a development that dictated the decline in the number of children in Russian families and the surge in divorce. "Matrimonial" relationships were not simply determined by kinship (as in the patriarchal family) or childbirth (as in the child-centred family), but by the specific cooperation of men and women of different generations, the aim of which was to provide each individual with opportunities for self-realization.

Although village families also went through transformation from the complex multi-generational patriarchal family (a kind of mini-community), through the smaller complex family (parents, children and at least one side relative, usually the husband's brother) prevalent at the turn of the twentieth century, to the modern small nuclear family, the archaic patriarchal family model based on kinship interdependencies still prevails in Russia. In a Mary El family, for example, the idea of the "man as head of the family" (marked by 80 per cent of the respondents in the 1970s) is still unshakable, over 90 per cent of families preserve the traditional "gender" division of occupations (Pankratova 1990). The trend towards total marriage, a significant indicator of the traditional family, was still found in the Siberian countryside in the 1990s (Mikheeva 1993). Traditional principles have also been sustained in the towns and cities of Central Russia, albeit in less obvious form (Golod 1996) – kinship identification is patrilinear, the wife adopts the husband's surname, the register of family names is used in selecting a name for the child. Although the nuclear family prevailed in Russia in the 1980s, at least among the urban population, and raising one or two children was considered optimal (Problemi Semyi 1989, 157), a public opinion poll in March 2001 showed that for most Russians (84 per cent of respondents) family in the wider sense represented the highest value (Zorkaya 2003).

A second branch of studies on kinship ties is based on the "social network" approach and comprises two lines of research. The first – the anthropological research line – focuses on the symbolic meaning of exchange. Peasant studies, for instance, focus on the peasant community institution responsible for the distribution and administration that aimed at collective survival, and analyse the specific nature of the Russian archaic traditionalism based on emotional links within the wider family and among the members of the community (Akhiezer 1999). However, the village community institution was activated only in a crisis; as a rule, interfamilial cooperation and resources were at work, which explains the surprising popularity among peasants of joint labour and common daily practices even after the revolution of 1917. The more hostile the state, the more organized and wide-scale family and community survival cooperation became, and, conversely, once the state assumed several key social functions, informal cooperation weakened and shifted to the level of cultural, spiritual and psychological support (Fadeeva 1999). Now that the patronage function of the state has obviously grown weaker, the kolkhoz-sovkhoz system disintegrated and the new powerful economic actors are unwilling to bear the burden of social obligation, networked mutual assistance has once again come into effect (Nikulin 1998).

The anthropological and economic approaches to exchange are different (Ashkerov 2001): the economy proceeds from the fact that every object has its market price; in anthropology, on the other hand, exchange is interpreted as reciprocal gift-giving and an act of symbolic recognition, an expression of solidarity that creates or confirms social ties between individuals or groups, i.e., the act of giving appears to be more significant than the gift itself (Shruder 1999). In the framework of economic exchange, the equation is between the object and the commodity, whereas social exchange equates the object with the service. Thus, commodity market relations, where people have no established ties with each other or the objects around them, are diametrically opposed to the relations involved in gift-giving. In the latter, the gift is an instrument used in maintaining social networks – both non-kinship networks based on the universal exchange of resources according to the principle "you give me, I give you", and kinship or clan networks.

The second – the network – research line stresses the functional significance of networks as the structural base for various social processes (Economicheskaya Sociologiya 2002). Kinship networks are established on the basis of long-term loan giving: parents unilaterally invest in relations with their children for decades, while the children provide their parents with support in their old age, i.e., reciprocity is ensured at the generational level. According to the frequency of investment in the form of gifts, various types of networks are invested in heavily, occasionally or rarely. The first type includes family networks of close relatives; the second, networks of friends, acquaintances and neighbours; the third involves "sleeping" networks that call for individual gifts "of gratitude" for certain services, i.e., "using personal contacts (channels, networks) to gain access to public resources: commodities, services, sources of income (e.g., education, jobs, positions) and privileges" (Ledeneva 1999).

Hence, the main aim of the article is to give readers a kind of "inner"-Russian insight into the evolution and transformation of the kinship ties and forms of family support that prevailed in Russian society in the twentieth century.

National family policies: prerequisites and consequences

In pre-revolutionary Russia (at least in the European part) the patriarchal extended family, consisting for the most part of three generations and a great number of children, was the common family form. This explains why the system of education at an early age (up to ten years) was interfamilial (Sudbi Ludey 1996). The patriarchal-authoritarian family system presupposed the domination and control of men over women and of older over young family members, i.e., a strict gender-age hierarchy where the head of the family controlled its members. It also established the priority of the family as a whole over the demands and interests of its individual members. Family support or "family unity" was a key factor in career development for the younger generation, where adult life was dominated by the corporate European model of achieving success with the leading role of the family and close relatives. Although the small family had also become a widespread legitimate form of family life by the beginning of the twentieth century, internal family relations were slow to change, and the plodding tempo of democratization and emancipation was particularly evident. Russia remained a peasant country up to the middle of the twentieth century, with "archaic forms of family organization in urban areas fading over a period of approximately fifty years, i.e., two generations [...] or even three, more rapidly than in the rural areas" (Mironov 2003, Vol. 1).

While the family in Soviet Russia inherited the authoritarian-patriarchal style of interfamilial relations, it was at the same time going through rapid modernization under the influence of a state family policy that was "limited, non-systemic, associated with the social policy [...], did not specify and consider the family's institutional interests" (Darmodekhin 2000). After the revolution of 1917, state educational policy was based on bringing up workers without social roots or an interest in preserving their family or class traditions. Arbitrarily, state family policy was subdivided into several periods, differing in essence in its goals and impact on internal family relations and the family structure (Rabzhaeva 2004):

1917–1921

The years from 1917 to 1921 were a period of rapid destruction of traditional family relations, of dramatic refurbishment of the institution family and the sexual revolution (Chuikina 2002), "of freeing the family from private ownership foundation and appropriation of family functions by the state" (Antonov and Medkov 1996). The soviet state "rooted out" the permissive elements in marriage contracting by approving the universal procedure of civil marriage registration as the only legitimate form, thereby rejecting the church registration practised before the revolution; established freedom of divorce – the divorce procedure became secular, simple and accessible (it took place by mutual agreement in a registry office, with one spouse filing a suit in a court of law); abolished the concept of "natural" and "illegitimate" children; allowed abortions to be carried out in hospitals, which was the first instance of legalized abortion in European history, allowing Russian women to control their own sexual lives and their fertility; proclaimed the family, political and legal "equality" of women and men.

As a result, "kinship feeling became a less solid tie than party comradeship" (Sorokin 1992). This period saw an increase in the natural birth rate (against the background of an overall decline), there was a rise in the number of divorces, and the marriage rate soared. The "freedom of marriage ties" legally proclaimed in 1918 gave women freedom and access to public life, on the one hand, but weakened family ties and transferred the function of bringing up children to state institutions, on the other. The new proletarian laws aroused a storm of discussion on the development of the proletarian "family unit" (Antonov and Medkov 1996): the works of A.M. Kollontai, devoted to the "women's issue", proclaimed children, husbands and the home as relics of the past. In her view, the future belonged to home communes, mechanized canteens, combines, crèches and kindergartens, all of which would emancipate the woman, "save" her from her husband and "tyrant" parents, and free her from maternity, while the family would disintegrate and be abolished. There was a wide gap, however, between the revolutionary rhetoric on women's equality with men and its implementation: with the simplified divorce procedure, embryonic social services and absence of compulsory and fixed state support, women, especially those with young children, were economically dependent on their husbands. Hence, single (divorced) mothers were condemned to a life of poverty.

On the whole, 1917–1926 became for Russia a decade of bolshevist experiment in the sphere of conjugal family relations, ideologically based on the stipulations of classical Marxism and the social democrats. It suggested the "inevitability" of establishing emancipated gender relations in the new socialist society (Kazmina and Pushkareva 2004). At the same time the state persevered in strengthening and encouraging a system of monogamy marriages, contrasting the "layman-intelligentsia-peasant commonplace marriage of convenience" with the "proletarian, civil, love marriage". However, equal opportunities for men and women in the professional sphere and in terms of family responsibilities and parental duties were no more than a declaration: the reality of family life and the simplified divorce procedures left women completely responsible for the children; the newly established soviet state did not have the resources to implement the declared programmes of liberating women from housework and the responsibility of raising children (Chuikina 2002).

1921–1929

From 1921 to 1929 the "NEP" ("New Economic Policy"[1]) period created conditions for social dualism in the family: family policy became more

1 The New Economic Policy (NEP) was officially decided in the course of the 10th Congress of the Communist Party of the Soviet Union and promulgated by the decree of 21 March 1921 "On the replacement of foodstuff and natural resource assessment by a natural tax". This allowed peasants to lease and hire labour, which is more capitalistic than socialistic, and to keep a surplus after having paid a certain amount of tax to the

liberal, although it did not entail abandoning the general course of deinstitutionalizing the family. This period was characterized by a growing number of divorces, which was linked, for instance, to the fact that official permission was granted in 1925 to use paid labour in farming. So-called "seasonal marriages" began to break up on a wide scale, since their aim was to attract an additional workforce in the course of intensive agricultural work. There was an obvious increase in fictitious divorce, a means of obtaining property and other benefits. The New Family Code of 1926 targeted the nuclear family.

At the turn of the 1930s, legal recognition of conjugal relations required proof that the couple lived together (shared a household) and proof to third parties of matrimonial relations, i.e., mutual material support and joint upbringing of children. When the new economic policy began to yield to the growing totalitarianism of the state, the norms of sexual and matrimonial behaviour favourable to soviet ideology became "incontestable". The real "Soviet" was to be converted to monogamous marriage (divorce on a professional record was viewed as a "stain" and could hamper career growth). The return to patriarchal norms of Christian morality led to double standards. Thus one set of norms required that marriage should be entered for love, whereas others stipulated that everyone must marry and no one should indulge in illegitimate liaisons. The toughening of moral norms and the limitation of sexual freedom took its toll on the attitude to abortion. In 1926, abortions were banned to women in their first pregnancy and to those who had undergone an abortion less than six months

government. Under the NEP, private ownership was restored to small parts of the economy, especially farming (but not to the land itself). The NEP also relaxed trade restrictions and tried to regain alliances with foreign countries. In explaing the NEP, Lenin declared "We are not civilized enough for socialism", referring to the fact that Russia was still a primarily agrarian nation, with a very small urban population and a weak industrial base. By 1928, the NEP had made a successful recovery after the devastating effects of the First World War, the Russian Revolution and the Russian civil war, over a period of five years, NEP allowed industrial and agricultural output to rise to its pre-war levels. The NEP was generally believed to be intended as an interim measure, and proved highly unpopular with the strong Marxists in the Bolshevik party because of its compromise with several capitalistic elements, such as the reappearance of the profit motive and labour competition (many women were fired by managers who considered them more costly to employ than men). Stalin introduced full central planning, renationalized the economy, and from the late 1920s onwards introduced a policy of rapid industrialization. Stalin's collectivization of agriculture became the most destructive departure from the NEP approach. The NEP period resulted in a clamp-down by the state and a reversal of morally substantiated interests.

previously. An anti-abortion campaign was launched, denouncing the "egoistic" women who had no desire to have children. The next step was to introduce a fee for abortion. The refusal of the state to control fertility was linked, on the one hand, to the total lack of resources to implement the Utopian social policy of the initial years of soviet power. On the other hand, the scope of demand for abortions came unexpectedly for the first soviet rulers and legislators, all of whom held traditional patriarchal views. Abortion was later banned unconditionally in soviet medical institutions, making it legal to prosecute the women, the doctors and the intermediaries concerned.

1929 to mid-1950s

The years from 1929 to the mid-1950s were a period of repressive family policy measures, the introduction of repressive legislation in relation to the family, and of men and women taking responsibility for sexual relations and parenthood (Chuikina 2002). This period was associated with forced industrialization, collectivization and the establishment of totalitarian government methods. In essence it renounced the idea of abolishing the institution of family and proclaimed a course aimed at strengthening a new type: the soviet family. Economically, this policy was based on the total involvement of women with children (women-mothers) in professional activities, which led to the virtual impossibility of looking after the home and the family as well. The country saw the establishment of the etacratic marriage order: in Stalinist Russia the right to marriage became a public duty imposed on the individual by the state.

The family policy measures intended by the state to create favourable conditions for family functioning provoked mass clandestine abortions, an increase in female-induced infertility and a high death rate; large one-time allowances for women existed only on paper and were not designed for the numerous and reproductive peasant women; divorce became a lengthy and extremely formalized process, which led to a decrease in the official divorce rate. In the 1930s, the small (nuclear) family became widespread almost as a "by-product" of Stalin's industrialization, and was a consequence of mass migration and a move towards greater closeness in private life. The nature of interfamilial relations began to change as the pattern of authoritarian-patriarchal relations gradually gave way to more democratic and more equal relations between spouses, parents and children.

During the Second World War, the role of women in the family changed utterly (Aarelard-Tard 2003): the ideal in the 1930s was that of the wise and skillful housewife, a model "home fairy". In the 1940s, women were obliged to manage the home and their children without male help, and to rely purely on themselves. The shortage of men in the post-war years caused many young women to become single mothers; a new family structure emerged (grandmother – mother – children), where the absence of fathers was quite common. Soviet ideology saw the equality of men and women as the norm. Women were encouraged to choose "male" professions (tractor drivers, construction workers, administrators) and worked on collective farms as much and as hard as men.

Soviet state family policy in the 1940s evolved towards stricter legislation. The decrees gave legal status to registered marriages only (those who had entered matrimonial relations between 1926 and 1944 were obliged to have their marriage registered, since it would otherwise be declared as invalid); toughened the divorce procedure (an obligatory court hearing of divorce cases was introduced); banned establishing paternity in relation to children born of an unmarried couple, which de facto reintroduced the concept of "illegitimate" children (the child was given the mother's surname, and the birth certificate carried a dash where the word "father" appeared). "These decrees threw our legislation back a century [...]" (Antokolskaya 1999, 77), placed the responsibility for a liaison on the woman (and later on her child) and partially on the legislation itself, since a monthly allowance was promised for each child born out of wedlock.

These changes in family legislation fulfilled two tasks in the sphere of family policy, which were both significant and ambivalent: the practical task of encouraging people to have children at a time of war and of correcting the demographic discrepancy between the female and the male population (shortage of men); the ideological task of stabilizing society and introducing norms for the small family. In the grave conditions of war, mass migration, evacuation, the taking of prisoners, and occupation, families began to fall apart, while the state made attempts to limit personal freedom and mobility by restricting divorce. On the other hand, the actual shortage of men both during and after the war led to the establishment of a new norm for everyday life – the maternal family. This explains the need to introduce on a wide scale the concept of the "normal" family, consisting of father, mother and child/children, by construing the notion of the incomplete family, discrediting unregistered marriages and maternal families, and introducing the concept of the "illegitimate" child.

On the whole, legislative policy between the 1930s and the1950s shifted towards "forced family stabilization" (Antokolskaya 1999), but the destructive forces of inertia remained active (Kharchev 1979). Besides, the slogan "children are not responsible for their fathers" proclaimed by Stalin at the start of repression became the ideological base for putting the idea of dissolving family ties into practice; it meant that the civil identification of each Soviet citizen had priority over all others, including their family ties.

Late 1950s to mid-1980s

The late 1950s to mid-1980s were a period of consolidation, but did not change the overall direction of transformations in family relations. The gradual disintegration of the state from the 1960s onwards provided the family with a certain autonomy (due to mass transition from communal life to people living in their own flats and the emergence of various secondary schools). Families were granted more opportunity to affect the life and education of their offspring and the system of kinship ties resumed its significance. However, by this time the family as a social institution had generally lost its inner educational potential, and public opinion humbly accepted the idea of "let the state educate", since women had been widely involved in public production since the 1980s (Socialniy Potencial Semiy 1988).

During this period the state began to "soften" the practices of standardizing family and interfamilial relations: it abolished criminal liability for clandestine abortion in the 1950s, permitting abortion on social and medical grounds; in the 1960s, divorce procedures were simplified to a great extent (through a registry office or, in disputed cases, via the courts), abortion was legalized as the woman's personal option, the right to establish paternity voluntarily or by court order was recognized, the mode of shared property for spouses and regulated alimony payment was confirmed; "socio-democratic" protection measures contained in social policy with regard to women-mothers were implemented in the 1970s and 1980s (Grigorieva 1998). By the early 1980s, women were heavily involved in public production, a process initiated in the early 1930s and that presupposed a state solution to the issue of child-raising in the form of child-care institutions, schools and mass public organizations (Socialniy Potencial Semiy 1988). Consequently, women's traditional ideas on the gender division of labour also began to change (Problemi Semiy 1989): over 50 per cent of respondents believed that if both spouses worked, housework ought to be divided according to their workload and inclinations; only 10 per cent of women preferred the "traditional" division of domestic duties into "female" (e.g., cooking, washing, cleaning) and "male" (e.g., fixing electric appliances, repairs).

The period from the 1960s to the 1980s was characterized by total marriage and the predominant dependence of the young on their parents as a result of the then work-pay system – low level and slow growth – and acute housing shortages (Talalai 1986). Besides, and similar to private life in general in a totalitarian state, although the family ceased to play a significant role in transmitting social experience and family cultural capital, its adjustment to the new social conditions was manifested, in particular, in the practice of drawing the older generation into the upbringing of their grandchildren. According to a broad poll of the age cohort born between 1965 and 1967 in Moscow, about a third were living with their grandmothers when they started school (1970s), while another 45 per cent saw the latter at least once a week. In other words, most adults of the modern generation were brought up with the direct participation of their grandmothers.

Mass involvement of women in the system of public production drove families, at least temporarily, to resort to the assistance of grandmothers during the pre-school years of their children. Even where the family had lived separately from their parents before they had a child, grandmothers "were summoned" from another town or village to perform household functions and take care of the child. Consequently, despite the impact of destructive factors, the three-generational family has remained quite a common, statistically significant family type up to the present time. In 1970, of all families with married couples, 23.7 per cent were extended families (included the parents or relatives of one of the spouses and common grandchildren), by 1979 their share had dropped to 19.7 per cent, and by 1989 to 17.1 per cent. However, compared to Western countries, these figures were incredibly high. In the 1980s, the USA only showed 1.5 per cent multigenerational families (Matskovsky 1993). At 39.6 per cent, the share of extended families among young couples was even higher, i.e. in the early stages of family life and during the period of having children, most couples lived in their parents' home. Overall during this period, the external factors of family stabilization no longer carried much weight, while mutual aid, support and care, and the close communication that gives satisfaction in family life became key in providing marriage stability (Govalo 1984).

The second half of the 1980s and the 1990s

The second half of the 1980s and the 1990s saw the aggravation of crisis trends during the disintegration of the soviet system and the transition to the market economy. From the mid-1930s up to the period under discussion, the family was seen as the most important institution in soviet society, maternity was considered a significant social function on the part of women and was both morally and financially supported by the state, which took upon itself the lion's share of responsibility for the upbringing, education and health care of children. However, the entire social sphere, including family issues, moved to the background of state interest, so that the married couple with one child, and exceptionally with two or more children, and the so-called incomplete family became the prevailing family model (according to the 1994 micro-census, every fifth family, i.e., 20 per cent of all families with children under eighteen, was incomplete).

The current trend in state family policy of "eradicating social dependence" (Luniakova 2004) shifts the responsibility for children and the family onto the family itself, thereby creating a situation of general uncertainty, social vulnerability and constant poverty. The spreading of unregistered marriages and the growing readiness of young people to postpone starting a family until they had reached a certain level of education and material and social status led not only to a decline in the share of official marriages, but also to an increase in the average age of contracting a "legal marriage" (Zakharov 2002a). At the same time, the average age of women at first birth also increased (Zakharov 2002b). The time gap between the age at first sexual relations and the age at marriage increased: up until recently, the beginning of regular sex relations, first marriage and the first child embraced a time span of one to three years (this resembles the pattern of traditional Russian sex education), in the 1990s, sex relations, marriage, having children and raising them became increasingly independent values.

The reasons for the far-reaching changes that took place in Russian society in the 1990s in terms of marriage and family (see table 9.1) are threefold: the natural transformation of the demographic pattern, the abolishment of tough state control (e.g., the external "regulator" in the form of the party committee) and the socio-economic hardships of the transition period.

Table 9.1: Some indices of demographic modernization in Russia

	1897	1927	1939	1959	1989	1996
Part of urban population	15%	18%	33%	52%	74%	73%
Life expectancy (years)						
Men	29.4	33.7	34.9	63.0	64.2	61.0
Women	31.7	37.9	42.6	71.5	74.5	73.1
Infant mortality rate (in 1000 births)	260	205	213	36,6	17,8	17,4
Coefficient of total birth rate	7.5	6.73	4.91	2.63	2.02	1.28
Coefficient of reproduction	1.4	1.681	1.367	1.186	0.953	0.603
Number of divorces (in 1000 people)	–		0.9	1.4	3.9	3.8
Number of abortions in 100 births	–	16	10	–	206	203
Average family size (number of family members)	5.5	–	4.1	3.6	3.2	2.84
Urban family	4.9	3.9	3.6	3.5	3.2	2.84
Rural family	5.6	5.6	4.3	3.8	3.3	2.85
Percentage of families consisting of five and more members						
Urban families	44.5%	30.4%	23.6%	20.4%	11.2%	10.5%
Rural families	64.5%	–	42.0%	29.9%	16.4%	14.1%

Source: http://www.demoscope.ru/center/popul/popul1.html

For decades, social institutions in Russia had centred their activities on the need to guarantee maximum employment for the whole population. Consequently, they focused on the individual, while the family became an "outside" link in the relationship between the individual and society, a personal matter. Moreover, the family and its size often transpired to be a negative factor at crucial moments (e.g., education, getting a job, career development) (Problemi Semiy 1989). Those who, despite objective difficulties, desire to have several children, are frequently confronted with a negative attitude in their environment (usually expressed by the phrase "Why procreate poverty?"). A family with no children, on the other hand, when explanations have been exhausted (e.g., studies, no accommodation), tends to be perceived as abnormal (Golod 1984). Studies conducted between 1999 and 2003 indicate that between 70 and 89 per cent of respondents agree with the statement "The couple should have children" (Solodnikov 2004).

Thus, notwithstanding the experiments carried out in the USSR in the sphere of marriage and family relations, once the state ceased to interfere in the domain of private life, marriage and family in Russia moved noticeably closer to relations that prevailed in Western Europe. In particular, the gap between registered and non-registered marriages narrowed substantially in terms of partner status, consequences and attractiveness for those contracting marriage. However, Russian society is characterized by the comparatively high significance of marriage bonds for starting a family, even among the younger generation, although interpretations of the meaning of marriage and the role patterns of spouses/partners do vary. The traditional marriage pattern still exists (the husband as breadwinner and the wife as keeper of the "home fireplace"), but a modernized arrangement (both spouses are almost equally responsible for the financial provision of the family, for keeping house and bringing up the children) is now becoming more common.

Women and gender relations

Summing up the results of current gender research, it can be said that the woman's role in terms of correlation between the "house" and a "professional" career is as follows: at the beginning of the twentieth century the woman was, first of all, the keeper of the home fires; combining professional and family roles, albeit with the emphasis on professional activity, was typical of the soviet period; today the role of women in the family is gradually being recognized again, an aspect that is related to the shortage of places in pre-school institutions, the absence of child-care support from relatives and difficulty in finding a suitable job.

E. Zdravomyslova and A. Temkina (1996) conceptualize the specific nature of the above-described family-marriage relations within the framework of the soviet gender system as the basic gender contract of the "working mother". Under this contract, which legalized the "double" burden on women-mothers, the state provided women with additional "safeguard" rights, benefits and social infrastructure. In other words, the soviet woman combined full-time work with the organization of family life and raising children, whereby state institutions shared to a great extent the burden of child care (Temkina and Rotkirkh 2002). The creation of the gender contract for the "working mother" was preconditioned by the 1917 revolution, the civil war, the forced reorganization of rural life in the 1930s, the updating of urban life, more active contact between rural and urban populations, and finally, the Second World War, when the number of men who found themselves far away from their families was legion: the paternalistic communist state sought to "replace" the former patriarchal power of the master of the home with support for new, secular, matrimonial practices (Ransel 2004).

By the 1970s, however, the quality of the social services offered by the state and the level of consumer goods production had not met the requirements of the emerging "consumer society". Hence mothers were obliged to resort to the help of grandmothers and neighbours: the "legitimate gender contract implied other parties besides the woman and the state" (Tartakovskaya 2004). Grandmothers not only brought up their grandchildren, but also became the institution that performed the role of retranslating family culture and their own cultural status (Semenova 1996).

The abandonment of the basic gender contract of the "working mother" valid in the soviet era is the root cause of the overriding conflict between the professional and family roles of the modern woman (Zdravomyslova 2003). The crisis-stricken post-soviet period in Russia led to cutbacks in the budgeting of child-care institutions, while at the same time family income levels dropped. This meant that indispensable child-care services could no longer be afforded. Daily child care once again became the responsibility of the mother, a development that would ultimately lead to an ousting of women from the labour market (Khotkina 2001). According to Goscomstat data, of the more than five million housewives in Russia in 1999, a little over a third (35 per cent) did not want to work outside the home; although they were housewives, the other 65 per cent wanted to work (they are in fact unemployed). Due to the collapse of the pre-school child-care infrastructure, numerous women prefer to have no children at all rather than lose a good job as a result of forced maternity leave.

Another reason why it seems problematic for women to combine professional and family roles is the persistent inequality in the distribution of household chores between the spouses. Although Khruschev's reforms raised the status of housework to a profession (housekeeping was a school subject) with prestigious knowledge and skills previously underestimated, there was never any doubt about the economic or social value of these skills (Reed 2004). According to Barsukova and Radaev (2000), most Russian families fall into the "transitional type" category, distinguished by the combination of egalitarianism and traditionalism, i.e., husbands help their wives, but the distribuition of work is far from equal (about 30 per cent of the wife's contribution). Besides, if the husband's employment on the labour market becomes more time-consuming, so does the housework to be performed by the wife. There is no reverse process. When the woman's workload outside the home increases, the domestic chores are not taken over by the man but performed by other members of the family or remain undone.

Thus, having unilaterally "dissolved" the gender contract of the "working mother, the state had nothing to offer in return, which is why "success in implementing life strategies now almost depends entirely on the individual resources (e.g., family support, personal ties) of concrete women" (Zdravomyslova 2003). Today, in an attempt to find their place in the labour market, many women are reappraising their position in the family: they could make a move to change the order of things in the family (look for a job and re-distribute responsibilities) or radically change their attitude towards it (divorce). On the demographic level, Russian women solve the socially significant gender problem of combining family and work with a compromise: "as the woman's biography unfolds in time, she first gets married and has children, then professional tasks are met" (Ustnaya Istoriya i Biographiya 2004).

Several researchers claim that the seeds of change in the dominant ideology on the family and the role of women were already discernible in the USSR at the beginning of the 1980s – the incessant decline in the birth rate forced the government, among other things, to expand benefits to working mothers, to extend maternity leave, and to generally limit women's workload in favour of family responsibilities. A transition from the double to the single-income family, i.e., raising the male – "breadwinner" – wage, appeared to be a way of giving women the freedom of choice between a professional career and the family. Thus, a discourse on the masculinity crisis and the drawbacks of maternal upbringing began in the media and in sociological publications. Such trends were not merely a response to the official ideology of egalitarianism, marking almost a "renaissance of the patriarchy" that had existed in the public subconscious mind, but also reflected the crisis of the socialist "welfare state" and the inefficiency of its family policy. By the end of the 1990s, the crisis of the economy was virtually the only justification for the introduction of former soviet principles of gender egalitarianism. Women's salary was an indispensable and often decisive contribution to the family budget, although this was now interpreted as a largely unwanted consequence of the economic crisis or as a legacy of the communist system.

Today the dominant gender ideology is "post-soviet traditionalism" in various forms, with a number of common characteristics (Zhurzhenko 2004): the absolute status of the family as one of the highest social values; a sharply negative attitude to the practices and results of the soviet gender policy – "systematic, consistent and purposeful alienation of the family from the upbringing of so-called 'new soviet people'" (Gasparyan 1999); critique of the violation in soviet society of the "natural" division of roles, which led to the break-down of authority within the nuclear family into two opposing parental authorities (reducing the father's and strengthening the mother's); priority of the collective interests of the family as a non-differentiated unity, and defense of the active position of the state in the family domain, which is expected to resurrect "the family-building culture of society, lost over a long history" (Antonov and Medkov 1996).

Researchers see the source of today's traditionalism in the 1960–1970s period, when sociologists and publicists, far from doubting the correctness of soviet family policy as a whole, criticized the infringement of men's responsibility for the newly established family from a moral point of view and the couple's unwillingness to have children (Kharchev 1979). The growing conservatism in terms of family and marriage fitted well into the official ideology, which in turn was linked to the communal cultural traditions still predominant in mass consciousness. "The ban on abortion, divorce restrictions, non-recognition of unregistered marriages, excessive interest in the "moral image" of people appointed to high posts, "public" interference in family matters, and the exaggerated chastity of official art were some of the topics consonant with the traditional system of ideas about the ideal family "of good character", according to nineteenth-century village standards and the methods of social control over them" (Vishnevsky 1998).

With regard to gender aspects of contemporary Russian society, several researchers have addressed the problem of alcoholism, which gives women the dominant role of maintaining the family and establishing aid relations in kinship and neighbourhood networks. Heavy drinking has a long tradition in Russia and led numerous commentators to argue that it is so ingrained as to be impossible to tackle. Historical evidence reveals that this culture was to a large degree created by successive governments, i.e., by producing and distributing cheap alcohol, it contributed substantially to the problem at various times. Nevertheless, taking into account the considerable variation in Russia's drinking culture, in terms of geography, gender and socio-economic strata, coupled with the strong fluctuations in alcohol-related mortality rates in the 1980s and 1990s, commentators have been forced to admit that heavy drinking is not an inevitable feature of being Russian.

We address the topic of alcoholism for several reasons: 1) Russian alcohol consumption is a major factor in lowering male life expectancy to the very young age of 57–58 (many Russians die of alcoholism before they retire), a situation that seems to worsen in proportion to the instability of people's lives – alcohol consumption among males has doubled since 1990. 2) One of the chief contributing factors to the high level of alcoholism in Russia is social custom – regardless of age or social standing, drinking carries almost no negative connotations. An alcoholic in the family is rarely a target for blame. Instead, people express sympathy for the "suffering" wife, children and relatives. Many women in these circumstances are forced to become the rock in the family and take care of its members, i.e., to earn a living, run the household, bring up the children, look after the elderly, and maintain kinship support networks.

Overall, Russian social networks have a distinct gender character: men tend to help men, and women support other women, thereby reflecting Russian gender culture and proving the dominant position of homo-social groups in everyday leisure and communication practices. Women more often than men receive monetary and material transfers, and then mostly from women, who are in charge of the family economy and can hence as a rule dispose of these resources. Large loans and occasionally gratuitous financial assistance are habitually provided by men, since they are generally in possession of more resources. In terms of "gender" kinship support, men view the family as the object of social assistance, proceeding from the number-of-children parameter, whereas women see the material situation of the family as the chief criterion for support (Solodnikov 2004). Elderly men help friends and acquaintances less frequently than women, an aspect related to the more variable and informal character of women's networks in contrast to the more business-oriented male contacts. Besides, the compensatory significance of close relatives and friends grows with time/age, especially for women. Men over sixty and women over forty or fifty years of age tend to lose their self-sufficiency more quickly, and their willingness to rely on relatives and friends increases dramatically (Dubin 1999). On the other hand, helping grown-up children gives meaning to elderly women's lives and becomes the most important source of positive identity proof (Tartakovskaya 1997).

Networks of Russian kinship ties

The network resource re-emerged in the final decades of soviet society, when informal legal regulations outweighed the realm of statutory law. The long-standing domination of customary law in the USSR led to fundamental shifts in social life (Vite 1996): "the deformation of the legal space was compensated by the 'balancing' deformation of the communication space." In the official public domain, soviet life had a semblance of Utopia, which was contradicted by everyday experience, however, and the genuine diversity of social life. The network resource mechanism was "grooved in" during the post-soviet period. In some cases networks were established or rebuilt, but many simply depreciated and became defunct. Consequently, opportunities to mobilize network resources today are limited for many Russians and inaccessible for the majority (Clarke 2002).

Studies on private transfers in Russia (1992–1999) provide data on the number of households that exchange resources. Between 36 and 80 per cent of all Russian households are constantly involved in mutual processes of supplying/receiving money, food, clothes, labour and "non-material" assistance (information and connections) from their relatives and friends. Low percentages are usually related to the fact that several Russian regions have been included in the data under review; if regional differences are not taken into account, the final results are distorted. Furthermore, exchanges in urban settings are more intense than those in the country, and the frequency of private transfers increased after the crisis in 1998 (Gradoselskaya 1999).

Analysis of the RLMS (Russian Longitudinal Monitoring Survey)[2] data collected between 1996 and 2000 allows for the following conclusions: the most intensive exchanges occur between parents and children, both in number and size; the bigger the settlement, the more widespread the help among friends (not only relatives) and vice versa, whereby most transfers take place in town settlements and the least in villages; in private transfers, exchange priority is given to generational ties, i.e., children and parents practise mutual assistance, whereas redistribution of transfers from the older generation over the middle to the youngest generation in the family is almost non-existent. Transfer exchanges between households with different incomes vary, with the poorest households distributing 46 per cent of their income and the richest, no more than 16 per cent. The average rich household transfer in rubles is twice the size of that in poor households. The structure of the exchanges observed indicates that all households are connected by equal and stable flows.

In summing up the different types of transfers and variables, we see that the poorest households, in addition to money and food, appear to be the most active consumers of labour assistance, albeit helping only themselves. The most prosperous households supply all resources to the poorer households, and receive in return only labour and connections. The gener-

2 The Russia Longitudinal Monitoring Survey (RLMS) is a series of nationally representative surveys designed to monitor the effects of Russian reforms on the health and economic welfare of households and individuals in the Russian Federation through precise measurement of individuals' health status and dietary intake as well as household-level expenditures and service utilization etc. Data has been collected thirteen times since 1992: in the initial two years the main goal of the RLMS was to work with the Russian State Statistical Bureau (Goskomstat) and the All-Russia Center for Preventive Medicine in order to create a representative profile of the economic and social dimensions of the population and the first national sample frame, allowing surveys to be representative at the national level. Beginning from 1994, the RLMS changed the emphasis of its work from institution-building to providing timely, high-quality information.
The new RLMS sample was smaller, but the number of primary sampling units was doubled to enhance the representativeness of the survey. RLMS survey instruments were designed by an interdisciplinary group of Russian and American social science and biomedical researchers with extensive experience in survey research. For other details see: http://www.cpc.unc.edu/rlms. The report on the research results was given by the authors G. Gradoselskaya and E. Gantman.

alized indicators for all RLMS surveys between 1996 and 2000 show (see tables 9.2 and 9.3) that the gradual growth in the average size of private transfers emerged during this period. During the crisis 1998, many households changed their behaviour, i.e., the isolation strategy worked: the majority of households moved to the independent category, whereby the donors were particularly actively (54 per cent). Assistance for parents increased substantially, and help for children gradually; the largest contribution to the total received transfer was related to the presence of pre-school children. The most insignificant transfers came from the state and had a minimal effect on the eventual size of received and given transfers, i.e., informal transfers constituted a separate domain, parallel to the state system of social relief. Moreover, the inefficiency of the state system led to the formation of the powerful informal system of transfer exchange.

Table 9.2 Participation in transfer exchange

Year	supporting households	Average "size" of transfers, Rubles	households being helped	Average "size" of transfers, Rubles
1994	3.3%	106.45	21.4%	164.39
1995	22.8%	250.02	19.8%	327.39
1996	23.1%	294.09	216%	441.87
1998	24.5%	371.08	23.0%	448.09
2000	28.8%	768.34	25.1%	1093.03

Source: RLMS results, 1994–2000

Table 9.3: Types of participation in transfer exchange

Year	1994	1995	1996	1998	2000
Donor	23.0%	17.3%	16.8%	17.9%	21.1%
Recipient	13.1%	14.3%	15.1%	16.4%	17.5%
Exchange	8.3%	5.4%	6.3%	6.5%	7.6%
Independent	55.2%	62.7%	60.6%	58.9%	53.6%

Source: RLMS results, 1994–2000

Data on the Russian monitoring of the economic and health conditions of the population (the "Russia" project) (Bessokirnaya 2002) shows that every fifth Russian urban dweller turned to relatives for material help, and every tenth person to friends, considering this move a survival strategy in adjusting to new circumstances (see table 9.4). According to the urban residents' assessment, asking relatives or friends for material help appeared to be one of the most effective methods of adjustment, while turning to a social relief agency or other state organization seemed least beneficial. Orientation towards kinship support is guided by the fact that most migrants (73 per cent) from bordering countries decide to live in Russia where their relatives are (Amelin 2002).

Table 9.4: Spread and effectiveness of Russian urban population adaptation strategies

People have been using the following ways of adaptation	Used such a method	Effectiveness index
Saved on buying clothes and shoes	69%	-0.21
Saved on buying foodstuffs	57%	-0.24
Saved on vacation	55%	-0.21
Asked relatives for material help	24%	+0.34
Changed job	22%	+0.07
Grew vegetables and fruit at subsidiary small-holding	17%	+0.32
Asked friends for material help	11%	+0.18
Found supplementary job	10%	+0.29

Source: Bessokirnaya 2002

Researchers note a contradiction between the renewal of organizational communal forms and the breaking-down of commune relationships (Nefedova 2003). At the beginning of the twentieth century, the commune moulded a specific socio-psychological peasant type, with steadfast traditionalistic aims passed from generation to generation (Danilov and Danilova 1996). The soviet state did not plan to use the commune in its reconstruction of the village. On the contrary, the socialist system of land tenure began by destroying the commune and establishing in its stead a new type of public land tenure based "on the principle of single economic governance" (Kabanov 1997). Nevertheless, in the absence of an effectively run system of land tenure, it was the commune that redistributed confiscated lands and coped to perfection with the fiscal tasks.

Certain elements of communal life have now been actively restored in a modified form: in the 1990s, a substantial number of lands was passed over to the rural administration's regulating land tenure. However, restoration of the outward collective forms has been accompanied by a decay in the collectivist mind, typically a more rapid occurrence in regions with a predominantly Russian population. The priority of personal initiative and an active position has not yet taken shape in the Russian peasant psyche (Khisamova 2002; Efendiev and Bolotina 2002), and in the depopulated Russian villages, those in search of a foothold find shelter in a mini-environment (relatives or close neighbours). T. Nefedova questions (2003) the Russian readiness "to give gratuitous assistance" (Shkaratan 2002) identified by sociologists – in the modern village practically everything is done for money: odd jobs are a vital source of real money and often the only one, with the exception of close kinship and neighbourly ties.

The rural population claims to need kolkhozes and sovkhozes to help with private households, but also because people are afraid of coming face to face with the hostile outside world. This does not imply a desire for collective work; elementary cooperation is rare even where necessary (e.g., in selling farm produce). Modern farmers have taken on numerous social functions previously performed by kolkhozes and sovkhozes, but they cannot be "charity institutions" for the weak, as in the case of many collective agricultural enterprises (Nefedova 2003). If they heightened their labour productivity and improved their organization, farmers would need only a small workforce. Since they cannot support the private production of the entire village, they confine themselves to helping their workers and pensioner, whose land shares they use. As a result, a large number of people are excluded from the habitual symbiosis of the collective enterprise and the individual production farm, which in turn find themselves without the traditional informal support, either direct or indirect.

The long-drawn-out economic crisis in the agrarian sector conditioned the need to consolidate the inner resources of the rural family (Fadeeva 1997): the family farm became more important, its production compensating the family budget deficit. Exchanges and assistance among relatives, acquaintances and countrymen intensified, as the data of budget reviews shows: almost all rural families are engaged in exchange or aid relations; the family farmyard rarely provides for the needs of one family only; more than half of rural families belong to exchange networks, even when these exchanges are not usually equal. Exchange flows "ply" not only between the village farmyards, but also between rural and urban residents: the practice of supplying relatives in town with foodstuffs, besides observing family etiquette, has a certain secret meaning, i.e., it is a way of "paying for" past and future requests for various services. Rural practices still continue to imply the importance of the "neighbourhood" institution. The village community remembers how to come to the rescue of those in trouble (e.g., to help those whose house has burned down) (Fadeeva 1999). Considering the acuteness of the rural employment problem, patronage appears to be necessary to attain even modest posts such as that of a cleaner or night watchman. The transparency of the village and the destinies that are intertwined bring together an array of grounds for mutual services, e.g., collective work, friendly relations, exchange obligations and other accompanying services.

There may seem to be a contradiction between our two statements "in the modern village practically everything is done for money" and "almost all rural families are engaged in exchange or aid relations". The truth is, however, that both trends can in fact be observed. Aid relations "free of charge" predominate in very close kinship and neighbourly ties. In other cases people prefer, on the one hand, to avoid helping "for nothing" and save resources for "their own people", on the other, to pay for help received and not owe a debt of gratitude or gain a reputation as a "hanger-on". On the whole, Russian society has maintained the solidity of family ties and traditions of "collective action" that compensate the weakness of social policies with redistribution within kinship economic networks, although aid is not based on full equivalence, but on principles of reciprocity and mutuality. These principles fit into the model of survival of the peasant community proposed by J. Scott in his "moral economics" theory (Scott 1976): the aim of peasant family economics is to provide a survival opportunity for all, albeit at the lowest level, which was the purpose of traditional Russian community institutions. Since the early 1990s, "horizontal" resource flows have been intensifying to integrate peasant households into a specific communal socio-economic network of kinship, neighbourly, friendly and partnership relations.

Investigating forms of kinship support and family exchange

Methodologically we can identify a few quite obvious approaches to investigating forms of kinship support and family exchange in the area of sociological (and often economic) studies, including the biographical method, public opinion surveys and the study of the motivation for transfers and their size in interfamilial exchange as a type of informal economy. The combination of all three approaches provides the most precise and most thorough knowledge of the topic investigated.

Through the analysis of narrated personal experience we can reconstruct family stories embracing several Russian generations in the changing social context of the twentieth century and identify both the typical nature of survival and the adaptation strategies employed under new socio-economic and historical conditions, and their unique character as a possible particular manifestation of socio-typical phenomena (Sudbi Ludey 1996). Among them: 1) the unique experience of preserving the customary method of keeping house in an individual family in a village in the Urals, by creating the formal semblance of a kolkhoz at the time of collectivization (in order to avoid repression, a kolkhoz was established for the sake of appearances; as a rule people looked after their old property, attempting to work their former plots; for the sake of form, one person was moved out; he built a hut on the outskirts of the village and lived there all his life); 2) "family-shared flats" as a strategy to avoid the intrusion of "strangers" into the private living space during the period of the settling-apart policy sanctioned by the state in the 1920s and 1930s. The broad campaign in Moscow during this time to withdraw "surplus" housing and "reduce living space" deprived many families of the total living space at their disposal. In this situation some related families preferred to move in with their relatives rather than share a flat with "strangers". In the 1930s, for example, about fourteen close and distant relatives lived in the Voronovs' flat, and attempted somehow to occupy the "surplus" living space[3]. During the Patri-

3 The selection of respondents for the biographical project "The century of social mobility in Russia" was made on the basis of the representative longitude "Generational paths in Russia" (carried out at the Sociology Institute from 1985–1993 and that included social trajectories of the age cohort born in 1965–1967; the project was led at different stages by M. Titma, L. Koklyagina and V. Semenova). The longitude provided representation of respondents from different social groups and, as in terms of time, the post-revolutionary history of Russia corresponds to the life-spans of tree relative generations. "The count back" from the generation of "children" (born in 1965–1967) made it possible to embrace the entire period of Soviet history: the grandfathers (as a rule, born between 1900 and 1920) saw the destruction of traditional Russian society, the parents (mostly born in between 1930 and 1940) witnessed the establishment and development of the "classical" soviet system, and the children have lived through its collapse and the country's choice of further development. Eventually, sixty-eight families were selected from the sample. From each of these, between two and three family members of differ-

otic war and with almost no male assistance, the women in the Voronov family survived as a result of kinship ties and family support (sought a post that enabled them to acquire foodstuffs and help the family) (Sudbi Ludey 1996).

The extent of mutual assistance in the village is characterized by a further example: in a village in Ryazan province, the paternalistic attitude of the landlord towards the peasants persisted for many years after serfdom was abolished (the master built and maintained a three-year village school, twice a year – at Easter and Christmas – he organized festivities for the village children, and opened a library and a hospital for the peasants). After the revolution the peasants refused to allow commissars from the town to burn down his country estate (it was used for kolkhoz purposes), apportioned a house to the old landlord and took care of him till he died, a form of thanks for his humane attitude towards them.

The harsh living conditions after the revolution, if anything, brought many family dynasties even closer – mutual assistance was preserved even between the most distant of relatives and helped people to survive during the years of reaction and war. The survival of those in the former elite groups was guaranteed in the soviet period, on the one hand, due to the absence of their own intelligentsia and administration elite. The soviet state was obliged to form its elite on the basis of the "former" social classes, which, as a rule, possessed considerable family-cultural capital and professional expertise acquired in pre-revolutionary Russia. However, a full appreciation of the specialists who survived the years of state repression only came when political persecution was over (Sudbi Ludey 1996). On the other hand, members of these "former" social classes sought to preserve their unity of estate, since personal ties with their estate group helped them to survive financially and fit into the new social structures, although they were fraught with the danger of repression.

Leaning on personal ties had always been typical of Russia, a mechanism that reached its peak in the final stages of establishing the bureaucratic system and soviet nomenclature. On the other hand, the soviet "blat" institution began to set in immediately after the revolution, while the traditions of making use of personal ties had also thrived in tsarist Russia (fathers passed on their social connections to their sons). After the revolution the connection channels were largely destroyed; those that remained

---

ent generations were interviewed, a procedure that facilitated the reconstruction of family histories from the turn of the century to the present day.

helped to find decent jobs and, consequently, a means of subsistence. The only possibility of survival for older family members, originating from classes swept away by the revolution, was their children, who could be reintegrated into the new society, master the desired profession and help them to survive. Almost all others were excluded from the new society, and deprived of income and social relief, many of them died of hunger. People from this social circle who lived in the urban centres had very little chance of survival. According to P. Sorokin, who refers to soviet data, the population of Petrograd dropped from 2.42 million on the eve of the revolution to 1.47 million in 1918, and further to 0.74 million in 1920. Moscow's population was halved from two to one million inhabitants between February 1917 and the 1920s (Sudbi Ludey 1996).

Biographical data and family stories alone are not in themselves sufficient to gain an understanding of the main tendencies in developing kinship ties and types of family support in Russian society throughout the twentieth century, since they do not explain the substantial mechanisms of social interaction, which is why we have to address kinship relations under the umbrella notion of network and the model of informal relations. The study of the informal economy presupposes combining institutional and anthropological approaches in the analysis of stable mechanisms of social interaction in soviet and post-soviet society. The domestic economy links the formal and informal economic sectors; home production determines the degree and intensity of its members' participation in the informal economy, substituting private interfamilial control for state control. In today's market economy, home production has not lost its position. On the contrary, it has become an "island" of stability and, in the light of an endless need for money, a means of survival.

Social networks of mutual assistance and collective survival in the village are determined by interpersonal ties and relations of a traditional nature: kinship, marriage and neighbourhood. The community of "one's own people" is local, with closed membership and a limited volume and variety of resources. Passive survival is possible within and with the assistance of the network; it can help to solve problems or improve situations to a certain degree, as distinct from facilitating individual or collective development. Another specific social phenomenon is the network of useful acquaintances, i.e., sporadic interaction in an emergency, determined by the position of the "donor" of a service in a formal institution. Other instances include hospitalization and medical care, avoiding conscription, entry into institutions (kindergarten, school, university). Services provided are standard rather than superior quality.

The outcome of private transfers is that underpaid or unpaid workers in the budget sphere continue to work and survive, particularly due to the fact that the relatives concerned work in a non-state organization, for example, receive a high salary and provide assistance to several "budget" relatives, usually students or pensioners (Neformalnaya Ekonomika 1999). Traditionally, economists have merely considered two sides exchanging transfers. e.g., parents and children, and in the network pattern also include transfers between distant relatives and friends, which are sometimes not only more intense, but also differently motivated. The identification of transfers is based on different types of support provided by members of a kinship network: most members in the network (about 60 per cent) render some form of emotional support, small services or become partners; between ten and 16 per cent provide substantial monetary or informational assistance.

A feature common to all transfers is their informality, which is why they escape control by the state. Private transfers hinge on such urgent matters in today's Russia as poverty, state support for households, taxation, and household survival strategies. For instance, determining the direction of transfers (the flow from which group to which and the type of resources involved) facilitates adjustment of state social policy. If state transfers are allotted to a group that represents an intermediate link in the chain of private transfer exchange, and passes these resources on, they can reach groups the state has no intention of helping.

Public opinion surveys seem an excellent supplement to biographical and network research. They demonstrate that the collapse of the centralized state system at the turn of the 1990s led to paradoxical consequences (Gudkov and Dubin 2003, 32): on the one hand, state power was viewed by the people as thoroughly corrupt, venal, and egotistical; on the other hand, it was from the state that the population, deprived of their own resources and of the institutional means of obtaining them, expected help. In 1990, 20 per cent of Russians believed that most people in Russia would be able to get by without the constant care and guardianship of the state, 63 per cent flatly disagreed with this; in 1997, the respective figures were 17 per cent and 72 per cent. However, only 9 per cent of respondents turned to state agencies to solve their problems, whereas 29 per cent have recourse to informal channels (acquaintances, relatives or friends), only 4 per cent turned to public organizations or private companies (services, consulting, intermediaries). These figures illustrate that in the experience of the ordinary person, informal networks and ties give the best results, most of which is achieved by turning to relatives (40 per cent of successful problem-solving), acquaintances, colleagues and friends (33 per cent).

In the new socio-economic environment, young people's expectations of help from the state to realize their aspirations, e.g., a future job, education, purchasing a flat, are coming to naught. Surveys on youth carried out between 1985 and 1995 (Magun 1996) show that although young people count on "some help", in particular when buying a flat, their expectation of aid from the state and other agencies is far less than what they expect in "parental" help. Hence, the younger generation are sceptical about the participation of state organizations and banks, as well as the companies they plan to work for, in solving their housing problems.

In 2001, young people relied more on help from their parents, relatives and friends than in the mid-1990s or in 1985, the reasons for which are diverse (Magun and Engovatov 2005). In the late 1980s, figures for expected help indicated a passive strategy. At the end of the 1990s, however, the figures pointed to a stronger focus on the active strategies of young people, who now now longer set their sights on assistance, but mobilized their own and other people's resources to become more active. Beginning with the early 1990s, each new generation of young people has become more and more aware, firstly, of their growing opportunities as a result of a good education and a good job. On the other hand, they see the diminishing ability of their parents to help them directly to buy a home and other consumer goods. As a result, the preferred "flows" of parental help were redistributed in favour of a good education, a reasonable job and a first-rate reputation. Another important argument was that parental help could still come in the form of the human, moral and social capital at their disposal rather than from material and financial resources that were in short supply.

Conclusion

Throughout the twentieth century, the family in Russia, as in all modern societies, was becoming more child-centred and gradually smaller in size.

Changes in marriage forms and birth rates as a result of modernization took place and have preserved under the impact of establishing a consumer society, developing a contraceptive industry and, most importantly, of greater emancipation of women and a shift in the notions concerning gender roles in the family and in society, and the striving for emotional and intimate community of the couple. On the other hand, there is an opposite trend, which W. Beck has called "the growing attraction of matrimonial community", whereby against the background of global and local social instability, the family (in broad terms) becomes a long-wished-for island of stability and affection in a sea of "boundless individualism". Overall, Russian society is evolving towards a diversity of family types and interfamilial relations.

Individual assistance of an informal nature was quite widespread up to the beginning of the twentieth century in the Russian village, along with the organized community help for those in need and unable to survive on their own. T. Shanin explains village solidarity as follows:

> "The interests of the rich and the poor in each village varied considerably, but the community of destiny or conflict, in the face of nature elements, the state, landlords and even the market provided ever growing and generally more prevalent causes for cooperation and mutual support. The experience of past centuries had taught the village dwellers that such unity was necessary for the survival of most of them" (1997, 275).

From the 1920s to the 1930s, peasants still had a large number of children, almost half of whom died at a young age. Medical care was non-existent, not a single doctor could be seen for miles around and only the fittest survived. Peasants accepted their children's death humbly, saying that "God gives, God takes away", so that abortion in the village was rare; babies were delivered in the knowledge that hardly any mother would be spared a funeral. Thus a typical peasant household in Russia included blood relatives of two or three generations with their wives. However, the determining factor of mutual support was not the degree of kinship but the amount of involvement in the life of the family: living together under the patriarchal control of the head of the family, close cooperation in everyday work, a "common purse" and complete confluence of man and the household.

Collectivization in the 1930s removed from the village its organizing and protecting social nucleus in the form of a commune, which led people to rely on kind consent and mutual assistance up to the 1960s. In the soviet era, the kolkhoz retained the features of the commune, where everybody knew each other, was in the know about "life details", no matter what happened. Everyone had a wide circle of relatives, including second and third cousins, ex-husbands and godparents. The customs and rites of good neighbourliness were held sacred – it would be a shame not to help with a funeral, even if you were not on speaking terms with the deceased (Kozlova and Sandomirskaya 1996) (e.g., in North Osetia even today the entire circle of acquaintances comes to the funeral and participates in the funeral repast, which lasts a month; after the funeral the mistress of the house where someone had died gives small symbolic gifts to those who helped).

From the 1970s to the 1980s, certain social functions were taken over by the kolkhozes, thereby decreasing the need for informal cooperation among countrymen (e.g., housing construction, hospitals, kindergartens, pension provision). Accordingly, the tactic of interfamilial relations changed: the older generation regretted the loss of the former universal assistance among villagers, now no longer in demand. What was left were some small obligations and the mutual exchange of services. At the same time, a new type of dependence began to assert itself: those who made decisions on the distribution of deficit resources, means and privileges were suddenly seen as "necessary" and "useful" (e.g., head of a kolkhoz and chief experts, party and trade union leaders). Professional and occupational duties now came under the pressure of family and friendship ties. Perestroika in the mid-1980s and the subsequent economic reforms undermined the basis of the former kolkhoz-sovkhoz system, refocusing it on the tasks of efficient production at the expense of the old patronage social functions and guarantees. Private family farms were once again viewed by village dwellers as the main means of subsistence, and the survival of the family was primarily achieved by exchanges and mutual assistance among relatives, acquaintances and countrymen.

Since the 1920s, life in the urban setting had changed utterly: people who moved to town from the country first of all rented a flat and finally built a shed in a suburb of Moscow because they could not afford a house. In this sense the situation resembled life in the country – water had to be fetched from the well, the toilet was outdoors, the oven had to be fired, but unlike the country, people could not own land. Women had to find jobs to secure the supply of food. Although peasant women previously had a negative attitude to abortion, considering it an extreme measure, lack of child-raising support and the harsh realities of poverty forced women to have abortions. In fact, the destruction of behavioural norms in terms of reproduction triggered the eradication of village culture (Sudbi Ludey 1996).

Beginning in the 1920s, the shift in the status of former peasants who had become urban dwellers took three generations. In the initial years after the revolution, links forged between neighbours as a result of close proximity in one place were the main institutionalized form of self-regulation and control, and the relations of mutual assistance were based on the exchange of services. When urbanization brought about the disintegration of local ties, disconnection and isolation replaced solidarity. Urban culture, where respect for the privacy of others became a cardinal value, was in the process of being established. The disruption of collective psychology, collective identity, and alienation from the "neighbours" began when people moved into flats. This new welfare had a double effect: on the one hand, money could buy the comforts of life and, on the other hand, it broke the traditional ties forged at a time of existential insecurity and abject poverty. People felt nostalgic about village life, a social space that once guarded the traditional life of the peasant community. These processes were prompted by a gradual penetration into network relationships of formal and modern motives of action and generalized means of exchange (money, aspirations of higher standards of living), which led to the disintegration of primary solidarity links of those equal in poverty (Gudkov and Dubin 2003): in the early 1990s, corporate solidarity among the intelligentsia began to evaporate, similar to the kinship and neighbourly ties in the modern village.

The investigations conducted in different regions of Russia revealed two opposing trends in informal cooperation: in some cases (usually in the urban centres) cooperation does not go beyond the relationship between children and parents; people encapsulate themselves in their family world (which, in the rural areas is the result of poverty, where families do their utmost to survive, severing almost all ties in the process). On the opposite pole we have, for example, the Kuban Cossack stanitsa, rich in mutual obligations, where exchanges are conditioned not only by traditional peasant thrift (to sell or merely give away the surplus and avoid waste) and redistribution of obligations in the sphere of official "privileges" and opportunities ("exchange in access channels" removes the need to make purchases, allows for saving money), but by preserved communal traditions of giving interfamilial and good-neighbourly aid to "one's own".

Today, where the patronage function of the state is obviously weaker, the kolkhoz-sovkhoz system has perished and the current major economic actors are unwilling to bear the burden of social obligation, networked mutual assistance is once more at work; exchanges and assistance between relatives, acquaintances and countrymen have intensified. The peasants themselves evaluate the significance of exchange and present-giving as follows:

"And though we visit each other less often, we do help each other. We give whatever we have. Otherwise we would never survive. You can't live without it, especially now. How can we live without it? What was it like before? You steal here, you pinch there, and now you just ask those who have access [...] So we go and beg them. And help each other [...]" (Vinogradsky 1999, 44).

Despite the fact that the monthly volume of mutual exchange, present-giving and labour services makes up almost a quarter of the family budget turnover, these flows are hard to pinpoint: the peasants themselves see them as insignificant, secondary and unimportant. They dissolve in their daily lives to such a degree that they become virtually invisible, so extensive are these "implements of the weak". They are stable, systematic, traditional and widespread. However, this is precisely what constitutes their problematic character – they construct solid structures of vital social "patience", which engender passive and inert peasant adaptation strategies to the new socio-economic conditions of life in Russian society.

Bibliography

Aarelalard-Tard, A. (2003), "Problemy adaptacii k novym kulturnym realiyam v zerkale biograficheskogo metoda", *Socis*, 2.

Akhiezer, A. (1999), "Khozyaistvenno-ekonomicheskie reformy v Rossii: kak priblizitsya k ponimaniyu ih prirody?", *Pro et Contra*, V.4, 3.

Amelin, A. (2002), "Socialnaya adaptaciya vinujdennyh perecelencev v polyetnicheskom prigranichnom regione Rossii (sociologicheskiy aspekt)", *Monitoring obschestvennogo mneniya: economicheskie i socialnye peremeny*, 3 (59).

Antokolskaya, T. F. (1999), *Semeynoe pravo*, M.

Antonov, A. I. and F. A. Borissov (1990), *Krizis semiy i puti ego preodoleniya*, M.

Antonov, A. I. and F. T. Medkov (1987), *Vtoroy rebyenok*, M.

— (1996), *Sociologiya semiy*, M.

Ashkerov, A. J. (2001), "Economicheskaya i antropologicheskaya interpretaciya socialnogo obmena", *Sociologicheskiy journal*, 3.

Barsukova, S. and F. F. Radaev (2000), "Legenda o gendere. Principi razdeleniya truda mezhdu suprugami v sovremennoy gorodskoy semie", *Mir Rossii*, 4.

Bessokirnaya, G. P. (2002), "Strategii vizhivaniya gorozhan i ih socialnye posledstviya", in T. Karakhanova (ed.), *Obraz zhizni gorozhan v obiectivnyh i subiectivnyh pokazatelyah*, M.

Chuikina, S. (2002), "Byt neotdelim ot politiki": Oficialnye i neoficialnye normi polovoy morali v sovetskom obschestve 1930–1980-h godov, in E. Zdravomjslova and A. Temkina (eds.), *V poiskah seksualnosti*, SPb.

Clarke, S. (2002), *Making ends meet in contemporary Russia: secondary employment, subsidiary agriculture and social networks*, Cheltenham.

Danilov, F. P. and L. F. Danilova (1996), *Krestyanskaya obschina i mentalnost*, in *Mentalitet i agrarnoe razvitie Rossii (XIX–XX)*, M.

Darmodekhin, S. F. (2000), "Semya i gosudarstvo", *Monitoring obschestvennogo mneniya: economicheskie i socialnye peremeny*, 3.

Dubin, B. (1999), "Zhizn po privichke: bit pozhilym v Rossii 90-h godov", *Monitoring obschestvennogo mneniya: economicheskie i socialnye peremeny*, 6(44).

Efendiev, A. G. and I. A. Bolotina (2002), "Sovremennoe rossiyskoe selo: na perelome epoh i reform. Opyt institucionalnogo analiza", *Mir Rossii*, V. IX, 4.

Fadeeva, O. P. (1997), *Strategii vyzhyvaniya selskih semey v krizisnom obschestve*, in *Krestyanovedenie. Teoriya. Istoriya. Sovremennost*, Ezhegodnik.

— (1999), Mezhsemeynaya set: mekhanizmy vzaimopodderzhki v rossiyskom sele, in T. Shanin (eds.), *Neformalnaya ekonomika. Rossiya i mir*, M.

Gasparyan, J. A. (1999), *Semya na poroge XXI veka: Sociologicheskie problemy*, SPb.

Govalo, B. I. (1984), *Studencheskaya semya (Populyarnaya demografiya)*, M.

Golod, S. I. (1984), *Stabilnost semiy: sociologicheskiy i demograficheskiy aspekti*, L.

— (1995), "Monogamnaya semya: krizis ili evoluciya?", *Socialno-politicheskiy journal*, 6.

— (1996), *XX vek i tendencii seksualnih otnosheniy v Rossii*, SPb.

Gradoselskaya, G. F. (1999), "Socialnye seti: obmen chastnymi transfertami", *Sociologicheskiy journal*, 1/2.

Grigorieva, I. A. (1998), *Socialnaya politika i socialnoe reformirovanie v Rossii v 90-h godah*, SPb.

Gudkov, L. and B. Dubin (2003), "Institucionalnye deficity kak problema postsovetskogo obschestva", *Monitoring obschestvennogo mneniya: economicheskie i socialnye peremeny*, 3(65).

Kabanov, F. F. (1997), *Krestyanskaya obschina i kooperaciya v Rossii XX veka*, M.

Kazmina, O. and N. Pushkareva (2004), "Brak v Rossii XX veka: tradicionnye ustanovki i innovacionnye eksperimenty", in S. Ushakin (ed.), *Semeynye uzi: Modeli dlya sborki*. Kn.1, M.

Kharchev, A. G. (1979), *Brak i semya v SSSR*, M.

Khisamova, S. (2002), "Chto podumaet sosed Vassiliy", *Ekspert*, 38.

Khotkina, S. A. (2001), "Genderniy podhod k analizu truda i zanyatosti", *Genderniy kaleydoskop*, M.

Kozlova, N. N. and I. I. Sandomirskaya (1996), *"Naivnoe pismo": Opyt lingvosociologicheskogo chteniya*, M.

Ledeneva, A. (1999), "Blat i rynok: transformaciya blata v postsovetskom obschestve", in T. Shanin (ed.), *Neformalnaya ekonomika. Rossiya i mir*, M.

Luniakova, L. (2004), "Chem muzhika kormit, luchshe rebenka vospityvat odnoy": socialniy portret materinskih semey", in S. Ushakin (ed.), *Semeynye uzi: Modeli dlya sborki*. Kn.2., M.

Magun, F. S. (1996), "Revoluciya prityazaniy i izmeneniya zhiznennyh strategiy molodezhi: 1985–1995 gody", *Sociologicheskiy journal*, 3/4.

Magun, F. S. and T. F. Engovatov (2005), "Mezhpokolennaya dinamika zhiznennyh prityazaniy molodezhi i strategiy ih resursnogo obespecheniya: 1985–2001 gg.", in Y. Levada and T. Shanin (eds.), *Otci i deti: Pokolencheskiy analiz sovremennoy Rossii*, M.

Matskovsky, T. (1993), *Semya v krizisnom obschestve*, M.

Mikheeva, A. R. (1993), *Selskaya semya v Sibiri: zhiznenniy cikl i blagosostoyanie*, Novosibirsk.

Mironov, B. N. (2003), Socialnaya istoriya Rossii perioda imperii (XVIII – nachalo XX v.). Genezis lichnosti, demokraticheskoy semiy, grazhdanskogo obschestva i gosudarstva. V.1. SPb.

Nefedova, T. G. (2003), *Selskaya Rossiya na pereputie: Geograficheskie ocherki*, M.

Nikulin, A. (1998), "Predpriyatiya i semyi v Rossii: sociokulturniy simbioz", in T. Zaslavskaya (ed.), *Kuda idet Rossiya? Transformaciya socialnoy sferi i socialnaya politika*, M.

Pankratova, M. G. (1990), *Selskaya zhenschina v SSSR*. M.

— (1989), *Problemy semyi v sovetskoy sociologicheskoy literature (nauchno-analiticheskiy obzor)*, in *Evoluciya semyi v sovremennom obschestve. Referativniy sbornik*, M.

Rabzhaeva, M. F. (2004), "Istoriko-socialniy analiz praktik semeynoy politiki v Rossii XX veka", *Socis*, 6.

Ransel, D. L. (2004), "Posidelki, pridanoe, svadba: organizaciya zamuzhestva v selskoy semye XX veka", in S. Ushakin (ed.), *Semeynye uzi: Modeli dlya sborki*. Kn.1, M.

Reed, S. (2004), "'Byt – ne chastnoe delo': vnedrenie sovremennogo vkusa v semeynuyu zhizn", in S. Ushakin (ed.), *Semeynye uzi: Modeli dlya sborki*. Kn.1, M.

Rimashevskaya, M. N. (1997), "Rol semyi v usloviyah socialnyh transformaciy", in V. Tishkov (ed.), *Semya, gender, kultura*. M.

Rimashevskaya, N., Vannoy, D., Malisheva, M., Mescherkina, E., and Pisklakova, M., (1999), *Okno v russkuyu chastnuyu zhizn. Supruzheskie pari v 1996 g.*, M.

Semenova, F. F. (1996), *Babushki: semeynie i socialnie funkcii praroditelskogo pokoleniya*, in *Sudby ludey: Rossiya XX vek. Biografii semey kak obiekt sociologicheskogo issledovaniya*, M.

Scott, J. C. (1976), *The moral economy of the peasant: rebellion and subsistence in south-east Asia*, London.

Shanin, T. (1997), *Revoluciya kak moment istiny*, M.

Shkaratan, O. I. (2002), "Informacionnaya ekonomika i puti razvitiya Rossii, in Rossiya v sovremennom mire: poisk novyh intellektualnyh podhodov", *Tretie Sokraticheskie chteniya po geografii*, M.

Shmeleva, M. N. (1997), *Nekotorye problemy etnograficheskogo izucheniya sovremennoy gorodskoy semyi russkih (metodologicheskie aspekti)*, in *Problemy i metody issledovaniya sovremennoy semyi*, M.

Shruder, C. (1999), *Ekonomicheskaya antropologiya*, SPb.

Solodnikov, F. F. (2004), "Socialno dezadaptirovannaya semya v kontekste obschestvennogo mneniya", *Socis*, 6.

Sorokin, P. A. (1992), "Sovremennoe sostoyanie Rossii", *Noviy mir*, 4.

— (1988), *Socialniy potencial semyi*, A.I. Antonov (ed.), M.

— (1996), *Sudby ludey: Rossiya XX vek. Biografii semey kak obiekt sociologicheskogo issledovaniya*, M.

Talalai, M. (1986), "'Zhenatyh ne propisyvaem': vzglyad sociologa na problemy molodezhnyh obschezhitiy", *Pravda*, 29 Sept.

Tartakovskaya, I. N. (1997), *Sociologiya semyi i pola*, Samara.

— (2004), "Socialnye seti i povedenie na rynke truda", *Sociologicheskiy journal*, 1/2.

Temkina, A. A. and A. Rotkirkh (2002), "Sovetskie gendernye kontrakty i ih transformaciya v sovremennoy Rossii", *Socis*, 11.

Ushakin, S. (2004), "Mesto-imeni-ya: semya kak sposob organizacii zhizni", in S. Ushakin (ed.), *Semeynye uzi: Modeli dlya sborki*. Kn.1, M.

Vassilenko, I. F. and N. F. Ivanenko (1999), *Nravstvennye koordinaty vnutrisemeynogo soznaniya*, in *Muzhchina i zhenschina v sovremennom mire: menyayuschiesya roli i obrazy*, V.1. M.

Vinogradsky, V. G. (1999), "'Orudiya slabyh': neformalnaya ekonomika krestyanskih domohozyaistv", *Sociologicheskiy journal*, 3/4.

Vishnevsky, A. (1998), *Serp i molot. Konservativnaya modenizaciya SSSR*, M.

Vite, O. (1996), "Izbirateli – vragi naroda? (Razmyshleniya ob adekvatnosti elektoralnogo povedeniya i faktorah na ee uroven vliyayuschih)", *Etika uspekha*, 9.

Vorontsov, D. (2004), "Semeynaya zhizn – eto ne dlya nas: mify i cennosti muzhskih gomoseksualnyh par", in S. Ushakin (ed.), *Semeynye uzi: Modeli dlya sborki*. Kn.1, M.

Wolf, C. (1955), "Institutions and economic development", *American Economic Review*, 45.

Zhurzhenko, T. (2004), "Staraya ideologiya novoy semyi: demograficheskiy nacionalizm Rossii i Ukrainy", in S. Ushakin (eds.), *Semeynye uzi: Modeli dlya sborki*. Kn.2, M.

Zakharov, S. F. (2002), "Vozrast pri registracii brakov povyshaetsya", in A. Vishnevskiy (ed.), *Naselenie Rossii. Ezhegodniy demograficheskiy doklad*, M.

— (2002), "Rastet li rossiyskaya rozhdaemost?", *Naselenie i obschestvo*, 68.

Zdravomyslova, O. M. (2003), *Semya i obschestvo: Gendernoe izmerenie rossiyskoy transformacii*, M.

Zdravomyslova, O. M. and M. J. Arutunyan (1999), *Rossiyskaya semya na evropeyskom fone*, M.

Zdravomyslova, E. and A. Temkina (1996), "Socialnaya konstrukciya gendera i gendernaya sistema v Rossii", in E. Zdravomyslova and A. Temkina (eds.), *Gendernoe izmerenie socialnoy i politicheskoy aktivnosti v perehodniy period*, 4. SPb.

Zorkaya, N. (2003), "Problemy povsednevnoy zhizni semyi. 'Bednost' kak fokus vospriyatiya povsednevnyh problem", *Monitoring obschestvennogo mneniya: economicheskie i socialnye peremeny*, 1(63).

Kinship in transformation: measures and models

Siegfried Gruber and Patrick Heady

Introduction

One of the paradoxes of this volume is that, for most countries over most of the twentieth century, we have few direct and comparable measures of the central topic of KASS: namely the extent to which kin help each other. There have of course been particular studies of specific places at various times – but detailed representative and internationally comparable studies of intergenerational helping behaviour amongst kin have only got under way at the start of the 21st century, with the SHARE (2005) study of intergenerational exchanges (Kohli et al. 2010). The data collected in KASS's own Kinship Network Questionnaire (KNQ) is the first attempt to extend such comparisons to wider kinship ties.

We have not drawn on SHARE or KNQ findings in this chapter. But even if we had, the data would not have enabled us to make before-and-after evaluations of the historical effect of increases or reductions of various forms of state support on the amount of help provided to each other by relatives themselves – for the simple reason that there is no comparable data from past decades on which to base the comparisons. Retrospective comparisons will become possible in future decades when and if it becomes possible to compare SHARE and KNQ findings with those of future surveys using comparable methodologies. However, at this point in time, any statistical conclusions about the "crowding-out" or "crowding-in" effects of state support derived from SHARE or KNQ data must be based on cross-sectional analyses, or in the case of SHARE, on panel effects between the first two waves. Analyses of these kinds will be reported in Volume III of this series.

Nevertheless we cannot leave the issue of historical comparisons there. For over a century, politicians and public have been convinced that kinship relations have been undergoing change. Part of the evidence has come from changing demographic patterns, and much of it has also emerged implicitly through the awareness of social crises – as documented in each of the national studies in this volume. If we cannot yet say much about the impact on family and kinship of the policy choices discussed in these chapters, might we not be able to trace the impact on kinship relationships of the fundamental economic transformations that occurred during the twentieth century?

The answer to this question turns out to be "yes", for two reasons. The first reason is that the changes were so massive that quite crude measures of kinship assistance are sufficient to give an idea of their extent and direction – and we do have some such measures reaching back to early in the twentieth century. Two in particular that we will focus on below are household composition – particularly the proportion of single-person households – and the proportion of the economically active population who were engaged in unpaid labour for family enterprises. The second reason is the development in the last decade or so of a number of broad measures of family attitudes and behaviour and their implementation in comparative social surveys such as the International Social Survey Programme (ISSP) and the European Values Study (EVS). Though they lack the specific detail of mutual assistance collected by SHARE and KASS, they nevertheless present a clear and revealing picture of several aspects of kinship interactions. Reher (1998) and Murphy (2008) use data of this kind to contrast contemporary kin relationships in northern and southern Europe. The findings presented below are consistent with their analyses, but focus specifically on the eight KASS countries.

Contact and co-residence

As we shall see in Volume III, the extent of mutual cooperation between kin is closely related to the extent of social contact between them. Residence matters, because co-residence itself can be a way of offering care (or subsidised accommodation) and because, as figures 10.1 and 10.2 show, higher levels of co-residence are associated with higher levels of contact generally – both between parents and adult children and between adult siblings. In these and all following figures the countries of the study are abbreviated to their first letter.

Figure 10.1: Contacts with adult child with whom respondent has most contact

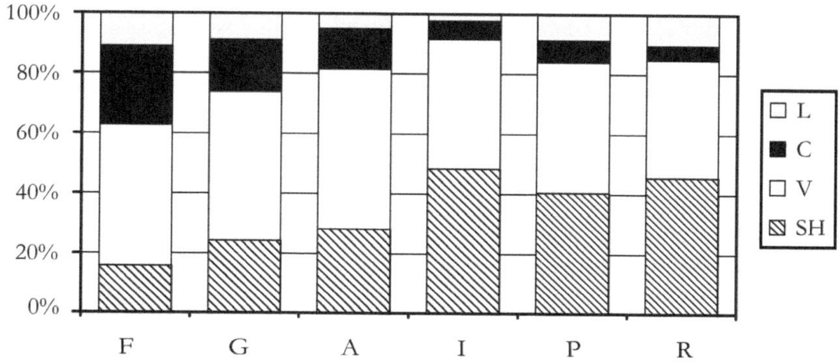

Source: ISSP 2001, SH: lives in same household, V: visit at least once a week, C: other contact at least once a week, L: less contact Base: all respondents having at least one adult child, with whom they have some contact – For further details see appendix

Figure 10.2: Contacts with adult sibling with whom respondent has most contact

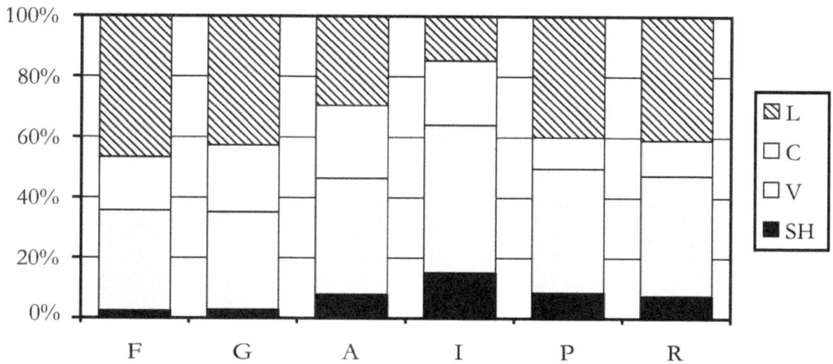

Source: ISSP 2001, SH: lives in same household, V: visit at least once a week, C: other contact at least once a week, L: less contact – Base: all persons having at least one adult sibling, with whom they have some contact. For further details see appendix

Of the six KASS countries covered by figure 10.1, we see that Italy has the highest proportion of parents who cohabit with an adult child (nearly 50 percent) and the lowest proportion (only 9 percent) who go a week without seeing an adult child. In France, by way of contrast, only

17 percent live with their adult children while 37 percent see their adult children less than once a week. (Had a Scandinavian country been included in this chart, the level of contacts would probably be lower still.)

This suggests that we can use the extent of co-residence between kin as one indication of the level of practical kinship solidarity. However, though family historians have produced numerous case studies of household composition in particular communities, the nationally available time series data from censuses is classified into different household composition categories – and the effect of co-residence is confounded with the effect of different fertility levels. For this reason we have used the only available measure that is relatively unaffected by fertility, namely the proportion of one-person households, as a rather crude indicator of the evolution of residence patterns over the twentieth century (figure 10.3).

Figure 10.3: One person households as a percentage of all households

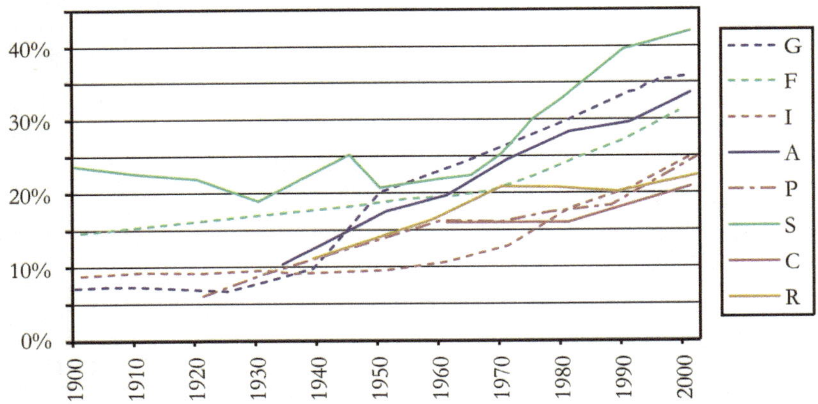

Sources: see appendix

Though the measure is crude, the results are dramatic. For all countries the trend has been upward, and the rapid rise still continues. While a number of factors may underlie the rise, there is no denying that it represents a move away from kinship solidarity. Whether willingly chosen by the person themselves, or implicitly imposed on them by unwelcoming relatives, living alone represents a renunciation of close companionship with other family members. Only in Russia has the increase in recent decades been minimal, partly because of the lack of available apartments.

Models of kinship

Might the different rates of co-residence and contact between close kin, recorded in figures 10.1 and 10.2, be accompanied and perhaps explained by different attitudes to family ties? Figures 10.4 through 10.10 explore this possibility – and they start with a surprise. One might expect that people in societies that maintain more contact with close kin would also be more likely to say that their families were important to them. But this is not the case.

Figure 10.4: Percentage agreeing to "Family is very important in my life"

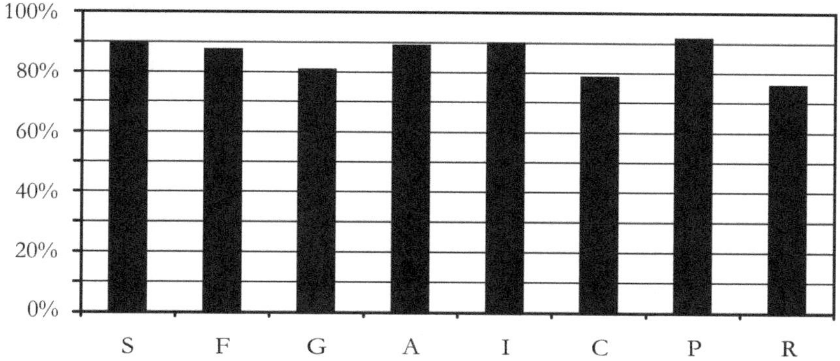

Source: EVS 1999. Base: all respondents. For further details see appendix

Figure 10.4 shows that huge majorities in all societies say that their families are very important to them and the proportion is just as high in countries with less regular kin contacts as in those with more. Nor is there any obvious difference in this respect between countries with high and low divorce rates. It may well be the case that people in different countries have different people and relationships in mind when they refer to whatever word is translated as "family" – but they seem unanimous that, whatever the bundle of relationships covered by the term, these relationships are very important indeed.

What seems to vary is the importance accorded to other relationships. Figure 10.5 compares the countries according to the importance informants attached to friendship (which is also more important for younger and urban people), and a comparison with figure 10.1 shows a fairly clear inverse relationship between the importance attached to friendship and the closeness of contact that adults maintain with their family of origin. The less the contact with the family, the more importance is given to friends.

Figure 10.5: Percentage agreeing to "Friends are very important in my life"

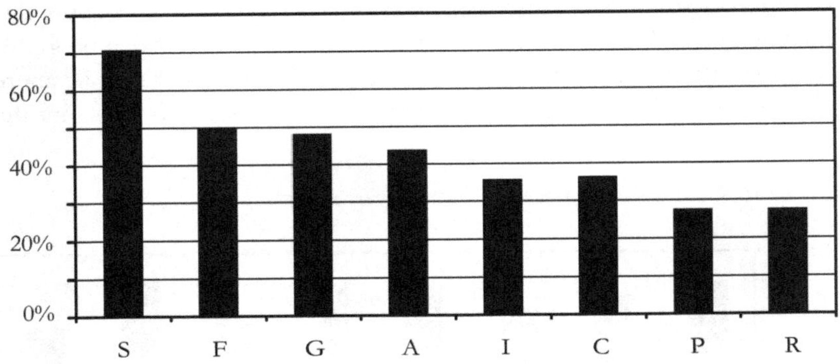

Source: EVS 1999. Base: all respondents. For further details see appendix

Figures 10.6 and 10.7 show a further inverse association between an emphasis on family ties and openness to other relationships. Thus, with one exception, people in the countries which emphasise friendship are most likely to *disagree* with the statement that "a job is alright but what most women really want is a home and children" – but are likely to *agree* with the general statement that "most people can be trusted".

Figure 10.6: Percentage of agreement to the statement "A job is alright but what most women really want is a home and children"

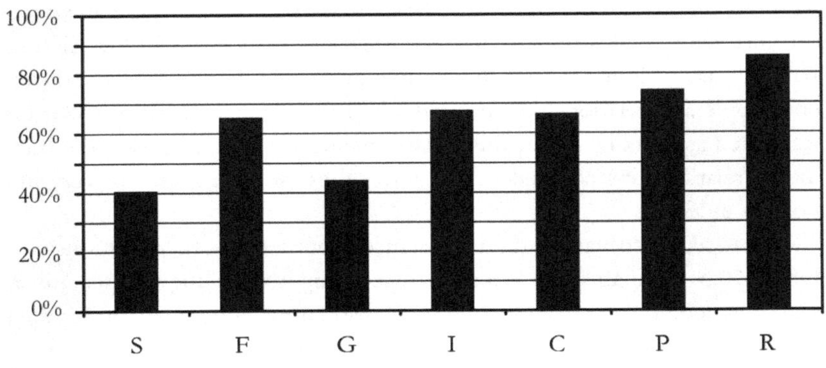

Source: EVS 1999. Base: all respondents. For further details see appendix

Figure 10.7: Percentage agreeing to "Most people can be trusted"

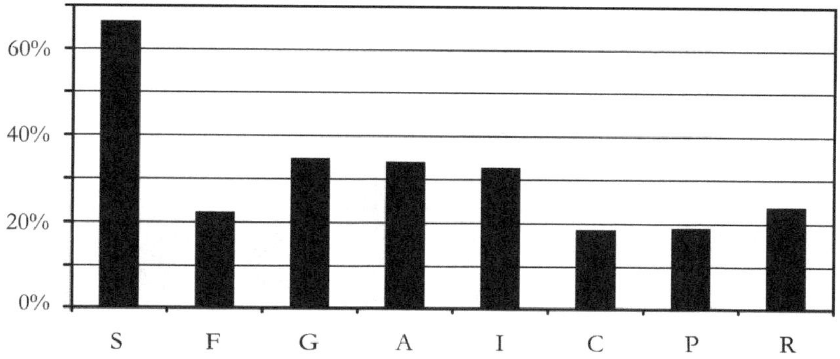

Source: EVS 1999. Base: all respondents. For further details see appendix

This data suggests that more is at stake in the question of regular contact with close kin than a matter of generosity or selfishness in respect to the individuals concerned. Relatively infrequent contact now looks less like a failure of filial or parental duty, and more like a principled act of openness to a wider community – while frequent contact between close kin emerges as part of a strategy for maintaining close relations with a relatively narrow but trusted group. Such a characterisation would surprise neither ethnographers nor family historians. Many ethnographic studies of communities which stress the maintenance of kin ties, particularly in southern Europe, also note an emphasis on intense local patriotism and a marked preference for marriages that reinforce existing links by local endogamy or by re-knitting ties between a set of intermarrying lineages (Segalen 1991; Just 2000; Heady 2003). Family historians, on the other hand, have noted that the countries of northwest Europe, where contacts between kin are least closely maintained, are the same countries where hundreds of years ago it was the custom for young people to leave home well before marriage to work as servants or apprentices some way from their families of origin (van Poppel et al. 2004). France appears to be an interesting special case – since it appears to favour practical openness to the outside (figures 10.1 and 10.4) while also restricting real trust to a narrower circle and emphasising women's role as homemakers (figures 10.6 and 10.7).

Figure 10.8: Percentage mentioning imagination being important as child's quality

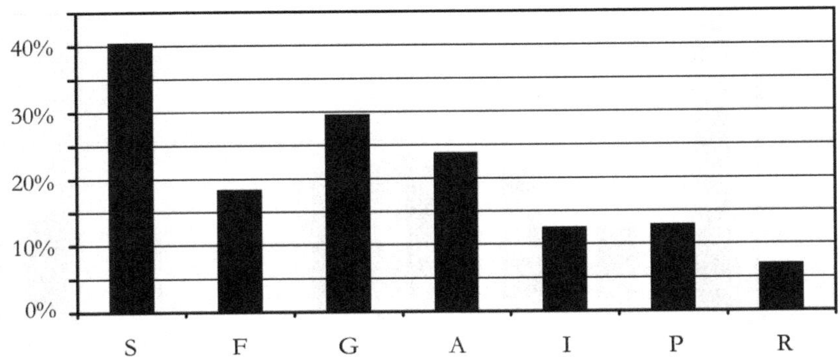

Source: EVS 1999. Base: all respondents. For further details see appendix

Figure 10.9: Percentage mentioning obedience being important as child's quality

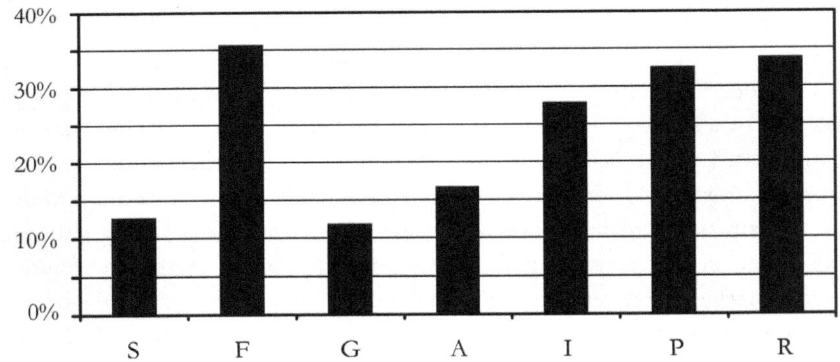

Source: EVS 1999. Base: all respondents. For further details see appendix

Issues of authority are involved as well, as can be seen from the contrasted attitudes to child rearing that are associated with the different approaches to kinship and social life. Where the social world is seen as a relatively closed sphere, dominated by kinship, obedience takes precedence over the fostering of imagination, while the opposite is the case in the societies that emphasise openness to wider ties reaching beyond kinship (figures 10.8 and 10.9). It is as though the former group see themselves as responsible for maintaining order in their relatively narrow social worlds, while the latter group are either less worried about order or, perhaps more likely, willing to delegate the problem of order to extra-familial institutions such as the state.

There is an interesting association between these attitudes and religious affiliation (figure 10.10). The countries with a more closed and authoritarian view of social life, centred round kinship, also have more authoritarian versions of religion – Catholicism and Orthodoxy (in both of which the priest is referred to as "father") – while in Sweden and Germany a relatively open view of social relations is associated with a greater or equal attachment to Protestant churches. The two countries where lack of faith is most widespread present an interesting contrast. In Russia this attitude is associated with communism – a creed which was as at least as authoritarian and exclusive in its own way as Orthodoxy and Catholicism. In France, on the other hand, it is associated with republican ideals of equality and reason: and the almost equal division of the country between this open vision and the more authoritarian and parochial tradition of Catholicism is perhaps another reflection of the tension between openness and closure that we noted a couple of paragraphs back.

Figure 10.10: Religious confession

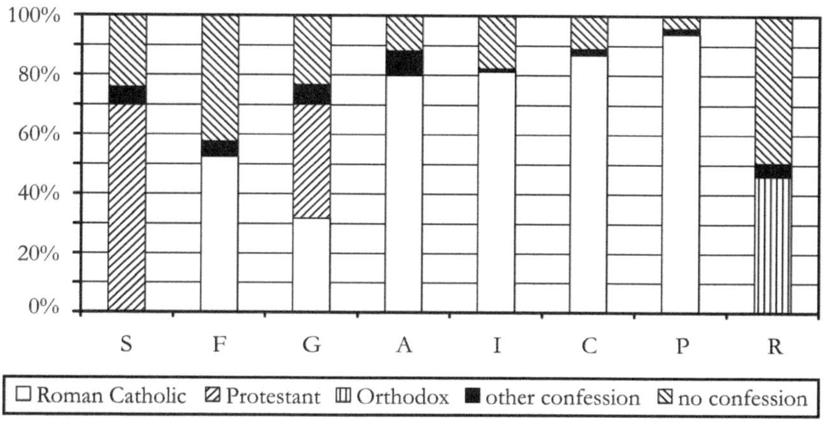

All confessions of a country besides the dominant one are grouped together.
Source: EVS 1999. Base: all respondents. For further details see appendix

However, the fundamental point that emerges from this analysis is a more general one. More or less frequent involvement with close relatives does not only have implications for those directly concerned – it reflects contrasting ways of constructing the whole social world. In this sense relationships with immediate family members cannot be fully understood in isolation: they have to be seen as part of a wider system of kinship and other ties.

Family relationships and economic change

But there is a paradox here. If the system of kinship ties rests on fundamental values, why should the pattern have changed – as, to judge from Figure 10.3, it seems almost everywhere to have done? Perhaps one clue relates to the association between an emphasis on kinship and a stress on the value of obedience. This might simply be a question of the value attached to order in an abstract way, or it might reflect a quite specific emphasis on the willingness to accept and carry out instructions – as is needed in any joint economic enterprise. It is well known that in some parts of Europe (for instance certain parts of Italy) family firms play an important part in the economy but the importance of family-based enterprises in many parts of Europe was far greater two or three generations ago than it is today.

Figure 10.11: Proportion of male labour force working as unpaid family labour

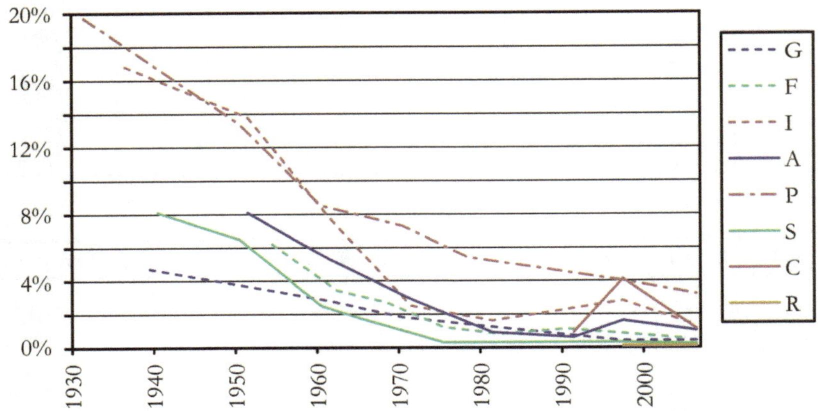

Sources: see appendix

Figure 10.12: Proportion of female labour force working as unpaid family labour

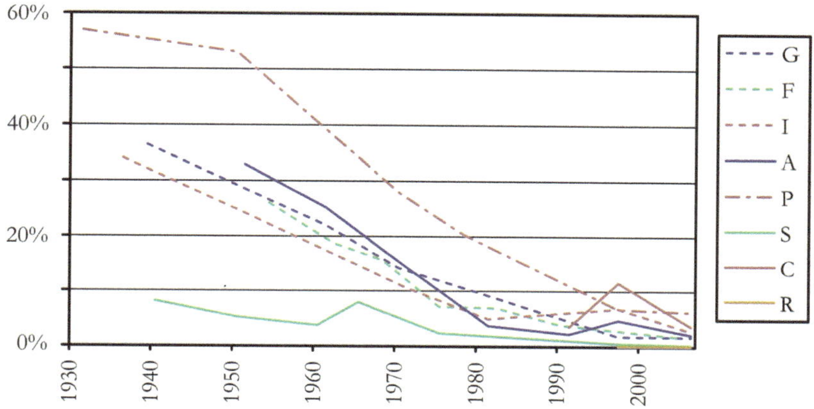

Sources: see appendix

The frequency of unpaid labour in family-owned productive enterprises declined dramatically during the 20th century. Figures 10.11 and 10.12 trace this decline. In the 1930s more than half of the female workforce and almost a fifth of the male workforce in Poland belonged to this category. In Italy a third of the female workforce and a sixth of the male workforce were employed without payments. In Germany it was also a third of the female workforce, but only 5 percent of the male workforce and in Sweden only 8 percent of both sexes, who were working without payment. In Poland the shares dropped to 5 percent of the male workforce and a fifth of the female workforce by 1978. In the 1990s the median of OECD countries was only 1.3 percent of female employment (ILO 2001, 21).

Most of this work was done in the agricultural sector: about 90 percent in Poland, Italy, and in Germany in the 1930s (United Nations 1949, 245, 247). And so, much of the decline in kinship based economic activity can be attributed to the decline in overall agricultural employment (shown in figure 10.13) that accompanied the mechanisation of agriculture and the rise of other economic sectors.

Figure 10.13: Proportion of labour force working in agriculture

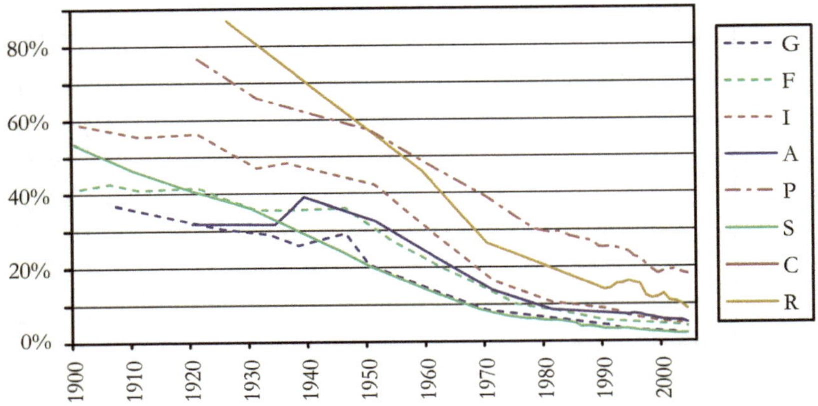

Sources: see appendix

The association between agriculture and the stress on kinship is very marked in the contemporary studies – both ethnographic and quantitative – reported in the second and third volumes of this series, and their findings confirm what is already implicit in the discussion above: namely that the practical work of family farming is interconnected with a world of social meanings. As will be apparent from those studies, more is involved in family farming than the practical decision that economic cooperation would be mutually beneficial – essential though that judgement is. Family farms are inherited, and someone who inherits the farm contracts moral obligations to their forbears, as well as to their siblings and to the neighbours who expect them to play a part in maintaining a community with its own skills and ways of doing things, both materially and socially.

The decline of agricultural employment and the growth of services (figure 10.14) has another important implication for kinship ties. Unlike agriculture, in which (at least until recently) the family could provide most of the training that the next generation would require, urban service occupations have increasingly required – or at least demanded – formal training outside the family context.

Figure 10.14: Proportion of labour force working in services

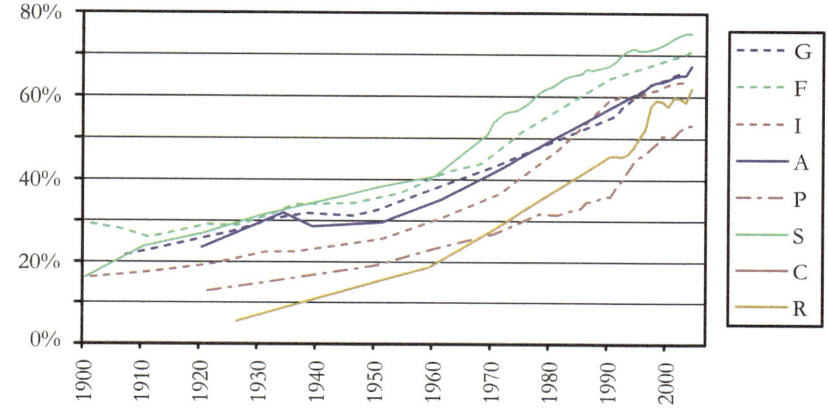

Sources: see appendix

Figure 10.15: Net enrolment ratio of secondary education

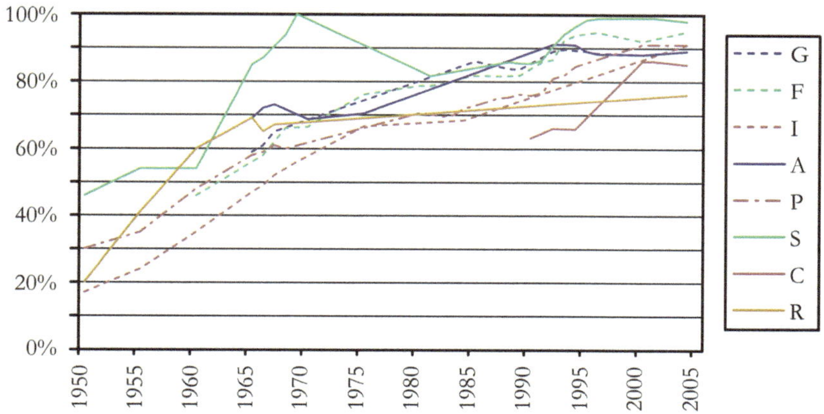

Sources: see appendix

There was an explosion of secondary education from the 1950s onwards (figure 10.15), which has been followed by a similar expansion of tertiary education (figure 10.16). It is not clear what impact this expansion would have had on the sense of obligation that young people feel towards their parents. On the one hand, the financial sacrifice demanded of parents for a child's education is far greater than it was formally. On the other hand the education itself is provided by others, and is likely to create a feeling of obligation to those who provide it – and a commitment to carrying forward their values – rather than the obligations to the world of kin to which the young people are connected through their parents.

Figure 10.16: Gross enrolment ratio of tertiary education

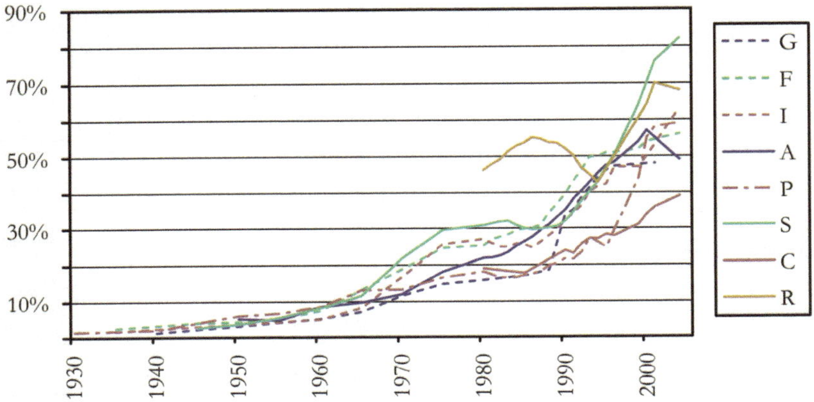

Sources: see appendix

The impact of this shift in educational roles from the private to the public sphere is particularly dramatic in the case of women since not only do they, like men, acquire an obligation to perpetuate the ideals of their public educational institutions, they may also experience this obligation as competing with the child-rearing role that was an important part of the former kinship-based model of social life (see figure 10.16). It is not surprising then, that the participation of women in paid work is continuing to rise. An initial glance at figure 10.17, suggests that the rise in female "economic activity" (according to the definition used in official statistics, which excludes women's domestic roles within their own families) dates only from the 1960s. However, it should be remembered that much of the non-domestic female activity recorded in the first part of the century was unpaid activity within family-based productive enterprises. In terms of direct contact with the external labour market, the rates of female participation have been steadily rising for three generations or more.

Figure 10.17: Activity rates of women

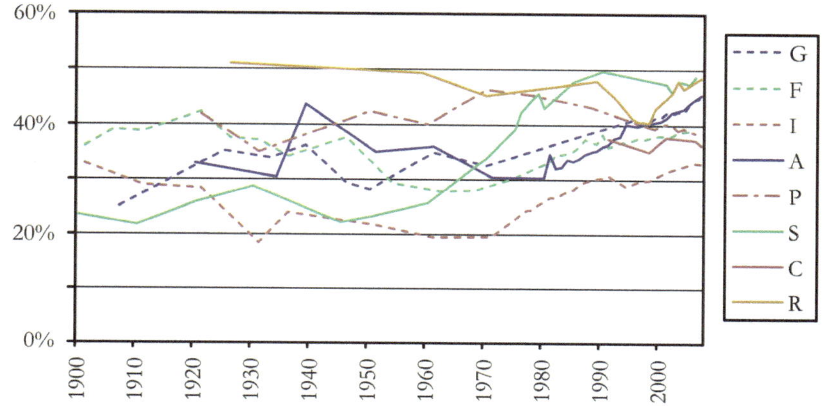

Percentaged on the entire female population from birth upwards
Sources: see appendix

Figure 10.18: Activity rates of men

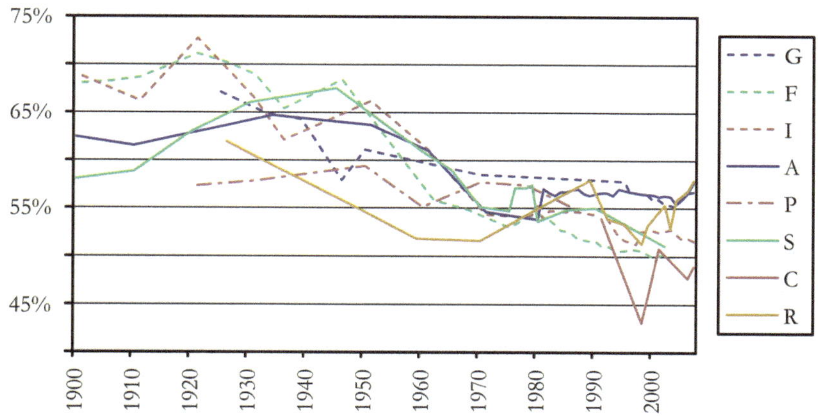

Percentaged on the entire male population from birth upwards
Sources: see appendix

Figure 10.18 presents male economic activity rates on the same basis: that is the number reckoned by the statistical offices to be employed, self-employed or unemployed, expressed as a proportion of the entire male population from birth until extreme old age. In contrast to women, the trend for men is steadily downwards, reflecting increased years of study and of retirement. (Of course the increases in study years and in overall life span apply to women too; but since fewer of them were "economically active" at the start of the century the downward effect on economic activity rates was less.) Overall, the picture is of a steady convergence between male and female rates of participation in paid work. However the convergence is not complete: female participation rates continue to be lower than those for men, and a higher proportion of women work part time.

Kinship and modernisation

Though the data we have looked at are very limited, they suggest an interconnection between the extent of contact and care for close kin, an overall attitude to social relationships (as either close and dominated by kinship ties, or wider and more open to non-kin and strangers), and the role played by family and kinship ties in economic subsistence. They also suggest certain broad differences between societies: changes over time as agriculture gives way to manufacturing and then to services; and different contemporary combinations of kinship behaviour, attitudes and religious allegiances. Much of the present volume is about how the processes became publicly visible and how different national polities attempted to come to grips with them. The chapters in the second and third volume will try to understand and document the individual motivations and social dynamics that connect economic arrangements, help between close kin, and the form and extent of wider social ties. The ultimate aim is to improve the link between policy making on the one hand, and empirically grounded understandings of the patterns and sources of mutual assistance on the other.

In this we are contributing to a debate that has been under way in most European countries for the last two centuries. Since the ideas and practices of the industrial and political revolutions started to spread from England and France, people in many countries have asked themselves whether and how they could combine their social systems with the benefits of economic modernity, in whatever form it took at the time. The 19th century German debates about a possible *Sonderweg*, the Russian controversies between slavophils and modernisers, the clerical versus lay debates of Third Republic France, and the century-long history of Italian argumentation about the problems of the *mezzogiorno* are all specific manifestations of this debate. Nor has the debate lacked academic formulations: indeed it directly inspired many of the classic works of early sociology, including Tönnies' distinction between *Gemeinschaft* and *Gesellschaft* (Tönnies 2001), Durkheim's work on *The Division of Labour in Society* (Durkheim 1964), and Weber's ideas about the protestant ethic, and the bureaucratic rationalisation of society (Weber 2001). Three recent contributions to this long-running debate have been Inglehart's work on modernisation, Putnam's (1994) work on civic traditions and social capital, and van de Kaa's (1987) theory of Europe's second demographic transition – to all of which we shall be returning at various points throughout these volumes.

Inglehart and Welzel argue "that socioeconomic modernisation, rising liberty aspirations, and the quest for democratic institutions all reflect the common underlying process of human development" (Inglehart and Welzel 2005, 9). Survey data (especially the EVS/World Values Survey) "demonstrates that the basic values and beliefs of the publics of advanced societies differ dramatically from those found in less-developed societies – and that these values are changing in a predictable direction as socioeconomic development takes place" (Inglehart and Welzel 2005, 1). In the post-industrial phase of modernization there is a shift from survival values to self-expression values, which increase human freedom and choice (Inglehart and Welzel 2005, 5). Inglehart and Welzel add a number of qualifications and clarifications: the process is not deterministic; traditional cultural heritages including religion are not dying out; cultural modernization is not irreversible; the process of cultural change is not linear; and modernization is not Westernization (Inglehart and Welzel 2005, 46f.).

Nevertheless the picture they present remains very clear. There is a strong association between a country's *per capita* income level and the values of its citizens: high income is associated with self expression and secular-rational values while low income is associated with survival and traditional values (Inglehart and Welzel 2005, 57). According to the authors there is still a clear clustering of the countries in survival/self expression values and traditional/secular-rational values according to religious and political history: Protestant Europe having the highest scores for self expression and secular-rational values, followed by Catholic Europe, while English speaking countries are similar to Catholic Europe concerning secular-rational values, but have higher scores in self expression values. The ex-Communist countries are similar to Catholic Europe and the English speaking countries concerning secular-rational values, but they have much higher scores in survival values (the Orthodox countries even higher than the Catholic ones). Traditional values are much more common in South Asia, Latin America and Africa (Inglehart and Welzel 2005, 63).

Where Inglehart and Welzel focus primarily on individual values, Putnam is interested in social involvement, which he refers to as the "social capital" of the community in question (and one of his concerns is with the processes that sustain social involvement at all – a theme to which we return below). However, his work parallels Inglehart's and Welzel's, in as much as he draws a contrast between *positive* social capital, embodied in "civic traditions" of involvement in associations that enable the self-directed expression of civic virtue and implement the principle of equal rights of all citizens, and *negative* social capital, in which social involvement is under the particularistic and authoritarian auspices of family and church.

All this is very uncomfortable for the authors of this study, as it will not have escaped the reader that the values associated with strong kinship ties in the figures above bear a very close relationship with the narrow, authoritarian values that Inglehart and Putnam argue – with substantial empirical evidence – are associated with relative economic underdevelopment, and which they also transparently dislike. Though the authors of this study are not particularly partisans for strong kinship ties, most of us do at least have a sympathetic interest in a range of different kinship systems – and are understandably disinclined to classify extended kinship as inherently "a bad thing". At the same time we have to be aware that the anthropologists' gut reaction of siding with the supposed values of the societies they study, against the "orientalising" prejudices of people in the most economically successful societies, will not do either. Critiques of clericalism, familism and the rest are not primarily made by outsiders, but form part of the internal debate of the societies concerned. Outsiders who uncritically espouse traditional rural values, in countries where much of the population (and particularly the female population) has been trying to escape from them, can be at least as offensive as overt critics. As Herzfeld (1997) points out, the way people handle the tension between what they perceive as modern and traditional ways of doing things, can itself be a central feature of their sense of identity.

The moral of this story, if there is one, is that we should not expect to avoid controversy when investigating fundamental issues that are controversial in the very societies that we are studying. We should certainly not ignore the arguments of the modernisation theorists – given the substantial evidence, from both statistics and ethnographic studies, that much of Europe is continuing to move further in the direction of what they describe as "modernity". The implication that kinship ties may be set to weaken further should at least make policy makers hesitate before shifting more of the welfare burden from the state back to the "family".

However, nor should the apparent contrast between an apparently narrow set of kinship values and a wider universalistic set of values associated with modern citizenship be taken at face value. It does seem to be true that strong kinship ties are frequently associated with a more general distinction between insiders and outsiders – but both the ethnographic and the quantitative data presented in the next two volumes suggest that the set of perceived insiders can number several hundred (see particularly Capello and Colclough 2010; Seiser and Schweizer 2010). It should not be assumed that the actual range of acquaintance in more kinship based rural communities is narrower than in more "modern" urban settings, or that the level of altruistic involvement is lower. In either case, it is at least as important to understand the general processes that help to build, or block, the formation of social ties as it is to construct a comparative classification of different community types.

Values and demographic change

As Grandits points out above, changing demographic trends have long been one of the main publicly available indications of changing social values. Some authors have argued that the value changes associated with "modernity" have contributed to two of the trends highlighted in chapter 1: the loosening of marriage ties and the fall in fertility levels (e.g. van de Kaa 1987; Lesthaeghe 1983). A great deal has been written about this, and it is also discussed in Volume III (Bernardi and White 2010; Heady et al. 2010). Here we look briefly at the correspondence between demographic indicators and some relevant attitudes.

Figure 10.19: Extra-marital births as a percentage of all births 2007

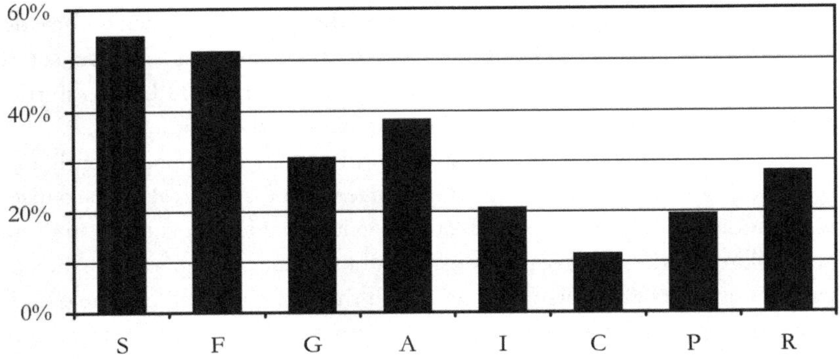

Source: see appendix

Figure 10.20: Total divorce rates 2002

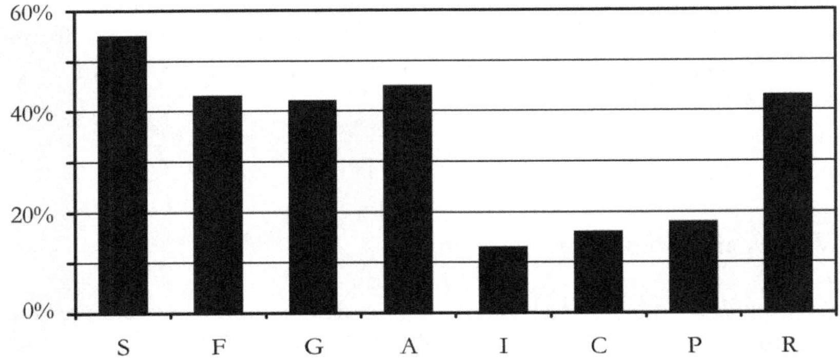

Source: see appendix

Extra-marital births and divorce rates are two of the main demographic indicators of declining commitment to formal marriage. Figure 1.1, chapter 1, showed the rapid rise in the proportion of extra-marital births in the later decades of the 20th century. Figure 10.19 compares the national percentages in the first decade of the 21st century. The overall pattern is quite close to that for the importance of friendship (shown in figure 10.5) and the more open, less authoritarian attitudes with which this is associated – but the inverse of that for contact between parents and adult children, and of support for women's home-making role. Figure 10.20, which compares

Total Divorce Rates – the percentages of contemporary marriages that can be expected to end in divorce given current rates of marriage break-up – shows a somewhat different picture. There is a sharp dichotomy between five countries in which over 40 percent of marriages can be expected to end in divorce, and three countries in which the divorce rate is still below 20 per cent, in contrast to the more gradual gradient between less and more "familistic" attitudes shown in figure 10.19 and earlier charts. Nevertheless, there are some points in common with the earlier distributions. The three countries with the lowest divorce rates – Italy, Croatia and Poland – also appeared to be highly familistic in earlier graphs; while Sweden – the one country in which a marriage is more likely than not to end in divorce – also emerged as the least familistic country in the earlier measures. The main difference is the position of Russia which combines traditional attitudes to gender roles and child rearing with a high divorce rate, and a medium percentage of extra-marital births. All in all, the demographic indicators of marriage-strength do appear to be broadly consistent with other behavioural and attitudinal measures of commitment to family ties.

A rather more complicated picture emerges in the case of fertility. Van de Kaa (1987) has linked the decline of fertility to increased individualism and alienation from the formal institutions of family and marriage – and a comparison of the downward fertility trends shown of chapter 1 with the various socio-economic trends shown in this chapter is clearly consistent with the hypothesis that attitude changes accompanying modernisation might have contributed to lower birth rates.

But a closer look at the national fertility trends shows features that are less easy to account for in this way. Figure 1.2 in chapter 1 showed how TFRs (Total Fertility Rates – estimated on the basis of the different age-specific fertility rates in the year concerned) developed during the post-war period. Although the overall downward trend was unmistakable it was hard to separate out the trends for different countries because of short-term fluctuations. Figure 10.21 displays the trends in a different way, by showing the completed life time fertility of cohorts of women born before the end of the 1960s. This shows far fewer short-term fluctuations than the TFRs making it possible to distinguish the relative positions of the different countries.

Figure 10.21: Completed cohort fertility by year of birth of mothers

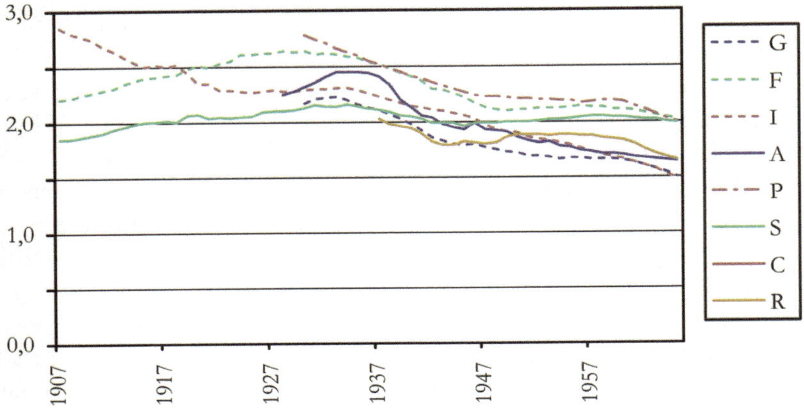

Sources: see appendix

In Sweden lifetime fertility has hovered around 2.0 for all cohorts born in the twentieth century. The other countries all[1] show a decline over the last several decades, but their relative position hardly changes. There are two relatively high fertility countries – France and Poland – which converge on the Swedish level; and four lower fertility countries – Germany, Austria, Italy and Russia – for which the completed fertility of women born in the late 1960s had sunk to about 1.5 children per woman. The striking thing about these groups is that they show no obvious association with our previous ranking of more and less familistic countries.

Of course most of the fertility of the cohort of mothers born in the late 1960s will have occurred during the 1990s. If we want to see how fertility has developed since then we are forced to turn back to TFRs. Figure 10.22 compares the national TFRs for 2005, showing much the same pattern, with one major difference: that Poland has now joined the group of low fertility countries.

1 We have not included Croatia in this graph, for reasons explained in the appendix.

Figure 10.22: Total fertility rates 2005

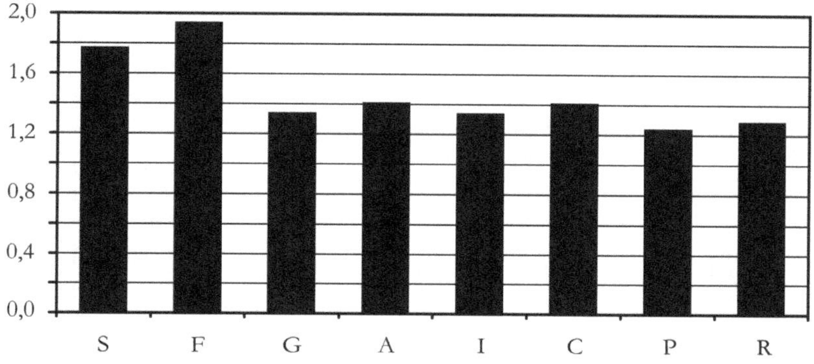

Source: see appendix

The picture shown in figure 10.22 is faintly reminiscent of the ordering of countries between less and more "familistic" values – in as much as the two least familistic countries, Sweden and France, are contrasted with the remainder. However, the ordering is the opposite of what would be expected from Van de Kaa's analysis, since it is Sweden and France – the least familistic of our eight countries – which currently have the highest birth rates. This negative association between fertility and strength of family ties, which has emerged over the last couple of decades and currently holds for European countries as a whole, has led some demographers to argue that low fertility rates result from the *persistence* of familistic values in the context of a modern economy (le Bras 1997; Micheli 2000; dalla Zuanna 2001). Can this argument be supported from the available attitudinal information?

A crucial point in this connection is that, despite low levels of actual fertility, there is little indication that the idea of having children is out of fashion. Figure 2.23 shows the distribution of opinions about the ideal family size that were reported by survey respondents in the mid 1990s – indicating the climate of opinion in which the latest cohorts of mothers shown in figure 2.21 were deciding on whether to have children themselves. Though the average size of the ideal family was slightly larger in the countries with higher actual fertility, two children was the most popular option in all six countries included in the chart, and even in the four low fertility countries more informants named ideal family sizes of three or more than chose family sizes of one or (extremely rare) zero.

Figure 10.23: Ideal number of children 1994

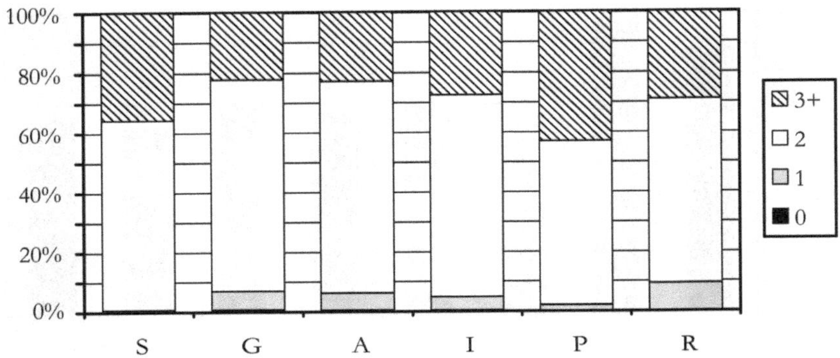

Source: ISSP 1994. Base: all respondents. For further details see appendix

Figure 10.24: Ideal number of children, by age and sex of respondents

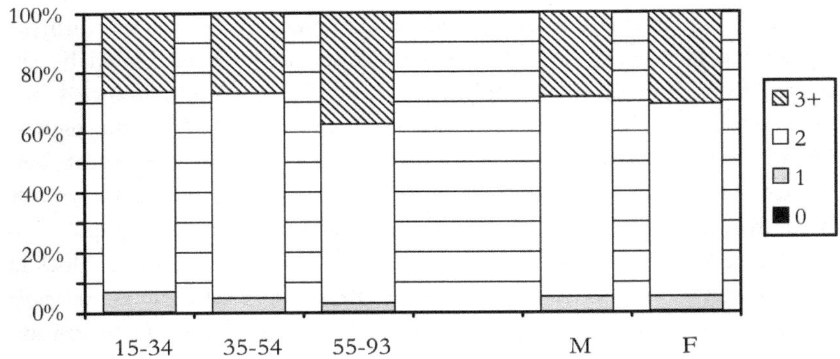

Source: ISSP 1994. Base: all respondents. For further details see appendix

Table 10.24 shows that the preference for families of two or more was almost as strong amongst the cohorts of current parents as amongst the over-55s – and was held equally by women and by men. Since then the average ideal family size has remained at two or more for most of our countries – though it dipped below 2.0 for Germany and Austria in a Eurobarometer survey carried out in 2001 (Goldstein et al. 2003), and the Austrian preferences remained a little below 2.0 in the subsequent Eurobarometer survey for 2006 (Testa 2006). These later surveys varied the question, asking respondents to state both the number of children they thought ideal in principle, and the number that they felt would be right for them personally. The two questions gave very similar results, effectively countering a suggestion that the earlier findings might have reflected abstract ideals to which the respondents were not personally committed.

If the desire for children itself is rather resilient, the question arises of whether low fertility can be explained by conflicts between family size ideals and other more variable desires – for instance the desire to play a full role in the modern economy. So it is interesting that, as figure 10.25 shows, Sweden and France – the two countries whose fertility is still near to replacement level – are those which seem best able to combine the high valuation of the mother-child tie with women's participation in the labour force.

Figure 10.25: Percentage of strong agreement to the statement "A working mother can establish just as warm and secure a relationship with her children as a mother who does not work"

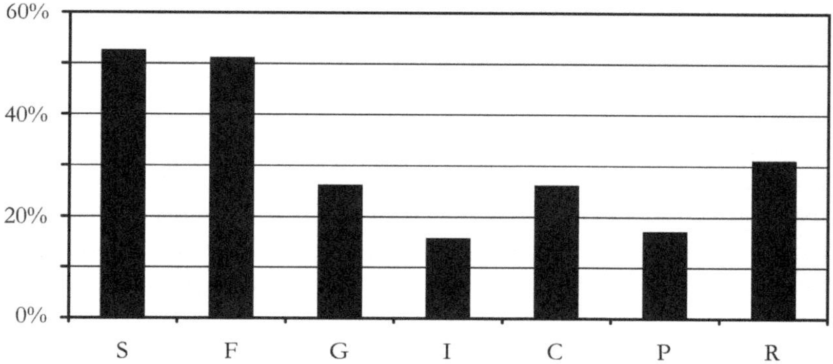

Source: EVS 1999. Base: all respondents. For further details see appendix

This would be consistent with a general tendency for fertility to decline because women who took advantage of the increasing opportunities of economic employment felt that the role of employee was hard to combine with that of motherhood – but for the conflict to be much sharper, and the downward pressure on both motherhood and employment to be greater, where traditional attitudes emphasised the incompatibility of the two roles. This combination of motherhood with economic production was, as we have seen, also typical for many women in the early twentieth century, though at that time much of the women's labour was unpaid work within the family context. This suggests that one issue may be the boundary between private and public life, implying a need for cultural changes that once again enable both sexes to readily affirm their worth through both their productive and reproductive roles.

However, appealing though this argument is, it would be wrong to read too much into the similarity between figures 10.25 and 10.22. The higher levels of both fertility and approval of working mothers in Sweden and France might reflect the influence of public policy – which in both countries is relatively supportive of working mothers – rather then cultural attitudes to working mothers. Or, if attitudes are crucial, the attitude to working mothers might simply be one of a number of non-familistic attitudes which, in ways we do not fully understand, make parenthood easier in contemporary conditions.

Conclusion

If some of the discussion in this section has been frankly speculative, the reason has been at least in part because the amount of available data is still so thin. As we noted at the start of this chapter, KASS is just one of several studies that are now bringing a great deal more evidence to bear on these questions. In the meantime, we hope that our brief discussion of some of the key available facts, and the controversies surrounding their interpretation, has helped to clarify the common agenda underlying these volumes.

In this book the agenda has mostly been addressed at the national level, based on historical sources and nationally collected statistics. In the next two volumes we will draw on the detailed information generated by KASS's own field studies of two or three specific localities in each of the eight countries. Volume II presents a series of "views from below": ethnographic accounts of interactions between family members in the context of their local communities and of their wider kinship networks. It also presents an initial overview of quantitative findings from the same localities – based on kinship network interviews, which are analysed in greater depth in the first part of Volume III. We will use these resources to present a more detailed picture of mutual assistance and social contacts between relatives than is currently available from national sources. By combining network information about who helps who, with the accounts of ideas, emotions and motives provided by the ethnographies, we hope to gain some understanding of the ongoing processes of social interaction that underlie both the shared trends, and the apparent differences, that have been discussed in this book.

Bibliography

Bernardi, L. and R. G. White (2010), "Close kin influences on fertility behavior", in P. Heady and M. Kohli (eds.), *Family, kinship and state in contemporary Europe, Vol. 3: Perspectives on theory and policy*, Frankfurt and New York: Campus, pp. 181–208.

Capello, C. and N. Colclough (2010), "A moral familism? Family clusters, neighbourhood and social welfare in a south Italian community", in P. Heady and P. Schweitzer (eds.), *Family, kinship and state in contemporary Europe, Vol. 2: The view from below: nineteen localities*, Frankfurt and New York: Campus, pp. 269–330.

Dalla Zuanna, G. (2001), "The banquet of Aeolus: a familistic interpretation of Italy's lowest low fertility", *Demographic Research*, 4 (5), pp. 133–162.

Durkheim, E. (1964), *The division of labour in society*, Translated G. Simpson. London: Collier Macmillan.

Goldstein, J., W. Lutz and M. Testa (2003), The emergence of sub-replacement fertility ideals in Europe", *Population Research and Policy Review*, 22(5–6), pp. 479–496.

Heady, P. (2003), "Conscripts and Christians: representing kinship and affinity in the Carnian Alps", *Journal of the Royal Anthropological Institute*, 9 (1), pp. 77–95.

Heady, P., S. Gruber and Z. Ou (2010), "Family, kindred and marriage", in P. Heady and M. Kohli (eds.), *Family, kinship and state in contemporary Europe, Vol. 3: Perspectives on theory and policy*, Frankfurt and New York: Campus, pp. 31–70.

Herzfeld, M. (1997), *Cultural intimacy: social poetics in the nation-state*, New York and London: Routledge.

Inglehart, R. and C. Welzel (2005), *Modernization, cultural change, and democracy: the human development sequence*, Cambridge: Cambridge University Press.

Just, R. (2000), *A Greek island cosmos: kinship and community on Meganisi*, Oxford: James Currey.

Kohli, M., M. Albertini and H. Künemund (2010), "Linkages among adult family generations: evidence from comparative survey research", in P. Heady and M. Kohli (eds.), *Family, kinship and state in contemporary Europe, Vol. 3: Perspectives on theory and policy*, Frankfurt and New York: Campus, pp. 233–258.

Le Bras, H. (1997), "Fertility: the condition of self-perpetuation: differing trends in Europe", in M. Gullestad and M. Segalen (eds.), *Family and kinship in Europe*, London: Pinter. pp. 14–32.

Lesthaeghe, R. (1983), "A century of demographic and cultural change in western Europe: an exploration of underlying dimensions", *Population and Development Review*, 9(3), pp. 411–435.

Micheli, G. (2000), "Kinship, family and social network: the anthropological embedment of fertility change in southern Europe", *Demographic Research*, 3(13).

Murphy, M. (2008), "Variations in kinship networks across geographic and social space", *Population and Development Review*, 34(10), pp. 19–49.

Putnam, R. D. (1994), *Making democracy work: civic traditions in modern Italy*, Princeton: Princeton Paperback.

Reher, D. (1998), "Family ties in western Europe: persistent contrasts", *Population and Development Review*, 24(2), pp. 203–234.

Segalen, M. (1991), *Fifteen generations of Bretons: kinship and society in lower Brittany 1720–1980*, Cambridge: Cambridge University Press.

SHARE (2005), *Survey of health, aging and retirement in Europe*, Mannheim: Mannheim Research Institute for the Economics of Aging (MEA).

Seiser, G. and P. Schweitzer (2010), "Houses, families, and the making of community: the Austrian rural case", in P. Heady and P. Schweitzer (eds.), *Family, kinship and state in contemporary Europe, Vol. 2: The view from below: nineteen localities*, Frankfurt and New York: Campus, pp. 91–128.

Testa, M. (2006), *Childbearing preferences and family issues in Europe*, European Comission: Special Eurobarometer.

Tönnies, F. (2001), *Community and civil society*, edited by J. Harris, translated by J. Harris and M. Hollis, Cambridge: Cambridge University Press.

van de Kaa, D. J. (1987), "Europe's second demographic transition", *Population Bulletin*, Vol. 42, No. 1, pp. 1–57.

van Poppel, F., M. Oris and J. Lee (eds.) (2004), *The road to independence: leaving home in western and eastern societies, 16th – 20th centuries, population, family and society, Vol. 1*, Bern.

Weber, M. (2001), *The protestant ethic and the spirit of capitalism*, London: Routledge.

Appendix: data sources and derivations

This appendix gives details of the data sources for the charts in chapters 1 and 10.

Charts based on comparative social surveys

The European Values Study

This EVS is a large-scale, cross-national and longitudinal survey focusing on social values. Specific themes include: the family, children, work, institutions, religion (http://www.europeanvaluesstudy.eu/). The EVS started in 1981 with 16 countries and has gradually expanded in geographical coverage and scope. From 1990 it has been linked to the World Values Survey (http://www.worldvaluessurvey.org/). The data used here is taken from the public use data base derived from the 1999 wave of the study (http://zacat.gesis.org/webview/index.jsp), which includes all the countries in our own project.

The International Social Survey Programme

The ISSP (International Social Survey Programme, http://www.issp.org) is an annual programme of cross-national collaboration on surveys covering topics important for social science research. It started in 1983 and, like the EVS gradually expanded in geographical coverage and scope. The topics are grouped in modules, and the national research teams decide which modules to participate in. We have used data from two modules: "Social Networks and Support Systems", carried out in 2001; and "Family and Changing Gender Roles II" carried out in 1994. The coverage is shown in Table 10.1.

Sample sizes and weights

Table 10.1: Achieved sample sizes (unweighted)

	Austria	Croatia	France	Germany	Italy	Poland	Russia	Sweden
EVS 1999	1,522	1,003	1,615	2,036	2,000	1,095	2,500	1,015
ISSP 1994	977	–	–	3,421	1,018	1,597	1,998	1,272
ISSP 2001	1,011	–	1,398	1,369	999	1,221	2,000	–
Fig. 10.1	558	–	583	538	413	583	896	–
Fig. 10.2	764	–	1,128	970	736	970	1,400	–

Table 10.1 shows the actual (unweighted) number of interviews carried out for each survey, since that is the best single indicator of the amount of data on which the figures are based. However, the percentages in our figures have been calculated using data that has been weighted to allow for sample design and non-response.

Notes on particular survey-based charts

- *Figure 10.1* ISSP 2001, combination of variables v10 and v11, all respondents having at least one adult child, with whom they have some contact.
- *Figure 10.2* ISSP 2001, combination of variables v6 and v7, all respondents having at least one adult sibling, with whom they have some contact.
- *Figure 10.4* EVS 1999, variable a001.
- *Figure 10.5* EVS 1999, variable a002.
- *Figure 10.6* EVS 1999, variable d062. Not asked in Austria.
- *Figure 10.7* EVS 1999, variable a169.
- *Figure 10.8* EVS 1999, variable a034. Croatia omitted because of anomalous data.
- *Figure 10.9* EVS 1999, variable a042. Croatia omitted because of anomalous data.
- *Figure 10.10* EVS 1999, combination of variables f024 and f025.
- *Figures 10.23 and 10.24* ISSP 1994, variable v28.
- *Figure 10.25* EVS 1999, variable d056. Austria not included in data file.

Derivation of population statistics charts

This section sets out the sources we have used for each of the population statistics charts in chapter 1 and 10. For most charts we have drawn on several different sources. There are three main reasons for this.

(1) The main international offices that produce contemporary statistics (Eurostat, ILO, UNESCO, United Nations Statistical Office) do not usually cover the first part of the twentieth century. For the first part of the twentieth century we have drawn where possible on the compilations of historical statistics produced by Mitchell and Rothenbacher.
(2) Where the main source of contemporary statistics is Eurostat, Russia and Croatia are generally not covered, and the coverage of other countries can depend on when they joined the EU. In these cases we draw on national statistics.
(3) A number of other sources fill particular gaps.

The sources for particular charts are as follows. (Bibliographic details of each source are given below.)

Figure 1.1:

- Eurostat online database: Statistics database/Database/Population and social conditions/Population/Demography/Demography – National data/Fertility/Fertility indicators (demo_find)/nmarpct
- INED online database: Population in figures/Europe and developed countries/Database/One indicator for various countries/Extra marital births (per 100 live births) for Croatia, Poland and Russia since 1950
- Rothenbacher (2005): table 4A on CD-Rom for each country
- Statistisches Bundesamt: online database: Population/Table Births, deaths and marriages from 1946 (only in German language)
- Gisser: pp. 28f.

Figure 1.2:

- Eurostat online database: Statistics database/Database/Population and social conditions/Population/Demography/Demography – National data/Fertility/Fertility indicators (demo_find)/totferrt
- Rothenbacher (2005): table 4B on CD-Rom for each country
- INED online database: Population in figures/Europe and developed countries/Database/One indicator for various countries/Total Period Rate for Germany, Croatia, Sweden and Russia since 1950
- Chesnais: p. 548
- United Nations, Demographic Yearbook, Historical Supplement, table 4

Figure 1.3:

- Eurostat online database: Statistics database/Database/Population and social conditions/Population/Demography/Demography – National data/Population/Population structure indicators on 1st January (demo_pjanind)/pc_y60_max
- UNO: online database: Panel 2 Detailed data/Population 60+ for Italy, Poland, Croatia, and Russia
- Statistics Sweden: online database: Population/Tables and Graphs/Swedish Population (in one-year groups) 1860–2008
- Statistik Austria: online database: Population/Population by Demographic Characteristics/Population by Age and Sex
- INED: online database: Population in figures/Metropolitan France/Population structure/By age (Total)

Figure 10.3:

- Destatis (Statistisches Bundesamt Deutschland) online database: Population/Households/Size of Households

- Eurostat online database: Statistics database/Database/Population and social conditions/Population/Census/National level census 2001 round/Households (cens_nhou)/a1
- Statistik Austria online database: Population/Households, Families, Living Arrangements
- http://www.perepis2002.ru/index.html?id=87online database: 2002 All-Russian Population Census/Basic Result/Table 3.6
- Afontsev et al (2005): pp. 39, 56.
- Crostat (2006): p. 23.
- Rothenbacher (2002): pp. 105, 256, 293, 449, 568, 661.
- Rothenbacher (2005): pp. 98, 284, 338–340, 536, 675, 797.

Figure 10.11 and 10.12:

- ILO (1990): pp. 314–317, 336–341, 354–357, 368–371, 378–381.
- ILO (2007): pp. 275f., 279, 281, 285f., 288.
- United Nations (1949): pp. 242–249.
- United Nations (1973): pp. 372, 374.
- United Nations (1980): pp. 975–978.
- United Nations (1986): pp. 866, 869f., 874f.
- United Nations (1990): p. 1133.
- United Nations (1996): pp. 856, 859.

Figure 10.13 and 10.14:

- ILO online database: ILO Data/ILO, Labour statistics Yearbook Database (LABORSTA)/Employment by sex and industry branch, ISIC 2 and Employment by sex and industry branch, ISIC 3 (both in absolute numbers)
- Mitchell (1992): pp. 3f., 6f., 141, 145f., 149, 151f., 154.
- United Nations (1996): pp. 916f.
- The older Russian data is actually that of the USSR

Figure 10.15:

- UIS (UNESCO) online database: Statistics/Data Centre/Custom Tables/Education/Participation/Net enrolment rate/Net enrolment rate. Secondary. All programmes. Total
- UNESCO (1970): pp. 91–98.
- UNESCO (1971): pp. 102–105, 108.
- UNESCO (1972): pp. 115–117.
- UNESCO (1995): pp. 3–63.
- UNESCO (2004): pp. 87, 89.
- UNESCO (2006): pp. 97, 101.
- Definition of net enrolment ratio: Enrolment of the official age-group for a given level of education expressed as a percentage of the corresponding population (UIS, Education Indicators, Technical Guidelines).

Figure 10.16:

- Eurostat online database: Statistics database/Database/Population and social conditions/Population/Demography/Demography – National data/Population/Average population by sex and five-year age groups (demo_ppavg)/Y20_24
- UIS (UNESCO) online database: Statistics/Data Centre/Custom Tables/Education/Participation/Gross enrolment rate/Gross enrolment ratio. ISCED 5 and 6. Total
- Mitchell (1992): pp. 878–883.
- UNESCO (2004): pp. 106, 108.
- UNESCO (2006): pp. 120, 124.
- United Nations (1949): pp. 133, 138f., 143, 146f., 149.
- United Nations (1999): table 3.
- Definition of gross enrolment ratio: Total enrolment in a specific level of education, regardless of age, expressed as a percentage of the eligible official school-age population corresponding to the same level of education in a given school-year (UIS, Education Indicators, Technical Guidelines).

- Up to 1965 (Germany: 1988) the ratio is the proportion of the number of students to the population 20–24 years old.

Figure 10.17 and 10.18:

- Eurostat online database: Statistics database/Database/Population and social conditions/Labour market (including LFS – Labour Force Survey)/Employment and unemployment (Labour Force Survey)/LFS series – Detailed quarterly survey results (from 1998) (lfsq)/Activity and activity rates – LFS series/Activity rates by sex, age groups and nationality (%) (lfsq_argan)
- ILO online database: Statistics and databases/LABORSTA – database of labour statistics/Total and Economically Active Population/Economically Active Population Estimates and Projections 1980–2020 (EAPEP)/Statistics: 1980–2020
- Mitchell (1992): pp. 3f., 6f., 141, 145f., 149, 151f., 154.

Figure 10.19:

- Eurostat online database: Statistics database/Database/Population and social conditions/Population/Demography/Demography – National data/Fertility/Fertility indicators (demo_find)/nmarpct

Figure 10.20:

- Eurostat online database: Statistics database/Database/Population and social conditions/Population/Demography/Demography – National data/Marriage and divorce/Divorces rates by duration of marriage (reached during the year) (demo_ndivrt)/total

Figure 10.21:

- Council of Europe online database: country tables 9 (Longitudinal data on fertility and female first marriage)
- Rothenbacher 2005: table 4B on CD-Rom for France, Italy, Sweden
- We have omitted Croatia, as there appeared to be discontinuities in the recent data.

Figure 10.22:

- Eurostat online database: Statistics database/Database/Population and social conditions/Population/Demography/Demography – National data/Fertility/Fertility indicators (demo_find)/totferrt

Population statistics bibliography

Reference details of the sources mentioned above are as follows.

Reference volumes on historical statistics

Afontsev, S., G. Kessler, A. Markevich, V. Tyazhel'nikova and T. Valetov (2005), *Urban households in Russia and the Soviet Union, 1900–2000*, IISH-Research Paper 44, Amsterdam.

Chesnais, J.-C. (1992), *The demographic transition: stages, patterns, and economic implications: a longitudinal study of sixty-seven countries covering the period 1720–1984.*, Oxford: Clarendon Press.

Gisser, R. (1979), "Daten zur Bevölkerungsentwicklung der österreichischen Alpenländer 1819–1913", *Geschichte und Ergebnisse der zentralen amtlichen Statistik in Österreich 1829–1979. Beiträge zur österreichischen Statistik*, Heft 550, pp 403–424, und *Tabellenanhang* (Beiträge Heft 550a), pp 23–31. Wien: Österreichisches Statistisches Zentralamt.

Mitchell, B. R. (1992), *International historical statistics: Europe 1750–1988*, Third Edition, New York.

Rothenbacher, F. (2002), *The European population 1850–1945 (the societies of Europe)*, Basingstoke, New York: Palgrave Macmillan.

Rothenbacher, F. (2005), *The European population since 1945 (the societies of Europe)*, Basingstoke, New York: Palgrave Macmillan.

Official Sources

CoE: The Council of Europe provides also demographic data for its member states
(http://www.coe.int/t/e/social_cohesion/population/demographic_year_book/2003_edition/04 Country Data/Default.asp#TopOfPage).

- *Council of Europe* (2006), *Recent demographic developments in Europe*, Strasbourg: Council of Europe Press.

Eurostat: The statistical office of the European Union provides a wide range of data including data about population and social conditions and economic data
(http://epp.eurostat.ec.europa.eu/portal/page/portal/eurostat/home/).

ILO: The *International Labour Organization* provides data about labour statistics. (http://www.ilo.org/global/lang--en/index.htm)

- ILO (1990) Yearbook of Labour Statistics: Retrospective Edition on Population Censuses 1945–1989. Geneva: ILO.
- ILO (2001), World Employment Report: Life at work in the information economy, Geneva: International Labour Office
- ILO (2007) Yearbook of Labour Statistics 2007: Time series. Geneva: ILO.

National statistical offices: *The national statistical offices of the countries* in this study also provide useful data.

- Austria: Statistik Austria (http://www.statistik.at/web_en/)
- Croatia: Državni zavod za statistiku (http://www.dzs.hr/default_e.htm), Crostat (2006) Statističke Informacije 2006.
- France: Institut National de la Statistique et des Études Économiques (http://www.insee.fr/en/)
- Germany: Statistisches Bundesamt Deutschland (http://www.destatis.de/jetspeed/portal/cms/Sites/destatis/Internet/EN/Navigation/Homepage__NT.psml)
- Italy: Istituto Nazionale di Statistica (http://www.istat.it/english/)

- Poland: Główny Urząd Statystyczny (http://www.stat.gov.pl/gus/index_ENG_HTML.htm)
- Russia: Federal'naja Služba Gosudarstvennoj Statistiki (http://www.gks.ru/eng/), http://www.perepis2002.ru/index.html?id=87: results of the 2002 census of Russia
- Sweden: Statistiska centralbyrån (http://www.scb.se/default____2154.aspx)

UNESCO: The Institute for Statistics of the United Nations Educational, Scientific and Cultural Organization provides statistical data about education
(http://www.uis.unesco.org/ev.php?ID=2867_201&ID2=DO_TOPIC).

- UNESCO (1970), Statistical Yearbook 1969, Paris.
- UNESCO (1971), Statistical Yearbook 1970, Paris.
- UNESCO (1972), Statistical Yearbook 1971, Paris.
- UNESCO (1995), Statistical Yearbook 1995, Paris: Lanham.
- UNESCO Institute for Statistics (2004), Global Education Digest 2004: Comparing Education Statistics Across the World, Montreal.
- UNESCO Institute for Statistics (2006), Global Education Digest 2006: Comparing Education Statistics Across the World, Montreal.

United Nations Statistics Division: The United Nations Statistics Division provides an online database for demographic data
(http://esa.un.org/unpp). There is also a common statistical database at the UN website (http://data.un.org/), including ILO and UNESCO data.

- United Nations (1949), *Demographic Yearbook 1948*, New York.
- United Nations (1973), *Demographic Yearbook 1972*, New York.
- United Nations (1980), *Demographic Yearbook 1979*, New York.
- United Nations (1980), *Historical Supplement to the Demographic Yearbook, 1948–1978*, New York.
- United Nations (1986), *Demographic Yearbook 1984*, New York.
- United Nations (1990), *Demographic Yearbook 1988*, New York.
- United Nations (1996), *Demographic Yearbook 1994*, New York.
- United Nations (1999) Demographic Yearbook Historical Supplement 1948–1997 CD-ROM.

Authors

Georges Augustins is Professor of anthropology at Paris Ouest Nanterre La Défense University. His researches pertain to peasant societies and kinship organisation, and relationships between hierarchy and local organisation. More recently he has specialised in conciliating Darwinism and the anthropological theory of kinship. He is the author of *Comment se perpétuer? Devenir des lignées et destins des patrimoines dans les sociétés paysannes européennes* and of *Les marques urbaines du prestige. Le cas d'Evora au Portugal.*

Leon Dyczewski is Professor of Sociology at the John Paul II Catholic University Lublin and Director of the Postgraduate School of Social Communication and Journalism. He has published many books and articles on culture, family, and the media. The themes covered include: cultural stability and cultural change, life styles and values in modern society, small groups and their culture-creating functions, dominant and alternative culture, ethnic and cultural identity, integration of ethnic groups, national culture and European culture, changes in the family, electronic media in society and family. He is the author of: *The Family in a Transforming Society"* and *"Values in the Polish Cultural Tradition.*

David Gaunt is Professor of History at Södertörn University Stockholm and has worked since the 1970s on the historical anthropology of Swedish family and kinship. He has published extensively on historical and contemporary kin relationships, in his book *Familjeliv i Norden*, and in international journals and anthologies. He was formerly director of social services research for the city of Stockholm, and has also written on the history of Swedish bureaucracy, old age, and the labour movement.

Christine Geserick holds a research position at the Austrian Institute for Family Studies at the University of Vienna. She has conducted several research projects in the field of family relations, focusing on gender and the transition to adulthood. She received her M.A. degree in Sociology, Social Anthropology and Psychology from the Westfälische Wilhelms-Universität Münster, Germany. She is currently completing her Ph.D. at the University of Vienna.

Hannes Grandits is a Professor at the Department of History at the Humboldt-University in Berlin and a former senior associate for Southeast European history at the University of Graz. In his research he works comparatively with historical-anthropological approaches to family and social security in Europe. Further fields of interests are socialist and post-socialist South-eastern Europe as well as the history of the late Ottoman Balkans and the late Habsburg Empire. Recently published books are *"Familie und sozialer Wandel im ländlichen Kroatien, 18.-20. Jhdt."*; *"Distinct Inheritances. Property, Family and Community in a Changing Europe"*, co-edited with P. Heady; *"Birnbaum der Tränen. Lebensgeschichtliche Erinnerungen aus dem alten Jugoslawien"* co-edited with K. Kaser; and *"Herrschaft und Loyalität in der spätosmanischen Gesellschaft. Das Beispiel der multikonfessionellen Herzegowina"*, or *"Yugoslavia's Sunny Side. A history of Tourism in Socialism (1950-80s)"*, co-edited with Karin Taylor.

Siegfried Gruber is a Post-doctoral fellow at the Max Planck Institute for Demographic Research in Rostock. He received his doctorate in Southeast European History at the Karl-Franzens-Universität Graz in 2004. His work on family history and historical demography is about household structures, life-courses, different demographic patterns within societies, and urban/rural differences. The regional focus of his research is South-eastern Europe.

Patrick Heady originally studied economics and statistics, and worked in quantitative social research before turning to social anthropology. Interested particularly in cooperation, identity and kinship, his anthropological publications include an ethnography, *The Hard People: rivalry, sympathy and social structure in an alpine valley*, and two jointly edited volumes: *Conceiving Persons: ethnographies of procreation, fertility and growth* with Peter Loizos and *Distinct Inheritances: property, family and community in a changing Europe* with Hannes Grandits. He was the main originator and coordinator of the KASS project, and is currently a research associate of the Max Planck Institute for Social Anthropology, and of University College London.

Alexander Nikulin is Director of the Centre for Peasant Studies and Agrarian Reforms, at the Moscow School for Social and Economic Sciences. He has edited several books and published articles on the informal economy in Russia, rural families and societies, and on agrarian history.

Johannes Pflegerl is a lecturer in sociology and sociology of the family at the University of Applied Sciences in St. Pölten, and a researcher at the Ilse Arlt Institute on Social Inclusion Research. Until 2005 he was a researcher at the Austrian Institute for Family Studies in Vienna. He has conducted several projects in the area of family research and he is author of several publications dealing with family and migration, family and youth welfare, family and violence. He is currently working on generational relations and care for the elderly.

Heidi Rosenbaum, is Professor Emeritus of European Ethnology at the Georg-August-Universität Göttingen. After her doctorate (Philipps-Universität Marburg) and her habilitation (Göttingen) in sociology she concentrated on family studies, later complemented by research on the history of childhood. She is author of many books and articles. Among these are *Familie als Gegenstruktur zu Gesellschaft*; *Formen der Familie. Untersuchungen zum Zusammenhang von Familienverhältnissen, Sozialstruktur und sozialem Wandel in der deutschen Gesellschaft des 19. Jahrhunderts*; *Proletarische Familien. Arbeiterfamilien und Arbeiterväter im frühen 20. Jahrhundert zwischen traditioneller, sozialdemokratischer und kleinbürgerlicher Orientierung*; *Private Netzwerke im Wohlfahrtsstaat. Familie, Verwandtschaft und soziale Sicherheit im Deutschland des 20. Jahrhunderts. Ein Überblick* with Elisabeth Timm. She is completing a monograph on the everyday life of children during the Nazi regime.

Martine Segalen is Professor Emeritus of Anthropology at the department of Sociology of the University of Paris Ouest Nanterre La Défense. She has published extensively on family, kinship, rituals and cultural heritage. She has been co-editor of History of the Family; and her *Sociologie de la famille* first published in 1981 is now in its sixth edition. Among her recent works is *Grands-parents. La famille à travers les générations* with Claudine Attias-Donfut. She is currently director and editor-in-chief of Ethnologie Française.

Elisabeth Timm is university assistant at the Institute of European Ethnology of the University of Vienna. Her work on the history and anthropology of kinship includes *Private Netzwerke im Wohlfahrtsstaat. Familie, Verwandtschaft und soziale Sicherheit im Deutschland des 20. Jahrhunderts* together with Heidi Rosenbaum; and *"Ich bin Glied einer Kette." Entgrenzung, Personalisierung und Gouvernementalität von Verwandtschaft heute am Beispiel der populären Genealogie* in Erdmuthe Alber et al. (eds.), Verwandtschaft heute. Berlin (forthcoming).

Irina Trotsuk is an Associate Professor in the Department of Sociology in the Faculty of Humanities and Social Science of the Peoples' Friendship University of Russia. She if the author of many articles and books dealing with sociological research methods, survey techniques, textual analytical tools and sociological approaches to measuring the values of different social and demographic groups. Among these are *Narrative Analysis in Sociology: Theory and Practice*; *Caucasian Youth: the Past and the Future – Somewhere in between*; *Methodology of Sociological Research: Practical Guide and Tests.* Her present research involves the comparative analysis of trends in young people's values in different post-socialist countries.

Pier Paolo Viazzo is Professor of Social Anthropology at the University of Turin. He is the author of several books including *Upland Communities: Environment, Population and Social Structure in the Alps since the Sixteenth Century*; *Introduzione all'antropologia storica*, *The Decline of Infant and Child Mortality: The European Experience, 1750-1990* with C. A. Corsini; and *Oltre le mura domestiche. Famiglia e legami intergenerazionali dall'Unità d'Italia ad oggi* with A. Rosina.

Francesco Zanotelli received his doctorate in Anthropological Sciences from the University of Turin in 2005. He is currently a research associate at the Institute of Philosophy and Social Sciences of the University of Siena studying the shift from ethnic self-ascription to national identity in Jalisco (Mexico), and the economic and identity role of kinship in contemporary Tuscany (Italy). He is adjunct professor of Economic Anthropology in the same institute and adjunct professor of Applied Anthropology at the University of Bologna. He has published articles on money circulation and exchange in rural Mexico and recently co-edited two books on the anthropology of work and migration *Emigrare nell'ombra* and on the anthropology of development *Subire la cooperazione?*.

Index